CHRISTIANS IN THE MARKETPLACE SERIES
Biblical Principles and Business: The Foundations

Richard C. Chewning, Ph.D., Editor

NAVPRESS

A MINISTRY OF THE NAVIGATORS
P.O. BOX 6000, COLORADO SPRINGS, COLORADO 80934

The Navigators is an international Christian organization. Jesus Christ gave His followers the Great Commission to go and make disciples (Matthew 28:19). The aim of The Navigators is to help fulfill that commission by multiplying laborers for Christ in every nation.

NavPress is the publishing ministry of The Navigators. NavPress publications are tools to help Christians grow. Although publications alone cannot make disciples or change lives, they can help believers learn biblical discipleship, and apply what they learn to their lives and ministries.

© 1989 by Richard C. Chewning
All rights reserved, including translation
Library of Congress Catalog Card Number
  88-63590
ISBN 08910-9556X

Second Printing, 1989

Scripture quotations in this publication are from several translations: the *Holy Bible: New International Version* (NIV). Copyright © 1973, 1978, 1984, International Bible Society. Used by permission of Zondervan Bible Publishers; the *New American Standard Bible* (NASB), © The Lockman Foundation, 1960, 1962, 1963, 1968, 1971, 1972, 1973, 1975, 1977; the *Revised Standard Version Bible* (RSV), copyright 1946, 1952, 1971, by the Division of Christian Education of the National Council of the Churches of Christ in the U.S.A., and are used by permission, all rights reserved; and the *King James Version* (KJV).

The individual authors of this book have used the following translations: Chewning—NASB: Kanzer—NIV, NASB, RSV; Wogaman—RSV; Augsburger—NIV, NASB, KJV; Kaiser—NIV; Krabbendam—NIV; Grounds—NIV; Gaffin—NIV; Geisler—NIV; Middelmann—NIV; Wauzzinski—KJV; Barker—NIV, NASB; Davis—RSV.

Printed in the United States of America

CONTENTS

SERIES EDITOR

Dr. Richard C. Chewning is the Chavanne Professor of Christian Ethics in Business at the Hankamer School of Business of Baylor University in Waco, Texas. He received baccalaureate, master's, and Ph.D. degrees, all in business, from Virginia Polytechnic Institute, the University of Virginia, and the University of Washington, respectively. He began formal academic training in business ethics and corporate social responsibility as a doctoral student and pursued postdoctoral study in comparative ethics at St. Mary's College, the seminary arm of the University of St. Andrews in Scotland.

Dr. Chewning began teaching at the University of Richmond in 1958 where he taught finance, served for some years as a department chairman, and also as an academic dean. In 1979 he was invited by the business faculty to develop and teach courses in the field of business ethics. He moved to Baylor University in 1985. He has published over forty-five essays and articles integrating Scripture with business and economics, and he has authored and coauthored books in the field of ethics and business from a biblical perspective.

For years Dr. Chewning has been a consultant to government bodies, trade associations, and corporations in matters of both finance and ethics, while maintaining a busy schedule of public lectures and seminar participation.

CHRISTIANS IN THE MARKETPLACE

What are God's thoughts about the issues we face as we subdue and rule the earth? How are we in the business world to cocreate, share, and distribute the wealth within the private and community sectors? Literally thousands of such questions flow from our God-ordained involvement in the marketplace.

Business, economics, and public policy, by their very scope, present a bewildering array of disciplines, functions, and structures. Does God, through Scripture, really address the important questions faced by the people working in these areas? How specifically does God speak to issues faced by Christians involved in marketing, accounting, real estate, foreign trade, public education, national defense, etc.? Are there just a handful of biblical principles that apply to the entire range of subjects, or are there many biblical concepts that we can bring to bear on such questions?

Answers to these questions can be found in this series of books known as CHRISTIANS IN THE MARKETPLACE. Four books have been designed. The first two books, *Biblical Principles and Business: The Foundations* and *Biblical Principles and Economics: The Foundations*, address around sixty to seventy basic questions, such as: Does the Bible prescribe a set of economic principles that are best satisfied in a particular economic system? How are Christians to resolve the tensions that exist between individual responsibility in a free market economy and society's need for some control to promote the social good? On what basis should Christians conduct business with nonbelievers: the principles of special revelation in Scripture or the principles of general revelation in nature?

Most of the chapters of the first two books are written by theologians, philosophers, and historians who were assigned predesigned topics and asked to address specific questions related to their subjects. Because there are multiple authors in each book, writing styles will vary between chapters, but the content is universally solid and generally free of the "technical language" so frequently associated with such discussions. The chapters have been written for contemplative Christian businesspeople rather than for theologians and philosophers. The thoughts are challenging. Some of the ideas are soul-stirring. Not all of the material is conceptually easy, but the vocabulary employed is not hostile to a well-read Christian.

Books 3 and 4 are survey books in which twelve areas of business (management, marketing, accounting, insurance, etc.) in book 3 and twelve issues in public policy (public welfare policy, national unemployment policy, national policy on income distribution, etc.) in book 4 will be examined in the light of Scripture. Specifically, contributing scholars were asked to (1) identify as many serious questions or topics as possible in their area that need to be explored from a biblical perspective; (2) identify as many biblical principles as possible that have application to their subjects; and (3) illustrate applications of biblical principles to the questions raised.

The scholars selected to work on the theological foundations books were chosen on three grounds: (1) they all have a very high view of Scripture as the authoritative Word of God; (2) they are representative leaders from different theological schools, thus their methods and systems of biblical interpretation (hermeneutics) offer an orthodox but creative range; and (3) their assigned topics fit their demonstrated interests.

The entire series is written by men and women who are committed to the full authority of Scripture. Those of us who govern the selection process are deeply aware of the controversies in the Church at large today over this matter of scriptural authority. These books do not address this issue; they assume the full authority of Scripture. There may be an occasional chapter author, however, who formulates his or her expression of scriptural authority in a nontraditional way. But the reader will find that all material has been handled in a completely orthodox manner.

The scholars do represent a diverse background of Biblical interpretation, however. This is part of the design of the series. The Bible presents many subjects that need to be kept in *balance* if Scripture is to be fully understood, appreciated, and lived out. And many of the exciting and encouraging mysteries of God seem to reside at the inscrutable juncture of these balancing truths. For example, we are individuals who are members of a Body of believers—we are one community. God is absolutely sovereign, and we are morally responsible creatures. Who can comprehend completely such wonderful truths? Both absolute equality and human diversity are affirmed—another truth that must be kept in balance. In order to seek balance, these scholars were selected because they come with diverse emphases that will allow us to step back and examine the significance of the tensions created.

Scripture does, at times, point to a mystery at work in two or more dynamic truths that, from the human perspective, seem to compete with one another—God's sovereignty and man's responsibility, for example. Many Christians have expended considerable energy over the centuries trying to solve such mysteries. This series makes no attempt to eliminate mysteries generated by truths held in tension. In fact, it is our conviction that God's truths are already in balance as revealed, and that the mysteries we so often want eliminated are divinely intended to reveal the incomprehensible nature of God so that we may hold Him in absolute awe. We make an effort to identify and explain the significant benefits derived from holding these particular truths in tension. We also try to avoid getting on one side or the other of these tensions, but we do emphasize them and seek their biblical balance.

The three overarching objectives of the series are (1) to encourage the development of a mature Christian world view (defined and expounded on in chapter 1) that encompasses business, economics, and public policy; (2) to demonstrate the application and integration of Scripture with the concerns of business, economics, and public policy in order to assist the development of a Christian world view; and (3) to encourage a *response* to God's revealed will regarding business, economics, and public policy, so that *justice* will be done in the marketplace. The first two are means to this end: doing justice. God has called us (hundreds of times in Scripture) to *do* justice, and many of these calls come in the context of the marketplace. The prophet Micah's call "to do justice, to love kindness, and to walk humbly with your God" (6:8) was in such a context (see 2:1-2,9; 6:9-13; 7:1-6). This series of books is devoted to stimulating a response to God's active call.

It is probably apparent by now that the series does not offer the reader a "fast-food" menu. We believe a banquet is more in order for God's children—a banquet, if you will, served in a number of courses. The menu does not offer simplistic answers; it provides serious food for contemplation. If we are to live by every word that proceeds from the mouth of God (see Deut. 8:3; Matt. 4:4), then we must examine all of life in the light of Scripture and obey its intent. Therefore, the call of this work must ultimately be understood as a call to Scripture—a serious examination of business, economics, and public policy in the penetrating light of God's revealed will.

A word of appreciation is very much in order for the director and editors of NavPress, the publisher of the series. If there is a valid vision associated with the series, there is also a corresponding risk, and they have been willing to assume the latter in order to support the vision. That takes faith, courage, and a commitment to imaginative service of Christ. I pray their risk will be rewarded with a Christ-serving impact from this series.

Richard C. Chewning
Chavanne Professor of Christian
Ethics in Business
Hankamer School of Business
Baylor University
Waco, Texas

CHAPTER 1

THE MAKING OF A CHRISTIAN WORLD VIEW
Richard C. Chewning

I s there really such a thing as a Christian world view or life view, a Christian way of looking at people and things? If we speak of a Christian world view, are we thinking of one particular way of interpreting life's reality, or are we allowing for a number of perspectives on the same subject? Is there a "Christian" perspective on capital punishment? Is there a Christian perspective on capitalism and the free market economy? Is there a Christian ideal regarding the spread of wages that should exist between managers and laborers? (The spread is 4 to 1 in Japan and 10 to 1 in the U.S.A.) Is there a distinctively Christian perspective on anything? If there is, how would we define it, and how does it come into being?

Yes, there is a Christian perspective. It is not simply a perspective held by a Christian, however. Christians have both right and wrong perspectives. So the person holding the perspective is not the determining factor of whether or not a specific view could be designated as Christian. Neither does the fact that someone quotes the Bible or applies Scripture to the situation automatically make the view Christian. It generally indicates an effort to present a Christian view, but does not in and of itself determine how successful the person may have been in doing so.

A Christian world view reflects the renovating work of the Holy Spirit on the human mind through the use of Scripture. Such a world view is incremental and developmental in character. It is both micro and macro in dimension. Furthermore, it embodies knowledge, understanding, and wisdom.

The Apostle Paul comments that "a natural man does not accept the things of the Spirit of God; for they are foolishness to him, and he cannot understand them, because they [spiritual things] are spiritually appraised" (1 Cor. 2:14).

What are "the things of the Spirit of God" Paul has in mind when he speaks of the undiscerning natural man's refusal to accept them? The "natural" or fallen man will not, for example, accept the truths and implications about mankind's fallen nature—our righteousness is self-righteousness; our motives are predominantly self-centered; we make God in our image and reduce Him to an acceptable psychological size so that we can justify the pursuit of our own desires; and so forth.

Paul goes on to state in 1 Corinthians 2:16, "But we have the mind of Christ." Paul is saying that the Christian, the reborn person (see John 1:13, 3:1-8; 1 Peter 1:23), is enabled to discern and understand things more and more from the perspective of God. As Christians we are being transformed by the renewing of our minds (see Rom. 12:2). With the mind of Christ being formed in us (see Gal. 4:19), we acquire a Christian's view of the world and of life. But how does this happen?

HOW A CHRISTIAN WORLD VIEW IS FORMED

Scripture and the Holy Spirit—How is a Christian world view formed? We cannot answer this "how" question as a scientist would, but we can describe some discernible realities about how a Christian world view comes into existence. Just as the physical eye can be woefully impaired in its vision by the presence of a cataract, so can one's spiritual discernment be blinded by an encrusted heart.

Biblically, the heart is descriptive of the innermost depths of our *intellect* (thoughts and reason), *will* (desires and ability to seek their fulfillment), and *emotions* (feelings). A hard heart is insensitive to the perspectives of God so that the things of God are suppressed and rejected (see Rom. 1:18). The mind of an employer, for example, can rationalize things so that his employees are simply factors of production to be treated as any other natural resource—exploited, discarded, manipulated, etc.—rather than perceived as authentic image-bearers of God whose very existence and capacities are extremely important to God.

Just as laser beams may be used to emulsify and remove a cataract from the physical eye, so the Holy Spirit uses the Word of God to clear away obstructions from our spiritual eyes and to cleanse us (see John 15:3, 17:17; Eph. 5:6; Titus 3:5). Paul, in fact, prayed that the eyes of the Ephesians' hearts would be enlightened to see and understand the things of God (see Eph. 1:18). The Spirit can not only wield the Word of God as a sword against God's enemies, but He can also use it as a scalpel for heart surgery on His children (see Eph. 6:17).

God uses the Scripture to transform our minds. God's Word is the antidote for the poison administered by the forces of darkness. There is no other test to which we can put our moral perceptions and hope for godly discernment than to examine them in the light of God's revelation. Biblical Christianity is not to be confused with existential or experiential Christianity, where one's intuition, feelings, or personal experiences become the governing realities for determining what is right and wrong. God is the author of our intuitive and emotional capacities as well as sovereign Lord over our experiences, but we are to judge and examine them all under the light of Scripture. He has promised to use His Word to guide us; He has not promised to use our personal perceptions and experiences to provide us with truth.

The fact that God has promised to use His revealed Word to teach and guide us, instead of using primarily our personal experiences and reason, is significant for us to comprehend. How long one has been a Christian is not a reliable indicator of whether or not he or she will have a developed Christian world view. A Christian view will emerge only to the degree that one is integrating and allowing scriptural truth, rightly applied, to govern personal perceptions of reality. Being adopted into the family of God is the first require-ment for the creation of a Christian world view, but being a Christian is not sufficient in and of itself to develop a view that is consonant with God's perspective.

The Christian view is incremental and developmental—The Christian perspective, if it is to be truly Christian in character, is developed by degrees. It is incremental and developmental in character. It is, if you will, the practical manifestation of the great biblical doctrine of sanctification. Biblically, the doctrines of justification and sanctification are inseparably yoked. If one of them exists in truth, the other one must of necessity exist.

Justification, the great Magna Charta of our faith, is the biblical teaching that we are unconditionally accepted by God (justified), not by any righteous-ness either infused in us or found in us, but by having our sins pardoned for Christ's sake and having His righteousness judicially imputed to us through our faith in Him (see Rom. 4:5-8, 8:30; 2 Cor. 5:19,21; Phil. 3:9; Titus 3:5,7). Faith is itself a gift of God (see Rom. 12:3; Eph. 2:8). If justification is a personal reality, sanctification will accompany it, for God will not leave His children infants. God wants us to grow and mature in Christ (see Eph. 4:11-16).

Sanctification is a work of renovation, not imputation. It is a work of transformation. The Holy Spirit, who regenerates the hearts and spirits of God's children, also nurtures and feeds the "new babies," first with the "milk of God" and then the "meat"—the Word of God—as they mature. By receiving the Word in faith, Christians are empowered by the Spirit to "put off the old man" and to "put on the new man." They do, in fact, become renovated more and more to the true likeness of Christ. Christians actually become holier by degrees and live more righteously. This process, however, is never completed (they are not perfected) in this life, but healthy Christians *will* continue to grow throughout their lives (see John 17:17; Rom. 6:5-6,14; 8:13; 2 Cor. 7:1; Gal. 5:24; Col. 3:5; Heb. 12:14; 1 John 5:4).

It is in the context of our sanctification that our Christian world view will be formed and lived out. One may ask, "Can a Christian world view be intellectually acquired through biblical study and not be practiced?" We must respond, to a degree yes, and to a degree no. This will be discussed later in the chapter.

As sanctification is a "putting off of the old nature" and a "putting on of the new nature" over time, a Christian world view is a perspective that grows. It is planted, weeded, fertilized, pruned, thinned, cultivated, rotated, and harvested. As in a garden, some fruit (our view of advertising, for example) may be ripe (in conformity with a biblical set of standards) before other understandings are mature (our perspective on foreign trade or employee rights). Our personal Christian world view cannot be either universal or evenly developed. Only pride encourages people to speak freely on all subjects as if they were resident experts in everything.

Micro and macro qualities—If our world view may be unevenly developed, it also has micro and macro dimensions. Biblical truth that constitutes the standard through which we are to evaluate perceived reality is itself micro and macro in character. The individual verses and paragraphs of Scripture, expressing a truth, constitute a microcosm taken from within God's truth. We begin our life in Christ with the gathering of individual biblical *propositions*—individual statements that are true. The Spirit uses these to cause us to do something, alter our perception about something, or store it for application in the future.

To illustrate, a new Christian might be reading Ephesians when the statement, "Let him who steals steal no longer" (4:28), almost jumps from the page and elicits the inner thought of, "Oh, I must stop having Bob [a motel clerk] write me a $60 room receipt every week." Our imaginary new Christian had been in the habit of staying in a $45-a-night room while on a routine weekly business trip to a neighboring city. Even deeper moral issues may surface that require contemplation: "Do I confess to Sam [his immediate superior] that I have been doing this for three years? Should I find a way to pay it back?"

Christians, new and mature, are constantly harvesting biblical propositions to use immediately or to integrate with previously learned insights. This integration takes two forms. We may integrate the specific biblical proposition with a growing array of applications (stealing as it relates to money, merchandise, proprietary information, taking credit for another person's accomplishments, etc.), or we may connect the individual propositional truths together to form biblical principles.

Biblical *principles* are propositions that recur a number of times, so we can conclude there is a body of teaching on the subject. In the wonderful and broad subject of "salvation," theologians over the centuries have discovered that numerous important issues are repeatedly covered from Genesis to Revelation, and that these have become doctrines of the Church: the Trinity, justification, sanctification, grace, and so on. These doctrines may then be related and connected to one another to form a body of systematic theology.

Are there a number of biblical principles that should be applied in our business and public policy interactions? For example, is the teaching that God is not a respecter of persons a biblical principle that can be widely applied in business and public policy? The concept certainly appears in Scripture frequently enough (e.g., Deut. 10:17; Acts 10:34; Rom. 2:11; Eph. 6:9; Col. 3:25; James 2:1-9; 1 Peter 1:17). Should customers who buy in large quantities get better service from us than ones who buy in small quantities? Should a superior's word be automatically accepted over the statements of a subordinate in determining justice in an internal business situation?

Does the doctrine of the Trinity give birth to biblical principles related to equality, and principles related to diversity and inequality? The biblical truth that each member of the Godhead is equally God, possessing every attribute of God in full measure and worthy of all worship and honor, is incredibly significant when we contemplate the implications of our own equality with all other humans and their equality with us. This concept has many things to say to managers and professionals about the dignity and worth of all workers. How we treat people—affirm their worth, show respect, seek justice for all—should be governed by this truth.

At the same time, however, each member of the Godhead has assumed certain roles. These roles reveal a submission and authority relationship within the Godhead. This, too, has something to say to each of us as we struggle at times with the issues related to authority and submission at work or elsewhere. Christian business professionals in leadership roles, for example, need to wrestle with what it means to be "servant leaders," and Christians in subordinate positions need to take seriously their testimony as they work out what it means to be "servant followers."

Biblical *principles* as we have defined them—recurring *propositions* (single pieces of biblical truth) that present a larger picture and understanding of a biblical subject—eventually begin to define for us a complex entity (macrocosm) within the still larger context of all of Scripture.

The Christian world view the authors of this book hope to present, expand on, and encourage is the macro one. We take this approach for five reasons. First, we believe that the macro view will demonstrate that a high degree of unity is possible among Christians regarding the principles that should guide our conduct in the business and public policy arenas and at the same time will provide ample room for a diversity of emphases. The larger Church is fractured theologically; we should not extend that division behaviorally.

Second, we believe that the truths held in tension within Scripture can be illustrated to be complementary and supportive of each other, and not at odds, through the macro model. This we even dare to hope will spill over into some reconciliations of our interpretive theological differences. Many theologians— teachers, pastors, and laypeople—avoid systematic theology because it can lead to a highlighting of differences, and they prefer to "get on with the work of the Church." That is valid *if* the study of Scripture, from a macro perspective, is limited to a focus on the system itself and leads to endless debates, which can themselves become a substitute for heeding God's Word. But a macro view of Scripture—the development and application of biblical principles—is essential for the development of Christian leadership.

The third reason for this emphasis is its function in developing Christian leadership in the areas of business and public policy. The writer of Proverbs said it well, "Where there is no vision, the people are unrestrained" (29:18)—they have no guiding direction. Certainly one leadership activity is to provide direction, a vision. Visions are generally macro in nature, not micro. Christian professionals who want to lead in the marketplace would be helped more by understanding God's revealed principles as they apply to business and public policy than they would by limiting their learning to micro applications of particular biblical propositions.

The fourth reason for our macro approach is that it helps greatly in overcoming a perennial problem associated with any application of Scripture: How do we know that Scripture is being applied correctly? Humans cannot guarantee that it is, but it is much more likely to be applied correctly if we are applying a recurring biblical theme to a situation (our biblical principles) than if we are applying an isolated verse, parable, or paragraph (our micro data). This does not imply that micro applications are wrong at all; it merely means that the macro ones should have an internal biblical check on them before we begin making our application.

Knowledge, understanding, and wisdom—Our fifth reason for pursuing this macro approach focuses on knowledge, understanding, and wisdom. The Spirit of God who rested on Christ was described by the prophet Isaiah as "the spirit of wisdom and understanding, the spirit of counsel and strength, the spirit of knowledge and the fear of the LORD" (11:2). Knowledge, understanding, and wisdom generally represent an ascending scale of completeness. They tend to flow from a micro level—knowledge is an aggregation of facts about things, events, people, Scripture—to an understanding of the dynamic relationship that exists within the mix of known things so that they are understood. (Knowledge is the static dimension of information; understanding is the dynamic interpretation of information.)

Knowledge and understanding are prerequisites of wisdom, which is the ability to discern or judge rightly and then offer courses of action that will encourage godly outcomes. True wisdom is to behave and act as God desires. This is why Job reports, "Behold, the fear of the Lord, that is wisdom; and to depart from evil is understanding" (Job 28:28). The fear of the Lord—terror that becomes awe with reconciliation—motivates God's children to seek His knowledge, understanding, and wisdom, an inseparable trilogy when governed by wisdom, its crown.

It would be the height of arrogance to presume that any human work could bring about true godly wisdom. But to the degree that our efforts promote the searching and study of God's Word where the Spirit can teach us, our work is appropriate. The reader is called on to test the work of the contributing scholars and the series editor against the Scripture. Have we been faithful to God's Word? Are our conclusions truly biblical principles? If they are, have they been properly applied in our illustrations? Are we maintaining a biblical balance, or are we pushing a particular interpretation of Scripture? Or are we ignoring other balancing positions? Our desire is to be faithful to Scripture, but we, too, struggle with the task.

WHAT FOLLOWS

Chapters 2-13 are organized into six pairs of chapters. Each pair of chapters is designed to illustrate a biblical tension in balance. The first section (chapters 2 and 3), for example, wrestles with the tension so frequently experienced by Christians regarding the question: Is the Scripture calling us to evangelize on the job, to work for the fulfillment of the creation mandate to subdue and rule the earth, to seek personal holiness, and/or to go forth and transform society? Surely this is a foundational question for Christians to resolve as we work in either the private or the public sector.

All six sections of the book address such fundamental theological questions, but some overarching questions transcend the particular biblical tensions we are seeking to put in balance. For example, to what extent does our personal experience shape how we perceive and interpret the Bible, and to what degree does the Bible help us perceive the world's reality?

Another tension we face as Christians is how to put what we hold as truth in our faith into practice in the marketplace. It is one thing to affirm with the prophet Micah that we know we are "to do justice, to love kindness, and to walk humbly with [our] God" (Mic. 6:8). It is something else to flesh out what it means "to do justice" in the marketplace. But we are called *hundreds* of times to do righteousness and justice, and the scriptural calls are frequently illustrated with ungodly examples from the marketplace.

We will begin by addressing the question: To what extent should Christian business professionals be motivated by making profits, helping others, improving society, and witnessing for the gospel?

BALANCING BIBLICAL COMMANDS:
The Creation Mandates and the Great Commission

At the very beginning of human history (before the Fall), God told Adam and Eve, "Be fruitful and multiply, and fill the earth, and subdue it; and rule over the fish of the sea and over the birds of the sky, and over every living thing that moves on the earth" (Gen. 1:28). This was the beginning of God's instructions to us concerning *family* and *work*. These two commands are often referred to as God's "creation mandates." Actually, there are three of them. The third one concerns His establishment of a day of rest (see Gen. 2:1-3).

Our primary interest here, however, revolves around just one of them: our need to fully understand God's expressed will concerning work and where it fits in our life's priorities. We were created to work—not as the sole purpose for our creation, but as a vital element in God's glorification through the disclosure of His awesome personage, creation, and sovereign will, which are partially disclosed through our cocreative activities.

We do not know how long our first parents lived in the garden before their fall, but that event set into motion a whole new set of conditions and consequences. Adam and Eve became morally discerning people (see Gen. 3:7). The ground was cursed and work became toil (see Gen. 3:17-19). They were driven from the garden to keep them from eating from the "tree of life," which would have resulted in their remaining eternally in the state of their newly acquired fallen nature (see Gen. 3:22-24). God's mercy was expressed both in their expulsion from the garden and in His statement that their seed (offspring) would eventually conquer Satan (see Gen 3:15). This was the initial reference to God's coming work of redemption. The rest of Scripture (see Gen. 3:8ff.) is the account of God's acts in mankind's history to secure our redemption.

The high point of God's redemptive acts, of course, is seen in the incarna-

19

tion, life, death, and resurrection of Christ. Just prior to His ascension, though, Christ gave His people another mandate, which has come to be known as the "Great Commission":

> "All authority has been given to Me in heaven and on earth. Go therefore and *make disciples* of all the nations, baptizing them in the name of the Father and the Son and the Holy Spirit, *teaching them to observe all that I commanded you*; and lo, I am with you always, even to the end of the age." (Matt. 28:18-20, emphasis added)

God's children, desiring to be obedient to His expressed will, have struggled over the ensuing centuries with just how to integrate the requirements of the creation mandate and the Great Commission. Surely the phrase in the Great Commission, "teaching them to observe all that I commanded you" means just what it says, but Christians have not always agreed on what is to be emphasized or practiced under its direction. Does this phrase embrace or supersede the creation mandate? And exactly what is embodied in the phrase, "and make disciples"? Does this phrase encompass our entire sanctification, or is it really directed toward our efforts to evangelize?

History discloses that some people have created dichotomies between the secular and the sacred, while others have established higher and lower priorities in their efforts to obey God's mandates—all quoting Scripture to justify their posture. There have been monastic movements. Asceticism has been recommended and followed by a few. Various separatist groups have been formed and have waxed and waned. Some preach that working for the Church is a higher calling, and others, as Martin Luther, see all honest vocation as a worthy and high calling. For example, Christians struggle with whether they are to witness to their faith in Christ on the job by being dedicated to good work or by actively seeking opportunities to present the gospel.

Some people feel strongly that we should never openly evangelize on our employer's time, for that is not why we are hired. Doing so is tantamount to stealing the employer's time in the name of God—a gross contradiction of values. Others, however, believe it is appropriate to evangelize on the job—hand out tracts, interject the gospel into conversations when possible, etc.—such as the army general who reported he was pressured to retire early because he evangelized on the job, declaring that he would rather be a private in God's army than a general in the U. S. Army. From his perspective, his job was of secondary importance, and evangelism was first.

This same body of tensions also surfaces in discussions (or private thoughts) as to whether God intends for us to apply biblical propositions and principles to the more formal policies and practices in our business. Should we make an effort to transform business and society in a way that will reflect godly standards, or is the primary thrust of Scripture more concerned with personal sanctification and holiness than with society's transformation? Just what ought to motivate a Christian in business: making profits, helping others, improving society, or witnessing for the gospel?

These many questions form a family of concerns that every Christian working in the marketplace faces and must resolve in some manner. They are deeper in importance than merely matters of emphasis. If they were merely matters of emphasis, we would have more tolerance with those who "do it differently." Our problem is really one of reconciling the relationship between the creation mandates and the Great Commission, and of understanding what is and is not included in "discipleship."

To help us focus on this tension, Kenneth S. Kantzer addresses the topic, "God Intends His Precepts to Transform Society," and J. Philip Wogaman addresses the topic, "Christian Faith and Personal Holiness." These two works will not cover every single question in the family of tensions we have exposed, but they will provide a strong biblical base for resolving them.

Each writer attempts to affirm his topic from a biblical perspective and not to defend it by attacking counter positions. It is important for the full positive pull of each topic to serve as the clarifying force for the issues. The legitimacy of Scripture's claim on countervailing positions must be felt and understood before reconciliation, synthesis, or a choice can rightfully be made. To do otherwise is to persist with a preconception. We must allow Scripture to reform us or we run the danger of reforming Scripture, something we are forbidden to do (see Deut. 4:2, 12:32; Josh. 1:7; Rev. 22:18).

Dr. Kantzer puts forth the premise that we are all created as interdependent moral beings, meaning that the observable characteristic of "exchange," the heart of business, is part of our very nature. We are created to exchange emotions, ideas, and things. From this, he builds a chain of biblically supported reasons: (1) God does intend His precepts to transform society; (2) Scripture does address directly the conduct of business; (3) God speaks to both the means and the ends of business; (4) the Christian businessperson is to promote the common good, foster justice, and seek fairness; (5) we are to seek good through mutually profitable exchange; (6) Christians come to business as stewards; (7) biblical goals and profits are not antithetical; and (8) a business profession is a calling from God.

CHAPTER 2

GOD INTENDS HIS PRECEPTS TO TRANSFORM SOCIETY
Kenneth S. Kantzer

Dr. Kenneth Kantzer is Chancellor of Trinity College and Director of the Ph.D. program at Trinity Evangelical Divinity School where he is also Professor of Biblical and Systematic Theology. He serves as the Dean of the Christianity Today Institute and is Senior Editor of Christianity Today. *Dr. Kantzer is an ordained minister (since 1948) in the Evangelical Free Church of America. He received his Ph.D. in History and Philosophy of Religion from Harvard University where he was a Hopkins Scholar. He has edited four volumes and contributed hundreds of articles to major magazines, journals, and symposia in the area of systematic theology and the application of Christianity to contemporary life and thought.*

CHRIST'S LORDSHIP AND THE BIBLE

Jesus Christ is Lord. Christians acknowledge Him to be their Savior; they also hold that He is God incarnate and, therefore, the divine Lord of the entire universe. Because He is true God as well as true man, it is the duty of all human beings to acknowledge His lordship. They owe Him their obedience and service.

Yet Christians, because they have publicly confessed Jesus Christ as Lord, are specially obligated to worship and obey Him. On His part, Jesus Christ gives His followers life and meaning, resources to sustain and strengthen them in their ongoing daily life, hope for the future, and guidance along the way. He provides this guidance in many ways.

He spells out His divine instructions infallibly in the Bible. He has also given Christians the Holy Spirit to enable them to interpret these instructions and to apply them to all aspects of life. The Bible, in fact, is His love book to the Church. All its ethical teaching can be summarized under the two great commandments: love to God and love to fellow humans. As Jesus noted, "All the Law and the Prophets hang on these two commandments" (Matt. 22:34-40, NIV).

The Bible is a divine love book in two ways; it shows us how love is both a principle of differentiation and a principle of motivation. As a principle of differentiation, it teaches us what is really right and what is really wrong. It guides us so that we will not be misled by what *seems* to be right according to our limited perception of reality. It instructs us as to what is true love according to the infinite wisdom of the omniscient God. This primary function is noted in the passage just cited from Matthew.

Love is also fundamental to a biblical ethic understood as a principle of motivation. God creates in us a love that enables us to desire to do what is truly loving and not to do what is unloving or hurtful to others. The Apostle John explicates love as a principle of motivation in the fourth and fifth chapters of his first Epistle: "We love, because He first loved us" (1 John 4:19, NASB). The Bible is a love book in this sense, too, because it guides us to the infinite resources of the omnipotent God, especially to the divine resources by which we can be regenerated and sanctified and thus come to be loving beings.

This does not mean that the Bible provides only broad principles for guidance. It presents all that we need to know so that we may be fully instructed as to what is God's will—that is, what is best for humans living in various situations that must be faced on planet earth (and, perhaps, beyond planet earth in whatever area of the universe we have an impact). For example, dumping garbage on a planet encircling Arcturus could be just as bad as dumping garbage on the streets of Chicago. And in the Bible, God also offers motivational resources through His creative, redeeming love. Then God instructs us as to how He has decided we may best obtain and appropriate these resources in our human experience.

In providing principles that distinguish between right and wrong, moreover, the Scriptures do not reveal minute instructions so that the Christian life becomes merely an application of precise actions for every situation. Rather, all instructions are implied in love, and love applies to all. Yet as finite creatures, we must work on the limited data obtained through our finite experience. God, therefore, graciously sees fit to give broad principles interpreting generally what love really means or requires.

Then beyond these general principles, in ever lower and more specifically directed hierarchies of application, He divulges certain information. The Bible does occasionally impart instructions for a particular person in a specific situation in space and time. David was guided to pick five stones for his sling rather than wear the armor of Saul when he went to defend the troops of Israel against Goliath, and Paul instructed Timothy under inspiration of God to fetch his cloak from Troas. But such examples are rare.

The level of generality or specificity in biblical instruction is, from our present point of view, set forth on an ad hoc basis. That is, the needs of the occasion at the time of the composition of each biblical text give rise to that specific command. Yet these ad hoc instructions are not due to an accident of history. They were arranged by the design of an omnipotent, omniscient God who loves us and wishes to provide the guidance and spiritual resources we need. Their divine purpose is to enable us to live the most full and useful lives possible according to our nature and lot in life as determined by the Sovereign God.

HUMAN DOMINION AND SERVICE

And how does all of this relate to business? By creation, human beings are social beings, never intended to live alone. Because of our social nature, we are specialized (each person is in one sense unique), interdependent and, therefore, necessarily dependent on exchange. Exchange is built into our very nature. And this *is* business.

So, it is not surprising that the first commandment recorded in the Bible is for humans to be fruitful and multiply (see Gen. 1:28). God set up in the human economy interrelationships of husband, wife, and children. Accordingly, the family is the original pattern for all human social life. It provides for individual differences, subordination of some to others, inequality within the members of the race accompanied by equal dignity and worth, mutual love, loyalty to the group, and service to one another and to the community as a common obliga-tion of all. Especially crucial for our understanding of business relationships is the principle of inequality—always to be accompanied by, even bathed in, love, thus safeguarding the personal dignity of each individual within a framework of subordination and inequality.

Immediately following Creation, God issued two further commands: to "subdue" and to "rule" the earth. These commands, which are given only to human beings, flow from their being created in the image of God. The Hebrew words for subdue and rule, *kabash* and *radah*, are extremely forceful. *Kabash* means "to tread down" or "to bring into bondage." *Radah* comes from a word meaning "to prevail against" or "to trample down" and suggests the image of one treading grapes in a winepress in order to secure their juice.

The extremely forceful image created by these two words, however, is balanced by the closely related command in the next chapter of Genesis: Adam learned of his new duty when "the LORD God took the man and put him into the garden of Eden to cultivate it and keep it" (Gen. 2:15, NASB). Here human responsibility is described by the Hebrew words *abad* and *shamar*. The first may be translated "to till" or "to work," but its most frequent translation is "to serve." *Shamar* can be translated "to keep," or "to watch," or "to preserve." Thus, this set of words indicates the way in which the earlier commands are to be obeyed.

Human beings are masters over the things of the earth (underlords under the Sovereign God), but they are to exercise their underlordship and mastery in such a way as to watch over and guard those resources and to serve them by seeing to it that they make their greatest possible contribution for the good of all humanity. This is the sense in which man has dominion over the physical earth and the animals.

The book of Ezekiel spells out the legitimate meaning of this divinely bestowed task by drawing an analogy. The prophet contrasts the proper role of humankind in relationship to nonhuman life with the role taken by Israel's leaders in relationship to the common people. God directed Ezekiel to instruct the shepherds of Israel, that is, the spiritual and political leaders of Israel, as follows:

> "Ho, shepherds of Israel who have been feeding yourselves! Should not shepherds feed the sheep? You eat the fat, you clothe yourselves with the wool, you slaughter the fatlings; but you do not feed the sheep. The weak you have not strengthened, the sick you have not healed, the crippled you have not bound up, the strayed you have not brought back, the lost you have not sought, and with force and harshness you have ruled them." (Ezek. 34:2-4, RSV)

In this passage, of course, the leaders of Israel are condemned for mistreating the people. But the proper relationship between humans and sheep is spelled out to provide the model or standard on the basis of which the shepherd-leaders of Israel stood rightly condemned.

This passage is especially relevant for our topic of how a responsible Christian should conduct business. An appropriate animal husbandry becomes a model for the guidance of our relationships with the sub-human world about us and with others in the human society.

Even more revealing is the passage from Isaiah 53, setting forth the divine model for dominion. Divine authority displays itself in a radical kind of servitude. The authority of the Lord, astounding as it may seem, is a dominion over humankind that is revealed in meekness and servitude.

The Apostle Paul picks up this same theme in Philippians 2. In relationships with others, human beings are called to an attitude like that of Christ, who did not choose to "lord it over others." The biblical God, who is a God of love, saw fit to humble Himself and to serve humankind. And so we human beings are to have this same attitude toward others.

The earth and all that is in it belong to God. We humans are only God's stewards entrusted with the administration and use of His creation. In his sermon on Ephesians, John Calvin catches this biblical theme:

> You may well say, I have worked hard in this or that. . . . There are a great number that take great pains in some occupation to get their living; and yet if a man examines what purpose it serves . . . he will find that it serves only to feed his pride and pomp. In short, it is an open provocation of God, and a wasting and perverting of what God has given to men with commandments to use it with sobriety and restraint. . . . Let him also see to it that he serves his neighbors, and that the use of his skill and occupation may redound to the common profit of all men.
>
> When men get to the point of saying, "Oh, such a man got on well by such a trade, and he made great profit out of it," then they rush in helter-skelter, and voice no question about examining whether the thing is just and right, or not.[1]

We are to safeguard physical life, including subhuman life and the physical resources of the earth. In Luke 16 our Lord teaches that in both the physical realm and the spiritual realm, we are accountable for how we use the resources God has placed at our disposal. We are to use them wisely for the good of all if we are to please God; we must not use them selfishly or for immoral purposes.

These mandates are parts of the creation ordinance. Mankind was destined to rule the world—as God made plain when He created humans in His image and drew the implications of that image for mankind's role in the world (see Gen. 1:26ff.).

This divinely ordained role for humankind was not negated by the fall of man into sin. The command is repeated to Noah and his sons:

> "All the beasts of the earth and all the birds of the air, upon every creature that moves along the ground, and upon all the fish of the sea; they are given into your hands. Everything that lives and moves will be food for you. Just as I gave you the green plants, I now give you everything."
> (Gen. 9:2-3, NIV)

Yet once again a caution follows immediately:

> "And for your lifeblood I will surely demand an accounting. I will demand an accounting from every animal. And from each man, too, I will demand an accounting for the life of his fellow man." (Gen. 9:5, NIV)

All this flows from man's creation in the image of God. And the New Testament reinforces the specific command not to murder because of the image of God in which man was created. That image has been defaced but not destroyed or completely effaced.

We live in a disordered, frustrated world. Humans engage in acts of violence that must be restrained by violence (see Gen. 9:6). Eventually, it is true, the whole world will be restored and placed under the lordship of Christ; "yet at present we do not see everything subject to him" (Heb. 2:8, NIV). For now, the whole creation continues to suffer and groan "as in the pains of childbirth right up to the present time." Now we wait in hope, eagerly looking forward to that day when all will be restored to complete obedience to Christ (Rom. 8:20-25).

For the meanwhile, the Holy Scriptures instruct Christians how to relate to other Christians and to individuals outside the faith. We are reminded that we are citizens of two worlds, and each carries its own set of responsibilities. As citizens of Heaven, we are responsible to God to serve His Kingdom of righteousness. As citizens of an earthly nation, we likewise have duties that require us to carry out our responsibilities toward the world. We are to love others (see 1 John 3:23). We are to be like the God we worship, who loves the whole world in spite of their sin, and so should we.

Paul spells out the duties of government to provide order, justice, protection, and the general welfare for all citizens (Rom. 13). And if this is true under an evil government like Nero's, how much more is it true under a good government. Moreover, since we live in a democracy, we *are* the government. *We* are responsible for bringing these good things to our fellow citizens. Constructive Christian citizenship is a part of the fulfillment of the ordinance first given at Creation, repeated after the Fall, and assumed everywhere in Scripture.

We are not simply to bear witness to the gospel. We are also commanded to do good works, which become the best evidence to nonChristians that we care for them and that Christianity really seeks the good of all human beings. Perhaps this verse best sums up the idea: "For it is God's will that by doing good you should silence the ignorant talk of foolish men" (1 Pet. 2:15, NIV).

We face a host of questions about how to understand and apply the Bible so that our divinely ordained civil duties do not conflict with our Kingdom duties. Is capitalism based on a principle of selfishness? If it is, must all good Christians become socialists? Is violence on the part of a good Christian permitted in order to enforce justice in an evil society? Some of these questions will be addressed in later chapters of this book.

APPLYING THE SCRIPTURE

The special concern of this chapter is to address certain broad, relevant questions. The following questions provide, or rather demand, a framework for a legitimate human role in relationship to the universe. Obviously, in turning to these general questions, we must assume certain positions addressed and defended in later chapters. It is equally clear that some of these assumptions are not accepted by all Christians. But the focus of this chapter will be on these specific questions.

1. Does God intend His precepts to reform society? Yes, that is their purpose, and His goal of a perfect society will be achieved. God will eventually vindicate His creation as good. Sin and disorder in the world are man's contributions that God deliberately chooses to permit for His own good ends, but He does not deliberately cause them.

Yet the world will never be completely transformed by the spread of the gospel and a gradual renewal of the whole world into a perfectly just society. The world is not now perfect, and it never will become perfect under the present course of events. Accordingly, scriptural instruction for Christians is not intended to guide them in a sinless world. It is true that the general command to transform and subdue the world was given before sin came into the world to wreak its havoc. That command has never been abrogated. It was repeated in the biblical instructions after the Fall and is still binding on mankind. It will remain valid and continue to guide all humankind in the future Kingdom of righteousness. Yet biblical instruction as a whole focuses on God's people in a state of transition. It seeks to guide Christians, who are forgiven sinners in process of becoming healed and perfect, to function in a world in rebellion against God.

The present state of society is a major justification for government and law, with their appropriate penalties for violations of the law, including the use of force. And in this world, moreover, good, creative, and constructive work of obedience to God is not wasted. Its value for society is significant for the good of humankind now in this transitional stage. We do not know how much of what we can do here and now will also be preserved beyond this stage to the permanent Kingdom that Christ will bring. At the Second Coming, the earth will not be destroyed but only judged and transformed. We have every reason to believe that we can make permanent contributions because the human lives affected are eternal. So, these "temporary contributions" are of infinite value.

In any case, we are instructed by our Lord, as His representatives, to do good to all men in His name. Every alleviation of pain and sorrow and hunger and thirst is good. Of course, we rarely know exactly what will be the results of our constructive labors; we only know that we are always to function in love if we would be obedient to our Lord.

Nonetheless, we have biblical grounds for believing that our ministry for the good of others is of permanent value because it affects personal beings who will, in fact, live forever and because the contribution we make will itself be a permanent one to human society. It is now our duty in a fallen world to bear witness by work *and life* to God's love for all human beings. In effect we set up a model that focuses on the gospel, but is not limited to the gospel in its narrow sense (i.e., 1 Cor. 15:3-4). Rather, it displays the providential care of God for all and the abundant resources He provides for us out of His infinite love for the whole world.

2. Do the Scriptures speak to the conduct of business at all? Yes, assuredly, they do. A Christian's involvement in business is a corollary of the creation ordinance. Human beings are social beings. God did not make us identical to one another. The welfare of humans, therefore, requires specialization and exchange. The family is a microcosm of the world. Although the New Testament idea of vocation or calling refers primarily to the gracious call of God to sinners in bringing them out of their lostness and alienation from their Creator into the family of the redeemed, Scripture also recognizes God's guidance of His children to various tasks in the world suited to their capabilities—capabilities that are theirs by right of creation and redemption and special gifts. Every person is to be faithful to the calling given by God.

Being in business is itself a divine call. In some sense it is a divine call to everyone, for all in normal life must share in the exchanges necessary for useful living. Others in a special sense are called by God to function in the business world.

3. Is the guidance of God for business related only to its ultimate goal? Or does His guidance include the ways and means by which business ought to be conducted? It is both. Everything that Christians do is for the glory of God. All our actions are to be motivated by love. We are to love all human beings. We are to serve God and all mankind for their good.

Part of our service is spiritual because it relates to the gospel, and part is physical or material, relating to life and health and earthly well-being. But the

Bible does not relegate these to separate categories. We are not to kill but to protect and to preserve the lives of our fellow humans. Moreover, we are to preserve their usefulness, so that they, too, can serve God and function effectively in society. We are to provide for their comfort and their legitimate wants. We should encourage them in all their values and desires that are good. But these are not unspiritual duties. They are a part of our spiritual service to God.

Of course, as citizens of the Kingdom of Heaven, we are to worship God, serve the Church, and work for the advancement of the gospel. The Bible affirms unequivocally that these are our *primary* duties. We are to seek first the Kingdom of God, and as we do so, God will take care of these other matters in their proper role and order (see Matt. 6:25-34).

But as citizens of an earthly kingdom, we also have duties not directly related to the gospel and salvation. These, too, are binding on us and must not be reckoned as apart from God. They are duties to God, who is the Lord of the nations as well as of believers. Under the guidance of God, each Christian is to conduct himself appropriately to a personal calling. We are to be honest. We are to seek the good of others and so serve them. We are to observe the laws of the land. We are to pay taxes. We are to pray for and honor those in authority. And to the degree that society allows, we are to participate in government.

In a democratic government such as ours, Christians are to rule justly and wisely. As rulers, we are responsible for the laws of our land and for their enforcement. And the method by which we are to rule is prescribed. Except where the freedom of one impinges upon the rights of others, we are not to use force. Christians are to respect the integrity of every individual and to preserve the rights and freedoms of all. In functioning as citizens and as part of the government, we are to seek to make humans morally good. We are to accomplish our social and political goals not by compulsion, but by persuasion, exhortation, example, and instruction. We are to seek directly laws that will guarantee justice and fairness and the general welfare of our society. The Old Testament rebukes rulers who do not work for the good of the society in which they live (see, for example, Amos 5-6). The New Testament spells out the proper role of government: to seek justice and fairness and the general welfare (see Rom. 13:1-7). Therefore, Christians living in obedience to God and under His direction must seek to create this kind of government when they are part of the government.

4. What are the implications of common grace for Christian believers who participate in business? The role of Christians in business is similar to their role in a democratic government. Here, too, they are to promote the general welfare and to foster justice and fairness. In this area, too, they are to speak and

do what can be done properly by private individuals. To enforce what they think is good for others is beyond their duty and, usually, beyond their power.

What they do as businesspersons participating in government, of course, depends on the kind of government in the society of which they are a part. Christians are to seek a government in which everyone has a role as part of that government in a democratic society. When they have a right to vote, they are to seek good leaders. In the United States, one one-hundred-forty millionth of the responsibility for all good or bad leaders and good or bad laws rests on the head of each Christian citizen in America. God will hold each one responsible for the laws in our democracy.

No Christian capitalist ordinarily seeks a *laissez faire* capitalism. It is the duty of government and, therefore, of Christians who participate in government to make sure that the rights of all are protected. Government is to protect persons incapable of protecting themselves. It is to prohibit and punish wrong-doing, which will include prohibiting monopolies that create artificial scarcity for the sake of increased profits. It is to prevent the exploitation of children, the aged, and individuals with handicapping conditions.

Government will do what cannot easily or well be done by the individual when there is no adequate profit to motivate a private person to do the task or when there is inadequate voluntary response within the society. The more moral a society is, the less government action of the latter sort is needed. But in a fallen world every society needs a responsive, socially responsible government.

5. Should Christians come to the workplace with a sense of responsibility limited to their personal moral conduct while functioning as Christians in an alien structure, or does their responsibility include striving to rebuild their sphere in the workplace under God's instruction? Every Christian is to seek the good of others in all endeavors. And so in business, one's duty is to provide a society that will be conducive to the good of humankind. For the Christian, business does not have the goal of fleecing others for all one can get. Rather, it involves mutually profitable exchange. Each participant is free to choose according to his or her own values. Thus, each gets a larger share of what he or she individually wishes.

We need to distinguish the acquisitive motive from greed. Greed is always bad. The acquisitive motive implanted in us at Creation is not bad; it represents a divine, providential motive for work and expenditure of energy for our own good. It is not selfishness but a sense of personal responsibility to support self, family, the Church, and society in general. It is part of our desire to become all that we were meant to be and to help others do the same.

Perhaps the major flaw in the thinking of Karl Marx was his inability to differentiate between the acquisitive motive and greed. Certainly his judgment that capitalism is necessarily and essentially based on greed shows a fundamental misunderstanding of any truly Christian view of a proper social and economic structure of society.

Max Weber thus notes, "The idea that modern capitalism is based on greed should be permanently consigned to the kindergarten of the mind." He then defines the essence of modern capitalism as rooted in the division of labor, a free market of exchange, and the use of capital available through delayed gratification.

A defensible capitalism has for its goal not just to prevent crime or to control other persons and institutions. Rather, when "properly understood, democratic capitalism, far from being the embodiment of greed, is the contemporary expression of enlightened self-interest harnessed for the advancement of the common good."[2]

The accomplishment of this aim means, of course, that certain restrictions must be brought to bear on the marketplace. The freedom of one is limited by the freedom of others. For example, beginning in 1988, several states will restrict the right to drive a car for those who choose to buy and use alcohol while driving a car. But within the limits of freedom to all, each person gains as a result of business transactions.

This is not to deny that most capitalists—and most humans—are greedy. That the individual capitalist often—perhaps in actual practice, always—functions, at least in part, on a selfish basis no one denies. But it is not necessarily so, and it ought never to be so. As a system of economics, capitalism is based on a free market in which each person participates on the basis of individual choice according to individual values. Mother Teresa, for example, may choose to live in poverty so she can give her life in service to the urban poor of India. But the point is, no one enslaves her or forces her to adopt her values and make the choices that she does. She chooses them in a free market on her own initiative. The essence of capitalism is individual freedom to choose according to one's own values with the limit of freedom for one restricted by the freedom of others.

6. Should Christians come to the marketplace to pursue personal gain so long as they maintain biblical standards of morality, or should they also seek to improve, and even rebuild, the marketplace? Obviously, the Christian is always to live in accordance with the divine guidance for a life that is pleasing to God. In addition, personal moral conduct becomes a part of one's witness, as Peter noted (see 1 Pet. 2:12-15).

Yet being a good witness is not the whole of the Christian's task. Changing the marketplace for the better is also an important duty, and that can include seeking greater justice and better government and creating better citizens and better laws. Since the individual's conduct is to be for the good of the whole society, the marketplace is not merely a place to secure goods needed or wanted with the least expenditure of one's own goods and wants that one can legitimately get away with.

7. Are Christians to pursue biblical values or profit? Early Calvinists were sometimes accused of seeking wealth purely to establish their own election and to secure private gain. But the true Calvinists of the Reformation and post-Reformation period were not misers or selfish money-grabbers. They reckoned themselves to be stewards of God, who were responsible to the community. The cutthroat capitalism based on greed for which capitalism sometimes became known at a later period—the kind that Marx analyzes, and to a much lesser extent Weber—was not true Calvinism. It was the result of a decline of Calvinism that brought the evils of a truly perverted capitalism. If we love all humans as God does, we shall seek their good. That means we shall refuse to function as businesspersons in the construction of a society that will harm others.

Hence, profit is not the only motive, and it is certainly not the ultimate motive of the Christian businessperson. The Christian in business will not lie or cheat and will not engage in a business to the hurt of others, such as the recreational drug business. No doubt, the Christian will face tension between promoting the good of humankind and, at the same time, securing a profit. There have to be limits on setting prices for what is sold. It must not be assumed that whatever is legal is morally right.

As one individual exchanges what he has for what another has so that each may secure what he wants more, both parties should profit. The goal is to make an exchange that will be mutually profitable. Moreover, the Christian does not just seek to gain things for personal consumption; he endeavors to secure those proper biblical values to which he is committed.

Profit is legitimate, for service has been rendered. Profit is the reward for a delayed expenditure of goods and for the risk a person takes in using capital. Unjust gains arise from falsely contriving a demand for what is not really good, creating false scarcity by planned and coerced monopoly, or misrepresenting a product by deliberate fraud.

The Christian is not to try to get government to set a just price by law. Such a practice fails to recognize the freedom of the individual to set his own values and to engage in business on the basis of them.

Of course, the government has a role of protection. It is, as noted earlier, to protect all who are incapable of protecting themselves—orphans, children of uncaring parents, the elderly with uncaring children, and individuals who are suffering from catastrophic illnesses. It is to impose limits on freedoms that destroy the freedom of others. Ordinarily, however, the Christian is to engage in *free* exchange, not *forced* exchange.

For any free economy, the free exchange itself is a safeguard against greed so long as there is no fraud or cheating or taking advantage of the absolutely helpless. The greedy person is neutralized in the exercise of greed because the buyer may not want the goods or be willing to pay the price asked. Usually greed will not harm others because what the greedy person offers for sale has no attraction for others at the price set. To function effectively in a free economy, the participant must know what others are willing to purchase and at what price.

8. How does all this affect the Christian businessperson making daily decisions? A business profession is a call of God, which is to be practiced for God's glory. Every business is good and legitimate for the Christian so long as it works ultimately for the good of humankind, and so long as business is conducted in a right and moral way. The businessperson is to make exchanges that will be profitable for both parties and thus enable both to function effectively for the common good in the role to which God has called each one.

EDITOR'S REFLECTIONS

History reveals that God's precepts have been used on numerous occasions to transform society. For example, John Calvin's ministry in Geneva (1541-1564) was a specific effort to have the Church and the state work together; Abraham Kuyper, premier of the Netherlands (1901-1905), strived to incorporate Christian principles into the political sphere; John Howard (1726-1790), a close friend of John Wesley, labored long and hard to change the conditions in the prisons of England; and William Wilberforce (1759-1833) led a successful fight in the English Parliament for the abolishment of slavery in the British Empire.

These illustrations are just a few well-known examples of Christians having an impact on society through their integration and application of biblical principles in the social order. The efforts of Howard and Wilberforce are particularly interesting because they took place in a time when the Christian faith was under enormous adverse cultural pressure. The popular intellectual currents of their day were definitely against Christianity. Deism, the darling of the day, held that God ruled His universe through a set of immutable laws which precluded the possibility of miracles, the Incarnation, or even the Trinity.

Voltaire (1694-1678), a popular writer of his day, openly scoffed at the Christian faith. David Hume (1711-1776), the Scottish philosopher, was a skeptic of the first order. Jean Jacques Rousseau (1712-1778), the romanticist, reacted against the rationalistic movement of the day, and moved the intellectual discourses toward a form of mysticism incompatible with Christianity.

But in sharp contrast to these intellectual streams was the spiritual revival of 1750-1815 that occurred in England, Western Europe, and the newly emerging American nation. The Wesleys (Charles and John), George Whitefield, and others were prominent in the movement, and Christian principles had a profound impact on individuals and society at that time. We have enjoyed many of the general fruits of that revival into our own day.

The very truth that God has, *at times*, sovereignly used His precepts to transform society should cause us to reflect that this is not the only way in which He uses His precepts in society. As Solomon tells us, "There is an appointed time for everything. And there is a time for every event under heaven" (Eccles. 3:1-8).

Christ tells us that we are the salt of the earth and the light of the world and that we are to "let [our] light shine before men *in such a way* that they may see [our] good works, and glorify [our] Father who is in heaven" (Matt. 5:13-16, emphasis added). The Apostle Peter, however, explains that the nonbelievers who observe our good works may not bother to glorify God (praise Him for the good works) until the Day of Judgment (see 1 Pet. 2:12).

So we see that God may also ordain His precepts to be used as standards by which the world will be judged. The Christian's role is to be obedient and follow God's precepts regardless of personal opinion about the probable outcome of applying the precepts in the marketplace. Ezekiel, for example, was told to go and preach the Word. He was told if he did not obey, the people would die in their sins, and they and Ezekiel would be held accountable. If they did not listen to him and died in their sins, Ezekiel would not share in their guilt (see Ezek. 33:1-9). His job was to obey. He was not responsible for how people responded to his efforts.

Christians may not refuse to labor in the marketplace "in such a way" (Matt. 5:16) that their light will bring glory to God without running the terrible risk of being found disobedient. Ultimately, the issue is not one of whether society is transformed—that may or may not be God's purpose at the time—but the issue is one of being obedient children to the glory of God.

There is still another tension to be faced, though. Are God's precepts given for the *primary* purpose of taking them as "light" to the marketplace—for judgment or for society's transformation—or are they fundamentally intended to produce personal holiness in His children? Do God's precepts have primary and secondary purposes, or only complementary, countervailing objectives? J. Philip Wogaman wrestles with this tension in his chapter, "Christian Faith and Personal Holiness."

Dr. Wogaman, while declaring that "biblical faith is unalterably *both* personal and social" in character, does rightly expose the truth that personal transformation must occur first, even though it "is not a *substitute* for attending to systematic (community) relationships." In fact, he sets forth the case that one (the development of personal holiness) should result in the other (love for neighbors expressed concretely and definitively to alleviate social injustices). Nevertheless, personal holiness is a foundational prerequisite for the Christian life.

CHAPTER 3

CHRISTIAN FAITH AND PERSONAL HOLINESS

J. Philip Wogaman

Dr. J. Philip Wogaman has been Professor of Christian Social Ethics at Wesley Theological Seminary (Washington, D.C.) since 1966. He was Dean of the seminary from 1972 to 1983. He is author of Economics and Ethics, The Great Economic Debate, Christian Perspective on Politics, *and numerous other books and articles. He is an ordained United Methodist minister and serves on the World Methodist Council. He is past President of the Society of Christian Ethics of the United States and Canada, and member of the American Theological Society. He received his Ph.D. in social ethics from Boston University.*

How do Christians perceive the relationship between "personal holiness" and "social transformation"? Which is prior to the other? Ever since the social gospel movement of the late nineteenth and early twentieth centuries, warm debate has been joined over which most fundamentally reflects the biblical faith professed by Christians.

The debate, as it usually proceeds, is terribly misplaced, for biblical faith is unalterably *both* personal and social. Those who seek to reduce the meaning of the gospel to social transformation have to overlook the deeply personal character of Jesus' ministry to individuals: the healing of individuals, the calling of individuals to be disciples, the challenge to individuals (such as the rich young ruler) to surrender their whole being to Christ, the parables (such as the lost sheep and prodigal son) depicting God's boundless love for each and every sinner, no matter how alienated and lost he or she might be. And they have to overlook the powerful witness of the letters of Paul to the personally transforming power of the gospel of Christ, as well as Paul's many moral admonitions and comments on the virtuous Christian life. And they must neglect the dramatic engagement of Old Testament prophets with malefactors of great power and wealth, the comforting words—often phrased in highly personal terms—of many of the psalms, and the explicit commentary of Ezekiel on our responsibility for the choices we make. So, a rounded biblical faith is deeply personal.

But the moment we are prepared to say that concern for society is only a "byproduct" of the personal transformation, we are reminded that the Bible is also profoundly social in character. Israel is a community formed by God, rebellious against God, forgiven and restored by God, directed by God, loved by God in covenant. God relates to Israel as a community, and its prophets address it as a community. But is that only an Old Testament faith, superseded by a more personal New Testament gospel? Hardly, for the New Testament is also relational through and through. Jesus proclaims the Kingdom of God throughout the gospel narratives while frequently engaging people in and through their relationships. Paul and other New Testament writers address the Church as a new social reality founded in Christ. And this Church is not a mere association of convenience among like-minded Christians—it is the *Body* of Christ whose members belong to one another as the various parts of the human body belong to one another. There is a corporateness, a *wholeness* to our belonging to one another in community—in the Kingdom of God and in its prefiguration on earth, the Church.

So any phrasing of the "individual versus society" debate among Christians is bound to be wrong if it does not recognize that we are *both* individual and social by nature. We are not just a part of society, for we have mind and will—consciousness and conscience—as individuals. But we are not just individuals, either, for a solitary individual is unthinkable. Even the language we employ to understand ourselves is the gift of generations of social interaction, and in deep and subtle ways we find we do, indeed, belong to one another. The Bible does not require us to make an artificial division between the individual and society; it recognizes that neither can be lost without both being lost.

This point having been recorded, there remains a sense in which we can conceive of an individual confronting the need to decide and act in a social setting. And in this sense, the personal *character* of that individual is quite fundamental to the quality of his or her deciding and acting. In a previous writing, I emphasized the fact that the analysis of social, economic, and political good presupposes the existence of good people who are willing to do it![1] That is a hard assumption to make, on Christian grounds, for the reality of sin pervades humanity to such an extent that even Paul exclaimed, "I do not do the good I want, but the evil I do not want is what I do" and "Wretched man that I am! Who will deliver me from this body of death?" (Rom. 7:19,24). So the character of people is very important to anybody who wants to see people act with deep moral insight in the social world. Christians have much to say about that.

WHAT IS PERSONAL HOLINESS?

In some Christian quarters, moral goodness is characterized as personal holiness. The word may require some explanation. I am not sure the average businessperson, any more than the average politician, would want to be known as *holy*. Something in the popular connotations of the word seems far removed from the practicalities of the world. Indeed, some of *Webster's* definitions of the word suggest this:

> Set apart to the service of God or a god: sacred . . . characterized by perfection and transcendence: commanding absolute adoration and reverence: spiritually pure: Godly: evoking or meriting veneration or awe: being awesome, frightening, or beyond belief: filled with super-human and potentially fatal power.[2]

Some of these characterizations for the word *holy* may indeed fit some personalities in the business world—such as "being awesome, frightening, or beyond belief"! But the net effect of such definitions is to remove whoever is holy from ordinary life altogether. That is compounded whenever holiness is visualized as the *mysterium tremendum* of which medieval mystics spoke or to which Rudolf Otto referred in his classic work, *The Idea of the Holy*.[3]

But that is not the best theological understanding of holiness. In fact, the more our understanding of the word *holiness* is removed from the realities of the world, the more it is also removed from its own root meaning—for the word originally meant to be "whole." *Holiness* meant "wholeness." To be whole is to be free of self-contradiction. It is to be an *integrated* person, a person of *integrity*. But it is also to be a person who is in harmony with the rest of God's creation. To be holy is to be in right relationship with God and with what God has made and with what God intends. It is to be reconciled to God and presented "holy and blameless and irreproachable before him" (Col. 1:22). It is to be "God's temple": "For God's temple is holy, and that temple you are" (1 Cor. 3:17). The word has much in common with the Hebrew *shalom*, which is translated as "peace," but which means "to be in a state of harmonious well-being with others and with God's creation."

It is easy to see how the word *holy* might have come to be interpreted in an other-worldly way, since it is almost always employed in the New Testament to emphasize the difference being a Christian makes in one's life. And yet, the Christian life (as Paul carefully explains) does not remove us from the world so much as it transforms our relationship to the world. To be holy in this biblical sense is to be freed from idolatry, no longer to embrace worldly values. So Peter addresses Christians with this admonition, "As obedient children, do not be conformed to the passions of your former ignorance, but as he who called you is holy, be holy yourselves in all your conduct; since it is written, 'You shall be holy, for I am holy'" (1 Pet. 1:14-16). These words are written not to a monastic community, safely removed from contact with the world, but to men and women who are in constant contact with a world in which they must struggle:

> Now for a little while you may have to suffer various trials, so that the genuineness of your faith, more precious than gold which though perishable is tested by fire, may redound to praise and glory and honor at the revelation of Jesus Christ. (1 Pet. 1:6-7)

To be holy, then, is to be one who is devoted to God. It is to be a person whose life is attuned to God's will first, one who has put aside the idolatries of the world. It is to be one who single-mindedly pursues God's agenda for the world, as best God's purposes can be known by fallible human beings who, in spite of all, are still tempted, still prone toward sin. A holy person, thus, is moral. But to be holy is more than to be *moral* as that term is generally used. We cannot and should not dispense with the theological context of the word. A holy life is one possessing a goodness that has its ground in God, that is responsible to God, that seeks God's will, above all, in all things.

THE CHRISTIAN BASIS OF PERSONAL HOLINESS

To be such a person is rather difficult. How does one go about accomplishing it?

The deep Christian insight—perhaps the deepest Christian insight of all— is that one does not do it for oneself. We are transformed by the power of God's grace, manifested through Jesus Christ. That is, we are holy not because we have set out to save ourselves, but because God has reached across the barriers of our self-centeredness with accepting love. Paul writes,

> For there is no distinction; since all have sinned and fall short of the glory of God, they are justified by his grace as a gift, through the redemption which is in Christ Jesus, whom God put forward as an expiation by his blood, to be received by faith. (Rom. 3:22-25)

We are, by God's love, freed from the necessity of trying to save ourselves, which Paul understood we could not do in any case.

Paul's own struggle—echoed curiously by such formative Christian leaders as Luther and Wesley in later centuries—was between a recognition of the imperative of righteousness and the impossibility of being righteous enough. Indeed, how can we be righteous enough if the Holy God, upon whom we depend for everything, has demanded perfection of us? But Paul was gripped at the center of his being by the enormity of the love God has for us, as manifested in Jesus Christ on the cross. Through Christ, we are liberated—not *from* righteousness, but *to* righteousness. In the Cross we see at once the immensity of human sin in all its deadliness and futility and the depth of saving love. When we are grasped by that love it is possible, as Wesley emphasized, to grow in perfection.[4] But Wesley did not think of *perfection* in abstract moral terms. *Perfection* meant "love." And so, using Wesley's terminology, we are *justified* by God's grace, received through faith, and we are *sanctified* as we grow in grace, our wills transformed by the power of the Holy Spirit as we move toward perfection in love.

The bearing of this upon personal righteousness or holiness is twofold. In the first place, holiness is no longer conceived of in terms of obedience to a set of negative laws. But in the second place, it is grounded in God's love and expressed as our own increasing capacity for loving response.

May I digress to comment that there is a good deal of practical psychological wisdom in this. Righteousness based primarily on conformity to law is likely to be self-centered and, ultimately, fragile. When we are righteous for the sake of gaining a reward or avoiding a punishment, are we not motivated principally by self-interest? And is that not far removed from love? And is love not the central law? But it is more than law; it is living reality. So the righteousness or holiness of which Christians speak is that transformation of the self occurring as we see that we no longer have to be preoccupied with self. We can trust God all the way and be free to live the life of love.

This reality still does not relieve us of the whole panoply of troubles and confusions to which human life is heir. But it does establish the basis upon which we can live in such a world without being defeated by it.

PERSONAL HOLINESS AND THE CHRISTIAN VIRTUES

The New Testament does not leave us with the doctrine of justification alone, though that is surely the basis for everything else one might say about the Christian life. It offers positive direction for the spiritual life by helping us understand the virtues or fruits of such a life. In the very books in which Paul insists upon grace and Christian freedom, he also writes concretely of the qualities of life that are to be sought or avoided. In Galatians, after an eloquent passage on Christian freedom, he goes on to caution us, "Do not use your freedom as an opportunity for the flesh, but through love be servants of one another" (Gal. 5:13). And not content with generalities, he tells us what to avoid: "Now the works of the flesh are plain: fornication, impurity, licentiousness, idolatry, sorcery, enmity, strife, jealousy, anger, selfishness, dissension, party spirit, envy, drunkenness, carousing, and the like" (Gal. 5:19-21). He issues a stern warning that "those who do such things shall not inherit the kingdom of God" (v. 21).

Is this a return to the legalistic morality from which we were supposed to have been freed by grace? Is Paul taking away with his left hand what he has set forth with his right hand? Hardly, for he is here warning about the effects of those things that are against love, against the Spirit within which we find freedom. Paul is reminding us that we cannot accept love unlovingly. God's love is deep and dependable. But the "works of the flesh" of which Paul reminds us are ways in which we refuse to accept the power of God's love in our lives.

The point is even clearer when we look at the positive virtues Paul lists immediately after his warning. He goes on to write that "the fruit of the Spirit is love, joy, peace, patience, kindness, goodness, faithfulness, gentleness, self-control; against such there is no law" (Gal. 5:22-23). And "if we live by the Spirit, let us also walk by the Spirit. Let us have no self-conceit, no provoking of one another, no envy of one another" (vv. 25-26). Is it not clear that he is primarily describing the qualities of love—what confirms it and expresses it as well as what stands in its way?

That is also true of many of the virtues underscored in Jesus' teaching ministry, such as the Sermon on the Mount, where the qualities of love are characterized and celebrated. The life of love is "blessed," even though the world, in its blindness, regards that life as weakness. The Sermon on the Mount does not leave the matter with abstraction, either. Offering illustrations that would have been painfully clear to His listeners, Jesus says,

> "You have heard that it was said, 'An eye for an eye and a tooth for a tooth.' But I say to you, Do not resist one who is evil. But if any one strikes you on the right cheek, turn to him the other also; and if any one would sue you and take your coat, let him have your cloak as well; and if any one forces you to go one mile, go with him two miles. Give to him who begs from you, and do not refuse him who would borrow from you." (Matt. 5:38-42)

The literature produced by Christians trying to get off the hook of such teachings is, by now, voluminous. But much of it misses the point that Jesus is confronting us with the centrality of love—He is not offering a new legalism. If one accepts the central premise of love, then the specifics can be taken in the spirit of being guided by love in all things. Even the more negative points in the Sermon on the Mount can be taken in that spirit, such as the warning against "practicing your piety before men in order to be seen by them" and "when you pray, you must not be like the hypocrites" (6:1,5). Hypocrisy is anxious, self-centered behavior; it is seeking dishonestly to "save oneself" by making an impression upon others while, at the same time, living by selfish standards.

First Corinthians 13 is possibly the best-known and best-loved listing of Christian virtues, and it is especially clear that virtues are an outgrowth of love:

> Love is patient and kind; love is not jealous or boastful; it is not arrogant or rude. Love does not insist on its own way; it is not irritable or resentful; it does not rejoice at wrong, but rejoices in the right. Love bears all things, believes all things, hopes all things, endures all things. (vv. 4-7)

If love, then, is the underlying meaning of the Christian virtues, what is the point in speaking of specific virtues and offering specific admonitions, as the New Testament frequently does? There is indeed a danger in pointing up specific virtues if they become a basis for some new legalism. Such a legalism becomes bizarre—even a bit humorous—as when we try to become more humble and, if we think we have succeeded, find ourselves becoming proud of it! But if one is secure in love—and that is what justification does for us—then the various virtues and moral admonitions are helpful as we seek to grow in love. Justification is the basis, the starting point, for Christian character. But we still need to grow. And it is still helpful to be alert to dangers along the way. There is still some point to moral instruction and to the development of the right kinds of habits in the moral life. Thinking about the qualities of Christian love in advance and learning from one's failures can help one be *instinctively* or *intuitively* loving in the future. One does not think about and practice the Christian virtues in order to score good behavior points with God. One does so because that represents the loving quality of life for which human beings were created and redeemed.

MAKING MORAL DECISIONS

Nevertheless, making moral decisions remains difficult in so confusing a world. Even the most mature Christians are quite capable of making mistakes. Being a holy person—as we have used the word *holy* here—does not in itself guarantee good results. Our intuitions, no matter how well disciplined by love, can be wrong, partly because we can have an erroneous perception of the facts—a problem with which everybody in business is more than familiar. Even the best data can be thoroughly inaccurate. And even when we have accurate objective data, we can misjudge what other people will do. And even when our data are accurate and we have correctly anticipated the reactions of others, we may not be clear about what is ultimately at stake. "New occasions teach new duties," as James Russell Lowell wrote, and "time makes ancient good uncouth."

For instance, throughout history large numbers of Christians have accepted the institution of slavery. No doubt many otherwise saintly people who just did not know any better may be included in that group. The striking thing about the pre-Civil War debates over slavery that racked Presbyterian, Methodist, and Baptist denominations in the United States is that people on both sides were so clear about being "right"—both citing Scripture and other sources of moral wisdom to make their points. In retrospect, it is clear to most people today that the proslavery position was flatly wrong, although the antislavery position was sometimes espoused in an unloving spirit and some of the antislavery people appear to have been tainted by racism as well.

Or, to cite another example, throughout history large numbers of Christians have treated women as inferiors by denying them equal political rights or equal rights of participation in the life of the Church. The struggles over this issue have also involved equally convinced Christians on all sides, with everybody also appealing to Scripture and to factual evidences of one kind or another. That struggle continues, though it is already evident to numerous Christians that it was a disservice to Church and nation to exclude the immense talents of one-half the human race from full participation.

New biological technologies, new forms of military capability, and new economic arrangements and possibilities challenge the judgment of even the most saintly Christians. And clearly it takes more than personal holiness to discern the will of God in such a changing world.

Then, is the Bible useless as a guide to moral decision making? By no means. The Bible is absolutely decisive in revealing what is ultimately at issue in all moral decision making. As we have seen, the Bible conveys our deepest insights into the gracious and creative character of God and also reveals the deepest insights into the character of Christian life. These are foundational to everything else.

But still, it is a mistake to treat the Bible as a detailed handbook of specific moral injunctions suitable for every occasion. At least three reasons explain why. First, many of the problems we face today were unknown in the ancient world. Second, one can get conflicting signals on specific problems from different parts of the Bible. And, third, some of the specific injunctions are not very adequate expressions of the Bible's own deepest truths.

I offer two illustrations, one from the Old, the other from the New Testament, to clarify further. If one turned to the Old Testament for insight into whether we should accept capital punishment in modern society, it would be clear from such books as Leviticus and Deuteronomy that we should. But we would be embarrassed to discover that capital punishment is prescribed not only for first-degree murder but also for all sorts of other offenses, including enticing people to follow other gods (see Deut. 13:6-10) and blasphemy (see Lev. 24:16). Under the U. S. Constitution, these acts are not even offenses, much less capital crimes! Or if one turned to the New Testament for directions on the role of women in church, one might encounter the proposition that women should always wear a veil in church (see 1 Cor. 11:5-15) and that they should not be permitted to speak there (see 1 Cor. 14:34-35).

Arriving at moral decisions by scriptural proof-texting is a notoriously unreliable method. But one can still learn much from the specific applications made in the Bible. Given the fact that such specifics are an attempt to apply the central truths of our faith to particular issues, Christians must take them seriously. I would go so far as to say that Christians should usually presume the rightness of a biblical application unless or until it becomes clear that (1) the particular injunction was intended only for the immediate historical situation in ancient Israel or the early Church, (2) the facts were not clearly known by the biblical writer, or (3) the particular application is plainly inconsistent with the deeper biblical witness.

IMPLICATIONS FOR THE BUSINESS WORLD

What are the implications of this point about making moral decisions for Christians in the business world? Indeed, is it even possible for a person to be

---

Editor's Note: Dr. Wogaman's Christology governs his view of Scripture. He subordinates Scripture to Christ. His understanding of Christ (scripturally derived) transcends in importance, for him, the Scripture itself. It is his understanding that the mind of Christ is such that he may make the three points above, which go beyond traditional orthodox thinking. Others of us (series editor, publisher, and other scholars participating in this book) are theologically convinced that this approach to the interpretation of Scripture opens the door to personalized emphases without a biblical check. The reader should note, however, that Dr. Wogaman's actual application of Scripture in this chapter is completely orthodox at every point except on the subject touched on in this illustration.

But it remains true that many problems confront us in the contemporary world that are not specifically anticipated by the Bible. Christians, no matter how saintly or how well-versed in Scripture, are called upon to *think*!

holy in the sense we have used that term and still be involved in business?

As I write, abundant evidence shows that it is not very easy. Wall Street insider trading scandals, fraudulent practices in the banking world—sometimes leading to bank failures and depositor losses or inconvenience—and problems with product safety suggest that many people in business are quite prepared to cut corners with the law, not to say with Christian ethics.

But one doubts whether those who engage in such practices are even trying to be Christian. Our concern is with people who are genuinely Christian and who, at the same time, sincerely *want* to apply their faith intelligently to their life in the business world.

The first word to such people obviously has to do with their motivations. What are their ultimate purposes in engaging in business? If their lives are characterized by personal holiness, they will not be motivated by idolatries of materialism or competitive success. On all hands we see people who *need* to be successful in business as a way of reassuring themselves that their lives matter. It is a way of "saving" oneself, peculiarly suited to the modern world.

Christians do not need this form of reassurance, having already the deeper reassurance of God's love in Jesus Christ. That is why it is deeply offensive to hear Christian preachers promise worldly success to those who live as faithful Christians—such as the nineteenth-century Episcopal bishop Lawrence's exclamation that "godliness is in league with riches" or twentieth-century counterparts who proclaim that "you have a God-ordained right to be wealthy."[5] And that is why it is even more offensive to see gross displays of materialism among certain televangelists of our time—though *pathos* may be a more apt word to describe this materialism.[6] But Christians do not need to be wealthy as a way of finding meaning in life.

That point granted, I do not think the business world *requires* anybody to be idolatrous. Many businesspeople are not at all materialistic in their lifestyles, treating their wealth as a trust for God and for others. Indeed, Max Weber's celebrated study *The Protestant Ethic and the Spirit of Capitalism* notes the influence of Calvinism in producing a form of ascetic capitalism in the Western world.[7] Ascetic capitalists considered it a serious responsibility to increase the sum of wealth in the world, but they themselves lived modestly. John Wesley's famous admonition to "gain all you can, in order to save all you can, in order to give all you can"[8] expresses something of that spirit, although it must be admitted that most of his followers were rather more successful in the first two points than the third! The great American steelmaker and philanthropist Andrew Carnegie expressed something of this spirit, insisting that wealth is a trust to be used wisely for the betterment of the community. He even took the view that those who die with wealth they have not given away have died as failures; by that standard he was something of a failure, even though his many philanthropies have blessed many American communities.[9]

What about business ethics, as such?

There are many different versions, some of which are plainly too narrow for Christians. For instance, there is Milton Friedman's 1962 comment that "few trends could so thoroughly undermine the very foundations of our free society as the acceptance by corporate officials of a social responsibility other than to make as much money for their stockholders as possible."[10] Behind this remark is Friedman's conviction that corporate officials should not remove from the stockholders the power to use their own money as they see fit. But it is utterly naive to think that only stockholders are influenced in a major way by the corporate decisions that must be made by corporate officials. Most morally sensitive business leaders would want to go further in acknowledging a responsibility to public health and safety, a responsibility to the well-being of employees, and a responsibility to be good corporate citizens of the communities in which they are doing business. It might be possible to make more money for the stockholders by disposing of waste products in the nearest river or by paying the lowest possible wages or by pandering to the lowest aspects of community taste through certain advertising campaigns. Such things are done. But ethically sensitive corporate leaders have higher standards.

But we are concerned here not just with high moral standards, but with *personal holiness*. To be a Christian businessperson is to care passionately about doing good. Such a Christian is motivated by far more than legal requirements or simple honesty in business dealings. Such a Christian wishes to approach the business world as his or her special calling, recognizing that business life can be a form of ministry. While such a businessperson may never have heard of Luther's views on the Christian calling, he or she would respond warmly to Luther's idea that a "calling" or ministry can be any activity that is needed for the well-being of society.[11]

Such a ministry has many concrete objectives, including the production and distribution of the goods and services needed for human survival and well-being, the provision of jobs for as many people as possible, the solution of practical material problems facing the community. The role of the businessperson is needed in all modern societies, including socialist ones. Their contribution is not at all inconsistent, in principle, with the deeper meaning of Christian life. Even the specific Christian virtues, such as those mentioned in 1 Corinthians 13, can be related creatively to the typical tasks of business life, including patience, kindness, hopefulness, and the capacity for endurance. A deeply Christian businessperson will bring these qualities to the business environment, seeking to do good as well as be good.

THE DILEMMA OF MARKET COMPETITION

There is a problem with leaving Christian responsibility at that level, however. A Christian can be a good person and *want* to do the right thing but still not be able to. Sometimes the real world is not receptive to good intentions.

It is possible for a very moral person to find himself or herself working for the wrong company. An unethical company—and there are a few—can make it pretty hard on an ethical employee. Then you have to change the company or get out—or work out some kind of compromise within yourself and just do the best you can. I recall one company personnel manager on the West Coast some years ago who discovered that his company's hiring policy was racially discriminatory. The policy was blatant, but it was also well-concealed. He was concerned about it, and he actually found a way to change it. But that is not always easy to do. Sometimes you just have to get out for the sake of your conscience.

But I am concerned about an even deeper problem. Sometimes the company is socially responsible, and its leaders and employees are decent, morally sensitive people. And *still* they find they cannot do what they want to do.

How can that be so? It can be so if market pressures force an ethical firm to compete against an unethical one. As we all know, the market "rewards" businesses that succeed in offering their products at lower costs than their competitors. If a firm can lower its cost of doing business by dumping its waste products in a river or by treating its employees like dirt or by engaging in dishonest practices, then its competitors will be penalized. That is the law of the marketplace.

Some force outside the market has to act in some way to make sure everybody is playing by the same rules. The point was made recently by Elmer W. Johnson, general counsel and vice president of General Motors:

> While GM management can exercise a considerable degree of discretion in attending to its responsibilities in areas involving important social interests, this autonomy is not without limits. The competitive market system very promptly penalizes and ultimately bankrupts the firm that would go very far in promoting social goals at the expense of private profit. Thus, when there are important social interests that the market fails to protect, even with the application of long-term enlightened corporate self-interest, management may have an obligation to support efficient government intervention or to cooperate with church and other groups to advance particular social reforms such as those embodied in the Sullivan Principles. Management should then utilize its experience and judgment in suggesting the best means for removing or overcoming competitive impediments to corporate social responsibility.[12]

A business leader who really cares about doing good will support the right kind of regulation. We have to pay attention to the overall system and not just to the narrow range of opportunities we have in one particular business. It is too bad somebody with Elmer Johnson's vision was not calling the tune when GM lashed out at Ralph Nader for exposing the safety problems of American automobiles. Instead of fighting the new federal regulations, farsighted industrial leaders would have *welcomed* them as necessary for the public safety and as necessary to ensure that no single company would have to bear the cost of improvements by itself.

Our larger point is that personal holiness is not a *substitute* for attending to systematic relationships; it *requires* it. Personal holiness, alas, does not guarantee wisdom in such matters. But it surely does mean that one struggles to attain wisdom, that one learns from one's failures, and that one has the courage to take risks for the sake of advancing God's purposes so far as one is given wisdom into the nature of those purposes.

There is, no doubt, room for a good deal of disagreement among Christians about such matters. I am struck by the frankness with which the New Testament informs us of disagreements among the great saints of the earliest Church. At the time it must have been terribly difficult to know whether Paul was right in his dispute with Barnabas over how to handle the young Mark—in retrospect, it is clear that Barnabas was right. Or whether Paul was right in his dispute with Peter over how to deal with Gentile followers of the Way—in retrospect, it is clear that Paul was right that time. The saints had to stew over such things until they got it right. In the process, they taught one another and learned from one another, and God's purposes were advanced.

I don't know very many Christian businesspeople who would want to be compared to a Paul, a Barnabas, or a Peter. Nonetheless, many are trying hard. They are relieved, by God's grace, of the necessity of being "right" about everything. But they are challenged by God's grace to respond wholeheartedly to the task of making this a better world and using their business opportunities and their roles as citizens as ways of doing so.

THE MINISTRY OF BUSINESS LIFE

We must return, in conclusion, to the observation that business life can be a real "ministry" for Christians, but only if one's Christian identity is primary, not secondary. To make this point more graphically, I will share an incident that occurred some years ago following a speech I gave to a church group. The speech dealt with the issue of the reform of the nation's welfare policies. I offered several proposals, which I set in a theological context and sought to spell out in practical, dollars-and-cents terms. During the discussion period, one man immediately voiced his objections: "According to my calculations," he announced, "your ideas would cost every one of us an additional five hundred dollars in taxes. And I'm not sure we can afford that much Christianity." He was almost certainly wrong in his mathematics, but that, to me, was not the main point. I was more interested in his comment about how much Christianity he thought he could afford!

To be Christians characterized by personal holiness is not to set a limit. To such Christians, God already owns all that we have. Indeed, Christians recognize that God owns us as well. The most important thing about us is that we are children of God. And in relation to every material question, we are simply God's stewards, responsible to God. There is room for debate on all issues of public policy and business policy, and Christians will sometimes disagree quite honestly about the course of wisdom. But there is no room for debate about how much Christianity we can afford. Our basic values are formed by God, in response to the incredible gift of life and grace that has been given to us; our values are not formed first and foremost by our business interests. But attending to business matters practically and creatively, seeking to solve problems of economic life and thereby to serve humanity, can surely be a worthy ministry for many Christians to undertake.

EDITOR'S PERSPECTIVE

Dr. Wogaman's conclusion is powerful—Christian business professionals have a true ministry in the marketplace, but only when our *identity* is in Christ and not in worldly success. The challenge he presents, and a correct one, is whether we will manifest the *character* and *conduct* of Christ or whether we will identify with the world's criteria for personal significance—power, wealth, prestige, and so on.

When we enter the marketplace, we encounter numerous opportunities to behave righteously or to compromise the very standards we know down deep are right. Our biggest temptations are associated with "doing right," not "knowing right." Our heart's desires—subconscious drives that support our identity—will ultimately govern our conduct because they really point to our first love. Will we exhibit holy conduct, as pleaded for by Peter (see 1 Pet. 1:13-16), or will we live in inner conflict by pursuing our self-will and rejecting the wholeness (holiness) God desires for us?

To what extent should Christian business professionals be motivated by making a profit, helping others, improving society, and witnessing for the gospel? Are God's precepts to be taken into the marketplace by His children and applied in a way to transform society, or are His precepts primarily intended to produce personal holiness? Are we to glorify God primarily by our work, in obedience to the creation mandates, or are we to evangelize in response to the Great Commission? This family of tensions revolves around our need to learn how to live as Christians in the world while not being part of the world.

No simple biblical prescription answers our family of questions. They are all important. We know we are not to be *conformed* to the world (see Rom. 12:2). Neither are we to withdraw from the world (see John 17:15). And while in the world, we are to let our "light shine before men *in such a way* that they may see [our] good works, and glorify [our] Father who is in heaven" (Matt. 5:16, emphasis added).

What does Christ mean by "in such a way"? This question is perhaps *the* key one to be answered. We are to have a good reputation in the world (see 1 Tim. 3:7). The unregenerate people of the world should see in us a good character that is manifested in our conduct. We should work hard for our employers, as unto the Lord (see Col. 3:23). Our integrity and behavior should be above reproach. We should pray to have the courage to stand for justice and righteousness in the marketplace. The biblical characterization of someone who compromises on this point is vivid: "Like a trampled spring and a polluted well is a righteous man who gives way before the wicked" (Prov. 25:26; Ezek. 34:18-19). We may compromise methods and procedures but not righteousness. We must stand for the good of our fellow employees, suppliers, customers, stockholders, community, and yes, even competitors—we must not spread false rumors, "steal" proprietary information, and so on.

The Spirit of God will provide the wisdom and discernment necessary to help us uphold the standards of God in everything we do and say at work—if we will seek His guidance. We also know that *how* we do something (kindly, patiently, etc.) is just as important as *what* we do in the world. Also, we must never be self-righteous or exhibit a holier-than-thou attitude. Everyone despises that. Besides, the world is incredibly judgmental, for unregenerate people constantly compare themselves with others. They become their own standards.

The two big issues confronting us, though, really rest beneath the family of tensions being addressed in this section. The first issue is, how are we to carry the name of Christ into the marketplace? Do we present ourselves to the marketplace as Christians or as excellent workers? Do we propose ideas to our peers with a distinctly Christian vocabulary, dropping Christian code words into our discussions? Or should we develop natural language with which to seek righteousness in the marketplace? These kinds of problems confuse our biblical tensions—are we to transform society or evangelize? The very concepts—transform society and evangelize—carry deep *methodological* expectations in our minds, and these expectations differ from person to person. Many of our conflicting opinions arise at this very point.

We have no biblical authority to go to the marketplace and present ourselves as Christian managers, Christian salesmen, or Christian typists. Some Christians are salespeople, but biblically we are not invited to attach Christ's name to our market vocation. We must be extremely careful how we carry His name. Yes, Christians are under the authority of Christ and are mandated to "do justice, to love kindness, and to walk humbly with [our] God" in the marketplace—the very context of this Micah 6:8 directive is the marketplace (see 2:1,9; 6:10-13; 7:1-6). But the very distinction between these two concepts—we have no authority to attach Christ's name to our market vocation, and we are under Christ's authority to act righteously in the marketplace—badly needs to be understood by Christians in business, politics, and elsewhere. NonChristians have not accepted Christ as their Lord. To ask them, in Christ's name, to institute a specific policy, take a certain action, or even hint that it should be done because we are Christians or ask for it in Christ's name is as ridiculous as asking a Russian to do something because an American president asks it. The citizenship loyalties are radically different.

Christ's kingdom on earth is not a temporal kingdom. His lordship is in the hearts of His children. Christ made this very clear to Pilate when He told him, "My kingdom is not of this world" (John 18:36). Evangelization is the presentation of the gospel message to effect a change in citizenship, not to bring about outward changes in behavior that leave the heart unaffected. On the other hand, Christians are to present righteous plans to the world that conform to God's revealed standards. We are to incorporate God's principles into all that we do at work and elsewhere.

The second major issue we need to comprehend can be called the problem of probable outcomes. Our basic desire must be to serve and please Christ—keep His commandments—but that does not *necessarily* mean our efforts to transform our work environment will be successful as a result of our obedience. We are to seek righteousness when it is within our legitimate power to do so, but God may be allowing others to thwart our efforts for reasons that transcend our understanding. If we are acting according to God's precepts, though, we can trust Him to work His larger will in the world. Christians are not told beforehand which battles will be won and lost in the marketplace. We are called to follow Christ—win or lose.

The issue of evangelizing in the marketplace is really a nonproblem, theologically. There is a time and a place for everything under the sun. It is all right to wear a bathing suit to the beach, but not to a formal 7:00 p.m. wedding. It is all right to evangelize, but not on an employer's time, perhaps not even on his property. Wasting time (working halfheartedly) and misallocating time (not working on an employer's assigned task, but evangelizing instead) are both comparable to stealing one's wages.

This caution does not mean that one should never share the gospel between 8:00 a.m. and 5:00 p.m. Natural opportunities to "give an account for the hope that is in [us]" (1 Pet. 3:15) may occur in God's kind providence at any time. Dramatic personal crises, for example, do occur in people's lives, and when they do, they spill over into the workplace. Love demands that we offer help and comfort. The gospel *may*, on specific occasions, be called for during a rest break, at lunch, or at any other moment, but the workplace is not a battlefield for staging evangelistic commando raids. Our place of employment is a place to work hard, as unto the Lord.

There are no rules by which the family of tensions discussed in this section are to be *balanced*, for life does not unfold before us predictably. We do know, though, that the Holy Spirit will guide God's children, and while doing so, He will *not* contradict other biblical principles. The commands for us to rule and subdue the created order are not in conflict or competition with God's directives to us to "go and make disciples." But our testimony to the watching world will be destroyed if we profess Christ as our Lord and neglect to serve our employers to the best of our ability. And to not love those with whom we labor by also caring for their eternal well-being is a superficial love, indeed. Oh, may our Savior lead us so our light will shine *in such a way* as to cause all people who see it to glorify our heavenly Father.

ETHICS OF THE COVENANTS:
Does the New Covenant Supersede the Old?

The precise relationship between the Old and New Testaments is as perplexing to many people as is the precise relationship between law and grace, dispensations and covenants, and Christ's discussion of old and new wineskins. Was there a new and elevated ethic introduced by Christ and His apostles in the New Testament, or was their teaching fundamentally a clarification or rounding out of the Old Testament teachings?

The nub of our concern in this section is this: Does the New Covenant, or New Testament, represent progressive revelation in the sense of (1) our learning more and more about an earlier revelation so that our understanding is enlarged (even though there is really only one unfolding ethic), or (2) an unfolding so great that it both effectively results in the redefining of earlier understandings of truth and calls for a different response and conduct on our part? An example of the second approach would be the question of whether capital punishment is no longer appropriate for the state in the same way as circumcision has been set aside as an ordinance. Is the New Testament a new covenant that supersedes the old one?

These questions must be wrestled with, for their answers shape many of our expectations for civil government and for our ethics in business. Part of the Old Testament has been clearly fulfilled in the Person and life of Christ, so that its ordinances related to sacrifice, for example, are no longer necessary or helpful except as they elucidate what Christ has done.

Many other Old Covenant regulations were civil in nature and intended to guide those who judged Israel with regard to community and civil matters. In our New Testament era, however, the Church has been scattered about the world, and God's theocratic state has been superseded. What functions have been transferred to the Church, what functions remain with the state, and what (if any) functions ceased with the transition?

The Old Testament is also full of admonitions that have direct application to our personal holiness. This means that the Old Covenant addressed personal, civil, and worship matters. The New Testament, on the other hand, seems to have a particularly heavy emphasis on doctrines of salvation and worship, as well as interpersonal attitudes and behavior, but only a small amount of discussion pertaining to our relationship to the civil community.

Do these differences of the weights between the focus of the Old and New Testaments tell us anything of significance about God's concern? If we believe the New Covenant supersedes the Old Covenant, this difference in weights would be significant, for the New Testament would then govern, to some degree, what should be brought forward into practice from the Old Testament. If we believe the New Covenant is an amplification and continuing revelation of the same truths—expanded but not altered in character—then the changed emphasis from the Old to the New simply reflects the shift from a theocratic state to a Church environment without significant theological implications regarding the content of revelation.

The importance of this matter is tremendous, for it opens the door to significant differences in our expectations of both the Church and the state, as well as our business ethics. To address this knotty topic, Dr. Myron S. Augsburger and Dr. Walter C. Kaiser, Jr., present cases representing the two positions—that the New Testament does or does not supersede the Old Testament.

Myron Augsburger's thesis is that the New Testament ethic supersedes the Old Testament ethic. It is important to decide if his case rests on a particular emphasis of a personalized Christological ethic or if there is a new ethic espoused by the New Testament. One could never question that Dr. Augsburger has a Christ-centered focus and emphasis. What is really the question here is whether our world view or life view, as described in the opening chapter, is as broad and complete as Christ's.

CHAPTER 4

THE NEW TESTAMENT ETHIC SUPERSEDED THE OLD TESTAMENT ETHIC

Myron S. Augsburger

Dr. Myron Augsburger is a theologian, pastor, and evangelist of the Mennonite church who currently finds himself serving the larger church community. He is President of the Christian College Coalition, an association of over seventy-five Christ-centered liberal arts colleges. He has served with Inter-Church as an evangelist since the 1950s. As an educator, he was President of Eastern Mennonite College and Seminary from 1965 to 1980. As theologian, he is an adjunct Professor of Theology at Eastern Mennonite Seminary and guest lecturer at other seminaries. He also served as senior pastor of the Washington Community Fellowship in the inner city of Washington, D.C., from 1980 to 1988. He is a member of several boards in the Mennonite church, the Presbyterian Ministers' Fund, and Evangelicals for Social Action. He has authored numerous books sharing his insights on Anabaptist theology.

A s we approach Scripture, we see that there is one overarching covenant of grace. And yet there are different levels of covenant within the Old Testament itself, from Noah to Abraham to David and to the promise in Jeremiah of a *new* covenant. The fact that there are Old and New Testaments, or "Covenants," suggests that we have a further disclosure from God in the New that more fully interprets the Old. Jesus Himself said, "Think not that I am come to destroy the law, or the prophets . . . but to fulfill," that is, to fill full, to provide the full meaning (Matt. 5:17, KJV).

To think of the New Testament as superseding the Old Testament is not to make it different in meaning but different in degree, in levels of understanding. In the Old, we have revelation in the acts and words of God telling us *about* God; in the New Testament, we have the presence of God incarnate in Jesus of

Nazareth. Jesus dared to say, "He who has seen Me has seen the Father" (John 14:9, NASB). This statement places Jesus in a different role from that of all other prophets.

We cannot now go back before the Incarnation and live at that former level of understanding. We recognize, however, that our understanding of the earlier "level" of disclosure helps us to understand the full disclosure in Christ. This is much like comparing elementary or secondary education with graduate studies; while there is a basic harmony, once we are in graduate school, we cannot go back and live at the sixth-grade level.

The Bible is not a flat book. Rather, it contains an unfolding revelation. Pre-Christian levels in the Old Testament outlined a higher ethical level for the people of God than what was known in the surrounding culture at the same time, but they were "sub-Christian levels" when compared to God's further revelation in Christ.

For example, we observe such issues as slavery, polygamy, attitudes toward women, attitudes on violence and on tribal wars, as the proof of the power of their particular deities, attitudes toward the nations, and so on. And yet the "Divine Imperative," God's claim upon people in the Old and New Testaments alike, is for us to be truly a people of God, not just to be an ethnic people with the religion of Jehovah.

A basic difference between the Testaments is in the answer given to the reality of the Fall and the sinfulness that perverts humanity. We have the law in the Old Testament as a pointer to the will of God and as a reminder of human sinfulness, while in the New Testament we have the reality of redemption in Christ and the quality and power of the new life and its potential for all who are regenerated by the Holy Spirit. Putting off "the old man" (the reign of sin), and putting on "the new man" (the reign of the Spirit), is now an actual reality for the disciple of Christ. We now live as actual participants in the "new order" as new creatures in Christ.

As God's new people, we live in the righteousness (right relatedness) of God in Christ. We now live with God's Kingdom, God's mission, God's purpose, and God's glory as our motivation. This focus creates a radical separation from the "spirit of the age," from the idolatry of mammon, and calls us to be in the world but not of the world, to use it but not abuse it. Although as a consequence of the Fall we are sinful, we have now been redeemed, and the new order and the power of the redeemed community provide our character. The call for us to recognize God's gift of creation and to have dominion over it is now given the meaning of ordering creation to achieve God's purposes for the human family.

When we speak of the culture of Israel and the culture of Canaan, we recognize that God was creating a different people in society as a witness of who Jehovah is as Israel's God. The New Testament witness of God supersedes a God of ethnic Israel and is witness to the God and Father of our Lord Jesus Christ who is to be known as God and Father for all *ethna*, all peoples.

In Elijah's clash with the prophets of Baal, the people were called to choose: "If the LORD is God, follow Him; but if Baal, follow him" (1 Kings 18:21, NASB). This decision involved a total lifestyle, a choice of being fully God's people. Actually, Baalism itself was more than a religious system; it was a way of life, an economic and political system, an ideology. As Wallace Hamilton points out, it grew from the word *baal* which means "owner," and was more an attitude toward property than a religion. A prince was called a *baal*; a slave's master was his *baal*; a woman's husband was her *baal*. It came to mean the aristocracy who owned the land, and then was attributed to a deity as the god of fertility, of prosperity. But God called the Hebrews to think not of ownership but of stewardship. God is the owner, the earth is the Lord's, and we manage it for Him, for His purpose, and by His principles. As Jesus taught us, we are to choose the role of servant, not of master, for the one who serves, who enables others, is as his Master (see Matt. 20:26-28).

The subject of business ethics cannot be addressed without some awareness of the need to contextualize the meaning of Scripture to be understood in our stage of the process of civilization. By civilization, I mean the rational activity of humanity through which the resources of creation are placed at our disposal to achieve chosen ends. Humans work, in contrast to animals, who are active by instinct, so that we may live and engage our goals or choices. And it is impossible to isolate oneself in work, for each is a part of the disciplines of the community in which we share.

The coordination of all who are connected by work requires ethical decision. For this reason, the matter of work and civilization constitutes a problem for theological ethics. Although some types of work may be morally neutral, work is to be considered ethically, for to be human is to be responsible. The context of our labor determines it as a service when it contributes to the need of the community, and this is of ethical significance. Emil Brunner has written, "The lowest kind of manual labor is of as much value as the 'intellectual,' if undertaken as the Divine commission to serve, and if it renders a real service to our neighbor."[1]

One of the higher principles having an impact on business ethics is that of love. Jesus said the first commandment is, "'You shall love the Lord your God with all your heart, and with all your soul, and with all your mind.' The second is like it, 'You shall love your neighbor as yourself'" (Matt. 22:37-39, NASB). When a person no longer loves God or people, he turns in his love of self to the love of things. This is a bondage, for the mania for things destroys community. An obsession with things, with acquisition, causes one to lose consideration for others.

It is in this light that we are to understand the Sermon on the Mount and, in fact, to apply Jesus' teachings to business rather than treat them as irrelevant idealism. Jesus says to us, "Seek ye first the kingdom of God, and his righteousness; and all these things shall be added unto you" (Matt. 6:33, KJV). The "things" are serendipitous, the extra assets of life, but things are not the heart of life, much less of life in the Kingdom of God. In Luke 10, Jesus tells the story of the good Samaritan to show us how we are to share as stewards, how we can be our brother's brother.

The Scriptures were given and written in quite different times, cultures, and phases of civilization from ours, and we need to contextualize the writings in their original setting for proper interpretation, from which we can then make applications to our setting. To do less than this is to do an injustice to the Scripture and to miss its meaning for today.

We can hardly say that the Scriptures teach one economic system, or that systems of the times reflected in Scripture fit our time. Instead of seeking to prove from Scripture that capitalism is the better economic system, I would affirm that by interpreting history with the present realities of the "global village" we can see capitalism as the more logical and potentially the more universally applicable and beneficial system. If used with such Christian principles as justice, love, and equity, with a stewardship that seeks God's direction in the use of His resources for the well-being of the total human family, the capitalistic system has a flexibility that can enable those of privilege to help those in poverty to achieve the means for well-being in their setting. But it is also true that if this system is used selfishly, to acquire rather than to enable, it will be exploitive.

For example, when the family of Emperor Haile Selassie laid claim to 60 percent of the land of Ethiopia, it robbed people of the very freedom for free enterprise that could have strengthened the nation. Consequently, the Marxist takeover has grasped a far greater control and further destroyed economic freedom as well as other freedoms. These insights come not from proof-texting but from discerning the basic principles of the New Testament on our Kingdom connection.

In earlier periods of history, people worked primarily for a livelihood, as a means of keeping body and soul together. Only the elite of royalty or of inherited means had wealth as power. In more recent centuries, with the free enterprise of our capitalistic system, the general public is able to work, save, and invest, to participate in capital growth, and to have the benefits of leisure and travel. Business is primarily a matter of resources, management, marketing, and profit. Christian ethics in business calls us to exercise these privileges with justice, love, and equity, or mutual freedom. Our task is to discover how the principles of Holy Scripture, especially the New Testament, interpret this exercise.

I. THE NEW TESTAMENT MAKES IT CLEAR AS A UNIVERSAL PRINCIPLE THAT PERSONS OF PRIVILEGE ARE NEVER TO EXPLOIT OTHER PERSONS.

The most important, the most valuable aspect of the world is humanity, you and me. Humanity is created in the image of God, though God has called *all* creation good. And the sin of humanity has subjected all creation to bondage (see Rom. 8:21). In fact, this eschatological passage of Romans 8:18-23 provides theological content for Peter's reference to the coming "new heavens and a new earth, in which righteousness dwells" (2 Pet. 3:11-13, NASB). Being saved in this hope of the ultimate fulfillment of God's purpose enables us to live now by the principles penetrating the earth in grace to hasten this fulfillment. And as children of God, we live by the principles that elevate humanity, recognizing the supreme value of persons in our total lifestyle, especially in the "orders of the common life."

Employer-employee relations are different in character from the master-slave relations referred to in various passages of Scripture, but these passages were given in contexts in which the latter was the practice. While the Old Testament had clear instructions about a Hebrew becoming a master of other Hebrews as slaves, these were outlined when the divine disclosure had not yet reached the level of the New Testament, where God's call for equity is applied to all peoples. A study of Paul's remarkable little letter to Philemon makes it clear that Christian faith injected a principle of love and equity between all peoples that could do nothing other than bring slavery to an end. This can well include the servile "slavery" of our market dependencies in the contemporary society.

The principles in Ephesians 6 and Colossians 3 can thus be applied to employer/employee relations in our modern context. The employer is to relate to the employee justly, knowing that he also has a Master in Heaven; that is, he answers to God for his management practices. The Epistle of James similarly confronts the employer with divine requirements for justice, equity, and freedom. In turn, Paul enjoins the employee to give honest work for his wage, not to render "eyeservice, as men-pleasers" (Eph. 6:6, NASB), but to serve the employer as one serves the Lord. In both cases the ethical appeal is our accountability to God in our exercise of the privileges of life. An application of these principles will free us from inequity, racism, and injustice in the marketplace.

Another case in point is the attitude taken toward women, that is, the place and role of women in society. Although there are a few illustrations in the Old Testament of women being granted business privileges, such as that of the daughters of Zelophehad (see Num. 27:1-7), the level of equity taught in the New Testament surpasses the teachings of the Old. Jesus and Paul taught in a cultural context where the rabbis negated teaching women. In fact, women were regarded as property, as chattel. Each morning as the Pharisee prayed, he included in his thanks to God his gratitude that he was not created a Gentile, a slave, or a woman. Into that culture Jesus injected the application of equity to women and men alike.

And Paul similarly taught that women are to learn, not without modesty, and to fill a complementary rather than a competitive role (see 1 Tim. 2:11). It appears that Paul's illustration from Eve emphasizes her mistake in usurping the individualistic role of making her decision apart from consultation with Adam. Rather, her relation to Adam was that of soliciting his participation in a decision she had already made. Adam and Eve were created in and for community, and for one to usurp the dominant role violated that community. These principles of equity and of community are expressed in various passages, but in sum they are grounded in the statement, "There is neither . . . male nor female . . . in Christ Jesus" (Gal. 3:28, NIV); we answer alike to our Lord.

The application of the principles implicit in the new male-female relationship, along with the teachings on modesty and purity, call for equal opportunity in business ventures. They also call for freedom from sexism in relationships, in advertising, and in social and business practices.

II. THE NEW TESTAMENT ETHIC OF THE SERMON ON THE MOUNT ELEVATES PERSONS ABOVE MATERIAL, AND RELATIONSHIPS OF *SHALOM* ABOVE LEGAL DEMANDS.

The Sermon on the Mount presents the priorities for the Kingdom of God. In Luke 6 and Matthew 5-7, we are confronted with a standard for the Christian life. These passages are as applicable to Christian ethics as are the parables and other discourses of Jesus. When we accept Jesus as Lord, we accept the whole Jesus, not just a part of Him. We acknowledge Jesus as the expression of God's will in what He said, in what He did, and in what He was as a whole person. Regarding what He said, we find some of His more explicit teachings on stewardship in Luke 12, teachings that confront us with the priorities of the Kingdom.

The emphasis on economics in the Sermon on the Mount calls us to first seek the Kingdom of God, to be honest and trustworthy, to refrain from alienating persons by a suit of law, to be clear about serving one Master, whereby mammon can be controlled, and not to have treasure on earth with an obsession with security in things but to share with those in need, especially when they ask of us.

Each area needs interpretation, and we can draw from the Old Testament various teachings or examples to help us do that. Abraham comes to mind as an example of decision making that places the Kingdom of God first. Isaac refused to fight the Philistines to keep the wells that he had dug. Boaz is cited for his kindness to the gleaners, especially to Ruth and Naomi. Naboth had a commitment to the will of Jehovah above profit in sales. The Rechabites are an illustration in the book of Jeremiah that God used to emphasize integrity. Daniel's life expresses the commitment to laying up treasure in Heaven rather than on earth. These Old Testament representatives help us understand the practical applications of Jesus' teachings.

The essential meaning of a passage, rather than a "wooden literalism," is to be applied in life. For example, "Give to him who asks of you" (Matt. 5:42, NASB) still leaves us with some choice as to what is best for us to give. Giving a handout may be easy but may not be genuine help, while giving opportunity, work, or security for credit can be a more significant, lasting asset.

For many years I have interpreted the way of Christ and His Kingdom as a "Third Way." By this I do not mean simply finding a middle-of-the-road position, but another level of ethics that is Christologically perceived and commensurately selective. This way is neither a rightist conservative stance nor a leftist humanistic stance, but is a Third Way that selects from both and critiques both from the priorities of the Kingdom.

In the March 1987 issue of the *New Oxford Review* is the article "Christ and Neighbor" by John C. Cort. He mentions that the U. S. Catholic bishops' pastoral letter on the U. S. economy refers to "economic democracy" as a "third way" between capitalism and communism. Although I have not adequately processed all of the meanings people read into "economic democracy," I like their statement as follows: "We believe the time has come for a similar experiment in economic democracy: the creation of an order that guarantees the minimum conditions of human dignity in the economic sphere for every person."[2]

Conservative Christians need to rediscover God's transnational vision for His people. As Tom Sine says, "Committing ourselves to work for a vision of messianic nationalism is committing ourselves to work for an agenda that is as secular as anything the humanists have dreamed up."[3] Too many evangelical Christians invoke the secular providence of Adam Smith for the larger economic world and invoke the God of Scripture to sanction their particular enterprise. We need to come back to Christ, to a Christology that holds faith and obedience together, that relates ethics to Christ in the same way that salvation is related to Christ, living out beliefs! This will enable us to penetrate the secular with the sacred.

III. THE NEW TESTAMENT UNDERSTANDING OF COMMUNITY IS THE LIBERATING OF ALL BELIEVERS TO MAXIMIZE THEIR POTENTIAL IN FULFILLMENT OF THE JUBILEE PRINCIPLE INTRODUCED IN THE OLD TESTAMENT.

God in Christ calls us into the new order that He is creating. This new community is called the Body of Christ, the body giving visibility to the Spirit of Christ within us by its expression in the social order. The people of God, born of the Spirit into the new order of the Kingdom, actually become a special expression of "community" within the larger social community. And the dynamic of community, as Dietrich Bonhoeffer wrote in *Life Together*, is that we always relate to one another in and through Christ. This relationship through the divine presence prevents us from misusing one another, from manipulating one another, or from seeing others as cogs in our wheel of success. Persons should never be a means to an end in our business practices; rather, as Kant has expressed it, persons are always an end in themselves.

The Old Testament teaching of Jubilee meant that every fifty years, very legalistically, every Sabbath of Sabbaths in the annual calendar, there was to be a release. Slaves from among their fellow Hebrews were released, debts were canceled, land was returned to the ownership of the family who had needed a mortgage or sale of their land for their own survival. In fact, laws on borrowing were drawn up with consideration given to the period of time the funds would be used until the Jubilee would call for their cancellation. To carry this over from a barter economy to a money-stock economy is not an easy task.

The New Testament takes the principle of the Year of Jubilee and applies it to the ethics of the Kingdom, calling us to live by the freedoms that liberate one another in the service of God. When Jesus read in the synagogue at Nazareth (see Luke 4:16-21, NIV), He chose the passage from Isaiah 61 announcing the Spirit's anointing for His messianic mission. Jesus concluded with the words, ". . . To release the oppressed, to proclaim the year of the Lord's favor." This last phrase is a reference to the Year of Jubilee, the release of all persons into the freedom of grace.

To apply this principle in our economy means to seek the freedom and fulfillment of each person, of each employee. It could mean profit-sharing plans, scholarship aid for the education of employees' children, and of course medical insurance, workmen's compensation insurance, and retirement benefits. Such social ethics have also been an undergirding factor in our nation in the practice of charitable contributions, which has led to building hospitals, providing for the arts, and making possible scientific research in areas that have enhanced social well-being. In the history of Christianity, it is clear that in the days of the early Church, the Roman Empire did not provide hospitals, care for the elderly, or care for children and orphans, but the Christian community created these benefits as an extension of their sense of Christian ethics.

In addition, it seems to me that in a money economy much more could be done to help persons who lack credit references due to their subsistence level of income. An illustration of how this can be taken seriously is seen in Robert Lavelle, executive vice president of Dwelling House Savings and Loan in Pittsburgh, Pennsylvania. Lavelle is called "a banker for the poor." His approach has worked because members of the bank staff spend time with the families who are borrowing, which in turn builds up confidence in their ability to manage.

It is not easy to help persons in a material way without creating other problems, such as dependency, low self-esteem, and irresponsibility. We must seek effective ways to enable a younger generation without giving them a "silver spoon." And we must find the way to help the poor, offering a hand-up rather than seeking to unhook from them with a handout. We need to develop apprenticeships, especially in the inner-city and urban context, which is now the majority pattern of the "global village," so that persons can learn the art of work. We need to recognize that there is something Christian about doing one's task well.

Martin Luther was once approached by a cobbler who wanted to know how he could give witness to the fact that he was a *Christian* cobbler. The cobbler's idea was to imprint the sign of the cross on every shoe he made. Martin Luther's reply was classic: "A Christian cobbler is not known by whether he makes a cross but by whether he makes a good pair of shoes."

IV. THE NEW TESTAMENT CALLS FOR US TO REACH OUT TO THE *ETHNA* (NATIONS OF THE WORLD) IN PATTERNS THAT SEEK THEIR WELL-BEING RATHER THAN TO HAVE PATTERNS THAT TAKE FROM THEM FOR OUR OWN SUPERIORITY.

We are not twentieth-century "Old Testament Israel"; we are an expression of the new people of God, the new Israel, the transnational and global community of God's people. Paul's letter to the Romans deals with how two peoples, Jew and Gentile, can become one people in Christ and live as one body with the diversity of its parts. In Ephesians 2, he shows how the Cross has broken down the barrier and made the two divisions, Jew and Gentile, one new humanity (see 2:14-18). As a consequence, business ethics are to seek equity and justice for each alike. This approach was tested first in the early Church at Jerusalem in the tension between the Grecian Jews and the Hebraic Jews with the need for deacons to serve in achieving equity (see Acts 6:1-7).

In Paul's missions, he sometimes worked as a tent maker, fitting into the economy of the community where he was serving. In addition, he took as a major role the gathering of funds from the more prosperous Gentile churches to help the needy in Jerusalem who were suffering from the famine in Judea. His efforts were an expression of a new sense of fellowship across national lines, at least across cultural lines as all were living under the Roman Empire (see Acts 24:17; Rom. 15:25-28; 1 Cor. 16:3; 2 Cor. 8:19-24).

During a preaching mission in India, I was impressed with the relevance of the statement that we should "live more simply that others may simply live." From the perspective of Third-World needs, Dr. Ronald Sider's book *Rich Christians in an Age of Hunger* is a prophetic word that we must all face with the honesty of Kingdom members. However, the answers are not so simple as "slicing the pie differently." We need to find ways to help more people come up with more of life's ingredients, sharing knowhow rather than simply sharing the produce.

Dr. David Barrett points out that Christians comprise only 32 percent of the world population, but receive 62 percent of the global income. And he says that we spend 97 percent of our income on ourselves and three percent on international missions. We are guilty of privatizing religious experience when we should be sharing God's compassion for the world. One example of trying to work at this creatively is expressed by several members of my congregation. Dennis and Eileen Bakke, along with other families, have created "The Mustard Seed Foundation" as a way for successful businesspeople to give start-up grants to Christian programs of witness or service. This ministry provides an opportunity to carry a sense of Christian vocation to one's occupation, expressing the discipleship of Christ in the occupational dimension of life.

V. THE NEW TESTAMENT EMPHASIS ON JUSTICE CALLS THE EMPLOYER TO FOCUS ON THE ULTIMATE WORTH OF THE EMPLOYEE AS A PERSON.

In the Sermon on the Mount, Jesus shows us that we can conquer anxiety by arranging our interests according to Kingdom priorities. He states, "Is not the life more than meat, and the body than raiment?" (Matt. 6:25, KJV). This hierarchy places things at the bottom, persons above things, and God at the top.

It becomes necessary to renounce some desires simply because the true self will not find satisfaction in them. The obsession with wealth is one of these.

Bishop Fulton Sheen distinguishes between natural wealth, which includes food, clothing, and shelter needed for a normal life, and artificial wealth, which is money, credit, stocks, and bonds.[4] He reminds us that the desire for possessions (artificial wealth) is never satisfied. It is in this light that Paul writes,

> But godliness with contentment is great gain. For we brought nothing into this world, and we can take nothing out of it. But if we have food and clothing, we will be content with that. People who want to get rich fall into temptation and a trap and into many foolish and harmful desires that plunge men into ruin and destruction. For the love of money is a root of all kinds of evil. (1 Tim. 6:6-10, NIV)

And a bit further in the same passage he adds,

> Command those who are rich in this present world not to be arrogant nor to put their hope in wealth, which is so uncertain, but to put their hope in God, who richly provides us with everything for our enjoyment. Command them to do good, to be rich in good deeds, and to be generous and willing to share. In this way they will lay up treasure for themselves as a firm foundation for the coming age, so that they may take hold of the life that is truly life. (1 Tim. 6:17-19)

In these verses Paul does not condemn the handling of money in business, but calls the person who is a steward of riches to be generous in sharing. And in his letter to Philemon he focuses this generosity on the relationship between Philemon and his servant as a brother, as an equal! James exposes the rich for hoarding their wealth rather than sharing with the needy, implying that their acquisition of wealth may have been at the expense of the less privileged (see James 4:13-5:9). Here especially, the tone of Scripture calls for special attention to equity, to justice, and to our mutual accountability before God.

Wayne Anderson applied these New Testament principles in the world of industry. Following an eighty-four-day strike at Pittron Steel, he came to the conviction that labor was not the enemy of management and that management was not the enemy of labor. Rather, he saw that management had become its own worst enemy, so he set out to correct himself and modify his management style. He began by taking positive steps of reconciliation. He threw away the scorecard, and he began to learn the names of the men and walk through the plant daily to chat with them. Dr. R.C. Sproul tells the following story:

One day he stopped to watch a chipper. Chippers had one of the hardest jobs in the plant. It was dirty, filthy work, demanding brute strength and endurance. The chipper's tool was a large hammer, like a jack-hammer, weighing about 30 pounds, which he used to chip away defects from large steel castings. Some of the castings weighed up to 300,000 pounds, and were the size of a small house.

Wayne stopped and shouted up at the man. "Hey, Tony, what are you doing?"

Stifling a curt reply, the man looked at the boss and said simply, "Chipping."

"It looks like hard work."

With a weary glance the chipper said, "It is."

Anderson said, "Let me have a crack at it."

With that, Wayne removed his suit coat, rolled up his sleeves, and climbed onto the casting. He asked for the hammer. As the chipper watched in disbelief, Wayne began furiously working with the hammer. His stamina lasted all of three minutes. Sweating profusely and gasping for breath, he said to the chipper, "How much money do you get paid for this job?"

The chipper told him, and Wayne breathed a heavy sigh. Shaking his hand, he said, "That's tough work. You earn every cent the company pays you."

Within five minutes every man on the floor had heard about the episode. Anderson, by his gesture, had dignified the least respected task in the plant.[5]

The concept "Value of the Person" became under Wayne Anderson the key to worker morale and reconciliation. We need to focus on how people are being treated and, as Anderson found, to emphasize love, dignity, and respect.

VI. THE NEW TESTAMENT EMPHASIS ON THE STEWARDSHIP OF THE TOTAL LIFE HOLDS EACH OF US ACCOUNTABLE TO THE MASTER IN EQUITY, JUSTICE, AND SHARING.

Our stewardship is not simply of things, but of our total lives. Stewardship is a lifestyle. We are instructed by Paul to "present [our] bodies a living sacrifice, holy, acceptable unto God, which is [our] reasonable service" (Rom. 12:1, KJV). He does not exclude the areas of manual labor or business enterprise, for Paul wrote to Titus, "Our people must learn to devote themselves to doing what is good, in order that they may provide for daily necessities and not live unproductive lives" (Titus 3:14, NIV). Paul wrote to the Ephesians regarding the character of the new life, "He who has been stealing must steal no longer, but must work, doing something useful with his own hands, that he may have something to share with those in need" (Eph. 4:28, NIV). Hence, Paul taught work, business management, profit, and sharing with others.

The New Testament would measure life by its service more than by status and material success. Over against the humanism of Job's "miserable comforters," who thought that if one is right with God he would not suffer physical or material difficulties but would be blessed with health and wealth, we find the New Testament measuring our blessedness by our Christlikeness in character and compassion.

Jesus said that the Gentiles lord it over one another, but that should not be the case among His disciples. To be truly great by God's standards, we must be servants (see Matt. 20:25-28). We must recognize that the desire to rule others is wrong. Jesus based this teaching on Himself as a role model, who "came not to be ministered unto, but to minister and to give his life" (Matt. 20:28, KJV). His teaching is further extended to the Great Judgment in which as Sovereign Lord He will divide the sheep from the goats, in these inimitable words:

> "Come, you who are blessed of My Father, inherit the kingdom prepared for you from the foundation of the world. For I was hungry, and you gave Me something to eat; I was thirsty, and you gave Me drink; I was a stranger, and you invited Me in; naked and you clothed Me; I was sick, and you visited Me; I was in prison, and you came to Me. . . . To the extent that you did it to one of these brothers of Mine, even the least of them, you did it to Me." (Matt. 25:34-40, NASB)

Clearly these passages emphasize looking out for the well-being of persons. The Father, who is no respecter of persons, who loves the whole world, and who desires that all should come to repentance, wants His people to handle the world's resources in a manner that will enhance His work for the well-being and the salvation of all people. John wrote of this, "If anyone has material possessions and sees his brother in need but has no pity on him, how can the love of God be in him?" (1 John 3:17, NIV).

VII. THE NEW TESTAMENT EXPOSES THE EVILS OF SYSTEMS THAT LIMIT, EXPLOIT, OR DEPERSONALIZE THE POOR.

Our world systems make "being," subservient to "having." Jacques Ellul, in *Money and Power*, makes this point very clear.[6] But we cannot resolve the problem by choosing between systems (i.e., capitalism and socialism), for the situation is pervasive. In capitalism, making money readily becomes the purpose of life. In socialism, individuals are submitted to production for society, and the economy is the purpose for their lives. For us to simply fight systems is to escape from responsible action at the level where change can actually be effected, change through the sense of partnership in God's grace where we function as His stewards in transcending a system by a community of love. We do not seek to set up another system and see it become legalistically imposed on society, but we call persons to the dynamic of being Christian in each time and setting as disciples of Christ.

In the well-known parable of the talents (see Matt. 25:14-30), Jesus shows that each person is responsible to the Lord as steward of his resources. The commendation is the same for the person who was faithful with five talents and the person who was faithful with two talents. The person given opportunity to be faithful in the use of the one talent was critical of the system and failed to exercise stewardship with his talent, and consequently he received the Lord's judgment. Ours is a call to faithful stewardship under God whatever the system.

Jesus opposed the way in which the religious leaders of His day subordinated religious practices to their interests in material gain. They would adjust Sabbath laws for the sake of their property, their animals, but not for the well-being of people (see Luke 13:10-17). He condemned their violation of Moses' teaching on supporting parents as He exposed their use of *Corban* (which means "dedicated"), laws governing property as devoted to God, so that they could keep the property for themselves rather than share it (see Mark 7:9-13). Jesus' dramatic act of cleansing the Temple, driving the business activities from the Gentile court to open the way for them to worship, is a witness to the servant role that business is to take in relation to the cause of the Kingdom (see Mark 11:15-18). And in a powerful story He contrasted the rich man, Dives, and the beggar, Lazarus, to focus our values on people and not on luxury (see Luke 16:19-31).

In the passage where Peter teaches us to submit ourselves to authority for the Lord's sake, he says, "Live as free men, but do not use your freedom as a cover-up for evil; live as servants of God" (1 Pet. 2:16, NIV). We are to use the world, but not abuse it; to enjoy the material, the created order, but not seek our fulfillment in material things.

In one of the final scenes of world history in which the destruction of Babylon is described, the merchants find their program collapsing with this world's system, yet the people of God can still say, "Hallelujah, the Kingdom of God lives on!" (see Rev. 18-19). Peter's advice about how to live remains timely: "Since everything will be destroyed in this way, what kind of people ought you to be? You ought to live holy and godly lives as you look forward to the day of God and speed its coming" (2 Pet. 3:11-12, NIV).

In essence the New Testament ethic for the Christian businessperson is to set one's financial management in direct relationship to Christ and His Kingdom rather than to a cultural or ethnic accountability. The business executive needs to work with the theologian in asking and answering how the reconciling gospel enables us to be socially responsible as ambassadors for Christ.

As agents of reconciliation, we discover a social mission in business, providing work, administering and managing effectively for persons and for profits, using the power of acquisition to enable others rather than to control them, sharing resources for the good of our neighbors, and becoming a presence of *shalom*, of wholeness. That one can be thoroughly Christian in business seems to be a calling of the New Testament, but it is difficult. Jesus said that "it is easier for a camel to go through the eye of a needle than for a rich man to enter the kingdom of God" (Mark 10:23-25, NIV). Yet in answer to the disciples' incredulity, He added, "With man this is impossible, but not with God; all things are possible with God" (Mark 10:27).

This awareness calls us to consider how to relate the social aspects of the gospel to the realm of business. The New Testament, bringing the whole of life under the lordship of the risen Christ, would call us to set the vocations of the common life in direct relation to His sovereign will, in quality, selectivity, integrity, justice, and equity.

As we look at those about us, we do not ask, "Who is my neighbor?" but as Jesus made clear to the lawyer (see Luke 10:25-37), we ask, "Am I being a neighbor?" Doing business with excellence is a part of our calling to do all things well to the glory of God, but doing business with a purpose to bless humanity, and not to secure our power and prestige, is a part of taking seriously our place in the community of Christ. Our gifts are gifts of the Spirit of God, and we are to use them so that everyone may profit (see 1 Cor. 12:4-7,27-31).

The moving account of the rich young ruler who came running to Jesus confronts us with life's most serious question: "Good Master, what must I do to inherit eternal life?" Jesus asked him a question that focused on seeing God in Jesus. Then He asked him to live by God's Law (citing the last six of the ten commandments). The young man cried out, "All these I have kept since I was a boy." Jesus responded, "One thing you lack. Go, sell everything you have and give to the poor, and you will have treasure in heaven. Then come, follow me" (Mark 10:17-22, NIV).

What is the one thing? It is to follow Christ above all, to let God be sovereign in one's life. If God is calling the shots, then anything that becomes a god to one is an idol and must go. Jesus did not tell Nicodemus or the woman at the well of Jacob to go and sell all, for their problems were not things but religious pride and sensual pleasure, respectively. He applied God's truth according to the need of the person, as He taught, "No one can serve two masters" (Matt. 6:24, NIV).

Similarly, Jesus taught by the parable of the rich fool that we are to beware of covetousness, "for a man's life does not consist in the abundance of his possessions" (Luke 12:13-34, NIV). On the other hand, giving up things does not in itself determine that one has a spiritual life. After Peter said, "We have left all, and followed thee" (Luke 18:28, KJV), the Master promised His special care and then called him to a more authentic understanding of the service of Christ. When St. Francis vowed poverty, he actually became greedy to be known as the poorest of men! It would appear that God has grace for people of means to live as good stewards (see Matt. 25:14-30), and He expects it as well as their caring for the poor who lack material goods.

Our free enterprise has the potential of stimulating one another, counseling and aiding one another, and at the same time permitting one another to achieve according to individual gifts. In the Christian community we should be able to assign persons with management gifts to function as counselors for persons who lack that ability. The safeguard from the power-blocks and class structures that seem inevitable in human selfishness is the worshiping community in which we have a communal program of enablement. We are called by God to assist one another in exercising our respective gifts in the freedom of the Kingdom of Christ. We are not lone, selfish individuals; we are a part of the new community, the people of God who are the salt of grace to the earth, the light of God to the world. We must always remember that "whatever [we] do in word or deed, [we are to] do all in the name of the Lord Jesus, giving thanks through Him to God the Father" (Col. 3:17, NASB).

Ours is a highly professionalized, very individualistic society. Even as Christians, we tend to see our work as our "vocation," thereby elevating it to the level of "calling." Our vocation is to be disciples of Christ; our work is our occupation, directed by our sense of vocation or calling (see Eph. 4:1-3). Only as our understanding of vocation is elevated to the level of God's calling in lifestyle discipleship can we be selective about occupations appropriate for a Kingdom member and the qualities of performance that reflect Kingdom qualities. This distinction, in my opinion, is the key to understanding New Testament ethics in business.

One of the members of my congregation, Dennis Bakke, is president of an applied energy business, which he helped to develop. As a dedicated Christian he has been able to share principles reflecting his values in such a way that they have been accepted by nonChristian colleagues, and together they have incorporated them into their business practices. They have articulated four values that are determinative in every decision with customers: integrity, fairness, social responsibility, and fun! They are employee oriented in their program and supportive of employee interests. This concern is expressed in one way by matching dollar-for-dollar all employees' giving to tax-exempt organizations including churches, giving away 30 percent of their profits in the first five years. This example of how Christian values can have an impact on business shows that it can, and does, work to the good of employees and employers.

The New Testament ethic supersedes the Old Testament ethic basically in that it is the full, universalized, and enabled expression of the will of God for the community of faith. As we are empowered by the Spirit of Christ, being a part of the Body of Christ, we are directed by our risen Lord. Glorifying Him is our first priority and is the distinction we carry into all of life. We are citizens of Heaven here in this world!

EDITOR'S REFLECTIONS

Before we leave Dr. Augsburger's thesis that the New Testament ethic supersedes the Old Testament ethic and turn to Walt Kaiser's position that there is one biblical ethic, it would be helpful to reflect on the interaction between the scholars when Myron Augsburger's position was set forth. The exchange was intense, but loving, penetrating, and enlightening. The effort was to clarify exactly what was embodied in the concept that the New Testament ethic supersedes the Old. It proved to be a difficult task. Was the old ethic in error? No! Was the old one merely more fully explained and expounded upon? Yes, but its superseding character means more than that. Just what does *supersede* mean? Is the old ethic set aside? Was it inadequate? The answer came back, yes and no! It was adequate for its day. It was and is God's truth, but the new ethic supersedes it. At times it seemed we were trying to define the indefinable.

The search for a precise explanation of the content of the concept proved to be very illuminating. It revealed the fundamental importance of our *personal perspective* on Scripture and how that shapes our Christian world view. For example, do we perceive that the law of God should determine the context and character of our business ethics, or should the redemptive work of Christ be the key? Do biblical precepts and law serve as the basic guide to our understanding of God's will for us in business, or does the embodiment of all truth in Christ (His character, acts, and teachings) provide us with a fuller understanding of God's will that supersedes the unincarnate revelation—Old Testament in particular? For example, does the embodiment of God's mercy in Christ mediate and interpret the judgment of God in such a way that capital punishment can be (is or ought to be) covered with mercy—death penalty delayed—so that mercy and reconciliation may have an opportunity to prevail?

74

Or to put it another way, can the blanket of compassion and mercy be pulled up over the body of the condemning features of the law so that an ethic of love may transcend (not invalidate, not annul, nor find fault with) the cold, harsh realities of an unincarnate code of law? Dr. Augsburger seems to answer yes. His Christology leads him to such a conclusion. Everything is to be viewed and integrated through Christ. The incarnate Word supersedes the unincarnate Word.

This position, then, introduces a new question. What will ultimately govern our view of Christ and keep it from going beyond the warrants of Scripture? If it should transcend Scripture, the "high" Christology will ultimately undermine the governing role of Scripture and result in a view of Christ that deviates from the biblical revelation. Can one have too high a Christology? Not if it is biblical; yes, if it is extrabiblical. Otherwise we abandon biblical Christianity.

What is the most basic governing agent for truth revealed to mankind: the Holy Spirit, the Scriptures, or a Spirit-informed biblical Christology (which allows us to interpret the Scriptures in the light of Christ)? The question is a very practical, not an academic, one. Of the three options set before us, only the Scriptures can be the objective standard on the human side of the God-man relationship if truth can be known without some form of existential experience. If, however, an existential experience is mandated (by the nautre of creation itself) before spiritual truth can be truly known, then one of the other two options—Holy Spirit or Spirit-developed biblical Christology—must govern truth. These are the implications of subscribing to a superseding New Testament ethic flowing from the redemptive work of Christ that comes to govern the continuing application of Old Testament precepts.

In his chapter, Dr. Kaiser maintains that reconciling the relationship between the Old Testament (law) and the New Testament (grace) is *the* most important single issue needing solution in the theological community. While acknowledging that there is discontinuity in certain areas—laws pertaining to temple worship and sacrifice, for example—he observes that enormous continuity remains between the moral law reflecting God's very character and the law to be written on the hearts of Christians by the Holy Spirit as we live under the grace provided through the substitutionary atonement of Jesus Christ.

Dr. Kaiser argues that the ethic of the New Testament does not supersede the Old Testament ethic and they are, in fact, one single ethic. After examining his position, we will look at how the difference between his view and Augsburger's can or cannot lead to material difference in our business conduct.

CHAPTER 5

A SINGLE BIBLICAL ETHIC IN BUSINESS

Walter C. Kaiser, Jr.

Dr. Walter Kaiser has served as Academic Dean and Vice President of Education at Trinity Evangelical Divinity School since 1980. He joined the graduate faculty at Trinity in 1966 and taught as Professor of Old Testament and Semitic Languages. He also serves as a member of the Board of Trustees of Wheaton College, Wheaton, Illinois, and as a commissioner on accreditation for the Association of Theological Schools of the United States and Canada.

Dr. Kaiser is the author of fifteen books, including Toward Old Testament Ethics, Toward an Exegetical Theology, Toward Old Testament Theology, *and* Hard Sayings of the Old Testament.

A ccording to conventional evangelical wisdom today, the Old Testament is not *our* testament. One such typical advocate of this position concludes,

> The Old Testament represents an old covenant, which is one we are no longer obligated to keep. Therefore, we can hardly begin by assuming that the Old Covenant should automatically be binding upon us. We can assume, in fact, that none of its stipulations (laws) are binding upon us unless they are renewed in the New Covenant. That is, unless an Old Testament law is somehow restated or reinforced in the New Testament, it is no longer directly binding on God's people (cf. Rom. 6:14,15) [i.e., ". . . you are no longer under law, but under grace."] There have been changes from the Old Covenant to the New Covenant. The two are not identical. . . .
>
> *Only that which is explicitly renewed* from *the Old Testament law can be considered part of the New Testament "law of Christ"* (cf. Gal.

6:2). . . . . No other specific Old Testament laws can be proved to be strictly binding on Christians, valuable as it is for Christians to know all of the laws.[1]

It is precisely this issue that illustrates why "the Old Testament problem . . . is not just one of many. It is the master problem c i theology," according to Emil G. Kraeling.[2] Put in its most elementary form, the problem is this: Does the Old Testament (hereafter OT) have any authority in the Christian Church, and if so, how is that authority to be defined and derived from the OT?

It is no wonder, then, that the OT is seldom, if ever, used as a source of norms or teaching on social, economic, or business issues. However, this negligence counters the clear claim that the Apostle Paul made for the OT: "All Scripture is God-breathed and is useful for teaching, rebuking, correcting and training in righteousness, so that the man of God may be thoroughly equipped for every good work" (2 Tim. 3:16-17).

But how "useful" is the OT? Paul answers with four clauses in which he sets two positive and two negative functions of the OT: (1) "teaching" (the OT contains three-fourths of God's word to humanity; some words are not repeated in the New Testament [hereafter NT]), (2) "rebuke" (e.g., Proverbs points out our sin and leads us to hate and leave it), (3) "correction" (God's standard, which sets straight what has been bent or twisted in our lives), and (4) "instruction in righteousness" (the rules given by a teacher to the child).[3] Particularly this fourth purpose of the "Scriptures," which are nothing less and nothing more than the OT itself in this context, points to the use of the OT for deciding what is "just, righteous, or upright." Righteousness is the state of being "just," of having "all as it should be." Surely such a claim directs the NT believer to the OT in order to make ethical and moral decisions!

Unfortunately, the arguments against applying Israel's law and history to a modern society come all too easily in the Christian community. It will be said that Israel is unique and therefore a special case. Since she experienced the special election of God and was ruled under theocratic principles, it is dangerous and hermeneutically irresponsible to transpose OT teachings given to her to a modern believer today. Consequently, it will be said, Christians should look to the NT for guidance on social, moral, ethical, economic, and business principles rather than the OT.

JESUS AND THE OLD TESTAMENT LAW

It would be altogether appropriate to place some of these key questions before the founder of Christianity, since Christians are wary of using the OT, especially the law of Moses, for fear that it might offend the very founding principles of their new faith. If we could arrive at some sort of consensus on what Jesus thought about the law, perhaps we might be in a more favorable position to decide how some of these same texts could be applied to modern issues raised in business.

Jesus' statement in Matthew 5:17-20 is certainly an extremely strong endorsement of the whole OT under the rubric of "the Law or the Prophets." He warned, "Do not think [apparently, some were on the verge of doing so or had already done so] that I have come to abolish the Law or the Prophets; I have not come to abolish them but to fulfill them."

Some Protestant commentators, such as Robert Banks,[4] have tried to show that the law has been "transcended" now that Jesus has come and fulfilled all that had been promised in the OT. In fact, Banks argued that the "commandments" of verse 19 ("one of the least of these commandments") refer to Jesus' commands, not the commands of the Torah!

David Wenham found all of Banks's arguments to be wrongheaded.[5] The termination point for the relevancy of the Law was not the appearance of Jesus, but the end of time itself when "heaven and earth pass away." Neither does "fulfill" mean to "establish and transcend"; instead it means to bring to completion and realization. Moreover, the "commandments" were those that had just been pointed to in verses 14-16, which were inscripturated in the OT, as the reference to the "jot and tittle" (v. 18 in KJV) proves.

Does such an endorsement of the Torah imply that all OT law is equally binding? No. Jesus taught, as did the rabbis, that we must differentiate between the "lighter" and the "heavier" commandments (see Matt. 23:23-24). For our Lord, the "more important matters of the law" were precisely those mentioned by Micah the prophet—"to act justly and to love mercy and to walk humbly with your God" (Mic. 6:6-8).

What makes some laws "heavier" than others? What gives some more endurance and applicability than others? If biblical interpretation is not to become the special preserve of a theologically sophisticated elite, there must be some fairly simple rules that the layperson can use and individually apply to the OT texts.

We believe that those laws directly based on the character, nature, and being of God are the ones meant to be permanent. The moral law found in the Ten Commandments of Exodus 20 and Deuteronomy 5, the holiness law found in Leviticus 18-20, which repeatedly urges us to "be holy because I, the LORD your God, am holy," and those motivational clauses attached to many forms of legal injunctions, such as "for I am compassionate" (Exod. 22:26ff.), all supply a universal basis—the character of God—for continuing to obey that law.

PAUL AND THE OLD TESTAMENT LAW

Usually, the debate shifts at this point to the Apostle Paul. Since Paul spoke of the law as having had a function for a definite period of time ("Before this faith came, we were held prisoners by the law, locked up until faith should be revealed. . . . [But] now that faith has come, we are no longer under the supervision of the law" [Gal. 3:23-25]), some argue that he meant that the new "law of Christ" (Gal. 6:2) has replaced the old law of Moses.

Paul's attitude toward the law is perhaps one of the most puzzling problems in all of biblical study, apparently for the same reason that the OT is the master problem of theology. On the one hand are those passages that appear to say that the law is abrogated and transcended (see Rom. 7:1-10; 2 Cor. 3:4-17; Gal. 2:19; Eph. 2:14-16). On the other hand, one can cite Paul as being just as certain that neither he nor any other Christian has by any means abolished the law by means of faith; in fact, the law turns out to be "holy, righteous and good" and "spiritual" (Rom. 7:12-14). Faith, instead of abolishing the law, only establishes it (see Rom. 3:31).

Even more spectacular is the discussion from Romans 9:30-10:13. Paul makes his strongest case that what he is preaching and teaching is precisely what Moses taught in Leviticus 18:5 and Deuteronomy 30:12-14, and also what Isaiah (see 28:16) and Joel (see 2:32) had urged (see Rom. 10:5-13). Christ was not the "end of the law" (Rom. 10:4) in the sense that He terminated it; He was its teleological goal or purpose. The two citations from Moses were not in opposition to each other ("Moses describes . . . the righteousness that is by the law. . . . But the righteousness that is by faith says . . ." [Rom. 10:5-6]), but were complementary and should have been translated as "for Moses described . . . *and* the righteousness which is by faith," just as the same Greek construction is rendered in verse 10, "For it is with your heart . . . *and* it is with your mouth."

Paul's contrast here (see Rom. 9:30-10:13) is not between the faith of the NT and the *law* of Moses; instead, it is between the homemade righteousness of his brethren, the Jews, ("pursued a law of righteousness"—note the word order in Greek [Rom. 9:31]; "as if it were by works" [Rom 9:32]; "sought to establish their own [righteousness]" [Rom. 10:3]) and the righteousness that came from Moses' law and from faith!

Accordingly, we concur with C. E. B. Cranfield[6] that much of our puzzlement over Paul's use of the word *law* comes from our failure to recognize that Paul had no separate word-group or term to denote what we now call "legalism," that unbiblical system by which a person attempts to earn salvation or to merit salvation from God. Paul was rightfully adamant on the point that no one could ever earn redemption from sin based on "observing the law" (Rom.

3:21-28). Yet he, like Jesus, appeared to have no objection to continuing to observe the ceremonies of the law as a mark of his solidarity with his kinsfolk (see Acts 16:3 on circumcision, 21:20-26 on vows and purification rites; and 1 Cor. 9:20-21 on being all things to all individuals that he might win some).

It is difficult to imagine Paul or Jesus teaching that the OT was not *our* testament. Even the very term "Christ's law" (1 Cor. 9:21; Gal. 6:2; cf. James 2:8) appears to reflect the OT once again. According to Galatians 6:2, this law was fulfilled by "carry[ing] each other's burdens." But James 2:8 notes that the "royal law of love" called for us to love our neighbor as ourselves, which is a command in Moses' holiness law (see Lev. 19:18).[7]

ISRAEL, THE CHURCH, AND THE OLD TESTAMENT

Some, of course, will concede the point that the OT was written for the Church as well as for Israel. However, with this concession there usually appears another problem: OT Israel is equated with the Church, and this equation governs the interpretation of the OT.

That there is some NT support for this connection between Israel and the Church cannot be denied. After all, the Church was described in 1 Peter 2:9 as "a holy nation" (the very phrase used to describe Israel in Exod. 19:5-6), and its members were labeled as "the Israel of God" in Galatians 6:16. Stephen also had used the term *ekklesia*, "the called-out [ones], the Church," when he referred to the Church or congregation in the wilderness (Acts 7:38). Most impressive of all was Paul's reminder that those in Christ had, previous to their conversion, been separated not only from Christ, but also "from the common-wealth [*politeia*] of Israel" (Eph. 2:12). The Church had been grafted into the root and trunk of the national Israel, even though some of the Jewish branches had been lopped off (see Rom. 11:13-21). Surely there is enough substantial evidence to argue for some kind of continuity between Israel and the Church.

But the real difficulty is that the NT never makes a direct equation between Israel and the Church. Israel remains a "commonwealth," a state with rulers, citizenship, and civil polity. Israel's military policies and responses do not and cannot guide the Church. Israel's installation of a king and her relationships with neighboring states do not and cannot set up norms for the Church in her relationships with institutions, both within and outside the state.

Membership in Israel was achieved by means of birth; in the NT, member-ship in Christ is achieved by the new birth and a salvation that comes as a gift of God's grace in Christ. Even though there is a closer relationship between believing Israel and the Church, the lack of a clear and total equation between the two is all the more obvious.

Therefore, although some analogies can be found between Israel and the Church, no direct equations between the two bodies are evident. To restrict our attention only to those portions where we can find some of these partial analogies between the believing remnant in Israel and the believing Church is to be overly selective and prejudicial in our use of the OT. And such highly selective usage will lead to reductionistic types of teaching and thinking about the OT, a state of affairs that Paul would condemn in 2 Timothy 3:16-17.

So we are caught in a bind. All of the OT is profitable for Christians' use, yet it must not be used as if it were directly addressed to the Church or as if we merely substitute the word *Church* every time we see *Israel*.

Is this the inevitable price we must pay for the specificity and particularity of the OT? Is it because the message given to Israel was so relevant to her day that its modern usefulness must be reduced to little more than a few general principles at a very high level of abstraction?

John Goldingay summarized Karl Barth's position on the OT in this manner:

> To try to apply the specific commands of God to a situation or to people other than those to which they were addressed is not merely difficult or impossible in practice: it is methodologically misguided. They are either so specific that they do not apply to us, or so general (as in the case of the Decalogue) that they only mark the boundaries of the area . . . in which concrete divine commandment and prohibition take place.[8]

Such estimates of the *applicability* of the OT to the modern scene and the Church are not found exclusively among those of liberal or neoorthodox theological persuasions; many evangelicals are just as anxious to avoid inappropriate application of the OT to our day lest the OT suffer from subjectivistic handling or from an unfair exposure. The concern is altogether fitting.

However, two responses must be given to this concern: (1) Jesus Himself warned us against relaxing "the least of these commandments" (Matt. 5:19), and (2) the prophets, Jesus, and the apostles were able to transcend this hurdle of cultural relativism, which had already become as much a difficulty in the first Christian century as it is in our day.

If it be objected that the warning of Matthew 5:19 is an isolated case, what shall we say about Mark 7:6-13? Our Lord was disgusted with the Pharisees who had "let go of the commands of God" (v. 8) and who had "a fine way of setting aside the commands of God" (v. 9), thereby "nullify[ing] the word of God" (v. 13). Would our Lord expect any less of us, His Church?

Furthermore, the changes in society between the time of Moses and the prophets, or between Moses and Jesus and the apostles, were often as great as some of the same we face today when viewing the OT. For example, both Jeremiah and Nehemiah faced very different situations from what Moses had to confront with regard to slavery laws, debt reduction, and taking of interest, but both appealed to the Torah as they made new applications of old laws. No less dramatic was Jesus' appeal to the creation ordinance when He faced the question of divorce. Time had not erased either the authority of the OT or (and here is the more difficult issue) its relevance and application.

The logical extension to this type of argumentation is to conclude that the NT also does not provide any ethical or moral guidance for us today since it was written almost two millennia ago. Roger Mehl advised that we will search the NT in vain for "precise norms of or even directions for a social ethic."[9] Likewise, J.L. Houlden opined, "There is, strictly, no such thing as the X of the New Testament. . . . It is at the cost of ignoring the individuality of each, in thought and expression, that the unified account can emerge. . . . There can be no initial assumption of harmony."[10]

Both the rejection of biblical authority as supplying norms for modern life and the rejection of a quest for the harmony advocated in the biblical texts on ethical and moral decisions are preemptory moves. The first objection sets up its own standard while deprecating the same alleged nonsense in others! The second was handled well in Oliver M.T. O'Donovan's counter comment: "In fact, the search for diversity is as much the result of prior methodological decision as is the search for harmony, and cannot be defended on purely empirical grounds. Empirical investigation reveals points of diversity and points of harmony, too."[11] Modernity and the scholarly community have placed too high a regard on diversity to the disregard, and even suspicion, of inductive investigations for evidences of harmony on moral, ethical, and theological principles.

The point of our discussion, then, is that there are no simple or direct equations between what was addressed to Israel and what is now addressed to the Church. One must also be careful not to indulge in "proof-text" ethics. "But," as Goldingay put it so concisely, "to be against proof-texting is no more adventurous than to be against sin."[12] The question still remains of what we are to *apply* to our generation and how the average reader will be able to recognize how and when this is to be done.

THE POSSIBILITY OF APPLYING OLD TESTAMENT ETHICS TO THE CHURCH

Three questions must be answered if the Church is to be able to apply OT ethics to itself and to the problems of the business world: (1) Does the OT contain "universal" ethical commands? (2) Are the ethical precepts of the OT in harmony with themselves and with the NT? and (3) Do the laws and commands of the OT have any *claim* on any other mortals than those living in ancient Israel? Each question demands a good answer before we can begin to lay the foundation for any type of biblical guide for the Christian conduct of business in the modern world.

1. Universality—Karl Barth's judgment was that the OT contained no "universal" ethical commands. For Barth, such a claim was an "untenable assumption," for "the command of God . . . is always an individual command for the conduct of this man, at this moment and in this situation."[13]

O'Donovan's response to Barth was that he had falsely equated "universal" with "generality" (i.e., Barth thought that a command had to be indefinite, imprecise, vague, or not specifically directed to a particular person or audience in order to be universal). O'Donovan stated,

> Yet moral philosophy since Kant has used "universal" as the opposite of "particular," not of "special" or "specific." A universal rule is one which applies to every case of a certain class, however minutely specified that class may be. [Furthermore,] a command or precept is "universal" whenever its content and the persons it addresses are indicated entirely by classification; where either the content of the command or its addressee is indicated by a demonstrative, a "this" or "that," a time reference, a proper name, etc. etc., it is particular.[14]

Moreover, the fact that some of God's commands have specific addressees in specific situations does not rule out the possibility that they may also be expressions of a universal principle. To treat all references to specificity or particularity as if they were somewhat random imperatives without attachment to any great body of morality would be to press the case for diversity and cultural relativism too far. Cultural continuity and canonical unity are just as worthy of having their claims examined and heard as are the claims of diversity and relativism.

In fact, "no command or principle . . . could be justified ethically except by a reference to a universal: an ethic without universals would be no ethic, a series of disconnected, arbitrary imperatives."[15] There lurks behind even such a specific command from Paul that begs, "I plead with Euodia and I plead with Syntyche to agree with each other in the Lord" (Phil. 4:2), an "implied assertion that agreeing together is something two Christian women ought to do."[16]

OT ethics is possible, then, even though some of its commands contain specific references and addresses. To be sure, some commands are limited to the person and the time in which they were expressed—for example, "Bring the cloak that I left with Carpus at Troas" (2 Tim. 4:13). But these are the exceptions that prove the rule rather than the instances that create the rule.

2. Consistency—What about consistency? All that is necessary here is to show that the biblical writer has given us more than just a bare list of unrelated imperatives. If the writer is writing out of a context of an antecedent theology and if the Bible is in existence at the time he is writing, then the writing is not a "stand alone" contribution. The way the writers explicitly quote, allude, and make inferences to previous events, characters and lessons learned from already inscripturated text is precisely what is needed to infer consistency and harmony in the ethical demands laid on all who heard and read this message. The writers believe they are supplementing and applying what has gone before, not supplanting it.

What connects the OT ethic with the NT ethic is the fact that both are revealed by the same God. Both are based on His character. Both return to the same "informing theology" or "antecedent theology" found in its quintessence in the Ten Commandments and in strands such as the holiness law of Leviticus 18-20. Evidence for such a claim can best be seen in some of the recent work on the laws of Deuteronomy. In a major breakthrough, Professor Stephen Kaufman published in 1979 his conclusions strongly suggesting that Deuteronomy 5:12-26 reflected the order and the particular application of the Ten Commandments to that day.[17] Behind all of the specificity of that large corpus of laws was the informing theology of the Decalogue!

3. Prescriptivity—The third and final question deals with prescriptivity. The OT purports to give more to its readers than mere advice or exotic information from the past. Since the source of the injunctions claims to be none less than God Himself, it is fair to assume that the OT is also laying a claim on our lives as well as on Israel. The fact that what the OT prescribes is also consistent with what we know of God from both the OT and the NT further leads us to heed its claims. Added to this is the fact that one can discern universal principles matching up to the character of God.

THE METHOD OF APPLYING THE OLD TESTAMENT TO CURRENT QUESTIONS

The OT teaches that God is king not just of Israel, but of all the nations (see Ps. 2; 47), and He is Lord over all events on earth (see Isa. 40:23-24). The standards of righteousness required of Israel are the same attainments God expects of all. His law sets the level for what is right and what is wrong for all the world. In fact, the Lord warns,

> "And if [all the wicked neighboring nations] learn well the ways of my people and swear by my name . . . then they will be established among my people. But if any nation does not listen, I will completely uproot and destroy it." (Jer. 12:16-17)

The same principles are set forth for us in even clearer terms in Jeremiah 18:7-10.

Therefore, in some senses, Israel was a model for all the nations. The morality she learned by revelation from God was not meant to be chauvinistic and distinctive to herself; it had been intended for publication among all the nations.

Yet in spite of this demonstration that God's law has relevance for nations other than Israel, we need to know what models or methods we can use to get from the OT to these nations and, much more personally, to our own day. Four such methods can be described and analyzed here: (1) the method of analogy, (2) the method of middle axioms, (3) the method of general equity as set forth in the Westminster Larger Catechism (Question 99, Section 3: "That one and the same thing in diverse respects, is required or forbidden in several commandments"; cf. Prov. 1:19; Amos 8:5; Col. 3:5; and 1 Tim. 6:10), and (4) the method of extracting legal precedents from earlier cases as a basis for making decisions in the contemporary world.

Since this chapter focuses on deriving ethical bases for making decisions in the business world, we will be more concerned with the interpretation of legal materials in the Bible, especially those sections called apodictic law (the case laws such as those found in the Covenant Code of Exod. 21-23) and those sections of wisdom literature featuring the practical application of legal principles for everyday life.

1. The method of analogy—Analogy presupposes that there is some sort of expressed comparison between Israel's laws and the Church. We have already seen that no such direct equation is made in the text of the OT or the NT, despite many assurances from modern commentators to the opposite effect. The only real analogy lies between redeemed Israel and the redeemed Church, but this comparison is too narrow for the questions posed by the business community and it is, as we have already argued, too selective to be a broad basis on which to base our model for applying the OT to modern situations.

2. The method of middle axioms—Interpreters have also attempted to obtain what was behind the specificity of the OT text by searching for what some ethicists have labeled "middle axioms." A middle axiom appears to be a principle that is somewhere between a general abstraction, such as "justice," and a specific, concrete action.

N. H. G. Robinson believes that this phrase may first have been used for ethical theory by J.H. Oldham. Oldham felt that statements like "obey the law of law" or "we ought to strive for social justice" were too broad and gave no direction on what we were to do in individual cases. On the other hand, precise instructions would rob individuals of their moral responsibilities. "Hence between purely general statements of ethical demands of the Gospel and the decisions that have to be made in concrete situations there is need for what may be described as middle axioms."[18]

But such hypothetical principles usually end up being altogether too general. They also lack the most needed ingredient: the demonstration that they are biblically derived from the same text where the particular law was being interpreted. Thus, while the Bible remains our authority, the middle axiom may or may not be normative.

Most devastating of all, this method never brings us back to any practical application or particular decision. What we ultimately need is not a batch of general principles, but specific bases for making decisions and for committing ourselves to a particular action.

3. The method of general equity —The Westminster Confession of Faith (and many of the earlier confessions) distinguished between the moral, ceremonial, and judicial laws of God. Generally the moral law was taken as the backbone for all law, just as we have argued here. Judicial laws were defined by the Westminster divines in this way: "To them also, as a body politick, he gave sundry judicial laws, which expired together with the state of that people, not obliging any other now, further than the general equity thereof may require" (xix. 4).

To speak of the equity of the law means that the law can apply to more cases than the one it particularly addresses. It can do so because a general principle lies behind every particular law. Thus, the law against muzzling an ox in Deuteronomy 25:4 has a legitimate application to giving Church leaders their salaries in 1 Corinthians 9:8-10 and 1 Timothy 5:17-18. The reason for this equity is to be found in the fact that giving engenders a spirit of generosity and gentleness in those who give. The concern was for the farmers, not the oxen!

This method's strong point is that it forces us to look for the one basic principle behind each judicial law and historical situation. Thus as James B.

Jordan of the theonomy movement points out, the same law, such as the prohibition on witchcraft, occurs in three different situations in the Torah: it is connected with adultery, for witchcraft is apostasy from Israel's divine husband (see Exod. 22:18); it is connected with submission to authority, since witchcraft is rebellion (see Deut. 18:10); and it is connected with separation of life and death in the context of the ceremonial law (see Lev. 19:31; 20:27).[19] Here, the laws of God have multiple equity in the areas of adultery, rebellion, and blasphemy against the name and work of God.

Thus, the equity of a statute, according to the *Oxford English Dictionary*, is "according to its reason and spirit so as to make it apply to cases for which it does not expressly provide." This is exactly what is needed if one remembers that in the case of Scripture we are not appealing so much to the "reason and spirit" of the law as we are to the informing theology of the moral law, which had already been published and which lies behind all of these individual enactments.

We are not saying that general equity means that we can apply case laws from the Bible cross-culturally minus their cultural expressions! We refer, instead, to the moral law of God, which stands behind these case laws. This method will help to define moral law behind most laws, but it will not tell us how to proceed from there.

4. The method of extracting legal precedents —The last method brought us close to defining the proper way to make ethical decisions in the business world from legal texts. The use of general equity is much like the use of legal precedents in our courts today. A previous decision is treated as an authority once it is determined that an analogous principle rests behind the previous decision.

The lawyer or judge reconstructs the *ratio* of the earlier case, which served as the main reason for deciding the previous case (the *ratio decidendi*). This legal principle is then applied to the new case, which demands a search for the moral point or the purpose behind the earlier case. Not all the facts or details of the previous case are relevant nor need they be appealed at this point.[20]

From this *ratio*, we can begin to build our "Ladder of Abstraction."[21] No matter which end of the two ladders we begin on, one ladder coming up from the OT and the other from the NT, we may begin either with the moral principle in hand and apply it to specific situations in the OT or NT context or with the specific application that will force us to seek the principle. The interpreter must be able to move from the ancient specific situation through the OT institutional or personal norm up to the general principle that embraces both the specific and the abstract statements of the text being studied. Once we are armed with the authoritative principle and the moral grounds behind that text, we may move down the NT and contemporary ladder to a new level of specificity appropriate to the modern needs and questions.

CONCLUSION

The ethical systems of the OT and the NT are not in tension with each other. The seeming disparity has been one of a proper method of interpreting legal texts. Perhaps even more determinative than this failure has been the artificial antagonism that we theologians have introduced between law and grace, i.e., between the OT revelation given by God to Moses and the promises divinely entrusted to Abraham, David, and the gospel writers.

Only when we realize that there is no such basic antagonism can we begin to supply the much-needed help that the business community requests. The NT cannot pretend to be all the revelation of God; neither can it always be expected to speak on issues that have already been taken up in the OT. Must the Church experience another fiasco similar to the one we faced at the beginning of the 1970s when the question of abortion was just beginning to rear its ugly head? Often, the unbiblical refrain was heard, "Well, I guess abortion is all right since the NT doesn't have anything to say on the matter in any direct way!" It took the Christian community until the 1980s to figure out that something was drastically wrong with that kind of hermeneutic. Have we learned our lesson well? Or will we repeat it in the area of economics and business?

This is not to say that this type of interpreting is easy or that it has no risks and no pain connected with it. It does! But we must be willing to listen patiently to the text and to place our questions before the appropriate texts with the proper method of eliciting the authority that that text has to offer on that subject.

Our conclusion is that an excellent case can be made for a single biblical ethic to be used in the business world. The moral principles are not only adequate for constructing such a case, but they will also supply us with the means for making particular applications at the most specific, mundane level.

EDITOR'S PERSPECTIVE

The key issue surfacing in the tension between Myron Augsburger's position (the New Testament ethic supersedes that of the Old Testament ethic) and Walter Kaiser's contention (there is only one biblical ethic) is the possibility that there will be human abrogation of part of God's biblical authority on the one hand or the imposition of humanly induced, extrabiblical authority on the other hand. Are we shortchanging or adding to the Scripture?

The heart of Dr. Augsburger's argument is that the redemptive work of God expressed fully in His incarnation in Jesus elevates mercy, compassion, forgiveness, and other redemptive aspects of God's character to a place of prominence. These aspects of grace supersede other parts of the law that mirror God's justice, judgment, and wrath, which now await their further manifestation on the Day of Judgment. He pleads for an ethic reflecting the work of redemption and not an ethic flowing from God's law.

Dr. Kaiser agrees with much of Dr. Augsburger's argument but contends it is a false dichotomy to divide Old and New Testament ethics in such a way as to see a new, superseding ethic. Rather, he believes we need to search for the *principles* embodied in the law and manifested in the incarnate Christ that are abiding universals reflecting the unchanging character of God. (More will be said in chapter 14 about *how* we are to discover the principles of Scripture.)

There is a progressive, unfolding revelation of God's character and conduct in Scripture. However, we must be very careful how we allow the latter revelation to guide us in our interpretation of the former. Scripture interprets itself for us when the prophets, the apostles, and our Lord quote other portions of Scripture and tell us the meaning. We do not always have the benefit of their input, though. We must seek Scripture's truth when there is less direct help, too, remembering that "no prophecy of Scripture is a matter of one's own interpretation, for no prophecy was ever made by an act of human will, but men moved by the Holy Spirit spoke from God" (2 Pet. 1:20-21). God gave us the Scripture, we are to live by "*every* word that proceeds out of the mouth of God" (Matt. 4:4, emphasis added), and we must rely on the Spirit to use the Scripture to help us interpret it. But how does the Spirit help us interpret the Scripture?

If the Scripture does not interpret the Scripture, we have no standard by which we may be corrected apart from our private thoughts and/or feelings. We are unable to resolve the debate over whether or not there is a superseding New Testament ethic, but it is appropriate to call every Christian to embrace *Biblical Christianity*—faith and response governed by the Word of God, not extrabiblical experiences—and to feed on and digest all of God's Word (Old *and* New Testaments).

Neither scholar—Augsburger nor Kaiser—plays down the importance of the Old Testament, even though some evangelical scholars do. Such a position is fraught with additional difficulties. For example, those who believe that only explicit New Testament directives are pertinent should remember that twice the New Testament states explicitly that God will put His "laws [plural] into their minds, and . . . will write them upon their hearts" (Heb. 8:10; 10:16). What laws does this refer to? The fact that God intends to write His laws on the hearts of His children is a biblical principle—a repetitive Old Testament and New Testament theme—and most certainly refers to God's precepts, both Old and New. The psalmist says God's law is written in his heart (see Ps. 37:31; 40:8; 119:11), and we are promised a similar experience in New Testament times. Surely we will have in our hearts what God has wrought in the psalmist's heart.

The practical implications for making business decisions are enormous. Individuals who limit their mental stimulation to the New Testament for the development of their spiritual sensitivities are apt to test God (a sin) and remain relatively immature in their understanding of God's will.

For example, the book of Proverbs is filled with God's wisdom, much of it having direct application in various business situations that run the gamut from dealing with personnel problems involving interpersonal conflicts (see Prov. 18:17) to the fact that driving a hard business bargain can be akin to an act of deception before the Lord (see Prov. 20:14). The Old Testament provides hundreds of examples, in many contexts, of God's mind on human activity in commercial settings.

What are businesspersons to do who promise to do a certain job for a specific price and then subsequently realize that the raw materials have gone up in price or, worse yet, an error was made in the cost-price calculation? Can we "escape" the problem by becoming legalistic and noting that nothing had been put in writing—there is no legal evidence of an agreement? Or can we simply deny that the particular price was ever really offered?

King David had a different perception of this situation. David wondered about who may abide in the presence of the Lord, and he answered his own question by saying, "He[who]swears to his own hurt, and does not change" (Ps. 15:1,4). God expects us to honor our word, even if it costs us because we erred. King Solomon happily tells us, though, we can plead our case with the person we verbally made the contract with, and if the individual releases us, we are free of the obligation (see Prov. 6:2-5).

We are to be holy, for God is holy (see Lev. 11:44; 1 Pet. 1:15-16; etc.). We really test God if we expect Him to stimulate us so that His principles of love and honor are written on our hearts, but we refuse to or fail to study the Scripture He has already given us. What right do we have to limit God to the New Testament revelation when He is the author of all the Scripture?

It is equally bad, though, for us to learn our lessons about business in the classroom and from the marketplace and then fail to examine these teachings in the light of God's precepts. We honor the marketplace more than God when we do this. Where, for example, will the Christian business professional wrestle with the market pressures that call for a changing relationship between a product's price and its quality? Can we arbitrarily alter these relationships without God's being interested? No! (Read Isa. 1:22.)

Product safety, issues of ecology and the environment, retributive justice, and many other contemporary subjects are covered more fully when we examine them in the light of both Old and New Testaments. Theologians will certainly continue to debate the relationship between the Testaments (and their relative importance), but if their debates distract us from feeding upon every word that has ever proceeded from the mouth of God, we'll develop spiritual malnutrition.

It is not being legalistic nor does it undermine grace to state that God's testimonies, precepts, ways, laws, word, statutes, commandments, judgments, and ordinances are to be written on the hearts of His children, and that the New and Old Testaments are harmonious. If they are not, God has a changing character or His house stands divided. The Word of God is powerless apart from the Spirit of God to impart life, love, forgiveness, and reconciliation, but the Word of God in the hands of the Holy Spirit becomes the very instrument by which He convicts, comforts, teaches, guides, and directs our lives. He feeds us a whole loaf, not a half-loaf. He does not feed us law; He gives us a living Word that builds us up in Christ. The law is transformed into purposeful love by the Holy Spirit when it is written on the hearts of God's children.

ABSOLUTES IN A SITUATIONAL ENVIRONMENT

Relativism, a world view holding that there are no absolutes, is the pervasive understanding of moral reality governing much of the business community's approach to moral decision making today. From such a perspective, there are no moral standards other than personal beliefs or culture's mores. In fact, the very notion of moral absolutes is quite passe in today's culture. People who hold to such a belief are generally depicted as naive and are frequently suspected of being antiintellectual.

Even many Christians have abandoned their beliefs in moral absolutes, succumbing to the world's mind-set that embraces situational ethics. They have shifted to such a position because Christians have not been taught to interrelate an accurate understanding of biblical absolutes with the necessity of making moral judgments in changing situations. In fact, this truth—there are biblical absolutes, but they do not eliminate the need for moral judgments—is so befuddling that many people perceive it to be internally contradictory. How can someone claim to believe in absolutes and simultaneously be left with the problem of making judgments about matters that have no absolute answers? What good are absolutes if they don't provide standardized or specific answers? In what respect, then, are they absolutes? After all, don't people who believe in absolutes have the right to expect absolute answers to real-life moral questions?

We have received little help for coping with this everyday reality. The Church, as a whole, has not done a good job of addressing the contemporary points of conflict between the culture's world view and God's revealed perspective on business-related issues. We will wrestle with the tension between believing in biblical absolutes and acknowledging that we must make moral judgments in many business situations. Biblical Christianity does not embrace

93

situational ethics where the situation determines the standard for "right." Biblical Christianity does, however, acknowledge an absolute standard of right that must be administered in vastly different situations.

To help us work through the tensions associated with these differences, Dr. Henry Krabbendam and Dr. Vernon Grounds address two biblical truths that are themselves in tension. Dr. Krabbendam discusses the fact that biblical propositional instructions can be objectively applied in the business world. Dr. Grounds addresses the truth that there are a number of demonstrable cases where the responsible application of biblical principles in business calls for a subjective moral judgment.

Dr. Krabbendam traces the shift in the Western world views from one greatly influenced by a belief in the "scriptural law" (God is the sovereign planner and controller of the universe) to that of interpreting reality through the "natural law" (the cosmos is impersonal, and there is no necessity for considering God) and finally to the modern "positive law" position (mankind is the sovereign seat of planning and control). This human-centered world view creates polarizations between such important tensions as being *individuals* while living in a *community*; balancing *freedom* and *control*; and contending with *diversity* and *uniformity*. These tensions give rise to the political, economic, and social struggles that wrack humanity.

Dr. Krabbendam believes reconciliation of these tensions is possible only through God's work of redemption, which brings people to the point of wanting to be personally obedient to the truths in God's unerring Word. Only in loving obedience to God's truth can mankind achieve the harmony, unity, and peace in the human community that God manifests within the Trinity.

The editor will end these two chapters by postulating that the presence of objective and subjective dimensions of reality is necessarily associated with the existence of and administration of biblical absolutes.

CHAPTER 6

BIBLICAL INSTRUCTIONS THAT CAN BE APPLIED TO THE BUSINESS WORLD

Henry Krabbendam

Dr. Henry Krabbendam is Professor of Biblical Studies at Covenant College. He received his undergraduate training in the Netherlands and his Th.M. and Th.D. degrees from Westminster Theological Seminary in Philadelphia. He has held pastorates in Canada, Pennsylvania, and California, is a frequent speaker in conferences and churches, and has contributed scholarly chapters on apologetics and hermeneutics in several publications. In recent years he has traveled frequently to Africa, specifically Uganda. He is the cofounder of the African Christian Training, Development, and Service Trust and is involved there in a wide variety of ministries, development projects, and businesses.

INTRODUCTION

This chapter consists of an introduction and two main sections. The two main sections focus on (1) the business world from the modern perspective and (2) a biblical perspective on the business world. The introduction presents three presuppositions, formulates three definitions, and makes some observations as the backdrop for the main sections. The three presuppositions pertain to the nature, authority, and relevance of Scripture. The three definitions are those of economics, business, and entrepreneur. The observations form the transition to the main sections.

Presuppositions—The first presupposition is that the Scriptures of the Old and New Testaments constitute a truly and fully divine-human book. They are the one uncompounded product of God as the divine author and of human writers as His instruments. In them the divine and human factors flow harmoniously together and at no point limit, suppress, supersede, or eliminate each other. The Scriptures are divinely perfect, inerrant and trustworthy in all that they assert, and humanly real, displaying the full humanity of the writers and addressing man in his full humanity.

The second presupposition is that the Scriptures of the Old and New Testaments are truly and fully authoritative. The cumulative nature of biblical revelation and the evident measure of discontinuity between the Testaments do not negate their organic continuity and underlying unity. Neither do they subtract from the binding force of the Scriptures in their totality as God's Word to man. Consequently, the Old Testament is not to be dismissed as abrogated, except where it is reconfirmed or repeated in the New Testament. Rather, the Old Testament has lost nothing of its compelling power, except where it is explicitly discontinued or clearly transcended by the New Testament. Similarly, the central scope of Scripture or any of its sections, however much it should receive the spotlight, never diminishes the truth of what may appear to be more peripheral or even incidental. Scripture is authoritative in whatever it teaches or touches,[1] whether it pertains to faith and practice, science and history, or economics and business.

The third presupposition is that the Scriptures of the Old and New Testaments are truly and fully relevant. They reflect the setting, the language, the culture, and the customs of their time. Historical, linguistic, archeological, and other auxiliary studies, therefore, can be expected to contribute and at times may even prove to be invaluable in bringing the original text in focus and displaying it in its true color. But this does not amount to a gap between the past and the present that cannot be bridged and ultimately relegates Scripture to the level of an antique. However venerable in age it may be, it remains young and is ever fresh. As the inerrant and authoritative truth of God, it addresses man everywhere and at all times in the total range of his predicament. It covers all occasions, settings, and circumstances as well as relationships, activities, and areas of his life, whether by injunction or promise, by pronouncement or warnings, by patterns or principles, by blueprint or in principle, directly or indirectly, explicitly or implicitly.

Definitions—The first definition is that of economics. Economics is stipulated here from a biblical perspective as a science that assesses and prioritizes the various human needs and aims at a disciplined, focused mode of administering a potential abundance of resources to meet them. Admittedly, this definition runs counter to the usual one that calls for economics to concern itself with satisfying unlimited wants by means of limited resources. In fact, they are completely opposite in the two pivotal areas that are covered. For one, the focus shifts from man's unlimited wants to his needs, which have inherent boundaries. For another, the dismal outlook fostered by ultimate scarcity is replaced by a bright prospect. The defeatist attitude in the face of an ever-threatening shortfall turns into expectancy and confidence.[2]

The second definition is that of business. Business is the activity of producing and/or marketing goods and services that aims at satisfying the needs of all involved. It appears biblical to hold that a godly society fostering a godly business climate will display a good measure of prosperity and wealth (see Deut. 28:1-14).[3]

The third definition is that of entrepreneur. An entrepreneur is an individual who by himself or in conjunction with others at an acceptable risk invests his resources, time, and energy in the organization and management of a business with the expectation that it will be profitable.[4] The risk factor is inevitable. The market conditions can suddenly and dramatically change. Only the entrepreneur himself can determine what risk is acceptable to him and what is not. But he should do so in the light of Scripture. It appears that debt financing should not be considered as an option (see Rom. 13:8).

Observations—The first observation is that Scripture is not merely a historical record of God's revelation to man, an accurate description of all His closely intertwined acts and words in the past. It *is* God's revelation in and by itself, and as such, it is a historical force in and for the present. It declares, interprets, and directs. It promises, provides, and protects. It diagnoses, treats, and cures. It addresses, demands, and grants. It does so and can do so because it is truth.

To be sure, not all truth is propositional, laid out in the form of a statement. A proposition is only a language medium to specify and convey truth. Neither are all sentences of Scripture propositions. Imperatives, questions, and exclamations as linguistic forms are by themselves neither factually true nor false. But Scripture most certainly contains propositional truth. Even in imperatives and the like, such truth is presupposed. Otherwise, they would be meaningless. In fact, it is the genius of Scripture that through its language, truth is communicated. First (capable of being) presented in a propositional form as objectively and universally valid, it is subsequently driven home to be believed and practiced by way of commands, promises, or other such linguistic forms.[5]

The second observation is that definitions are frequently neither neutral nor harmless. The opposing definitions of economics are a case in point. They are verbalized world views in collision. The one turns economics into a "dismal science," indeed. The ever-threatening scarcity must spell frustration and defeat. The other holds out the hope of abundance and wealth (locked into created reality by God and to be released under God), truly a different picture. It hardly needs to be emphasized that the latter definition is informed by biblical truth.

These two observations pave the way for the main body of this chapter. The first section aims to explain why the present-day business world by virtue of the modern prevailing temper, which incidentally has little desire and no ground on which to oppose the pessimistic definition of economics, does not have a particularly bright future and cannot be expected to be the powerful force for good that it should be. It sets the stage of the second section, the presentation of the only true alternative. This is the biblical perspective with its blueprint of propositional, objectively valid, and applicable truth and, therefore, with the explosive potential of healing a broken present and transforming a dismal future into a promising one.

THE BUSINESS WORLD FROM THE MODERN PERSPECTIVE

A business does not operate in a vacuum. It is closely intertwined with society in general, its practices and its goals, but above all with its philosophy. Even if it does not wish to reflect society's "spiritual" climate, a business is forced to take that into account.

Today's society has been called schizophrenic in ethical decision making.[6] This schizophrenia, however, is not just ethical. It has a philosophical, indeed "religious," finality to it, which produces a fundamental, ideological polarization in society that cannot but tear at its fabric. This polarization is bound up with the problem of the one and the many.[7] How can the individual and the group enjoy a relationship of harmony rather than conflict? Can the interests of both be served fully—and simultaneously? As the historical roots of the present-day polarization are now laid bare and its precise nature described, it should become clear why the Christian is persuaded that only he is able to provide the answer to these and similar questions.

1. The historical roots of the polarization —The polarization in today's society came about by a development that took place in two stages. The first one was constituted by a subtle but decisive shift. In it, Western culture was cut loose from its Christian moorings and put on a different footing. The second one was evidenced by a much more dramatic transformation. In it, secular humanism became dominant. In the early shift, the Christian "genetic code" was removed from the prevailing culture, although the latter remained formally intact for some time. Since it was severed from its roots, however, humanism could take it by storm and reshape it with relative ease.

The first phase of the development was marked by a shift from divine law to natural law, the second phase by a transition from natural law to positive law.[8] The shift from divine law to natural law was fundamental. Although it did not immediately tamper with the prevailing body of law and the generally accepted principles of order, they were nevertheless cut off from their origin. They were no longer considered as instituted by God to determine the predictability, orderliness, direction, and purpose of created reality (with the implications of the Fall as a complicating factor). Rather, they were presented as inherent to nature that virtually took the place of God. As such, nature was treated as basically infallible (with the consequences of the Fall nowhere in sight). The real became equal to the ideal, the "is" to the "ought," and description to prescription.[9]

Under the onslaught of Darwinism, however, the concept of an infallible nature crumbled and with it the prevailing structure of law and order. Reality was defined in terms of total randomness. The universe turned from a cosmos under God to nature as an impersonal cosmos with its own law structure to an intrinsically purposeless, lawless "multiverse."

At this point, a subtle twist comes into view. On the one hand, the notion of purposelessness is the deathknell not only for God (and nature) but also for man. He is just another link in the chain of being, essentially no different from the primeval sludge that produced him and therefore without any intrinsic dignity, fully expendable and disposable. This seems a steep price to pay for getting rid of God. On the other hand, the same concept of purposelessness opens the way for presenting man in a totally different light. Once God is removed from the scene, man becomes the "logical" choice to take His place as the zenith of the process of natural selection and at any rate the "fittest" to survive. He will now determine destiny, introduce design, provide purpose, set standards, and impose law. The era of central planning and positive law has, at last, arrived.[10] The notion of purposelessness seems to pay off handsomely after all. An incident, if not accident, of nature assumes sovereign control over nature.[11]

Against this backdrop two major, present-day trends in economics, business, and the marketplace come into focus. As they are analyzed, it will hopefully become evident that they are polarized because of their religious roots and are bound to perpetrate the often-prevailing conflict, disruption, and paralysis until a new spirit invades the business world and transforms it.[12]

2. The two trends in the polarization—The first trend stresses the centrality of the individual and is committed to the free market. Leave man alone. Do not regulate him. Allow him to deploy his entrepreneurial talents. Grant him his profits. Let him amass wealth. Encourage his business expansion. Such a system will benefit the "many" directly in terms of available goods and services, employment, and philanthropy. But it will also do so indirectly in that it will produce trailblazers, trend-setters, and models and patterns of success. To be sure, there are danger spots in any system. Some will abuse it. Others will fail. But consistent decentralization will be the best remedy. Have the aggregate of human brain power take a crack at failure and the aggregate of human effort tackle inequity. Progress and finally success should result. In a word, the total aggregate of thinking and acting individuals should gain the day.

Persons who were committed to an infallible nature with the imprint of order, harmony, and progress indelibly stamped upon it would naturally favor this approach. Why tamper with the free and spontaneous processes that have produced such an enormous legacy? Intervention leads to interruption, regulation to retardation, and coordination to fragmentation. A *laissez faire* attitude should prevail. Government should stay out of the marketplace. Let the businessman freely compete and knowledgeably interact with the forces of supply and demand. Interference simply short-circuits nature's laws. It is presumptuous and self-defeating.

But the early Darwinians who applied the principles of evolution to the socioeconomic realm were equally enamored by the free market idea. They appealed to the concepts of natural selection and the survival of the fittest. The former, inseparably connected as it is with randomness, cannot be reconciled to the imposition of control and design. The latter, as it is thrown upon its own resources, must be at odds with a guarantee of provision and success. Of course, there is a price to be paid. What cannot adapt itself, the misfit, and what cannot muster sufficient strength, the unfit, will be weeded out. But there is a reverse side. The competent and the resourceful will flourish, ultimately to the undoubted benefit of society in general.[13]

Within this framework, man is fully part of nature. This situation could not last indefinitely. Eventually man could not be content with anything less than full control over nature. The later evolutionists laid the theoretical foundations for this idea. After purposelessness had effectively negated the existence of God, it was time to move on. Natural selection and survival of the fittest were relegated to the background. Man is now called upon to eliminate waste and suffering and to secure productivity and well-being. Man, in a word, is poised to provide purpose and paradise. From one-among-many, he is transformed into one-of-a-kind, not individually but collectively. This brings the second basic trend into view.

The second trend emphasizes the collective approach and is committed to a controlled market. Leaving man alone will lead to misery. Competition will become cutthroat and will produce some (big) winners, but many more (big) losers. Let a man make healthy profits and expand his business. Allow him to capture the market and accumulate wealth. He will only be able to do so at the expense of the workers. And once he has arrived, he will seek to retain his economic dominance by monopolization, manipulation, elimination, oppression or other similar means. At the same time he will welcome a proletariat that through perpetual serfdom will enable him to maintain his position and lifestyle. To be sure, he will make goods and services available, provide employment, and make philanthropy a priority. But all of that will be designed to safeguard the status quo. Ultimately, the "many" will serve the "one."

To counter such rugged and destructive individualism, a central agency is indispensable, an agency that is responsible for purpose and direction, that takes dead aim at waste and suffering and secures productivity and well-being. To do its work, it should be at the heart of a scientific planning process, be in control of all of society including the marketplace, and have coercive power to enforce its will. To be effective, it should control the educational system, be in charge of the money supply, have authority over essential industries, regulate the utilities, have the right to tax unconditionally, and have enforcement agencies at its disposal. Of course, only a central government fills that bill. Never mind that it inevitably ends up as a dictatorship of the elite that imposes its will by means of an inefficient and wasteful (rather ironically) bureaucracy and only survives by living parasitically off the very masses it wished to liberate. The "many," it appears, extricated themselves from the service of the "one" in order to fall victim to the tyranny of the "few."

3. The radical nature of the polarization—The choice that the two trends offer appears rather grim. From the one perspective, the option is for an unimpeded freedom over a stifling and debilitating regimentation; from the other perspective, for necessary controls in the face of an irrational and unsettling conglomerate of self-serving decisions.

These two trends seem bigger than life. They are locked in fierce competition, and often in physical battle, nationally as well as internationally, economically as well as politically. But they do not come out of thin air. They are inseparable from well-defined, foundational, philosophical presuppositions, which goes to show that ideas shape the course of history. The Christian better be prepared and make his presence felt in the marketplace of ideas with a thorough understanding of what he encounters and a cogent presentation of his own position. The mind matters.

In the meantime it would arouse more than a little curiosity that both trends in their pitched battle inflict heavy, indeed lethal, damage upon each other without much apparent success.

The proponents of the free market argue that the socialist experiment is a failure. It has never caused an economy to flourish. It inevitably leads to poor quality goods, shortages, and a sullen society. It survives only through theft by "legal" means (taxation) or illegal means (confiscation). It always leaves debt in its wake (a third form of theft). Apparently it cannot make it on its own. These points appear to be well taken, and at times they are freely admitted.[14] These failings should be socialism's undoing or at least should put a question mark behind its philosophical foundations. Neither one, however, is the case.

On the other hand, central planners challenge the advocates of the free market to show how a decentralized, uncoordinated, unregulated, "irrational," unscientific, and chaotic conglomerate of random "free" market decisions *should* lead to a just and wholesome society. All they have managed to do thus far is to polarize the haves and the have-nots, to perpetuate greed and selfishness on the one hand and resentment and bitterness on the other. The theoretical point is certainly cogent. An evolutionary commitment to a random reality and a theoretical justification for the necessary success of the free market are mutually exclusive.

In sum, a collectivist system that has rational philosophical underpinnings but does not seem too productive is pitted against a free market system that appears to be productive but has no rational justification. Both have their Achilles heel cut by their opponent but both move right along, the one without much to show for, the other without much to go by.[15]

All this is curious indeed. But some further probing reveals an additional curiosity. The two trends appear to mutually and simultaneously presuppose and exclude each other.

They presuppose each other. Man as the central planner needs the raw stuff of randomness to exercise his control. It keeps him in business. Similarly, randomness cannot be introduced except against the backdrop of the idea of purpose. To put it differently, neither control nor randomness can be defined or exist except as a negation *of the other*.

But they also exclude each other. Total planning cannot allow for anything that is unpredictable and will seek to eliminate any kind of "freedom" as capricious, reactionary, and threatening. If it is not in control of everything, it is not in control of anything. Conversely, freedom will aim to remove any imposed order. If it is not free in everything, it is not free in anything. In other words, neither total planning nor freedom can be defined or exist except as a *negation* of the other.

If the Christian is to avoid falling victim to either trend or getting caught in the crossfire, a recognition that this is not a coincidence is crucial. What comes into view here is a fundamental dialectic (a polarity in which the two poles presuppose and exclude each other mutually *and* simultaneously). Because it has a religious grip on the modern predicament, it is worth exploring further.

4. The religious roots of the polarization—The fundamental dialectic emerges inevitably and inescapably when man renounces the living God. When God is dethroned, man is left with a "vacuum." Without divine control, reality cannot be anything else but contingent, discontinuous, and undetermined. Randomness reigns. Before long, this kind of "reality" is viewed as chaotic and unsettling. It poses a threat. Since nobody can live in such a "vacuum," the search is on for a principle of necessity, continuity, and determinism. Purpose is introduced. Order is established. The threat is gone.

Ironically, when discontinuity is replaced by continuity, the shoe soon begins to pinch the other foot. Control asserts itself, and it is perceived to be regimenting and stifling. The danger of a treadmill existence and zombielike reality begins to loom large. Because no one wishes to live in such an atmosphere, contingency, discontinuity, and indeterminism look inviting. Freedom enters. Personal choice is restored. The danger recedes.

Ever since the fall of man, this dialectic—with its pendulum swinging back and forth with monotonous regularity—has entered in the warp and woof of human history.[16] In fact, it has become the driving force behind all man's thought and action. Because the two poles presuppose each other, his ultimate aim is to reach a synthesis, an equilibrium where a perfect balance is achieved. Since they exclude each other, he will never be able to realize the aim of a well-balanced, peaceful coexistence. Inasmuch as the poles presuppose and exclude each other simultaneously, he can neither abandon his aim nor achieve his goal. As long, therefore, as he is in the grip of the dialectic, he will try again and again, however much he fails, and fail again and again, however much he tries. The dialectic appears to be a never-ending dead-end street, a veritable deathtrap indeed. It can only be sprung by the renunciation of apostasy.

I have argued elsewhere that all of the history of philosophy consists of one long string of abortive attempts to arrive at a synthesis.[17] It possibly needs to be underscored that the principal figures in that history were not in the posture of playing games, leisurely toying with ideas. They aimed at giving a universal accounting of their total experience. They meant business. The grim truth is that if they had achieved the synthesis, it would have effectively spelled the demise of the God of Scripture. It would have gone down in history as the absolute proof of a universe without God, which ultimately is the objective of all apostate thought.

This battle is not just fought in the higher regions of the human intellect, beyond the reach and comprehension of most. No, it rages throughout human existence, including the hustle and the bustle of everyday life. It is God's curse upon the human race that wherever apostasy prevails, the particulars and the universals, the one and the many, the individuals and the group, the few and the masses, no longer can be thought of or brought together anymore. They become mutually exclusive, however much they presuppose each other. Any effort to come to a synthesis, to arrive at harmony, to establish a peaceful coexistence, will shatter on the rocks of conflict of interest and hostility.

This problem certainly explains the perpetual tensions that plague mankind everywhere, including the business world. What management may perceive as simply the freedom to pursue the good, if not the survival, of the company (change in work rules, reassignment of jobs, early retirement, streamlining of operations, etc.), the worker may experience as damaging, if not destructive (heavier work load, lesser job, subsistence pay, unemployment, etc.). What the consumer may applaud as necessary protection (price ceilings, government regulations, inspections, etc.), the producer may judge to be a burden that may make him lose his competitive edge or even close him down (unprofitability, soaring costs, unnecessary interference, etc.). In short, what is freedom to the one is dissolution to the other, to be eliminated at all cost. Then, what is wholesome regulation to the one is a deathknell to the other, to be undone at any price.[18]

5. The principal solution to the polarization—What is a Christian to do in the schizophrenic frenzy of the modern predicament? He finds himself between a rock and a hard place in a post-Christian world. Of course, he will tend to avoid the Scylla of extreme totalitarian control as well as the Charybdis of absolute freedom. But he may unsuspectingly favor the approach of his secular counterpart, to add a "pinch" or more of continuity (control) when discontinuity gets out of hand (chaos) and similarly a "pinch" or more of discontinuity (freedom) when continuity gets out of hand (regimentation). Most governments follow this policy as they seek to resolve conflicts of interest and achieve a perfect balance by means of their own brand of "positive law."

This route, however, is not advisable for the Christian. He would implicitly admit that man is the measure of all things, the hallmark of all positive law. He also would fall into the grasp of the apostate dialectic. The Christian ought to recognize that the enemy is not freedom or necessity, control or decontrol. The world may tirelessly and endlessly debate the pros and cons of regulation versus deregulation, but to the Christian, the great enemy is first self and then sin. And his dilemma is first God and the neighbor versus self, and then holiness versus sin.

Against this backdrop, the proposed solution for the present-day predicament seems evident. The suggestion to return to natural law would definitely not be sufficient. For one thing, it would be impossible to turn back the clock historically. The times of belief in an infallible nature, which was the philoso-

!

phical underpinning for natural law, will never return. For another, natural law is basically empty. The "is" simply does not imply the "ought." Proponents of natural law invariably provide it with a content to which they already were committed in the first place.[19]

No, the Christian's solution, if it is going to turn the world "right side up," should go beyond that. His outline for the future should have renunciation of apostasy as the priority item; only that will break the grip of the dialectic with its deadly consequences. This activity would imply an old-fashioned call to repentance (see Acts 17:30). Love toward God and the neighbor as well as obedience to His Word, specifically His law, would follow in its wake. Then, wherever Scripture does not explicitly or implicitly call for a certain action, man should use his creative imagination, as created in the image of God, to advance His Kingdom and the cause of the neighbor. Finally, however, this plan can be implemented only by the grace of God, and at the same time, it may well lead to another kind of conflict, opposition from an apostate world.

These points are essentially summarized in the biblical summons to "fear God and keep his commandments" (Eccles. 12:13). This summons gains in significance in its context of cosmic, societal, and cultural futility (see Eccles. 1:2; 12:8), which incidentally is God's judgment on man's apostasy (Rom. 8:20).[20] Both a divine irony and a human tragedy emerge here. On the one hand, man is mandated to develop this earth (see Gen. 1:28; 2:15). Refusal to work makes him eligible for excommunication (see 2 Thess. 3:14). On the other hand, he is calmly told that all his labors and achievements in themselves are by definition futile. Man apparently cannot win for losing. Man is condemned when he works (to futility) and when he refuses to work (under judgment).

Although the "what" and the "that" of labor and achievements ultimately amount to nothing, the "why," "how," and "what for" count for everything. Concretely, in the case of the businessman, the production and marketing of goods and services that aim at satisfying needs—as well as the investment of resources, time, and energy to achieve all that—will not take on substance and meaning unless done in the fear of God (the dynamics of all acceptable conduct), in obedience to His law (the standard of all conduct) and, as the capstone, for the advancement of the cause and Kingdom of God (the goal of Christian conduct). This will now further be explored in the next section.

A BIBLICAL PERSPECTIVE ON THE BUSINESS WORLD

Christians in business do not necessarily run a Christian business or a business in a Christian way. To qualify as such, they must meet the requirements of a biblical motivation, a biblical standard, a biblical goal, a biblical decision-making process, and a biblical prospect. These will now be detailed. Of course, not every Christian in the business world may be able to implement all of them all the time.

1. The biblical motivation—The driving force behind Christian business-men's thoughts, words, and actions should be the fear of God, which is best defined as a heart's attitude of reverential awe toward God. That is, we are powerfully attracted to Him and desire to please Him to the extent that we consider His approval as our greatest delight and something to be gained at any price and His disapproval as our greatest dread and something to be avoided at all cost.[21] Where this fear is absent, one can expect anything up to and including murder (see Gen. 20:11). Where this fear is present, one can anticipate every-thing up to and including divestment of what is most cherished (see Gen. 22:12). This attitude applies to the business world as well.

It invariably produces love toward God (see Deut. 30:6) and the neighbor (see Lev. 19:14,18). This love is not capricious emotionality or mere action. It is a deep desire to be at one with its object, whoever or whatever that may be. It will give up everything and do anything in its power to achieve union. It takes great delight in reaching its objective. It will lavish time, energy, and resources on the object of its desire (before and) after the union is consummated. It is a reflection and an outflow of the love of God.

This love has amazing characteristics. It is not boastful or arrogant. It does not act inappropriately or in a self-seeking fashion. It is not easily angered and does not keep tabs on wrongdoings. It shuns unacceptable practices and delights in truth. There is no end to its trust and hope. No wonder that it has a history of success (see 1 Cor. 13:4-8). It is the love of Christ in man.

It also has wonderful company. It is conjoined with joy, peace, patience, kindness, goodness, faithfulness, gentleness, and self-control (see Gal. 5:22-23). This aggregate of virtues spells strength, harmony, commitment, care, a willing-ness to stick it out, and an ability to keep oneself in check. It is the fruit of the Spirit.

The combination of the fear of God, Christian love, and the fruit of the Spirit as the driving force of the business world would have a far-reaching impact. For one thing, the problem of the one and the many would once and for all be settled. In principle, the solution has its anchorage in the being of God with its perfect unity in diversity and its perfect diversity in unity. There is harmony among the Persons without their being forced to relinquish their identity. There is also a plurality in the Godhead without its causing any conflict. In practice, it is resolved when man reflects who God is in a combination of love (a desire to be one), respect (in recognition of someone's individuality), and self-sacrifice (service of one another).

For another, it would solve the problem of freedom versus necessity. On the one hand, God has all things under His sovereign control. He purposes everything that comes to pass according to His master plan. On the other hand, man is under no extraneous compulsion to do what, in fact, he is doing. On the contrary, he is fully responsible for what he does, has, and is. More precisely, both in and as a part of that master plan God has posited man sovereignly as fully and freely responsible. When man, in his aspiration to replace God, individually or collectively becomes the final and absolute (pre)determinant, he leaves a robotlike society in his wake. The dialectic with its mutually exclusive polarity devours him.

But what man never was able to accomplish, God could and did. He produced and runs a universe of total design down to its last and minutest detail without impinging in the slightest upon man as a freely responsible agent. This accomplishment shows that God is God (and, incidentally, that it is in man's best interest to renounce his rebellion). He transcends the dialectic and its distasteful and deadly dilemma. It is hardly surprising that in presenting this truth to the world of his day, Paul concludes with a doxology (see Rom. 11:33-36).

Moreover, the stage is set to undo the damage the dialectic has inflicted on the economic sphere in terms of depersonalization, dehumanization, and exploitation. Wherever the dialectic reigns, management and labor turn into impersonal forces that treat each other as simply a vehicle to achieve its own end and will take as much advantage of the other as possible. They are truly two poles that mutually and at the same time presuppose and exclude each other. The union contract aims to provide the synthesis and with it a peaceful, permanent coexistence, but it fails to do so. It is no more than a tenuous and temporary balancing act that is soon upset again by strikes (labor) and/or lockouts (management). Even the federal mediator with all the force of the government at his disposal is not able to produce a final settlement. The dialectic will not permit it.

Clearly, there is a need for Christian love to restore the personal touch, Christian respect to restore the human touch, and Christian self-sacrifice to restore the healing touch throughout the area of labor-management relationships. Bargaining tables, union contracts, strikes, lockouts, and federal mediators as they are known today will soon be things of the past. The relationships will be harmonious, peaceful, and productive and lead to abundance and wealth.[22]

What kind of conduct can one expect when Christian love, respect, and self-sacrifice enter the business world? The next section considers the possibilities.

2. The biblical standard—The entire Holy Bible constitutes the sole standard for all ethical conduct, providing commandments, prohibitions, principles, models, and patterns throughout. However, since the law of God as set forth in the Decalogue appears to be foundational, it will be the principal focus in the present context.

The Ten Commandments have been properly characterized as the only garment that fits the body of mankind. Since the First, Fourth, Fifth, and Eighth Commandments are particularly relevant, they will now be brought to bear on the business world, together with their own pertinent case laws[23] and supporting principles, patterns, or models mentioned in the rest of Scripture.

The First Commandment forbids man to make something or someone ultimate other than God. No one may hunger or thirst for anything or anyone more than God. He must be the desire of one's heart. No one may depend upon anything or anyone more than God. He is the source of everything. No one may listen to anything or anyone more than God. He has the final word.

Case law underscores that man must depend for his total existence on the Word of God down to its last detail. The treasure of abundance and wealth that is locked in created reality will apparently not be released apart from dependence on and obedience to that Word. A strong warning is given not to shift one's dependence to riches when that materializes (see Deut. 8:1-20).

The rest of Scripture echoes these concerns. Man should not be governed by a love of money (see 1 Tim. 6:10), nor should he put his trust in riches (see 1 Tim. 6:17). The implication for the businessman is evident. He should not make his money (see Matt. 6:24) or his business (see 1 Cor. 7:30-31) or his riches (see James 5:1-6) ultimate.

The Fourth Commandment addresses the issue of man's rest before and delight in his God. The case law informs us that rest is all-embracive and has strong socioeconomic implications. For example, payment of debt may not be exacted beyond the seventh year, the year of release, from the impoverished fellow member in the covenant society, whether the born Israelite or the resident alien. In fact, when people extend poverty loans, the year of release may not be taken into account. Such loans should be made freely, generously, and according to need. In this context, it is emphasized that loans may also be extended to foreigners, to whom, incidentally, the seventh-year rule does not apply. But under no circumstances may the Israelite enter into a state of indebtedness to them (see Deut. 15:1-11).

The debt issue is a concern of other Scripture as well. It lays down the principle that the Christian should not get into debt (see Rom. 13:8). It calls debt a judgment of God (see Deut. 28:44-45) and warns that the lender is always in charge and the borrower by definition a slave (see Prov. 22:7). Furthermore, the application of the rest factor to socioeconomic life comes to the fore in the legislation pertaining to the Year of Jubilee. The fellow Israelite must have both his land and his freedom restored to him (see Lev. 25:8-55). The delight factor enters when Scripture prohibits business dealings of any sort on the Sabbath (see Neh. 13:15-22). It is ultimately the day of the Lord and should be honored as such (see Isa. 58:13-14).

It appears that the businessman should avoid debt financing altogether. Genuine alternatives to bankroll an enterprise include "joint ventures, partnerships, or stock issues, with those who have the capital."[24] Also, economic freedom is evidently basic to all other types of freedom. Finally, the Lord's day is set apart for worship, not to conduct business.

The Fifth Commandment focuses on the authority issue. According to the case law (see Deut. 16:18-18:22) and other Scripture (see Eph. 5:22-6:9; 1 Pet. 2:13-3:7), society is held together by a network of authority structures—civil, ecclesiastical, marital, parental, and societal (such as the employer-employee relationship). Some of them are involuntary, others voluntary. Persons who exercise authority must do so with integrity, self-sacrifice, and concern for the well-being of those entrusted to their care. Theirs is a sacred trust for which there is a day of accounting. Those under authority should be in cheerful submission to and full support of those in authority. This is a sacred trust as well and also has a day of reckoning.

Furthermore, all authority in the purview of the Fifth Commandment is delegated authority with its own specific jurisdiction. No such authority may have the final word or encroach upon the jurisdiction assigned to another. Scripture warns against the totalitarian tendencies of a central government (see 1 Sam. 8:10-18; Rev. 13:1-18, esp. vv. 16-17) and, ironically, records the people's insistence on one (until, of course, it is too late; see 1 Sam. 8:19-20).

Again by way of implication, a businessman who has a heart for God as the absolute owner of everything, including his business (see Lev. 25:23), and as the final authority as to how to run it should have a commitment to the free market. Government intervention in the economic and business sphere is a disturbance of the created order. Any claim of ownership on the government's part ought to be contested. Property taxes are a prime indicator of such claim. Any insistence upon final authority ought to be protested as well.

The government's jurisdiction is determined by its function as the minister of distributive and retributive justice. It should resist its totalitarian tendencies, so tempting by virtue of the power—whether executive, legislative, or judicial—at its disposal, and not venture inside the boundaries of other jurisdictions. Man is ultimately dependent on and accountable to God alone and not on or to other men, whether individually or collectively. Of course, there will be little prospect for the government to retreat within its own boundaries for the proper reasons until the dialectic is broken. Be this as it may, the businessman should be in submission to his government, also in the area of taxes, unless he is required to transgress God's law.

Central to the Eighth Commandment is the absolute ownership of God, and corollary to this is man's stewardship of what has been entrusted to him. In the case law, God forbids man to make Kingdom contributions from illicitly acquired funds, to charge interest to fellow members of the covenant society, to insist on a crippling or life-threatening collateral, or to oppress an employee. At the same time, loans at interest to foreigners are allowed, gleaning privileges must be granted, and wages must be paid promptly so as not to put an intolerable burden on the wage earner (see Deut. 23:17-20,24-25; 24:10-14, 19-22).

In addition, Scripture sets forth the objective (even if not intrinsic) value of precious metals and stones (historically acknowledged by the market forces) (see Gen. 2:12), the necessity of just wages (see Exod. 12:35-36), the mutually enriching relationship of management and labor (see Ruth 2:4), the danger of illicit profits and a warning against unjustly acquired riches (see Prov. 15:27; 16:8), the tendency to perpetrate the oppression of the poor (see Eccles. 5:8), the judgment on illicitly and inhumanly acquired gain (see Amos 8:5-14), the inviolability of private property (see Acts 5:4), the evil of swindling (see 1 Cor. 5:10), the danger of greed (see 2 Pet. 2:14), and the sins of underpaying employees and preserving riches through murderous practices (see James 5:1-6).

So, the Christian businessman should be committed to integrity, honesty, service, and self-sacrifice. Concretely, this commitment translates into high-quality goods and services that satisfy the customer, affordable prices, appropriate treatment, meaningful warranties, and so on. It also translates into a living wage for the employees, proper working conditions, possible bonuses, special awards, incentives, special emergency funds, and retention of workers during slow periods—including proper planning to that end. Of course, employees are expected to give their best effort, display a good work ethic, and be committed to seeing the business or company they work for prosper.

In addition, the Christian businessman should take a dim view of the institution of debt capitalism and debt financing. It was made possible by the printing of paper money (the creation of phantom wealth out of nothing) and is now virtually out of control through the abandonment of the gold standard (which encouraged the accumulation of real wealth based on productivity). But the practice should be resisted because it produces money inflation (reduces the value of money and precipitates an increase in prices) and thus becomes a form of theft. All of this is a result of "positive" law.

3. The biblical goal—Ultimately everything must be done to the glory of God. But there is a direct and immediate way (see 1 Cor. 10:31) as well as an indirect and mediate way (see 1 Pet. 4:11). The former is usually a matter of one's motivation and possibly an affirmation of that: "I do this for the glory of God." But this rather ethereal way must be given feet, just as the Old Testament attaches a certain money value to a vow with which people consecrate themselves or their property to God (see Lev. 27:1-25). Thus, the vow achieves meaning. Here the indirect and mediate way of glorifying God comes into the picture. It sets penultimate goals as means to an ultimate end. One such goal, of course, is for the individual to conduct his business according to the biblical standard. Employees as well as clients should come to praise God as a result of that. But there is more.

The businessman should dedicate his business, however small or large it may be, to Kingdom service within the framework of the Great Commission. After all, the Kingdom encompasses all of life, and the Great Commission is its cutting edge. He has a goal *in* his (doing) business, to satisfy needs of people (to the glory of God), and also one *for* his business, to assist in promoting the cause of God, however, whenever, and wherever.

He may take his cue from Paul's injunction to the individual Christian to work so that there is something to share with the needy (see Eph. 4:28) and apply it to his business. This injunction indicates a central thrust of Scripture that untiringly promotes, if not requires, a giving spirit that will make the proper funding of the Kingdom a reality.

In the Old Testament, the giving runs from 10 percent of one's income (see Lev. 27:30) to well beyond that, through one-time offerings (see Exod. 35:22; Num. 7:3; 1 Chron. 29:3-4; 2 Chron. 24:10; Ezra 1:6), interest-free loans (see Deut. 15:7-11; 24:19-20), debt remission (see Deut. 15:1-2), gleaning privileges (see Deut. 24:19-21), and sharing at festival meals (see Neh. 8:12).

In the New Testament, the amount runs from 10 percent (see Matt. 23:23) to 50 percent (see Luke 3:11) and possibly beyond that (see Acts 4:34-37; 2 Cor. 8:1-4) up to 100 percent (see Luke 21:1-4).

Scripture indicates that, with the rock bottom of 10 percent, giving is always at the individual's discretion (see Acts 5:4), should not be forced (see 2 Cor. 8:8), and should flow from a cheerful heart (see 2 Cor. 9:7). But even at that, the giver must keep in mind a model, a rule of thumb, and a principle. The model is Christ who became poor that others would become rich (see 2 Cor. 8:9). The rule of thumb is that at the end (of the day, week, month, year?) the one with a lot has nothing left and the one with little has no lack (see 2 Cor. 8:15). The principle is that one will reap as one sows, scantily or abundantly (see 2 Cor. 9:6). Clearly, a godly pressure is on every Christian. The businessman may be well advised to start with paying 10 percent of his net business income to God while living off the remaining 90 percent, but strive toward living off 10 percent while contributing 90 percent to godly causes.

The distribution of charitable funds may assume many forms. It may be done by personal giving. A foundation or charitable trust is also an option, however, as long as the directors or trustees will not be able to thwart the godly purposes of the institution.

These purposes, of course, may vary. They may be formulated more or less broadly to include support for missions, education, relief agencies, or other projects at home or abroad. In all cases, they should serve the glory of God through thanksgiving (see 2 Cor. 9:11) or some other means.

The emphasis on the financial is no coincidence. The funding of the Kingdom has always been a major need in every time period. Since business is at the heart of the cultural mandate, it is in the best position to produce the economic freedom needed for the promotion of the Kingdom. In itself, it is doomed to futility, but by turning to the biblical motivation, standard, and goal, business becomes a powerful force for good. Christian entrepreneurs deserve a warm welcome.

4. The biblical decision-making process—The businessman will be faced with decisions in all phases of his enterprise, capitalization, location, organization, management, production, distribution, expansion, personnel, customer relations, and so forth. He will soon discover that the biblical injunctions, prohibitions, models, patterns, and principles do not cover every part of every phase. Even some evidently ethical decisions will not be covered by explicit biblical data. Beyond that, he will have to make judgment calls in nonmoral issues, such as what kind of cars to manufacture, whom to promote, whether to expand or not. Is there any way he can be aided in the wide variety of decisions he will have to make? The answer appears to be in the affirmative.

When explicit ethical patterns, principles, injunctions, or prohibitions come into play, there should be no doubt about the decision, however difficult it may be to implement.

When explicit biblical direction is missing, the model that James presents will prove to be of value (see James 2:1-13). He resolves the issue of partiality in three stages. First, he combines an incisive assessment with sanctified sense. You despise the poor, and eventually you will give an oppressor and a blasphemer an honorable welcome. Then, he measures it by the law of love and finds it, of course, wanting. If you love someone as you love yourself, you will not put him in a humiliating position. Finally, he applies the standard of the Ten Commandments, which gives substance to the law of love, to the problem. And he declares partiality a transgression of the Sixth Commandment, a sin of murderous proportions just as hatred. To make decisions and settle issues, therefore, that are ethical in nature, James invites us to assess a situation and search out possible implications with sanctified sense, determine how it looks in the light of the law of love, and apply the Decalogue, thus formulating in a sense a brand-new case law.[25]

When decisions need to be made that are outside the purview of the law of God, a new set of biblical parameters comes into play. As created in the image of God, man is endowed with creative imagination, and he should use it in his business. Of course, it should go hand in hand with sanctified sense. For some decisions, one should be knowledgeable; for others, one should possess skills; for all, one should count the costs.

In recognition of God's all-controlling plan, moreover, anyone will do well to closely observe His providence. So it may be advisable for the businessman to fill positions only by means of in-house promotions and to embark on gradual expansion. Of course, it may be necessary to make bold, creative moves when the time appears right, when "sudden" opportunities arise, or when deadlocks require a breakthrough. But by and large, God's long-term providence serves His long-term Kingdom plan. So the businessman should be involved in long-term thinking and long-term planning with long-term execution. He has time. Just as God is not in a hurry, he will not be, even less so when he understands the meaning of godly offspring. He will leave them a legacy. They may achieve what he has not been able to accomplish.

However, creative imagination and careful consideration of divine providence will not always lead to success. In the first place, and apart from the element of risk that every entrepreneur takes, no decision will ever be truly successful unless it meets three conditions. It must be made (1) on the bedrock of holiness, which includes integrity and kindness (see Prov. 3:1-3), (2) in total trust in and acknowledgment of God (see Prov. 3:5-6), and (3) out of delight in God and His cause (see Ps. 37:3-4). Every decision made in the fabric of a holy life is favorably received by God; each one made in acknowledgment of God will prove to have come about under His guidance; and each one made out of delight in God is underwritten by Him.

If a business flourishes with a decision-making process of this sort, God receives the glory, and His Kingdom stands to gain. If in spite of it a business fails, God will still accomplish His purposes and still receive the glory. The Kingdom of God never experiences defeat.

5. The biblical prospect—The Christian businessman is a biblical realist who knows that the abundance and the wealth stored up in created reality are enormous.[26] He also knows that the Fall has seriously jeopardized their release. He is aware that the fear of God and its concomitants of love and obedience spell life and prosperity (see Deut. 28:1ff.; Prov. 19:23). He is also aware that God's impoverishing judgments come upon sin (see Dan. 5:17ff.). He recognizes that at times strong advancements are made in spite of a disobedient lifestyle (see 2 Kings 14:23-27) and that reverses occur in spite of purposeful obedience (Job 1:1ff.).

It is clear to the Christian businessman, however, that a booming society without God has the seed of destruction already in it (see Gen. 4:16-24). It is also clear that while unrighteousness has no future (see Ps. 73:1-20), righteousness will gain the day (see James 5:11). Further, he is convinced that as long as unrighteousness is dominant, that day will not come (see Isa. 48:17-19). He is also convinced that righteousness must present a challenge to its dominance (see Matt. 28:19-20). Finally, he is persuaded that unrighteousness will never surrender without a battle (see Rev. 12:12) and that the victory is assured (see Rev. 12:12; 21:9-27).

Here the biblical prospect emerges. It is one of (spiritual) warfare and (ultimate) victory.

In the warfare, the fear of God (and its concomitants) is pitted against the fundamental dialectic. The two are mutually exclusive; the fear of God overcomes the dialectic or the dialectic the fear of God. Although acknowledging the reality of restraining grace, the notion of a pluralistic society in which all segments purposely do their utmost to arrive at a peaceful coexistence is a myth. To aim at such coexistence as an achievable ideal is at best naive and at times aiding and abetting the Enemy.[27]

This warfare is the real thing. Compared to it, the battle between the two poles of the dialectic is nothing more than an in-house squabble between *feindliche Bruder* ("hostile brothers") who will immediately close ranks when challenged by their common enemy, the fear of God, as to their common root, apostasy from God. Such challenge is not without danger. Casualties are inevitable. But for the fear of God not to issue a challenge, by identifying with one of the poles or out of a ghetto mentality, leads to a worse fate. It will either be neutralized or swept aside as irrelevant.

Both parties in the warfare aim to conquer, but here the resemblance stops. The dialectic, as a tool of the Enemy, seeks the death and removal of what is in reality its greatest friend. The fear of God, as a divine instrument, seeks the transformation and life of what is in reality its greatest enemy. The dialectic will avail itself of every conceivable weapon from its master's arsenal, including deception and murder. It also will use the disguise of the trust of God (in a fragmented, truncated, or warped form), without acknowledging the God of this truth, to achieve its end. It may even orchestrate proponents of truth for that purpose. The fear of God will turn to the prescribed weapons of *its* Master, such as *love* and *truth*.[28] It may use the various truths of God mined in the context of the dialectic to reach its aim, as long as the basic antithesis is not compromised. It may even welcome practitioners of the dialectic as cobelligerents for the purpose of intermediate goals.

Christian businessmen may differ in position, in function, in importance or influence, but they may not shun the warfare. Challenge they should, first themselves and then others, prudently and probingly, in the spirit of love and on the basis of (propositional) truth, to repentance and faith as the only way to break out of the grip of the dialectic. Their weapons do not seem to be a match for the Enemy. But the divine promise is that they *will* be the means of victory, the victory of the Kingdom *in* their various business enterprises and *through* their various business enterprises.[29]

In fact, this victory has been accomplished once and for all, is in the process of being achieved again and again, and will ultimately be a continuous state. It has been accomplished once and for all on the cross (see Gen. 3:15; Luke 10:18; Col. 2:15; Rev. 12:9). It is in the process of being achieved again and again throughout a Christian's life, also in his business and through his business. Victory does not bring the warfare to an end. The once-and-for-all victory did not; in fact, it intensified the warfare (see Rev. 12:12) as does every individual victory (see 1 Pet. 5:8). But the stage is set for the next victory and, of course, the next (see James 4:7), until the final victory at the return of Christ (see Rom. 16:20; 1 Cor. 15:57).

This triumph will usher in the Kingdom with a glory that is beyond all human imagination (see Rev. 21:1ff.) and a state of victory that will continue unabatedly.

EDITOR'S REFLECTIONS

Is Henry Krabbendam making such a strong appeal for the observance of the full range—every "jot and tittle"—of God's propositional truth (Old Testament law regulating debt, for example), thus implying necessarily a "theonomic" position? This question was put to him at the Scholars' Colloquium where these chapters were discussed. Henry was careful to answer that the full range of God's revelation includes promise as well as law, love as well as obedience, and that the relationship of the Testaments is one of progress as well as unity. He was fearful of an approach that was too "wooden" and appealed for the need of a living relationship with the risen Christ as a vital condition for all of God's unerring Word in order to produce love, obedience, and a "sanctified sense."

Dr. Krabbendam rightly points to the truth that God's children need the active leadership of the Holy Spirit if we are to do God's will and implement the scriptural propositions set forth clearly in the Word. He hastened to add that dependence upon Christ and the Holy Spirit is no substitute for responsible conduct. In fact, man is under strict obligation to meet all God's standards fully. His reliance upon Christ and the Spirit should be motivated by the recognition of this responsibility and the desire to meet it.

What personal freedom and moral judgment are we to exercise in the application of biblical absolutes? How bound are we to the propositional truths of Scripture? If we are bound, in what way are we bound?

Dr. Vernon Grounds presents the scriptural case for the responsible use of subjective judgments in applying biblical principles in the marketplace. This is the balancing position in our resolution of the tension between the reality of the existence of biblical absolutes and the necessity for our exercise of moral judgments. As you read, be careful to distinguish between Dr. Grounds's personal position and the arguments of others he presents that differ from his own. He does support the idea that Scripture has an abundant supply of propositional statements that are helpful to businesspeople navigating the treacherous waters of the marketplace. He does not believe, however, that all propositional statements, even though they are absolute truth, can be easily or immediately transferred from Scripture and applied in business without a lot of care, adjustment, and subjective judgment if it is to be done responsibly.

As stated previously, the editor will outline his reasons at the end of the next chapter for believing "that the presence of objective and subjective dimensions of reality is necessarily associated with the existence of and administration of absolutes." Henry Krabbendam has presented the objective side of the picture. Vernon Grounds now presents the subjective side.

CHAPTER 7

RESPONSIBILITY AND SUBJECTIVITY: APPLYING BIBLICAL PRINCIPLES IN BUSINESS

Dr. Vernon C. Grounds

A native of New Jersey, Dr. Vernon Grounds received his B.A. from Rutgers University (Phi Beta Kappa), his B.D. from Faith Theological Seminary, and his Ph.D. from Drew University, where he wrote a dissertation, "The Concept of Love in the Psychology of Sigmund Freud." He has been awarded the D.D. by Wheaton College and the L.H.D. by Gordon College.

After ministering as a pastor for ten years in Paterson, New Jersey, Dr. Grounds became Dean at Baptist Bible Seminary in Johnson City, New York. In 1951 he joined the faculty at Denver Seminary. After five years, he became Dean and ultimately President, a position from which he retired in 1979. Since then, while continuing at the seminary as a professor, he has been directing the Counseling Center that bears his name, serving as president of Evangelicals for Social Action, and participating in the work of various Christian agencies and publications. In addition to writing and editing, he lectures and preaches in the United States and overseas.

A.

Christians must be both concerned and informed about mundane matters like business if they are to live out their faith effectively. That is the judgment of British churchman Brian Rice. "The God of the New Testament," he writes, "is the God of social problems, of politics, of economic affairs, of international relations. These problems are theological problems and are among the most important areas of Christian obedience in our time." Indeed, Rice contends that "the Church must give priority to the study of political and economic problems and to action in these fields" if it is to be loyal to the New

Testament and relevant to contemporary life.[1]

Urbanologist Dennis Clark emphatically agrees. He points out that Christians in the United States are a significant segment of our technological society and therefore have an enormous opportunity to exert a constructive influence. "The problem of work and vocation in this society," he declares, "is incandescent in its prominence, historic in its challenge, and epochal in its significance for the good of mankind if it can be mastered." Hence, he insists that "a Christian devotion to its solution would be one of the most exciting departures of the modern era."[2] There is compelling reason to consider in depth what Scripture can contribute to the issues confronting business today and tomorrow. Does it embody insights and directives that are able to furnish needed guidance for both management and labor, principles that reach beyond the sanctuary out into the marketplace? Perhaps the best starting point for an answer to these queries is the text that evangelicals regard as foundational for their view of the Bible:

> All Scripture is God-breathed and is useful for teaching, rebuking, correcting and training in righteousness, so that the man of God may be thoroughly equipped for every good work. (2 Tim. 3:16-17)

Here the apostle sets forth a twofold function of divine revelation, its positive and negative contributions to human existence. Written under the unique control of the Holy Spirit, it teaches us what we ought to believe, what we ought not believe, what we ought to do, what we ought not do. Hence, its teaching must blanket all of our activities, whether so-called spiritual or so-called secular. Activities such as manufacturing, banking, administering, exporting, and importing—all business activities ought to be carried out within the parameters laid down by God's Word.

Traditionally, Protestants have adhered to the position that the Bible is an infallible rule not only of faith but also of practice. Typical of this tradition is the opening sentence in the Second Helvetic Confession adopted by Swiss Reformed churches in 1566: "In this Holy Scripture, the Universal Church of Christ has all things fully expounded which belong to a saving faith, and also to the framing of a life acceptable to God."[3] Typical, too, is the New Hampshire Confession adopted by the Baptist churches of that state in 1833:

> We believe the Holy Bible was written by men divinely inspired, and is a perfect treasure of heavenly instruction . . . and therefore is, and shall remain to the end of the world, the true centre of Christian union, and the supreme standard by which all human conduct, creeds, and opinions should be tried.[4]

The Protestant position was also enunciated in the Edwardian *Homilies*, probably written by Thomas Cranmer, officially issued in 1547 and regarded as a classic exposition of Anglicanism. One of these sermons urges believers to read their Bibles faithfully. Why?

> Unto a Christian man there can be nothing more necessary or profitable, than the knowledge of Holy Scripture, forasmuch as in it is contained God's true word, setting forth His glory and also man's duty. . . . Therefore, as many as be desirous to enter into the right and perfect way unto God, must apply their minds to know Holy Scripture; without which they can neither sufficiently know God and His will, neither their office and duty. And as drink is pleasant to them that be dry, and meat to them that be hungry, so is the reading, hearing, searching, and studying of Holy Scripture, to them that be desirous to know God or themselves, and to do His will.[5]

Protestants believe, accordingly, that Scripture provides us with more than a theological creed; it provides us at the same time with a kind of Baedeker for life's journey through the present world with all of its besetting complexities and perplexities.

But questions are raised by many (not this author) concerning this belief. Is every aspect of the human enterprise, business included, to be governed by Scripture? In fact, is it actually the purpose of divine revelation to be blindingly prescriptive in all areas of our life and activity? An ancient aphorism, it is argued, furnishes a succinct corrective of so exaggerated a view of the Bible's purpose and province: "Scripture does not teach us how the heavens go. It teaches us how to go to heaven." Just as God does not intend His Word to instruct the astronomer, so He does not intend that His Word instruct an entrepreneur. Any attempt to formulate an authoritative mandate for executives, financiers, and employers is bound to be abortive. The course of wisdom, consequently, is to refrain from making such an attempt.

For example, Roman Catholic ethicist Daniel Callahan deplores the notion prevalent among even his own coreligionists that "all we need to know is to be found in Scripture, whether the subject be the state, war or peace or economic life." Criticizing this gross oversimplification, he argues that sometimes, pressured by emerging quandaries, we are compelled to recognize the limitations of Scripture: "Many of the problems we now face—think of cybernation, genetic manipulation, electrical and chemical control of behavior, urbanization—are simply not amendable to 'Biblical' solutions."[6] And surely these limitations must be recognized when we are dealing with the industrial, financial, commercial, interpersonal, and transnational intricacies of our capitalistic economy.

Allen Hollis, for one, urges that we recognize these limitations, refusing to follow the lead of those mistaken biblical interpreters who "have shown enormous ingenuity in building elaborate superstructures on minimal foundations." Instead, we need to keep in mind the great differences between Old Testament days and our own age. He says,

> The ancient Hebrews were limited to what they could design with their hands and what they could cultivate in the fields, and the Bible writers did not have to contend with the depersonalizing effects on people of this massive juggernaut of productivity.

Hollis reminds us of "another phenomenon unknown to Bible writers," which we must appreciate:

> It is the enormous concentration of economic power in giant industrial firms. Accurate comparison is impossible, but it does not seem unreasonable to imagine that even a smaller firm like American Motors has more total worth than all of Biblical Israel. We do not have any detailed picture of how Solomon operated what was a sophisticated business operation during his reign, though we are sure it quite surpassed anything previously seen. But it was small potatoes to our firms. . . . As we face the problems of understanding how the Bible can speak to a world so different, we must be aware of the differences.[7]

Sir Josiah Stamp, an outstanding economist as well as a qualified New Testament scholar, also emphasizes these differences and the limited capacity of Scripture to serve as a guide for business activities in our century. He makes two points:

> (1) Christ's teaching had primarily a spiritual and not an economic bearing. Its economics, so far as they went, were directed to the conditions of His own time, which were quite different from those of to-day. This alone makes it difficult to transfer literally to the world of to-day.
>
> (2) The attempts made to derive direct guidance in economic affairs from the letter of Scripture have generally failed.

In view of this, Stamp sees no way of utilizing Scripture for business management except by "examining Christian precepts, and extending their action logically into economic relations to see how far they are workable, and how far they have an economic reaction."[8]

Our task, then, as we study Scripture is to determine, aside from unequivocal imperatives like the Ten Commandments and Ephesians 4:28 ("he who has been stealing must steal no longer"), when and if culture-transcending principles are embodied in a biblical passage. This assignment is undeniably not easy. It demands careful exegesis and proper hermeneutics. In their most helpful book, *How to Read the Bible for All It's Worth*, Gordon Fee and Douglas Stuart lay down two indispensable guidelines:

> First, we must do our exegesis with particular care so that we hear what God's Word to them really was. In most such cases a clear principle has been articulated, which usually will transcend the historical particularity to which it was being applied. Second, and here is the important point, the "principle" does not now become timeless to be applied at random or whim to any and every kind of situation. We would argue that it must be applied to *genuinely comparable situations*.

We can steer our way—admittedly not without risk—between the Scylla of biblical irrelevance and the Charybdis of indefensible literalism if we remember this imperative: "No proof-texting when there are not immediately relevant texts."[9]

At the same time, however, while recognizing limitations and difficulties in utilizing biblical materials, we must not minimize Scripture's value for guiding Christian disciples in our twentieth-century workaday world. Old Testament scholar Christopher Wright argues for a discriminating use of Mosaic rules and regulations that might at first glance seem unhelpfully archaic:

> We assume that if God gave Israel certain specific institutions and laws, they were based on principles which have universal validity. That does not mean that Christians will try to impose by law in a secular state provisions lifted directly from the law of Moses. It does mean that they will work to bring their society nearer to conformity with the principles underlying the concrete laws of Old Testament society, because they perceive the same God to be both Redeemer and Law-giver of Israel, and also Creator and Ruler of contemporary mankind.[10]

Keeping Wright's argument in mind, we can consider the Deuteronomic laws regarding gleaning a field, leaving a mother bird to care for its young, and permitting an ox to munch while treading out corn. Are they merely quaint, outmoded regulations for a relatively undeveloped agricultural economy? By no means! John Taylor explains their enduring value when he says,

> If we take the Bible seriously at all, then we must take seriously the idea that what was first offered to Israel was meant to be a model of the salvation that was to be experienced by all. And we would say the same of the Christian church in the world today. Of course the details will be entirely different because the cultures are different: only the cranks would deny that. But style of relationship, the order of priorities, the criteria, and the frame of reference, these are still valid and their demand on us has to be faced.

In fact, as he examines other Deuteronomic laws, Taylor discovers in them "the principle of an equipoise society."

> The stern pressure of circumstances are [sic] compelling us at last to recognize how essential is this balance in what we call the eco-system. But this is only a reflection of the balance which is equally essential for the true functioning of the even vaster system in which God, man and the rest of nature, the past, the present and the future, are held together, the kingdom of right relationships.[11]

Postulating, then, the abiding relevance of biblical principles, we are nevertheless constrained to admit that it is extremely difficult to apply these truths and teachings to our specific problems. This difficulty emerges all too plainly in the history of Christian theology and ethics. The most learned, spiritual, and prayerful of godly men and women have arrived at radically divergent conclusions on a wide range of beliefs and practices. At one in their adherence to a core of essential doctrines, leaders of the Church through the ages have quarreled over a host of matters. Often they have failed, as Anderson Scott reminds us, in thinking out "the practical applications of their religious principles in their relations with other men." Scott gives these examples:

> Richard Baxter, when he said, "A man must be a very obdurate Sadducee who would not believe in witchcraft"; John Wesley, when he said, "Giving up witchcraft is in effect giving up the Bible"; Martin Luther when he said, "He that says slavery is opposed to Christianity is a liar"; the Moravians in Germany (than whom no Christian community has earned a nobler reputation for their piety, self-sacrifice and zeal for the Kingdom), when they wrote to the Moravians in America, "If you take slaves in faith

with the intention to conduct them to Christ, it shall not be a sin but may prove a blessing"; George Whitefield, when he persuaded the trustees of Georgia to introduce slavery—"I should think myself highly favoured if I could purchase a good number of slaves, in order to make their lives comfortable (and lay a foundation for bringing up their posterity in the nurture and admonition of the Lord)."[12]

If, parting company with these Christian worthies, we no longer follow the Old Testament directives for killing witches, and if we are convinced that slavery is wrong, we realize that to unearth abiding biblical principles and apply them properly is in many cases a delicate task. We realize, too, that a subjective element inescapably complicates our interpretive task. With our different backgrounds of presuppositions and experiences, we study a text; we prayerfully seek the illumination of the Holy Spirit; we read the works of scholarly predecessors; we consult members of our own spiritual communities; we may even take into account the ideas of informed nonChristians, appreciating that God in His common grace operates outside the confines of professed faith in Christ to grant an insightful understanding of social structures and dynamics.

Yet in the end we must individually arrive at our own conclusions and make our own decisions as to what policies we will pursue and what actions we will take. To quote President Harry Truman, we are compelled ineluctably to aver, "The buck stops here." Or appealing to a higher authority than a mere American president, we turn to Paul's pronouncements in Romans 14. Concerning issues of belief and behavior on which God has given no definitive revelation, he asserts, "Each one should be fully convinced in his own mind" (v. 5). Then he adds, "Each of us will give an account of himself to God" (v. 12). Any Christian engaged in business, whether as employer or employee, will thus repeatedly confront situations for which no clear-cut biblical directives are available. At such a juncture, he must in keeping with his own conscience and shouldering the burden of personal responsibility choose the course of behavior that he believes most in harmony with biblical principles.

B.

Following this lengthy prelude, we now turn our attention to some basic postulates of Scripture, which can be cast in the form of propositions. Let us see how the double-sided approach of subjectivity and responsibility works out.

1. We consider, to start with, the proposition or doctrine that every human being is made in the image of God and therefore possesses incalculable worth and dignity (see Gen. 1:27; Ps. 8:3-7). As God's image-bearer, he is entitled to self-determination and self-fulfillment. According to our Declaration of Independence, he is the living repository of "certain unalienable rights." Seeking to concretize these rights, Dennis Clark suggests:

—Every man has a right to employment by virtue of his nature, dignity and need for personal growth.
—Every man has the obligation to work.
—Every man has the right to acquire an understanding of the cultural significance of work in general and his own and other related work, particularly through education at the adult level.
—Every man has the need and right to participate in vocational groups that foster occupational responsibility, protection, and co-operation.
—Work and the scientific and technical skills and instruments of work must be used with due regard for the integrity and balance for the natural and social environment.
—Work processes must be organized to insure respect for personal dignity and creative and knowledgeable work participation, and to promote appropriate vocational order, interests, investment, and rewards.
—Production, distribution, and consumption of goods are not ends in themselves, but creative activities to permit the development of working life and betterment cf man's intellectual, economic, and social improvement.[13]

Reflecting the image of his Creator-God, man for his fulfillment must feel that to some degree he is being creative; Erich Fromm speaks of productivity, Erik Erikson of generativity. If a person's work is too demeaning or stultifying or emotionally unrewarding, he will fail to actualize his potential. More than that, he may sense that he is a sort of valueless zombie. Feodor Dostoevski, the world-renowned Russian novelist, eloquently states this dire possibility of emotional damage:

To punish him atrociously, to crush him in such a manner that the most hardened criminal would tremble before such punishment—it would be necessary only to give his works the character of complete uselessness. . . . Let him be constrained in his work as to pour water from one vessel to another and back again, then I am sure that at the end of a short period he would strangle himself or commit a thousand crimes punishable with death rather than live in such an abject condition or endure such treatment.[14]

Obviously, therefore, human beings must not be treated as cogs in a machine, mere hands in a production process, faceless nonentities, replaceable employees whose feelings, needs, and relationships can be ignored. Their well-being as persons must concern Christian employers. No matter how seemingly insignificant an individual's role in a business enterprise, he is a brother in the human family, made—this truth must never be forgotten—in God's image, and God expects members of the Christian brotherhood to treat that individual with respect. Indeed, God requires that Christians give a caring response to Cain's insolent question, "Am I my brother's keeper?" The answer God requires is an acknowledgment of human kinship: "No, I am my brother's brother."

But how are we to implement this basic biblical truth in the competitive world of business, providing adequate wages, generous fringe benefits, an assurance of security and worth, and as far as possible some genuine participation in what may be a large, impersonal enterprise?

2. Next, we consider the proposition that man's chief end, in the well-known words of the *Westminster Shorter Catechism*, is "to glorify God and enjoy Him forever." An all-controlling text for a Christian in the whole round of his life and activity is Colossians 3:23: "Whatever you do, work at it with all your heart, as working for the Lord, not for men." John Mitchell, a layman involved heavily in religious and civic affairs, the one-time chairman of the Dallas Theological Seminary board of directors, himself president of a successful machinery manufacturing company, refers to this text in his book, *The Christian in Business*, and comments, "I recommend that motto as a basis for every Christian's business life, and for every company that professes to be Christian in its policies and activities."[15]

The supreme purpose of human existence is not to produce and reproduce, to get and beget. It is not simply to provide goods and services for common needs. Certainly it is not to accumulate money. From a biblical perspective, the vast structures of industry and commerce are means to the end of enabling people to live for God's glory.

The biblical imperative affirmed by the Apostle Paul in 1 Corinthians 10:31 ("So whether you eat or drink or whatever you do, do it all for the glory of God") and by Jesus in John 15:8 ("This is to my Father's glory, that you bear much fruit, showing yourselves to be my disciples") is plain enough, to be sure. But how can the glory of God be made a realistic guideline in business policies?

3. Briefly, let us consider a third scriptural principle. According to the New Testament, Christ is Lord as well as Savior, and His lordship extends over all reality. Paul impressively expresses this central truth of our faith, "For this very reason, Christ died and returned to life so that he might be the Lord of both the dead and the living" (Rom. 14:9). No smallest corner of human life lies beyond our Savior's sovereignty.

But once more the question arises: How do we implement this principle in the nitty-gritty hustle and bustle of a competitive capitalistic economy? And this question becomes more conscience-probing in the light of another question. Jesus in His Sermon on the Plain inquires of His disciples, "Why do you call me, 'Lord, Lord' and do not do what I say?" (Luke 6:46). Yes, lordship involves obedient activity. Yet how in the marketplace can that obedient activity be carried out?

4. We consider, for another thing, the proposition that any work a Christian does, whether a woman keeping house or a janitor sweeping floors or an executive administering a transnational corporation, is to be viewed as a calling, a providentially assigned vocation.

Martin Luther in particular brought out of obscurity the New Testament teaching set forth most clearly in 1 Corinthians 7:17-19:

> Nevertheless, each one should retain the place in life that the Lord assigned to him and to which God has called him. This is the rule I lay down in all the churches. Was a man already circumcised when he was called? He should not become uncircumcised. Was a man uncircumcised when he was called? He should not be circumcised. Circumcision is nothing and uncircumcision is nothing. Keeping God's commands is what counts.

Thus, no matter what place in an economy a Christian occupies, his task is to be imbued with dignity because it is God's appointed calling. Luther vigorously and repeatedly stressed the dignity of all labor:

> A cobbler, a smith, a farmer—each has the work of his trade, and yet they are all alike consecrated priests and bishops. . . . What you do in your house is worth as much as if you did it up in heaven for our Lord God. For what we do in our calling here on earth in accordance with His word and command He counts as if it were done in heaven for Him. . . . Therefore we should accustom ourselves to think of our position and work as sacred and well-pleasing to God, not on account of the position and the work, but on account of the word and faith on which the obedience and the work flow.[16]

But is this New Testament teaching an impracticable piece of religious idealism? Can it have a positive, even a powerful impingement on marketplace activities? Elton Trueblood maintains that it is a most relevant concept:

> If ours is God's world, any true work for the improvement of man's life is a sacred task and should be undertaken with this in mind. We sometimes suggest this by our frequent use of the word "vocation" but we have used the word so long that we have forgotten the degree to which it is a specifically Christian word. . . . The really crucial decision comes, not when a person decides to be a foreign missionary rather than a farmer; the really crucial decision comes when a man decides that he will live his whole life in what the late Thomas Kelly called "Holy Obedience"; whether that leads to farming or banking or evangelistic work in Africa is then wholly secondary. The major decision has already been made and the decision is that to allow one's entire life, one's channel of divine love. . . . It is just as important for one boy to decide to be a Christian businessman as it is for another boy to decide to become a Christian clergyman. . . . If our religion is united with the major steps of life, that is, the decisive ones, it ceases to seem either abstract or irrelevant. *No religion is irrelevant if it helps people to see the hidden glory of the common things they do.*[17]

And to Trueblood's persuasive argument, let us add the remarks of theologian Thomas Oden concerning the value of this biblical principle in the functioning of even today's giant conglomerates. He says,

> If one believes, as I do, that corporations despite their imperfections perform legitimate and socially constructive services at home and abroad, one is compelled to conclude that working for a corporation as a janitor or as a chief executive officer can be seen as a Christian vocation. . . . This vocational approach is perhaps the most effective way to insure the accountability of the corporation or, for that matter, the church, the state, or a university.[18]

5. Another scriptural proposition we need to consider is *stewardship*, a term appearing often in the *King James Version* of the New Testament (e.g., Luke 12:42, 16:1ff.; 1 Cor. 4:1-2; Titus 1:7; 1 Pet. 4:10). Let us join to the principle of stewardship the related concept of servanthood as incisively set forth by our Lord:

> "You know that the rulers of the Gentiles lord it over them, and their high officials exercise authority over them. Not so with you. Instead,

whoever wants to become great among you must be your servant, and
whoever wants to be first must be your slave—just as the Son of Man did
not come to be served, but to serve, and to give his life as a ransom for
many." (Matt. 20:25-28)

How does this conjoining of stewardship and servanthood affect a Christian's work ethic? Dynamically! Well, *ex hypothesi* it should, though no doubt it
often fails to do so. Yet as Wade Boggs perceives, it ought to have a forceful
impact.

> In Biblical terminology, all the economic activity concerned with process-
> ing, distributing, possessing, and using material goods goes by the name
> of *stewardship*. . . . Stewardship calls for an acknowledgment of God's
> sovereignty in areas of the production and distribution of material goods,
> management and labor, wages and prices, capital and profits, ownership
> of property, and use of the tools of production. . . . Man's relationship to
> land, minerals, water, air, and living creatures is one of stewardship, of
> obligation to use all these things in accordance with the will of the Sover-
> eign Creator.[19]

Basic to this concept is the belief that God is the Maker and hence the
Proprietor of everything on our planet. As Psalm 24 puts it,

> The earth is the LORD's, and everything in it,
>   the world, and all who live in it;
> for he founded it upon the seas
>   and established it upon the waters. (vv. 1-2)

Temporarily entrusted with the care of God's creation, Christians ought to
be the vigilant enemies of waste, pollution, and the selfish depletion of nature's
limited storehouse. Thus, the implications of stewardship are obviously enormous, impinging as they do on decisions concerning what products it is morally
right to make and market. Ought we as God's stewards to abstain from the
production and sale of superfluities and luxuries in a world where multitudes are
without the barest necessities? Such a decision is confessedly difficult to reach,
yet stewardship inescapably lays upon us the responsibility for a wise allocation
of the world's resources.
    Stewardship likewise places upon us the responsibility for understanding,
as we seek to serve our fellow mortals, the difference between need and want.
And achieving this understanding, as Paul Ramsey acknowledges, is no trivial

task. Assume "that the Reformation doctrine of vocation requires that Christian love penetrates everything a man does." Ramsey explains,

> This means that he has every possible stimulus for carrying on the philosophical quest for determining the universal needs of human beings, for ascending the scale of values as far as possible, for finding out about the highest good, for becoming as enlightened and effective in the attainment of these ends as his capacity allows. For his enlightenment also the Christian is "servant of all" the sources of information employed by the human mind and "subject to every one" of the ways his neighbor's true needs may be adequately found out and best served.[20]

This task as formulated is onerous enough to drive a businessman to despair. Yet what does it mean to be Christ's steward-servant in the marketplace?

A further implication of the steward-servant role is the determination to avoid shoddy, careless workmanship, holding instead to the highest standards. A still further implication is the willingness to go beyond average expectations and legal requirements, keeping in view our Lord's thought-provoking inquiry, "What are you doing more than others?" (Matt. 5:47).

6. We turn now to a New Testament proposition derived from a cluster of personality traits. Perhaps this proposition can best be stated in the traditional formulation of imitating Jesus Christ, reproducing in character and conduct the pattern set by our Savior.

What do we learn from these passages (Matt. 5:2-12; 23:23; 25:14-29; Rom. 12:8,17; 2 Cor. 8:11; 12:7; Gal. 5:22-23; Eph. 4:28; 6:3-7; Col. 3:22-24; 1 Thess. 4:12; 1 Pet. 2:22-23) to say nothing of the admonitions in the book of Proverbs? We learn that a Christian is to be just and fair, honest and diligent, caring and compassionate, a person marked by integrity and responsibility, concerned about the welfare of others as much as he is about his own (see Phil. 2:4).

If we turn again to John Mitchell's *The Christian in Business*, we find a whole chapter entitled "Whatsoever Things Are Honest." We find, moreover, an inventory of desired traits in an employee, which include honesty, intelligence, pride, consideration, loyalty, and enthusiasm. We are told that these mark, at least hypothetically, "a typical member of the Mitchell working force."[21] Allowing for a degree of hyperbole, we must nevertheless grant that some of these characteristics duplicate elements of Christocentric character as delineated in the New Testament.

Singling out honesty as a virtue essential for the successful ongoing of our industrial society, economist Kenneth Boulding says,

An exchange system, for instance, cannot flourish in the absence of a minimum of simple honesty because an exchange system is an exchange of promises, and honesty is the fulfillment of promises. If we extend the concept of honesty a little further into the fulfillment of role expectations, we see this also as essential for the successful operation of a system based on exchange. This is why the institutions of capitalism cannot operate successfully in the total absence of what might be called the puritan virtues.

With equal justice "the puritan virtues" might be called the biblical virtues, and these are indispensable for the functioning of our capitalistic economy. Unless they are cultivated and regnant, Boulding foresees "a general lapse into cynicism and the overt acceptance of a dishonest covert system"; and he prophesies, if and when that takes place, "a society is doomed."[22]

Much more might well be added with respect to just and fair wages, advertising, sales techniques, and management philosophy. But suppose we refrain from belaboring the obvious.

7. We will consider one more proposition, which in a way is a compendium of those propositions already mentioned and others that could be adduced. Neighbor-love, the issue and concomitant of love for God, is the key of the Christian lifestyle. In lapidary simplicity, Jesus summarized the essence of biblical ethics,

> "'Love the Lord your God with all your heart and with all your soul and with all your mind.' This is the first and greatest commandment. And the second is like it: 'Love your neighbor as yourself.' All the Law and the Prophets hang on these two commandments." (Matt. 22:37-39)

Our Lord restated this principle of neighbor-love in His so-called Golden Rule: "Do to others what you would have them do to you, for this sums up the Law and the Prophets" (Matt. 7:12).

If we appreciate that the neighbor-love commanded by our Lord is a steadfast commitment to an individual's highest well-being rather than a feeling-state, we are able to discern how this principle, carried into the business world, might govern its policies and objectives. If we perceive with John Calvin that "just as the law of love wants us to love our neighbors as ourselves, so it summons us to be caring for their welfare,"[23] we may start to lose our doubt that the Golden Rule can become the touchstone of our business transactions.

8. We have discussed biblical demands and principles as they impinge on Christians in the fields of management and labor. We have failed, though, to

mention an astringent warning that can readily be cast into a cautionary proposition: Guard against the enticement of mammonism. Jesus earnestly admonishes His disciples to avoid the danger of subtle idolatry, the spirit of covetousness that causes people to worship money and depend on it grovelingly for their security: "No one can serve two masters. Either he will hate the one and love the other, or he will be devoted to the one and despise the other. You cannot serve both God and Money" (Matt. 6:24). In His parables, like that of the rich fool (see Luke 12:16-21), Jesus sounds an alarm that individuals caught up in profit making would do well to heed. It is an alarm that sounds out again in 1 Timothy 6:9-10:

> People who want to get rich fall into temptation and a trap and into many foolish and harmful desires that plunge men into ruin and destruction.
> For the love of money is a root of all kinds of evil. Some people, eager for money, have wandered from the faith and pierced themselves with many griefs.

Profit making, moneymaking—that's the name of the game. Even a Christian in business cannot ignore the bottom line of the balance sheet. If he operates in the red, he fails; so does his business; and besides that, he fails his coworkers and any investors who have entrusted their funds to him. Profit making, moneymaking, is therefore a legitimate Christian concern. But what margin of profit and what personal rewards for skillful management are there? How does one's soul stay untainted by greed? How does one perform one's marketplace activities without once in a while flexing one's knees at mammon's shrine? This temptation compounds the difficulties we have been observing of implementing Christian principles in the competitive, unChristian arena of moneymaking.

Thus, at the end of our study we confront the inescapable issues of subjectivity and responsibility in the implementation of biblical principles, which is why the conscientious disciple prayerfully relies on a more-than-human Source of counsel and guidance. In the words of James, "If any of you lacks wisdom, he should ask God, who gives generously to all without finding fault, and it will be given to him" (1:5). Jejune as it may seem, we know why in some Christian companies there is an empty chair at meetings of directors. Presumptuous and pretentious as it may sound, that chair is reserved for the Senior Partner and Chairman of the Board, God.

EDITOR'S PERSPECTIVE

Dr. Grounds's chapter is clearly in touch with a commonly experienced reality—Christians in the marketplace do encounter situations that require the subjective application of biblical principles to their problems. For many Christians, this experience is so pervasive that they operationally, if not normatively, abandon the conscious process of looking for biblical absolutes to apply to their problems. It is easy to become encumbered by the cultural pressures that tell us all moral matters are relative and subjective in character; there are no objective absolutes to assist us.

It is in the face of this cultural assumption that Dr. Krabbendam's position—there are biblical absolutes that can be applied objectively in business—is apologetically postured. His argument and that of Vernon Grounds are completely defensible biblically and experientially. How can both positions be correct? How can there be knowable, objective moral absolutes and the simultaneous need to subjectively apply them?

Four things tend to obscure our understanding and application of absolutes. First, we can become confused about what is and what is not an absolute. We can fail to distinguish between what reflects an absolute and what is itself an absolute. Second, we can overlook the fact that we are finite beings seeking to administer absolute standards from a limited perspective. Third, the *foundational* absolutes we seek to understand are qualitative in nature and abstract by definition. Finally, the foundational absolutes speak first about attributes of character and are only secondarily related to behavior. Let's examine these complicating factors.

In matters pertaining to morality, virtues, right and wrong, and other normative concepts of moral perfection, God alone is absolute, the standard by

133

which all other ideas about absolutes must be examined and compared. God's character is the standard by which we examine human character, and His behavior is the standard by which we measure human behavior.

The attribute God uses most frequently to describe Himself is His holiness; it is the very essence of His being. Because we bear His image, we are called to be holy (see Lev. 11:44; 2 Cor. 7:1; 1 Pet. 1:13-16). This is one of the three characteristics Scripture refers to when describing what it means for us to be made in God's image—we have the *capacity* to be holy (see Eph. 4:24; Col. 3:10 for the three image characteristics—holiness, righteousness, and true knowledge of God). Often God uses this attribute to describe His other ones—holy name (encompassing all), holy arm (power), and so on.

Since God is absolutely holy in character, He is also of necessity perfectly righteous; all His acts are absolutely right. Scripture speaks of righteousness over four hundred times, and we, as God's image-bearers, are called to act righteously. We have the *capacity* to be righteous (see Eph 4:24). Note, however, that holiness and righteousness are both *abstract traits* describing God's character and behavior.

These abstract traits are absolute in both their quality and their quantity in God's case. So how can finite creatures know or possess them? We can come to *know them* objectively only as God reveals Himself to us and manifests Himself through His behavior. We can come to *possess them* only as we are renovated to Christ's image by the work of the Holy Spirit. When they are described in Scripture, though, the commands, laws, and precepts are illustrative and reflective. They speak of and point to characteristics and behavior that will mirror God's perfections.

Therefore, specific forms of volitional behavior can be described in absolute terms, and many biblical propositions do this. They point to the genuine possibility of our being like God. We can manifest Godlike character and behavior by not lying, not stealing, not committing adultery, not coveting, not failing to love God or neighbor. But even these forms of absolute truth merely reinforce the reality that we are morally responsible agents. They highlight the fact that we are to choose good and repudiate evil. We are not automatically holy and righteous in character and behavior. We have a fallen nature, and our "new nature" is ever struggling with our "old nature." As a consequence of the Fall, we are in a state of being that requires us to make moral choices.

We need to remember, though, that the situations we find ourselves in do not define what is right. Our biggest problem is contending with our own character and desires in different situations. (Scripture can help us know more of what God thinks, but it cannot, apart from the Spirit's reforming work, *cause* us to do God's will.) So we bring a character and self-orientation problem to the entire discussion of biblical absolutes.

Moral judgments are required of everyone, even the most sincere, dedicated, and mature Christians who earnestly seek to know God's will. Moral choice came with the Fall. God had announced the consequences if Adam and Eve disobeyed Him; they would come to know good and evil, necessitating their exercise of moral judgment (see Gen. 2:17; 3:7,11). Now even loving parents must decide if their three-year-old child should go to bed at 7:30, 8:00, 8:30, or 9:00 p.m. A just and righteous entrepreneur, who is making lots of money, must decide if he should give his surplus income to a mission program, reduce prices and benefit the customers, reinvest the surplus in new technology to enhance the operations of the business, pay his employees higher wages, or keep the surplus for future contingencies. Or is some combination best?

A true knowledge of God and His precepts aids us in making moral choices. When we have the opportunity to choose between obviously right and wrong alternatives, this knowledge will tell us precisely what to do in these clear-cut cases. Many times, though, we must choose from an array of good alternatives. Absolutes sensitize us to our responsibility and encourage us to seek the wise alternatives, but "righteousness" (a known, absolute standard of conduct) can only call us to make a morally accountable decision in the light of God's character and behavior. We call these the gray areas.

This is where Henry Krabbendam's statement that we need a "sanctified sense" is so appropriate. God leads His children, but His children make morally responsible and accountable decisions as agents created in God's image. We are responsible for our choices—absolutely responsible.

It is just as obvious, though, that Vernon Grounds's discussion on the subjective character of moral decision making, even in the full light of biblical absolutes, equally reflects God's truth. We must conclude that God's moral absolutes do not eliminate the need for our moral judgments. The absolutes become the guideposts and encouragers for godly behavior, but they do not automatically furnish clear, precise answers. The following common business decision clearly illustrates this point.

We are not to lie—a biblical absolute. When we advertise our products or services to their best advantage, though, ignoring their deficiencies, are we being completely truthful? What we don't say (silence) can be just as deceitful and misleading as an inaccurate statement. We must decide, before God, what is and what is not lying.

The regenerate Christian soon realizes that the real problems associated with this decision-making process are ones associated with the heart's attitudes, desires, and focus. If we desire honesty above wealth, our moral decisions are greatly simplified. If we have a strong drive for wealth and are wrestling with how far we can go with "puffery" in our advertising, we experience real moral tensions. Knowing the true condition of the heart, and guarding it ("taking every thought captive to the obedience of Christ" [2 Cor. 10:5]), is a prerequisite for godly decision making in business.

We need the Spirit's help. There is no way to be holy and possess a "sanctified sense" apart from God's regenerative and sanctifying work. May the Holy Spirit make us anew in the image of Christ in holiness and righteousness.

SCRIPTURAL LAW AND NATURAL LAW:
The Bases of an Ethical Appeal in the Marketplace?

Is a Christian to raise moral issues with nonChristians in the marketplace on the grounds of scriptural law or natural law? Can the natural law, as observed and filtered through fallen motives reflecting self-righteousness and prudentiality, produce the same moral behavior as that created under the influence of God's written law in Scripture? Can either natural law or scriptural law help the unregenerate make moral decisions, or are they so self-centered that there is only an appearance of morality that serves their own purposes? What are the bases of ethical business conduct in the secular environment? These are the kinds of questions we want to examine now.

Theologically, this family of questions comes under the topic of human depravity. Depravity concerns itself with the extent of our *sin nature* and how that influences and affects our relationships, abilities, and character. It deals with the biblical tensions arising from the beliefs 'hat the natural (fallen and unregenerate) man, although still in God's image, is dead to God (see John 5:25; Rom. 3:10-12; Eph. 2:1-7) and simultaneously is "without excuse" for he knowingly suppresses the truth (see Rom. 1:18-23).

We are not attempting to resolve the t'·eological debates about the nature of depravity (total or partial), however. We are going to explore the practical consequences of affirming that the unregenerate are dead to God and that they knowingly suppress the truth they have about God. If both are true, and they are, for Scripture affirms them both, then what can we learn about how to approach nonChristians on explicitly moral issues in the marketplace? Should we appeal to biblical law in our discussions, or should we point to the prudentiality of the natural law? This question is important for every Christian who desires to be salt and light in the marketplace.

As we read the materials prepared by Dr. Richard Gaffin and Dr. Norman Geisler to help us contend with this issue, we need to keep in focus the distinction between the "appearance of righteousness" and "true righteousness," which the Holy Spirit is developing by degrees in the sanctified believer. An illustration will be given to clarify the distinction.

We will assume that two executives (in different businesses) decide to increase their employees' pay by 20 percent. The two acts are behaviorally identical. If one executive acted righteously, then the other one did, too. Right? Both can certainly give the appearance of righteousness to the human observer. God, however, does not judge by what the eye sees or what the ear hears (see Isa. 11:3). No, God judges the intents and motives of the heart (see 1 Cor. 4:5).

Everyday marketplace ethics concentrate on the "appearance of righteousness." If an act is helpful and constructive from a personal and social point of view, it is deemed good. From this perspective, we are overwhelmingly a righteous people in our economic transactions. This is a fair judgment, isn't it? Good acts are righteous acts, aren't they?

Life is really more complicated than this. We may rarely know the motive of our neighbors, but we generally have some notion of our own motives if we stop to examine them. We soon discover, though, that even our own motives are often veiled to us and are generally mixed in their orientation. The more basic question is, What is God's perception of our "righteous" activity? Just because we declare that our activities are good does not make them so (see Prov. 14:12). God looks at the motives behind the behavior as well as the behavior.

Behavior that appears to be righteous is better than bad behavior, but it is not automatically righteous from God's perspective. Dr. Richard Gaffin discusses "total depravity" and its implications for business decision making and business morality. He draws us into the tension that exists between balancing a biblical understanding of "common grace" (God's activities in the world that aid and constrain all human behavior) and total depravity. He believes the level of a culture's general morality is a function of both God's moral law (written on each individual's conscience) and common grace. He does not believe it results from moral principles derived from the natural law.

Dr. Gaffin believes that God provides, through common grace, the economic stability necessary for us to sustain physical life; he does not think that we can depend on mankind for such stabilizing morality because, apart from common grace, the systems of this world would collapse under their collective weight of sin. Thus, Christians should not expect to elevate the general level of ethics in the business community by appealing to moral principles that are revealed by God in natural law.

CHAPTER 8

TOTAL DEPRAVITY AND BUSINESS ETHICS

Richard B. Gaffin, Jr.

Dr. Richard Gaffin is Professor of Systematic Theology at Westminster Theological Seminary, Philadelphia, where he has been since 1965. Born of missionary parents in Beijing, China, he studied at Calvin College (B.A. in history, 1958) and Westminster Seminary (Th.D., 1969). He is a minister in the Orthodox Presbyterian church and a frequent speaker at conferences and seminars. Among his writings are Perspectives on Pentecost *and* Resurrection and Redemption.

If the Bible teaches anything clearly, it is the reality of sin. That is the dark side of the clarity of Scripture, confessed by the Protestant Reformers—its unsparing portrayal of human sinfulness. From beginning to end, Genesis 3 through Revelation 22, the Bible documents the full range of sin and its consequences.

Sin is rebellion against God. (1) Specifically, human sin is *lawlessness* (see 1 John 3:4)—violation of God's law, prideful disobedience of the revealed will of God, the Creator, on the part of the creature made in His image and for His service. (2) Sin is *universal* ("There is no one righteous, not even one" and "all have sinned" [Rom. 3:10,23; cf. 1:18-3:10]); every human being is born a sinner ("Surely I was sinful at birth, sinful from the time my mother conceived me" [Ps. 51:5]). (3) Sin is also *intensive* or integral, its corrupting impulse resident at the core of human personality ("For out of the heart come evil thoughts, murder, adultery, sexual immorality, theft, false testimony, slander" [Matt. 15:19]). (4) The character of sin as transgression involves *guilt* (e.g., Rom. 5:12ff.) as well as corruption. (5) The ultimate punishment on the condemnation sin deserves from God, in fidelity to His holiness and righteousness, is *death*—eternal death

("The wages of sin is death" [Rom. 6:23]).

All the historic Christian traditions agree, more or less as stated, with these points; to deny the reality of sin is to deprive Christianity of any real meaning. There are differences, however, and among these is perennial dispute about the third point, the depravity or corruption of sin. Briefly stated, the issue is this: Is human depravity total or partial? Is the corruption of human nature complete, or is it limited in some respect? Is there perhaps left in people a remnant unpolluted by sin, some capacity or potential that sin does not govern? I seek to (1) show that the Bible, in fact, teaches that human depravity is radical and total and (2) answer, again on a biblical basis, certain apparently formidable objections to this teaching. That, in turn, will provide a necessary framework from which to (3) draw some conclusions, necessarily brief and general, for ethics in business and economics.

TOTAL DEPRAVITY

A good place to begin with biblical teaching on the depth and scope of human sinfulness is 1 Corinthians 2:14:

> The man without the Spirit does not accept the things that come from the Spirit of God, for they are foolishness to him, and he cannot understand them, because they are spiritually discerned.

The larger context is one of those passages where the Apostle Paul is concerned with the "big picture," to provide some fundamental perspectives on his gospel ministry as a whole (see 1:18–3:23). In sharp contrast to the false divisions and party spirit present in the church at Corinth (see 1:10-17), he sets out the true nature of the division created by the gospel. The result is nothing less than total conflict between God and "the world," "this age" (1:20), constituted and distinguished by sin and unbelief. In terms of the pairs wisdom-foolishness and power-weakness, this struggle is so unrelieved, the antithesis so absolute, that "Christ the power of God and the wisdom of God" is rejected as weakness and foolishness. For the unbelieving world, the gospel message of Christ's cross is thoroughly foolish, a "stumbling block." Conversely, in His "foolishness" and "weakness" God confounds and nullifies human wisdom and power (1:18-29).

Paul goes on to describe this antithesis in individual terms (see 2:14-15). The unbeliever is "the man without the Spirit" of God; the believer is "the spiritual man," that is, renewed, indwelt, motivated, and directed by the Spirit of God. Here, too, the antithesis is total and exclusive. All people fall into one of these categories; there is no middle ground, no third group.

(What Paul writes several verses later is only apparently an exception. When he calls Corinthian believers "unspiritual" and "carnal"/"worldly" [3:1,3], he is not providing a rationale for two classes of Christians, "spiritual" and "carnal," with unbelievers as the remaining third class of people. Such an understanding would soften and domesticate his intended point. The kind of spiritual immaturity present at Corinth is not merely "low-level" Christian behavior but decidedly unChristian; their "jealousy and quarreling" [v. 3], as he makes unmistakably plain elsewhere [see Gal. 5:20], is sin, a "work of the 'flesh,'" totally contradicting the "fruit of the Spirit" [Gal. 5:??].)

There are at least two pertinent comments about the unbeliever. First, his sinful condition is such that he does not accept the things of God's Spirit because he is *unable* to do so; "he cannot understand them." Paul plainly asserts the inability of the unbeliever. Second, what is the extent of this inability? What is the scope of "the things that come from the Spirit of God" that the unbeliever cannot comprehend? Verse 15 points to the answer. The believer, in contrast, comprehends and discerns "all things"; the things of the Spirit are "all things" (cf. v. 10).

Is there anything that restricts or delimits "all things"? Nothing in the immediate context appears to do so. Further, as already noted, the antithesis in 2:14-15 is part of the megaconflict between God and the sinful world, that struggle which in scale is nothing less than that between two "aeons," two world-orders (see 2:6,8), between two creations, the old and the new (see 2 Cor. 5:17). There is no warrant for restricting the inability in view to a religious or moral sphere, in distinction from other areas of human knowledge and endeavor. The inability of the unbelievers to understand, their epistemological inability, is comprehensive and total.

First Corinthians 1:18-3:23 is, in effect, a commentary on Jesus' teaching in Matthew 11:25-27 (cf. Luke 10:21-22):

> "I praise you, Father, Lord of heaven and earth, because you have hidden these things from the wise and learned, and revealed them to little children. Yes, Father, for this was your good pleasure. All things have been committed to me by my Father. No one knows the Son except the Father, and no one knows the Father except the Son and those to whom the Son chooses to reveal Him."

Present here is the same antithesis, the same countervaluation of human wisdom and understanding, encountered in 1 Corinthians 1-2. Specifically, again, what is negated is the knowledge of unbelievers; what is hidden from them, the "wise and learned" in their own eyes, is revealed to "little children," that is, believers (cf. Matt. 18:3-4; Mark 10:15). Again, too, there is an indication of the comprehensive scope of the knowledge at issue; what is hidden from unbelievers is "all things."

The context defines "all things." "All things" are "these things" (v. 25). The latter expression, in turn, refers in the immediately preceding verses not to an explicit grammatical antecedent but more generally to the account of things that have happened in several towns in Galilee: the rejection of Jesus and His miracles, a rejection that will serve as a basis for the condemnation of those towns at the Final Judgment (see vv. 20-24). Luke, in addition, brackets the passage with Jesus' vision of the eschatological overthrow of Satan and his rule through the mission of the seventy-two (see 10:17-20), and His pronouncement about the blessed advantage of His disciples in view of the new, consummation realities experienced by them in contrast to those of the old order (the "many prophets and kings" [vv. 23-24]).

All told, then, "these things"/"all things," hidden from unbelievers, are the things of the Kingdom of God/Heaven brought about by the coming of Christ (cf. esp. Matt. 11:11-13 and Luke 10:9). The mutual self-knowledge of the Father and the Son, sovereignly revealed to believers, concerns all that is revealed in the coming of the Kingdom.

According to the synoptic gospels, the Kingdom is at once both the center and the all-encompassing theme of the proclamation of Jesus during His earthly ministry. It is not confined to some restricted ("religious") sector of concerns. Rather, the Kingdom is a comprehensive eschatological reality. It is the consummate realization of the expectations created by God's covenant, the fulfillment of the promises made to the Old Testament fathers (see Luke 10:24). More specifically, the Kingdom is a matter of the eschatological lordship of God in Christ, inaugurated and presently being realized through His first coming and to be consummated at His return.

Nothing in the entire creation is irrelevant to this Kingdom or falls outside this eschatological rule of Christ. The reality of the Kingdom, in the words of Paul's subsequent commentary, is the reality of God's having "placed all things under his feet and appointed him to be head over everything for the church" (Eph. 1:22), the reality, already begun in His exaltation, of bringing "all things in heaven and on earth together under one head, even Christ" (1:10).

The Kingdom of God—its claim—is totalitarian in the most ultimate sense that the creature made in His image can know and experience. It resists and negates all efforts, be they pre-Kantian dualisms or post-Kantian dimensionalisms, to narrow its scope. All of life, including all knowledge, is "religious." For Jesus, as for Paul after Him, the cognitive inability of unbelievers is comprehensive and total.

The two passages so far examined express the unbeliever's total inability to know or understand. Both, however, plainly have in view an inability that is more than cognitive in the strict sense of having to do with the use of reason or the capacity to think. In fact, in both instances the inability in view manifests itself precisely through the exercise of that capacity. "Wisdom" is unable to understand the things of God's Spirit and so is bound to reject Christ and the gospel. In other words, it is an immoral, sinful inability.

Paul is clear on this point. The ignorance of the Athenians, revealed in their altar to "an unknown God" (Acts 17:23), is not innocent. Along with their "scientific" sneering at the proclamation of the resurrection of the dead and Final Judgment (see v. 32), their ignorance is culpable; it is ignorance that needs to be repented of (see v. 30).

Elsewhere (notably in Rom. 1:18ff. and Eph. 4:17ff.), Paul pictures the depth and magnitude of human sinfulness in the most unsparing fashion, largely, again, with the use of cognitive terms. Sinners, apart from God's saving grace, live "in the futility of their thinking" and are "darkened in their understanding" (Eph. 4:17-18; cf. Rom. 1:21); supposing themselves to be wise, they have become fools (see Rom. 1:22). They are "separated from the life of God because of the ignorance that is in them due to the hardening of their hearts" (Eph. 4:18). Accordingly, "having lost all sensitivity, they have given themselves over to sensuality so as to indulge in every kind of impurity, with a continual lust for more" (Eph. 4:19). They "suppress the truth by their wickedness" (Rom. 1:18); they have "exchanged the truth of God for a lie," the primal, perverse, and perverting lie of creature-worship in one form or other (Rom. 1:25). Consequently, God has abandoned them in their idolatry to the full range of corruption and immorality, some of it of the most degrading, even unimaginable ("unnatural" [Rom. 1:26]) kind (see Rom. 1:24,26-32).

Plainly, the depravity depicted in these two passages is both radical and total. It is rooted in the human heart, the controlling center of one's being, and nothing there mitigates it or otherwise checks it from completely permeating and dominating the entire person. That makes clear, then, the radical sinfulness of the cognitive incapacity in view above. That total inability to understand is a leading function of radical corruption; total inability is total depravity.

A couple of other facets related to the teaching of these passages need to be highlighted. (1) Total depravity is universal. That is one of Paul's points in Romans 1-3. The Jews, because they may not have committed some of the more conspicuous hard-core sins documented among the non-Jews, are not thereby to suppose that they are better, less depraved; in the matter of God's judgment on everyone "who does evil," too, the regulative principle is "first for the Jew, then for the Gentile" (Rom. 2:9). (2) Paul closes his indictment of the universality of human sin and depravity with a composite of citations from the Old Testament (see Rom. 3:10-18). This reflects the pervasive, overall unity of the biblical witness. New Testament teaching on total depravity is fairly seen as an amplification of Jeremiah 17:9, for one: "The heart is deceitful above all things and beyond cure" (*or*, "desperately corrupt").

Romans 8:6-8 can serve to close this brief survey: "The mind of sinful man is death, but the mind controlled by the Spirit is life and peace; the sinful mind is hostile to God. It does not submit to God's law, nor can it do so. Those controlled by the sinful nature cannot please God."

The same antithesis between believers and unbelievers found in 1 Corinthians 1-2 comes into view here. All people fall into one of two opposed groups; they are controlled either by their sinful nature ("flesh") or by the Holy Spirit. There is no middle ground, and nothing softens the conflict; it is an absolute, all-inclusive conflict, nothing less than life-and-death in magnitude. On the one side, the disposition ("mind") of sin and death—its ultimate end, eschatological death (cf. Rom. 6:23)—consists in an utter inability to please God or obey His law and in implacable hostility toward God. The basic dimensions of human depravity are death and enmity—a total inability to be or do anything for God and a total capacity, a radical heart commitment, to being and doing everything against Him.

The Bible never relativizes sin. To do so, it should not be forgotten, relativizes the gospel and gives rise to cooperative schemes in which we presumably contribute, no matter how minimally or covertly, to our own salvation. The Reformers, for one, clearly understood this; total depravity and *sola gratia*, grace *alone*, stand or fall together. The sheer graciousness of the gospel is revealed in what from the sinners' side is its incredible, impossible demand: its resurrection demand. The gospel is God's call to those who are *dead* in transgressions and sins to hear and live (see John 5:25; Eph. 2:1,5; 5:14).

We are not sinners because we happen to sin; we sin and cannot do otherwise because we are sinners. Absolutely nothing in sinful human nature alleviates or restrains its corruption. There is in us no remnant of goodness, either actual or potential, no corner or secret recess of human personality, no matter how attenuated we might conceive of it, that remains unpolluted by sin. Human depravity is total.

COMMON GRACE

The doctrine of total depravity has always had its detractors, both outside and within the Church. There are at least two reasons for that, apart from inadequate and confusing ways in which the doctrine may sometimes be presented. The deepest reason is our own sinfulness—our native resistance to acknowledging that we are sinners and the full magnitude of our sinfulness. Only the Holy Spirit can produce genuine confession of sin (see John 16:8-11).

But another reason especially warrants our attention here. The doctrine of total depravity seems to contradict reality. To confess radical human corruption, apparently, is in conflict with life as we experience it. Everywhere around us, outside the pale of Christianity and among those who make no pretense of being believers, are countless and evident instances—in the great as well as the small affairs of life—of kindness and helpfulness to others, of philanthropy and deeds of mercy, of attraction to what is good and right, noble and honorable, of efforts that advance peace and human well-being, of beneficial cultural and artistic accomplishment, of heroism and self-sacrifice, even to the point of death.

Further, we have no difficulty observing a wide spectrum of variations within the general condition of human sinfulness. We see the tireless community volunteer and the hardened criminal; relatively, some people are "good" and others are "bad." A perennially cited example is that of the Roman emperors: the moderation and equity of Titus and Trajan provide a sharp contrast to the cruelty and excesses of Caligula and Nero. In our own time, we think of Hitler and Gandhi.

It is a matter not only of our experience but also of what Scripture itself recognizes. Abimelech, king of the Philistines, displayed moral restraint and even a certain indignation (see Gen. 20:1-17; 26:8-11). Jehu, who did not abandon the false worship of the golden calves (see 2 Kings 10:29,31), nonetheless destroyed Baal worship in Israel and is said by the Lord Himself to "have done well in accomplishing what is right in my eyes and [to] have done to the house of Ahab all I had in mind to do" (vv. 28,30). Jesus taught that even corrupt public officials reciprocate love of some sort (see Matt. 5:46) and that evident sinners "do good to those who are good to [them]" (Luke 6:33). The inhabitants of Malta, though pagan (see Acts 28:4), showed Paul and those traveling with him "unusual kindness" (v. 2) and at their departure generously furnished needed supplies (see v. 10).

In view of our undeniable experience and this biblical evidence, then, is it not clear that the doctrine of total depravity exaggerates and distorts human sinfulness? Is not its portrayal of human nature entirely too grim and pessimistic, as its opponents have never tired of insisting? As some even urge, must we not resist this doctrine and its implications for the sake of nothing less than our humanity itself, to preserve what is truly human in human nature? Must we not, after all, maintain that all human beings are made in God's image and so there still remains in them, despite their sin (in some instances, certainly, of the coarsest or most horrifying kind), a remnant of goodness, some smoldering spark of desire for what is right and true that often finds expression?

To conclude that we can continue confessing total depravity only at the expense of our perception of reality and of our own humanity creates a false dilemma. After all, Scripture affirms both—radical human corruption in the face of the full reality of human existence. Paul, for one, does so within the span of a single argument (see Rom. 1:18-3:20). He says of the (on the still most likely exegesis, pagan or unbelieving) Gentiles that they "do by nature things required by the law" and "show that the requirements of the law are written on their hearts" (2:14-15); yet he goes on to include them in his unsparing universal indictment: "There is no one righteous, not even one; . . . there is no one that does good, not even one" (3:10-12). Essentially, Paul argues that within the totality of sinful humanity there are some who in a sense do what the law requires, yet, ultimately, they do not do good, nor can they please God (see Rom. 8:8). It will simply not suffice, biblically, to shade human sinfulness by entertaining the notion of a somehow uncorrupted remnant. Rather, the question is how to account for undeniable gradations and variations within the bounds of total depravity.

The answer, according to the Bible, lies not in us but in God—in His kindness, His graciousness, His patience. From one angle the entire message of the Bible from Genesis 3 on is a message of postponed judgment. The full measure of eschatological death and destruction that the sin of our first parents deserves is delayed. In banishing them from His fellowship-presence in the garden, God does so in hope, with a promise (see Gen. 3:15)—a promise that shows His purpose to have a people ("seed") for Himself, that is, to save them from the destruction their sin deserves and eventually to bring the entire creation to a state of consummate blessing and perfection, the "new heavens and a new earth" (cf. Rom. 8:20-21, a Pauline commentary, in effect, on Gen. 3; Isa. 65:17ff.; Rev. 21-22).

Consequently, this promise also entails the delay of the "everlasting destruction" of the unrepentant and disobedient "from the presence of the Lord," a delay that continues until His second coming (2 Thess. 1:9-10). God's covenant rainbow-promise to preserve "all life on the earth" made to Noah and his sons after the Flood—itself a grim pointer to eschatological judgment (see 2 Pet. 3:3-7)—confirms this delay (see Gen. 9:8-17; cf. 8:21-22). In effect, God's promise of delayed judgment is a promise that the human race will have a history; the delay period as a whole is human history in its fullness, unfolding toward its God-ordained consummation.

Ultimately, history (the delay) is for the sake and in the interests of eschatological salvation for the Church and the correlative renewal of the cosmos. But the continuation of history also entails postponement of deserved eschatological destruction for those who persist in unbelief. As such, we shall presently see more clearly, it embodies God's favor toward them—not merely negatively as a reprieve period but positively, in a full range of gifts and benefits. Inseparably intertwined and yet distinct from God's special—electing and saving—grace in Christ is His general, nonsaving kindness and forbearance toward every creature, a common grace that embraces the entire creation.

Biblical evidence for common grace is of two sorts—negative and positive. The essence of common grace is divine restraint. The delay of eschatological wrath and judgment, already noted, shows "the riches of [God's] kindness, tolerance and patience" (Rom. 2:4-5; cf. 2 Pet. 3:9). But that delay is bound up with a larger, overall restraint on sin itself and its consequences. God restrains not only His holy wrath but also the unholy disposition of the human heart. Sin is a positive, specific evil—not merely privation or limitation. It is lawlessness, rebellion against God and, as such, is inevitably ruinous and chaos-producing; its inherent tendency, left unchecked, is to destroy everything, including the sinner himself.

God's restraint on sin and its hellish consequences appears already at the time of the Fall. The exclusion of Adam and Eve from the garden—itself a punishment—seems also to have been intended to keep them from the gross, perhaps even eschatological sacrilege of eating from the tree of life (see Gen. 3:21-22). Clear examples are the protective mark put on Cain (see Gen. 4:15) and the explicit declarations of divine restraint present in the cases of Abimelech (see Gen. 20:6) and, later, Sennacharib, king of Assyria (see 2 Kings 19:27-28). Again, God spares some from the extremes of degrading depravity to which He "gives over" others (see Rom. 1:24,26,28), extremes to which, without exception, all are disposed.

The curse on Adam and Eve (see Gen. 3:16-19) compounds the futility, decay, and death permeating the entire creation because of sin (see Rom. 8:20-21). The environment becomes dangerous; predatory animals become a threat to human life; "natural disasters" are a reality. Yet, at the same time, the curse is pronounced in a way that moderates those perils and preserves from their unmitigated consequences. Though Adam's labor becomes frustrating toil, it remains productive; there will be genuine agri-"culture" (cf. Gen 3:23). Though childbearing becomes agonizing and painful, Eve is "the mother of all the living" (Gen. 3:20). All told, "Restraint upon sin and its consequences is one of the most outstanding features of God's government of this world—the history of this present world exists within an administration that is one of restraint and forbearance."[1]

There is also a positive side to this restraint and prevention. In His forbearance, God is also genuinely good toward all. His kindness to every creature involves a full range of gifts and benefits. The entire creation, animate and inanimate, is the constant recipient of untold blessing; a number of the psalms, especially, extol this universal generosity (e.g., 65:5-13; 104:13-24; 145:9,15-16). The whole of humanity, unbelievers as well as believers, enjoys God's bounty and favor. "All nations," including themselves, Paul tells his thoroughly pagan audience at Lystra, have this testimony from God, that "he has shown kindness by giving you rain from heaven and crops in their seasons; he provides you with plenty of food and fills your hearts with joy" (Acts 14:16-17). The seasonal ordering of crops, God's faithful maintenance of the food-producing capacity of the earth—despite the ravages of famine and drought—is a constant witness to God's goodness, a granting of "creature comforts" calculated to produce joyful contentment. Similarly, Jesus speaks of God's benevolence that is (as His disciples' love is to be) without limits, "He causes his sun to rise on the evil and the good, and sends rain on the righteous and the unrighteous" (Matt. 5:45); "He is kind to the ungrateful and wicked" (Luke 6:35).

Within this framework of God's general benevolence, His common grace, belong those phenomena of our experience confirmed in Scripture already noted: the frequent interest of unbelievers in what is right and good, their devotion to expanding the frontiers of knowledge, to developing the arts and sciences in a constructive and worthwhile fashion, to advancing society and promoting the well-being of the human race. In His common grace, God not only bestows good on sinful human beings; He also produces good through them.

Clearly, this aspect of common grace has a direct bearing on economics as a whole and business ethics in particular. Several ramifications are worth further reflection.

(1) We are faced here with what has been called the paradox of common grace, a paradox taught in Scripture itself. In the course of the same argument as we have seen, Paul seems to assert that the unbeliever can do good and cannot do good. No doubt, we encounter here the ultimately impenetrable mystery of the Creator-creature relationship, God's incomprehensible dealings with the creature made in His own image. But the apparent contradiction involved is reduced, though not entirely removed, with the help of a biblically based distinction. That, by the way, is not the distinction between natural good and religious good, the unbeliever presumably being capable of the former but not the latter. Such a distinction, in whatever form, is unbiblical; its tendency—inevitable, so the history of the Church in the West would seem to teach—is to domesticate religion, to make the worship and service of God increasingly unimportant, peripheral, even irrelevant and so, among other things, to deny total depravity.

Rather, the biblical distinction instructive here is that between conformity and obedience. What God incites in and elicits from unbelievers is a certain conformity but not genuine obedience to Himself and His will. Ultimately, this conformity to His law, though beneficial to themselves and others, is such that it does not please God but is compatible with hostility toward Him (see Rom. 8:7-8). Yet to neglect it would be "more sinful and displeasing."[2]

This conformity is not merely "external." Common grace is not, at least usually, an outward, mechanical-like constraint; it does not force the unbeliever to do something unwillingly. There is an inward dynamism to common grace; it is a positive restraint that enlists the person—the will, desires, emotions as well as intellect. And it is genuine mercy; it restrains and ameliorates sin and its effects in unbelievers and so makes them a means of blessing and good to themselves and others.

But—and this is critical—common grace, no matter how positive its effects, is *restraint*, not renewal. It is not a matter of the heart; it does not restore unbelievers at the core, in the integrity of their persons. It does not destroy the disposition of the "flesh"; nor does it create the mind-set of the Spirit, that renewing of the mind, that living sacrifice of praise without which God cannot be acceptably worshiped and served (see Rom. 8:6; 12:1-2). Its movement to good, in other words, is not a removal of total depravity. Only one "restraint" can accomplish that, only one limiting factor on our radical corruption—the saving, regenerating grace of God in Christ.

(2) In a real sense "common" grace is a misnomer; it is anything but indiscriminate. God's gracious restraint differentiates. It, not some self-determining capacity in ourselves, explains the wide, varied spectrum of attitudes and behavior in sinful humanity—virtue here and vice there, the conscientious law-conformity of some and the vicious unscrupulousness of others, why one is "given over" (see Rom. 1:24,26,28) to gross sinning to suffer its degrading consequences, while another is spared and enjoys a prosperous, happy life. In a real sense, in comparison with others, some unbelievers ought to acknowledge, "There, but for the grace of God, go I."

God's restraining and preserving grace is hardly predictable; it sustains anything but a static relationship to sinful human existence. It sovereignly cuts across all sorts of motives and many different lifestyles, and no one is in a position to bring all the factors involved under one denominator.

(3) Common grace also explains the "grayness"—the disconcerting and sobering ambiguity—that frequently results from comparing believers and unbelievers. As it has been put, too often the world exceeds, and the Church fails to meet, expectations; unbelievers, we must admit, sometimes put believers to shame. Seldom in life do we encounter an antithesis between full-blown

wickedness and undeviating holiness. Similarly, unrenewed human existence can display unmistakable parallels with the sanctified living of Christians; there can be a striking likeness between actions of unbelievers and the good works of believers.

(4) It bears repeating that the variations and ambiguity noted in (2) and (3) do not point to limitations on human depravity; they are not based on presumably uncorrupted remnants in unbelievers. The remnant notion is perhaps applicable but only in terms of the constant activity of God's restraining grace. The unchecked tendency of sin is to self-destruction, to efface the divine image in which we are made. So, to the extent that the functions and capacities constitutive of that image are preserved, we may speak of remnants of God's image in our fallen nature.

But—and this once more is the point—the existence of these remnants does not alleviate our depravity. To the contrary, human sinfulness finds its expression just in terms of these remnants. Sin has not destroyed God's image but has redirected its capacities totally, from the heart, in total hostility toward God; those gifts from God, incomparable in the entire creation because functions of His image, have been turned against Him. Sin has not annihilated our humanity; *man*—male and female—is a sinner. That is the appalling awfulness, the desperate culpability of our sin.

(5) Among the remnants mercifully preserved by God are the capacity to reason, volition, and the power of discrimination. One other factor, usually overlooked, deserves attention because it is especially pertinent to our topic: our sense of community, of common humanity.[3] God's restraining gifts are not only individual but corporate. The social side of sin's self-destructive tendency is alienation and eventual isolation from others; self-murder/hatred involves the murder/hatred of others.

God preserves humanity from destructive and chaotic self-isolation; He maintains in sinners, through a complex web of relationships, a need and desire to be with others, a concern, at various levels, to preserve community. But neither is this corporate, social dimension of the divine image to be thought of as an uncorrupted remnant; it is not "like the Sphinx in the desert sands of Egypt."[4] Racism and ever-present varieties of (covert or open) national aggression make it all too evident that there is solidarity in sinning ("They not only continue to do these things [that deserve death] but also approve of those who practice them" [Rom. 1:32]).

(6) What can/does the unbeliever know? The answer to this much-mooted question, also relevant to our topic, eludes easy formulation. In view of earlier discussion, we can be brief here. Scripture recognizes that unbelievers have knowledge and sees that as a gift from God (e.g., Isa. 28:26); technology

apparently begins (see Gen. 4:17, 20-22) and has certainly continued to develop impressively in the line of unbelief.

However, Jesus and Paul are emphatic that unbelievers understand nothing truly (see Matt. 11; Luke 10; 1 Cor. 1-2). They "suppress the truth by their wickedness" (Rom. 1:18). As the religious center of all human knowledge more and more comes into view, it becomes increasingly apparent that their knowledge is "ignorance" (Eph. 4:18); the most that can be said is that theirs is "futile" thinking and "darkened" understanding (Rom. 1:21; Eph. 4:18). The knowledge of unbelief, at best and in its undeniably impressive manifestations, is fragmented and ambiguous; its integrity is illusory.

Unbelievers, to use Calvin's evocative analogy, are like travelers at night after a momentary lightning flash;[5] for an instant the terrain around them has been illumined far and wide, but before they can take even a step, they are plunged back into darkness and left groping about aimlessly. To vary the figure, unbelievers are frozen perpetually in the split second after the firing of a flash attachment in a dark room—having a blurred and fading, still indelible impression of everything just illumined and yet now no longer seeing anything, knowing and yet not knowing.

BUSINESS ETHICS

The conclusions reached so far may be summed up in two controlling perspectives on business and economic life.

(1) Balance needs to be maintained between common grace and total depravity as two correlative, mutually qualifying poles; to ignore either or emphasize one without the other results in distortions.

(2) Until Christ's return for Final Judgment, we can count on the maintenance of at least some measure of economic stability, the continuation of available resources and structures for production, distribution, and exchange that ensure throughout the world—despite catastrophes, periodic disruptions, and ever-present, often widespread pockets of poverty—conditions of economic viability and, on occasion, well-being and even prosperity.

But for all that we rely on God, not man—not on presumed remnants of good will or common sense or conscience, or "enlightened" self-interest, or the social impulse in human nature, or even our instinct for survival, but on God's covenanted fidelity to sinful humanity and the creation (e.g., Gen. 8:21-22; 9:8-17; Acts 14:17). Left to themselves, sinners can reckon only on economic chaos and disaster, but thanks to God's preserving, restraining mercy, there will be a minimum at least, sometimes more, of economic order. Ultimately, this order eludes our calculation and control; under the ubiquitous pressure of human corruption, it constantly threatens to disintegrate.

These two general perspectives can be amplified by brief answers to several questions that could be posed.

(1) What can be derived for business ethics from general (natural) revelation? Strictly speaking, the answer is nothing. Taken by itself, general revelation will never provide the basis for a stable natural theology-ethics. Romans 1:18-25 makes that point. The world around us is plain enough; it clearly evidences God's eternal power (see v. 20). The world in its entirety is His creation—it depends on Him and exists for Him. The problem, however, is that all unbelievers are such truth suppressors (see v. 18); the most to be said for their comprehension of the environment is that ultimately it is "futile" and "darkened" (see v. 21). Apart from the acceptance, in faith, of God's special saving revelation in Christ and His inscripturated Word, a true and reliable understanding of general revelation is permanently excluded. Nor can there be a genuine ethics, business or otherwise, that is not living, in Christ, *coram Deo*.

Of course, various codes of business conduct are based on the (more or less strong) conviction that self-interest and the interest of others, at whatever level (individual, regional, national, international), need not conflict but ought to serve each other economically. Where such ethical codes function, they will, apart from the adverse effect of other factors, no doubt produce economic benefits, for a shorter or longer time and to a greater or lesser extent. But that will happen, despite human depravity, by God's common grace. And under the impact of that depravity, even these codes of conduct (and the theorizing supporting them) will constantly tend to be implemented in ways that result in economic injustice and exploitation.

(2) Is business conduct based on biblical revelation ethically superior to that based on general revelation? Here, in addition to the answer to the previous question, the comprehensive epistemological-ethical antithesis between belief and unbelief of 1 Corinthians 1-2 and Matthew 11:25-27/Luke 10:21-22 comes into play.

For unbelievers, special revelation functions much as does general revelation. As revelation from the true and living God, it is suppressed and rejected as foolishness. Nonetheless, when the "wisdom" of the world, in effect, takes over biblical principles (e.g., the Eighth, Ninth, and Tenth Commandments or aspects of the Sermon on the Mount) as unacknowledged "borrowed capital" (C. Van Til), that is likely to have more beneficial economic consequences than if those principles are neglected. But such *de facto* conformity to God's law is not true obedience; to think of it as somehow ethically superior is risky at best.

For believers, the problem with an ethics supposedly based on general revelation alone is not merely that it is inferior; it is an unbiblical abstraction, having no more promise than the efforts of unbelievers. The Christian has experienced the only limit there is to human depravity—God's resurrecting, regenerating grace in Christ, the renewing presence of the Holy Spirit. The only legitimate access to general revelation is, by faith, in the light of biblical revelation. The Scriptures are the indispensable "spectacles"[6] for rightly examining and perceiving the world about us, essential, among other things, for formulating sound business ethics.

Expanding on this last sentence would take us beyond the scope of this chapter. But perhaps one observation may be permitted here that is especially pertinent where human depravity and the curse on sin continue. Writing to the Church in the shortened time between the resurrection and the return of Christ, Paul exhorts his readers, "Those who buy something [should do so], as if it were not theirs to keep; those who use the things of the world, as if not engrossed in them" (1 Cor. 7:29-31). Paradoxical as it might at first seem, just where this eschatological "as if not" controls the economic life of Christians, they will prove useful as economic guides, both in theory and practice, for "this world in its present form" that is "passing away" (1 Cor. 7:31).

(3) Does capitalism cater to human depravity? Any economic system, including capitalism, is subject to exploitation by the deceit and perversity of the human heart; no system is immune to or a protection against that corruption. There ought to be no doubt about this reality, even on the assumption that private ownership and a free market economy are compatible with or even demanded by biblical principles. Individual or corporate possession of the means of production and distribution, geared to the acquisition of profit, carries an almost irresistible temptation to all sorts of economic manipulation and intimidation—sometimes blatant but often refined, veiled even to the perpetrators themselves.

It is not simply as an afterthought that the Bible warns against "love of money" (1 Tim. 6:10; cf. 3:3; 2 Tim. 3:2) and "dishonest gain" (1 Tim. 3:8; 1 Pet. 5:2), especially in those who would be leaders in the Church. It also teaches that the desire to be rich usually coexists with other vices in a snarled web working harm for others and one's own destruction (e.g., Eccles. 5:8ff.; 1 Tim. 6:9-10).

However else it is evaluated, capitalism abets the perverse inclination to secure ourselves rather than serve others. Like any other economic system, it will remain an instrument of misery and confusion until it functions under the transforming power of the Holy Spirit in that three-stage program of economic renewal announced, for instance, in Ephesians 4:28: "[1] He who has been stealing must steal no longer, [2] but must work, doing something useful with his own hands, [3] that he may have something to share with those in need."

To close this chapter on a somber but appropriate note, we are bound to acknowledge the inescapable, simply devastating biblical basis for the position taken at Summit III of the International Council on Biblical Inerrancy in Article XIII of *The Chicago Statement on Biblical Application*: "We affirm that human depravity, greed, and the will to power foster economic injustice and subvert concern for the poor."

EDITOR'S REFLECTIONS

Dr. Gaffin clearly sees people falling into one of two categories: the redeemed who are alive to God, and the unregenerate who are alienated from God. There is no third group. The regenerate children of God receive His moral law, which the Holy Spirit uses to do a loving work of renovation in them. The unregenerate, on the other hand, are self-serving and on an ultimate path of self-destruction, regardless of their outward behavior.

The outward behavior of the unregenerate may be borrowed from God's moral law if they perceive it will benefit them, or they may behave from prudential motives related to the culture's laws and customs. All their behavior, though, is self-serving. Even any declared allegiance to God would be feigned (see Ps. 66:3; 81:15). They may even be outwardly conformed to the moral law, but they could not be lovingly obedient to God from the heart because the unregenerate heart would still be dead to God and alive to self.

Richard Gaffin understands the unregenerate to be totally depraved and unable to have a true, God-oriented motive. Furthermore, he believes their behavior could only be a positive force in the marketplace as a result of God's common grace, and not because of any inherent good in them. Therefore, appeals to nonChristians in the marketplace on the grounds of either the scriptural law or the natural law could only be interpreted by them through a self-serving filter, which may or may not elicit good behavior.

Dr. Norman Geisler has a different perception of the problem Christians face when communicating with nonChristians about ethical issues. He does not believe that Christians, in the general everyday hustle and bustle of the marketplace, should make moral appeals to nonChristians on the grounds of God's special revelation. The only common ground available to everyone is the natural law, which Paul refers to in Romans 1:18-32, 2:12-14. In fact, Dr. Geisler sees both the context and the order of this well-known passage pointing to the important fact that nonChristians are capable of cognitively recognizing the truth of God in and through natural revelation. It is only after such cognitive recognition that there is a volitional act of suppression, which turns the truth to a self-serving interpretation (albeit destructive in the final analysis) that reveals their ultimate moral failure.

Dr. Geisler concludes that it is precisely through appealing to the natural law that Christians should approach others in the marketplace. He does not, however, argue that such an appeal will necessarily cause others to do what is socially and economically in the best interest of everyone. Nor does he imply or believe that nonbelievers are somehow less in need of God's grace because they might choose to do things that are mutually beneficial to them and society rather than harmful to either party in an economic transaction. He does believe that Christians are free to and would be wise to learn how to incorporate appeals to the self-evident moral truths of the natural order.

CHAPTER 9

NATURAL LAW AND BUSINESS ETHICS

Norman L. Geisler

Dr. Norman Geisler is a Professor at Dallas Theological Seminary. He earned his B.A. and M.A. at Wheaton College, his Th.B. from William Tyndale College, and his Ph.D. (in Philosophy) from Loyola University, Chicago. He has taught philosophy, ethics, and theology at William Tyndale College (1959-1966), Trinity College and Evangelical Divinity School (1966-1979), and Dallas Theological Seminary (1979 to the present). He is the author of over twenty-five books, including The Christian Ethic of Love, Options in Contemporary Evangelical Ethics, *and the forthcoming book,* Christian Ethics: Options and Issues.

I f the Bible is sufficient for believers in matters of faith and practice, then what need is there for natural law? In brief, because not everyone accepts the Bible, but no one can avoid natural law, which is "written on [the] hearts" of all men (Rom. 2:14-15). Only believers accept the Bible. But business must be done with unbelievers. Therefore, it is necessary for us to have some common ethical ground on which to engage in commercial transactions with them.

All business presupposes an ethical standard on which it is conducted. But whose ethical system should be used? In a pluralistic culture we cannot expect Muslims to accept the Bible as a basis for doing business with Christians. We cannot expect Christians to accept the Koran as the grounds for engaging in business with Muslims. And, of course, secular humanists will not accept either book. Whose ethical standard, then, shall we use?

We must utilize some moral standard, but no one religious group will accept the divine (scriptural) law of the other. Unless there is a moral law common to all men, regardless of their differing religious authorities, there will be no ethical basis on which to conduct business with nonChristians.

I. THE NATURE OF NATURAL LAW

God has two revelations: one in His world and the other in His Word. The former is called general revelation and the latter special revelation. Divine law is a special revelation to believers. Natural law is a general revelation to all persons.

A. Definition of natural law—Natural law is described in the Bible as that which human beings "do by nature"; it is the law written on the hearts of all men (see Rom. 2:14). Those who disobey it go contrary to nature (see Rom. 1:27). The natural law condemns such things as "wickedness, evil, greed and depravity." The actions opposed to it are "envy, murder, strife, deceit and malice." Those who oppose it are called "gossips, slanderers, God-haters, insolent, arrogant and boastful." They "disobey their parents; they are senseless, faithless, heartless, [and] ruthless" (Rom. 1:29-31). According to Paul, all of these actions are contrary to natural law.

B. History of natural law—Belief in natural law did not begin with Christians. It is found in ancient Hindu, Chinese, and Greek writings. Even before Socrates, the Greek philosopher Heraclitus believed in an unchanging Logos (Reason) behind the changing flux of human experience.[1] Plato held to moral absolutes.[2] The Stoics developed natural law theories well before the time of Christ.[3]

   1. St. Augustine on natural law—The concept of natural law has a venerable history among great Christian thinkers. Like others before him, St. Augustine believed that God gave the Gentiles "the law of nature."[4] He referred to it as "the system of nature."[5] This law is "implanted by nature" in all men.[6] Natural law is reflected in the image of God in man. To be sure, Augustine believed this image was marred by sin, but he insisted that "the image of God is not wholly blotted out in these unbelievers."[7] Thus, Augustine held that God was just in punishing unbelievers for not living in accordance with this "law written on their hearts."[8]

   2. Thomas Aquinas on natural law—Following Augustine's view on natural law, Thomas Aquinas declared that "natural law is nothing else than the rational creature's participation in eternal law."[9] Law is "an ordinance of reason made for the common good."[10] It is the "rule and measure of acts."[11] Eternal law is the divine reason by which God governs the universe;[12] natural law is simply the human participation in this eternal law. It is the first principle governing human action, as the laws of logic are the first principles governing human thought.

Aquinas distinguishes natural law, which is common to all rational creatures, and divine law, which is imposed only on believers. Natural law is directed toward man's temporal good; divine law is aimed toward his eternal good.[13] Divine law is for the Church; natural law is for society as a whole. The basis for human law is natural law. Since business is conducted in the context of civil laws, it is subject to both human laws and natural law on which they are based.

3. John Calvin on natural law—Just like Augustine and Aquinas before him, John Calvin believed that natural law is ingrained by God in the hearts of all men: "That there exists in the human mind, and indeed by natural instinct, some sense of Deity, we hold to be beyond dispute." He contended that "there is no nation so barbarous, no race so brutish, as not to be imbued with the conviction that there is a God."[14] This "sense of Deity is so naturally engraven on the human heart, in fact, that the very reprobate are forced to acknowledge it."[15]

This innate knowledge of God includes a knowledge of His righteous law.[16] Calvin held that since "the Gentiles have the righteousness of the law naturally engraved on their minds, [so] we certainly cannot say that they are altogether blind as to the rule of life."[17] He calls this moral awareness "natural law," which is "sufficient for their righteous condemnation"[18] but not for salvation. By means of this natural law, "the judgment of conscience" is able to distinguish between "the just and the unjust."[19] God's righteous nature "is engraved in characters so bright, so distinct, and so illustrious, that none, however dull and illiterate, can plead ignorance as their excuse."[20]

Not only is the "natural law" clear; it is also specific. It includes a sense of justice "implanted by nature in the hearts of men."[21] There "is imprinted on their hearts a discrimination and judgment, by which they distinguish between justice and injustice, honesty and dishonesty." According to Calvin, it is what makes them "ashamed of adultery and theft."[22] The natural law even governs "good faith in commercial transactions and contracts."[23] Even the heathen "prove their knowledge . . . that adultery, theft, and murder are evils, and honesty is to be esteemed."[24] Calvin summarizes man's "natural knowledge of the law [as] that which states that one action is good and worthy of being followed, while another is to be shunned with horror."[25]

4. Thomas Jefferson on natural law—The roots of early American natural law views derive from John Locke. He believed that the "laws of Nature" teach us that "being all equal and independent, no one ought to harm another in his life, health, liberty or possessions; for men being all the workmanship of one omnipotent and infinitely wise Maker."[26] This same view was expressed by Thomas Jefferson in the Declaration of Independence (1776) when he wrote, "We hold these truths to be self-evident, that all men are created equal, that they

are endowed by their Creator with certain unalienable Rights, that among these are Life, Liberty, and the pursuit of Happiness."

Jefferson believed that these unalienable rights are rooted in the "Laws of Nature," which derive from "Nature's God." On the Jefferson Memorial in Washington, D.C., are inscribed these words he wrote: "God who gave us life gave us liberty. Can the liberties of a nation be secure when we have removed a conviction that these liberties are the gift of God?" Here again it is clear that Jefferson's America was based on the concept of God-given rights grounded in God-given moral rules called "Nature's Laws." So for Jefferson, too, natural law was not a descriptive "is" but a divinely prescriptive "ought."

II. THE NEED FOR NATURAL LAW

In their zeal to advertise their commitment to God's infallible and inerrant revelation in Scripture, some evangelical Christians overstate their case. In so doing, they diminish or negate the need for natural law. John W. Montgomery, for example, recently declared that natural laws are, at best, formal, ambiguous, devoid of substantial content, and incapable of independent justification apart from that of Scripture.[27] But if this is the case, God is guilty of sending unbelievers to their eternal doom for not living in accord with purely formal, ambiguous, and vacuous natural revelation (see Rom. 1:20; 2:12). If there is no natural law, God is unjust.

A. The need for natural law in general—There are many strong arguments in favor of natural law. Several of these will be briefly stated here. First and foremost is the argument from God's justice.

1. The argument from divine justice—Paul's argument in Romans 1-2 indicates that he believed the justice of God in condemning the unbelieving Gentiles was based on the fact that God had clearly (see Rom. 1:19) revealed Himself through nature to all men and that His law was "written in their hearts" (Rom. 2:14). It certainly would be contradictory to divine justice to condemn people to eternal separation from God for not living according to a standard they never had and never knew. So, the fact of natural law is absolutely indispensable to the belief in divine justice.

2. The argument from social need—Furthermore, society cannot function without some kind of common moral code that binds people together in a social unit. Every society has a moral cohesive. If it did not, it would not be a society; it would self-destruct. But not every society accepts a divine law, such as the Bible or the Koran. Therefore, some kind of naturally available moral code is required to bind people together.

All the great cultures of the past and present manifest a common moral law. C. S. Lewis collected quotations from these cultures and correlated them under various headings (listed later). Vastly different and separate societies not only need such a moral cohesive but also have expressed them in their writings. This is ample testimony to the universal social need for some natural moral principles by which their conduct can be governed.

To argue that there is no adequate moral basis for society apart from special revelation runs contrary to the moral writings of the great cultures of the past. That is tantamount to saying that these great civilizations have not expressed moral character. And such a blatantly false statement is contrary to the biblical teaching on common grace and general revelation.

3. The argument from international law—Hugo Grotius saw clearly the need for a natural law basis for international affairs. He viewed it as a rational "method for arriving at a body of propositions underlying political arrangements and the provision of the positive [civil] laws."[28] Grotius's definition was "what [ever] God makes known as His will is law."[29] Nonetheless, in opposition to the ethical voluntarist (like Scotus), he believed that "God does not will a thing because it is lawful, but a thing is lawful—that is obligatory—because God willed it."[30]

However, Grotius was so convinced that natural law stood on its own two feet that he declared, "What we have been saying regarding the priority of natural law would have a degree of validity even if we should concede . . . that there is no God, or that the affairs of men are of no concern to Him."[31] The point is that, even apart from belief in God, natural law is necessary for ruling human societies. For his pioneer work in this area, Grotius earned the title "the Father of International Law."

As human technology developed, the need for a natural law basis for international affairs became even more apparent. The Nuremberg War Crimes Trials after the Second World War are a classic case in point. Hitler engaged in barbarous, inhumane, and cruel actions by masterminding the murder of six million Jews and another six million from "undesired" groups. Emerging from this holocaust was the collective recognition of a moral standard that transcended individual cultures and countries. For if Hitler's actions are judged from within the Nazi state, they are not immoral crimes but moral causes. Only if there is some natural law transcending given cultures and binding on all men can we justify calling the Nazis barbarous, inhumane, and cruel.

Further, efforts to redress the Hitler horrors led to the "human rights" movement. The United Nations drafted a "Universal Declaration of Human Rights." A.H. Robertson, spokesman for the European Convention on Human Rights, wrote,

> The perversion of democracy and the maintenance of the rule of law necessitated foundations . . . on which to base the defense of human personality against all tyrannies and against all forms of totalitarianism. Those foundations were effective protection of the rights of man and fundamental freedoms.[32]

The very concept of fundamental rights as humans, transcending all states, demands a moral law that is above and beyond all particular governments and religions. So the desire for a transnational moral code is a will-o'-the-wisp unless a natural law transcends all governments.

B. The need for natural law in business ethics— Business is conducted within pluralistic societies and among a multiplicity of nations. Within these social groups are various religious groups, and each has its own religious authority, whether the Torah, the Bible, the Koran, the Gita, or the Analects. Since no one group accepts the religious authority of the other groups, there is no way that any single religious book will, by common consent, become the authority for doing business with other countries. Thus, there is a pressing need for some moral standard on which the various religious groups can conduct mutual business.

Business cannot be conducted in a moral vacuum. Commerce depends on common ethical commitments. Parties doing business must assume general moral principles, such as honesty and good faith. They must assume promises will be kept and contracts honored. But since no one of the various religious authorities is acceptable to all the participants in the international community, the only recourse is some kind of moral law common to all men. This is precisely where natural law becomes necessary for business. But is there a natural law common to all men? Where is it found? How is it recognized?

III. SOME MANIFESTATIONS OF NATURAL LAW

One of the most commonly heard objections to natural law, as opposed to moral laws revealed in the Bible, is that natural law is not clear. Opponents claim that there is no place one can read these natural laws. It is vague, if not vacuous. Natural law can be easily distorted by depraved minds.[33] On the other hand, they insist that the Bible is clear and contentful. Let us briefly consider these objections.

A. Some objections to natural law—Before we discuss the role of natural law in business ethics, several objections to it need to be addressed. Some object to natural law, in favor of divine law in the Bible. However, there are serious problems with this position.

1. Which "Bible"?—Individuals who insist that the Bible should be accepted by governments as the basis for their society and business activity forget several important things. First of all, whose "Bible" is to be chosen as the basis for civil law? Each religious group has its own religious book, and each claims its book as *the Book*. There is no practical way to adjudicate this problem without offending the religious beliefs of all who are forced to live according to the religious tenets of an opposing religion.

Furthermore, even among those who accept the Christian Scriptures, there are vastly different ways of interpreting them. So the problem is compounded. Which interpretation of whose "Bible" do we follow? Conservative Christians who accept a "literal" historical-grammatical interpretation of the Christian Bible cannot agree on which of its moral statements still apply to us today. For example, are we still under the moral law given by Moses? Theonomists say, "Yes," and dispensationalists say, "No." Theonomists claim that we should still stone homosexuals, rebellious children, and adulterers.[34] Nontheonomists recoil at the very suggestion of such theocratic legalism. Theonomists engage in heated debates over whether Old Testament laws such as those against wearing garments with mixed fiber still apply today (see Deut. 22:11). (Think of what applying this law would do for Christians in the clothing industry!) The simple appeal to special revelation does not solve the problem of finding understandable and applicable moral rules for today's business decisions.

2. Is natural revelation unclear?—In their evangelical zeal to exalt God's special revelation in the Bible, some have overstated their case. Just because the Bible is superior in content to natural revelation does not mean that natural revelation is inadequate for its God-given task. True, sin impairs man's ability to apply natural revelation to his life. But the defect is not in the revelation but in man's refusal to accept it. According to Romans 1, natural revelation "is plain to them, because God has made it plain to them" (v. 19). The problem is that "the man without the Spirit does not accept the things that come from the Spirit of God" (1 Cor. 2:14). The revelation is *perceived* but not received.[35]

3. Is natural revelation distorted?—God has clearly revealed Himself in nature and in the conscience. So the problem with unbelievers is that they shun the truth natural revelation discloses to them (see Rom. 1:18). Rejecting the truth is not unique to unbelievers with God's general revelation. Believers do not always live according to the truth of God's special revelation, either.

To claim that general revelation is inadequate because unbelievers have distorted it is to reject special revelation for the same reason. Peter, for example, tells us that "people distort [Paul's writings], as they do the other Scriptures, to their own destruction" (2 Pet. 3:15-16). Everything God has revealed in Scripture has been subjected to similar distortions as those moral truths He has revealed to all men in His natural law. There is no defect with either of God's revelations. The problem is not with God's revelation but with man's rejection of it. The difficulty is not with God's disclosure but with man's distortion of it.

The existence of hundreds of religious sects and cults, all claiming that the Bible is their revelation, is ample testimony to the fact that even the teachings of supernatural revelation in Scripture are not immune to distortion. In fact, the distortions of the teachings of the natural law among various human cultures is no greater than the distortions of the teachings of supernatural revelation among the various cults. Careful examination of both areas indicates that in spite of the clarity of both revelations, depraved human beings have found a way to deflect, divert, or distort God's commands. So the teachings of the Bible have no edge on natural revelation in the matter of immunity from distortion.

4. Is natural revelation identifiable?—For many, the Bible has an advantage over natural law in moral matters in that the Scriptures have a specifiable content. We know where to go to get a Bible, and we can read what it says. But where does one go to read natural law? The biblical answer to this question is twofold: it is "written on [the] hearts" of all men, and it can be seen in what they "do by nature" (Rom. 2:14-15). The first manifestation is the inner side of the natural law, and the second, the outer side. Let us consider the areas in which natural law is revealed.

(a) Natural law impressed inwardly on the heart—What is written on perishable paper can be erased, but what is written on the heart of an imperishable person is not completely erasable. Virtually all theologians agree, no matter how Calvinistic they are, that the image of God is not completely destroyed in fallen man; it was effaced but not erased. As we have demonstrated, this was true of Augustine and Calvin. And it is also true of Luther.[36]

The Bible is very clear that even fallen men bear God's image. For example, the prohibition against murder is based on the fact that all men, even in their sinful condition, are still in the image of God. Moses wrote, "Whoever sheds the blood of man, by man shall his blood be shed; for in the image of God has God made man" (Gen. 9:6). Likewise, James says not to curse other humans because they "have been made in God's likeness" (James 3:9). If it is morally wrong to kill or curse human beings because the image of God includes some moral likeness to God, then we can understand something of God's moral nature by looking at our own nature made in His image.

The natural law is written in the most readily available place for people— in the heart. It is also written in a way everyone can read—intuitively. No lessons in language are necessary, and no books are needed. Natural law can be seen "instinctively" (Rom. 2:14, NASB). It is known by inclination even before it is known by cognition. We know what is right and wrong by our natural intuitions. Our very nature predisposes us in that direction. Being selfish creatures, we do not always desire to do what is right, but we do nonetheless desire that it be done to us. This is why Jesus summarized the moral law by declaring, "In everything, do to others what you would have them do to you" (Matt. 7:12). Confucius recognized the same truth by general revelation when he said, "Never do to others what you would not like them to do to you."[37]

The natural law is not hard to understand; it is hard to practice. We know what we want others to do to us even if we do not always want to do the same to them. The natural law, then, can be seen better in human reactions than in actions. That is, one's real moral beliefs are manifest not so much in what he does but in what he wants done to him. Some may cheat, but no businesspersons want to be cheated. Others may be dishonest in their dealings, but none of them like to be lied to in any of their deals.

(b) Natural law as expressed in reactions—Our actions are often contrary to our moral inclinations. That explains why our best understanding of the natural law comes not from seeing our actions but from observing our reactions. This is true because we know the moral law instinctively. We do not have to read it in any books; we know it intuitively since it is written on our own hearts. So when we read the natural law, we must be careful to read it from actions truly indicative of it. These are not necessarily the ones we do to others, but those that we desire to be done to us. Paul speaks to this point when he writes of the things we "do by nature" that "show" the moral law "written on [our] hearts" (Rom. 2:14-15).

Our moral inclinations are manifest in our reactions when others violate our rights. We do not see the moral law nearly as clearly when we violate others' rights. Herein is revealed our depravity; our sinfulness is found in our unwillingness to do the moral thing.

The kind of reaction that manifests the natural moral law was brought home forcefully to me when a professor I know graded a student's paper written in defense of moral relativity. After carefully reading the well-researched paper, the professor wrote, "'F.' I do not like blue folders." The student stormed into his office protesting, "That's not fair. That's not just!" The student's reaction to the injustice done to him revealed, contrary to what he wrote, that he truly believed in an objective moral principle of justice. The real measure of his morals was not what he had written in his paper but what God had written on his heart. What he really believed was right manifested itself when he was wronged.

(c) Natural law as expressed in writings—Contrary to popular belief, the great moral writings of the world do not manifest a total diversity of perspectives. There is a striking similarity among them. In fact, the similarity within writings expressing the natural law is just as great as that within writings on the divine law. That is, the great ethicists have read general revelation with as much agreement as theologians have read special revelation. Within both groups there are conservatives and liberals, rightists and leftists, strict constructionists and broad constructionists.

The stark truth is that it matters little whether it is the Bible, general revelation, or the U. S. Constitution; a bad hermeneutic can distort one as well as the other. The problem is not with the divine revelation but with the human interpretation of it. No revelation is immune from distortion by fallible and fallen human beings who wish to make it fit their depraved desires and actions.

In spite of human distortions of God's general revelation, there remains a general agreement among nonChristian writers on the nature of the natural law. C.S. Lewis has provided a noteworthy service in cataloging many of these expressions of the natural moral law. (Of course there is diversity of ethical expression among the great cultures, too, but this diversity no more negates their unanimity than diversity of belief among evangelicals negates their unity on the essential Christian teachings.) This general agreement is manifest in the following quotations:

1) The Law of General Beneficence
"Utter not a word by which anyone could be wounded." (Hindu)
"Never do to others what you would not like them to do to you."
    (Ancient Chinese)
"Men were brought into existence for the sake of men that they might do
    one another good." (Roman, Cicero)

2) The Law of Special Beneficence
"Surely proper behavior to parents and elder brothers is the trunk of
    goodness." (Ancient Chinese)
"Love thy wife studiously. Gladden her heart all thy life long." (Ancient
    Egyptian)
"Natural affection is a thing right and according to Nature." (Greek)
"The union and fellowship of men will be best preserved if each receives
    from us the more kindness in proportion as he is more closely con-
    nected with us." (Roman, Cicero)

3) Duties to Parents, Elders, Ancestors
"Has he despised Father and Mother?" (Babylonian)

"[There is a duty] to care for parents." (Greek)
"I tended the old man, and I gave him my staff." (Ancient Egyptian)

4) Duties to Children and Posterity
"Nature produces a special love of offspring" and "To live according to
Nature is the supreme good." (Roman, Cicero)
"The Master said, Respect the young." (Ancient Chinese)

5) The Law of Justice
"Has he drawn false boundaries?" (Babylonian)
"I have not stolen." (Ancient Egyptian)
"Justice is the settled and permanent intention of rendering to each man
his rights." (Roman, Justinian)
"Whoso takes no bribe . . . well pleasing is this to Samas." (Babylonian)

6) The Law of Good Faith and Veracity
"A sacrifice is obliterated by a lie and the merit of alms by an act of
fraud." (Hindu, Janet)
"Whose mouth, full of lying, avails not before thee: thou burnest their
utterance." (Babylonian)
"The Master said, Be of unwavering good faith." (Ancient Chinese)
"The foundation of justice is good faith." (Roman, Cicero)

7) The Law of Mercy
"I have given bread to the hungry, water to the thirsty, clothes to the
naked, a ferry boat to the boatless." (Ancient Egyptian)
"One should never strike a woman; not even with a flower." (Hindu,
Janet)
"You will see them take care of . . . widows, orphans, and old men, never
reproaching them." (Redskin)

8) The Law of Magnanimity
"There are two kinds of injustice: the first is found in those who do an
injury, the second in those who fail to protect another from injury
when they can." (Roman, Cicero)
"To take no notice of a violent attack is to strengthen the heart of
the enemy. Vigour is valiant, but cowardice is vile." (Ancient
Egyptian)
"Nature and Reason command that nothing uncomely, nothing effemi-
nate, nothing lascivious be done or thought." (Roman, Cicero)[38]

B. Manifestation of natural law in business ethics—The moral principles cited above apply to business as well as to any other area of human relations. The natural law teaches honesty, fidelity, and industry. It is opposed to lying, promise breaking, and laziness. Thus, the businessman can consult his own inclinations and expectations. When in doubt, he can ask, "What would I like someone else to do to me?" Through the "spectacles" of this question, he can read the natural law written by God on his own heart. All businesspersons, whether Buddhist, Christian, Jewish, Muslim, or secular humanist, can do this. Good moral principles are not unique to the Bible; they are written on the hearts of all men.

IV. SOME CONTRIBUTIONS OF NATURAL LAW TO BUSINESS ETHICS

Christians in business should meditate on God's Word day and night (Ps. 1:2), for they believe that "all Scripture is God-breathed and is useful for teaching, rebuking, correcting and training in righteousness, so that the man of God may be thoroughly equipped for every good work" (2 Tim. 3:16-17). They must be aware, however, that the nonChristians with whom they conduct business do not share this belief. Therefore, each Christian must seek to find that common ground he shares with the unbeliever by way of natural law.

Natural law makes significant contributions to business ethics. These are manifest in the ways it avoids the extremes of the alternative views.

A. Avoiding the extreme of antinomianism—There are two extremes in contemporary ethics: antinomianism at one end of the spectrum and theonomy (and biblionomy) at the other end. The former is a secular extreme, and the latter is a religious extreme. Contemporary antinomianism is manifested in a secular humanistic perspective that eschews all God-given moral absolutes. This view has been expressed in the *Humanist Manifestos I and II*. John Dewey and other influential Americans signed *Manifesto I* in 1933. They declared, "The nature of the universe depicted by modern science makes unacceptable any supernatural or cosmic guarantees of human value."[39] Humanists later added, "Values derive their source from human experience. Ethics is autonomous and situational, needing no theological or ideological sanctions."[40]

One of the signatories of *Humanist Manifesto II* was Joseph Fletcher, author of *Situation Ethics: The New Morality*. In this work, Fletcher argued that "only the end justifies the means: nothing else,"[41] and all "decisions are made situationally, not prescriptively."[42] He rejected all contentful ethical norms and insisted that we should avoid absolutes like the plague.[43] In the name of this moral relativism, *Humanist Manifesto II* approved total sexual freedom for consenting adults, abortion, euthanasia, and suicide.[44]

But these humanist ideas are contrary to their own human inclinations. Which of the signatories of the *Manifestos* was naturally inclined to believe that his mother should have killed him in her womb? What American believes that we should kill a little baby who is trapped deep in an abandoned well in the womb of the earth? Yet this is what happens to over four thousand babies every day who are trapped in their mother's womb.

Even the pagan Hippocratic Oath pledges, "I will neither give a deadly drug to anyone if asked for it, nor will I make a suggestion to this effect. Similarly I will not give to a woman an abortive remedy." Not only is our natural inclination against taking an innocent life, but so are the great moral creeds. Here again there is ample testimony that the natural law is understood by all men.

Even Seneca, whose Stoic philosophy allowed for abortion, nevertheless praised his mother for not aborting him.[45] But the natural law teaches that we should do to others what we would have them do to us. So Stoic speculative rationalizations were contrary to their own moral inclinations. The natural law is clear, but it must be read from our actual nature rather than from our theoretical notions. It must be read from our hearts, not from our minds. Natural law is the solution to antinomianism because, without appealing to any special revelation, its validity is manifest in the intuitively known moral principles within all men.

Furthermore, the denial of a natural law is self-defeating. This is painfully evident in Joseph Fletcher's attempt to deny all moral absolutes. In his futile quest for moral relativism, he insists that we should never use the word *never*. But this very statement does not avoid the word *never*.[46] The claim that we should always avoid the word *always* is equally self-destructive. And insisting that all is relative is tantamount to claiming that one is absolutely sure there are no absolutes. In each case, the moral relativist defeats his own argument because he uses absolutes to make his claim to relativism. As he wields his sword to behead the monster of absolutism, he decapitates himself on the back swing.

In short, the inconsistency of the relativist is that he is really standing on the pinnacle of his own absolute as he attempts to relativize everything else. The truth of the matter is that one cannot move the world unless he has some place to rest his fulcrum. Relativism self-destructs when it contemplates its own absolutism.

There must be some natural law or else moral judgments would not be possible. C. S. Lewis insightfully made this point in his *Abolition of Man* when he wrote,

This thing which I have called for convenience the Tao, and which others may call Natural Law . . . is not one among a series of possible systems of value. It is the sole source of all value judgments. If it is rejected, all value is rejected. If any value is retained, it is retained. The effort to refute it and raise a new system of value in its place is self-contradictory. There never has been, and never will be, a radically new judgment of value in the history of the world.[47]

Professor Allan Bloom makes a similar case for an absolute moral law in his recent best seller, *The Closing of the American Mind.* He chides the view that "there are no absolutes; freedom is absolute." Then he adds, "Of course the result is that . . . the argument justifying freedom disappears."[48] As to the oft-repeated claim that the study of different cultures proves that all values are relative, Professor Bloom responds, "All to the contrary, that is a philosophical premise that we now bring to our study of them." Furthermore, "this premise is unproven and dogmatically asserted for what are largely political reasons. History and culture are interpreted in the light of it, and they are said to prove the premise." The fact of different opinions on values does not prove value is relative. He notes, "To say it does so prove is as absurd as to say that the diversity of points of view expressed in a college bull session proves there is no truth."[49] There are absolute values, and they are undeniable.

The importance of a natural law ethic is that this approach can be taken into the business world without showing favor to any religious group. Without an objective ethical basis for our actions, there is no realistic alternative to antinomianism. But business cannot proceed as usual without an objective ethical standard common to all who engage in the business transactions. Thus, natural law is essential to a viable business ethic in our religiously pluralistic world.

Furthermore, a natural law basis for business ethics helps avoid another problem that arises out of using religious authorities (such as the Bible), which are private to one religious group. We sometimes hear public figures make statements like this: "I personally do not believe that it is right to do such-and-such, but I would not impose my belief on others." This bifurcation of private and public ethic often springs out of the mistaken idea that one's ethic comes out of his own private religious book. And, of course, he does not want to impose his religious beliefs on someone else.

A natural law ethic avoids this private-public split. Regardless of what one's private religious authority tells him, a public moral law binds all persons and institutions. Thus, on a natural law view, there is no difference between a private ethic and a corporate ethic. If it is wrong for a person to intentionally take innocent human lives, then it is also wrong for a corporation to do it. If stealing is wrong for citizens, then it is also wrong for companies. The natural law transcends both individuals and institutions.

The natural law opposes an "end justifies any means" ethic on both a private and a public level. This is particularly applicable in a capitalistic business context in which the profit motive is so dominant. Capitalism based on an antinomian ethic is destructive of society. It feeds on greed, produces poverty, and leads to revolution and war. Universal moral restraints, such as the natural law, are necessary to keep capitalism in check. Otherwise, money becomes the end. Moral principles are sacrificed for monetary profit. Here again a universal moral law that is binding on both national and international business is necessary to avoid antinomianism and its concomitant evils.

B. Avoiding the extreme of theonomy—Whereas antinomianism destroys the common moral basis for conducting business with anyone, theonomy destroys the common ground for doing business with unbelievers. The unbeliever does not accept the special revelation, or the divine law, of the believer. They have no mutual moral understanding, and without that, commerce breaks down.

Theonomy is an unworkable ethical basis in a religiously pluralistic society. Of course, a government could mandate divine revelation as its basis for civil law, but herein lies the evil of theonomy. Perhaps the easiest way for a Christian to understand this evil is to think of the Ayatollah's Iran. Would we like to live under a Muslim theonomy? Then on what grounds can we impose a Christian theonomy on others? Sooner or later the question arises, Whose religious book will be the basis for the civil laws? It is sheer religious bigotry to answer, "Mine."

Indeed, contemplating a Muslim theonomy is not necessary to make us recoil in horror. The Christian theonomy offered as an alternative is enough to give pause to Christians disgusted with the current secularization of America. Do we really think that the solution to the present antinomianism is, as theonomists claim, the execution of all kidnapers, adulterers, homosexuals, and even rebellious children?[50] Thoughtful reflection reveals that the "cure" of reconstructionism may be worse than the disease of secularism.

C. Avoiding the extreme of biblionomy—Another error of misapplication of the Bible to our society today is that of biblionomy. By biblionomy, I mean the belief that God ordained the Bible to be used as the basis for civil law. This view is like theonomy, only it does not insist that the Old Testament Law of Moses is still the basis on which society should operate. Biblionomists feel a kinship to theonomists because they both believe that divine law is the God-ordained basis for human law. They both reject natural law as the grounds for civil law. And both are dedicated to setting up a Christian society.

In one sense, biblionomy is more dangerous than theonomy because it is more deceptively appealing to Christians who are frustrated with the secular humanistic takeover of our society, with all its accompanying evils. This view has great appeal to those who long for the "good old days" when Christian values dominated our culture. They desire to get back to our Christian roots and reestablish a Christian America. This view has strong appeal for Christians who see themselves as fast losing their rights in an increasingly anti-Christian society. However, the biblionomist's cure to the extreme secularization of America is as bad as the disease. It would replace one religious law for another.[51]

How should a Christian use the Bible in his business dealings? What advantage is there in being a Christian? Much in every way! First, as Christians, we believe the Bible is God's only infallible and inerrant written authority for faith and practice, which includes business practice. So, the Christian in business will use the Bible as the divine authority for all business decisions. Of course, he cannot assume that unbelievers with whom he conducts business will do the same.

Second, the Bible does not contradict the natural law. Rather, the Bible complements and supplements natural law. After all, the same God whose moral nature is reflected in natural law has expressed His moral character in biblical commands to believers. Or to be more explicit, the eternal moral principles reflecting God's nature that are embodied in the Second Table of the Mosaic Law are the same as those expressed in natural law.

God's moral principles do not change any more than His nature does. This is not to say that believers are bound today to live according to Moses' Law. Paul clearly stated that we "are not under law, but under grace" (Rom. 6:14). Having the Law of Moses was the "advantage" over the Gentiles (Rom. 3:1-2), for the "Gentiles . . . do not have the law" (Rom. 2:14). Paul said that what "was engraved in letters on stone [i.e., the Ten Commandments]" has faded away since Christ came (2 Cor. 3:7-8).[52] He did this "by abolishing in his flesh the law with its commandments and regulations" (Eph. 2:15).

Paul informed the Galatians that now that Christ has come "we are no longer under the supervision of the law" (Gal. 3:25). The writer of Hebrews observed that "the law was given to the people" of Israel (Heb. 7:11), and there was "a change of the law" (v. 12) by which "the former regulation is set aside" (v. 18). The psalmist declared,

> He has revealed his word to Jacob,
>   his laws and decrees to Israel.

He has done this for no other nation;
        they do not know his laws. (Ps. 147:19-20)

Nowhere in the Old Testament are Gentiles condemned for not keeping the Law
of Moses. God always measured them by the truths that were part of the general
revelation.[53]

The fact that the Law of Moses was given only to Israel is not to say that
Christians have no law. We have the natural law, and we have the divine law of
the New Testament. Indeed, Christians have much to learn from what God
revealed to Israel in the Old Testament (see Rom. 15:4; 1 Cor. 10:11), and the
moral principles embodied in the Second Table of the Mosaic Law are restated
in the New Testament. However, we are not under the Mosaic Law any more
than we are under the laws of the state of Illinois when we violate a similar
traffic law in the state of Texas.[54] Just as each state codifies moral principles
differently, even so the revealed moral code for the Church is not the same as
that for Israel. For example, under the Law of Moses, adulterers were executed,
but in the New Testament, they were only excommunicated, with restoration
upon repentance (see 1 Cor. 5:5; cf. 2 Cor. 2:5-8). The same is true about the
moral duty to honor parents. When this moral principle is stated for Israel in the
Old Testament, it is given with the promise that they will live long in the land (of
Palestine) that the Lord would give them (see Exod. 20:12). In the New
Testament when Paul states a similar command to honor parents, the attached
promise has nothing to say about land promised to Israel. Rather, it simply
pledges "long life on the earth" (Eph. 6:3).

The Christian, then, is not under the Law of Moses, but he is bound by the
"law of Christ" (Gal. 6:2). Hence, in business he is bound not only by the natural
law he shares with unbelievers, but by a divine law he does *not* have in common
with them. This special revelation places some greater obligations on the
believer and deserves careful attention, which the limits of our topic do not
allow. Briefly, however, two things may be noted.

First, the Christian has greater duties than those of the natural law. The
moral principles of the divine law are the same in both Old and New Testaments
insofar as they both reflect the unchanging character of God. Christ did not
come to destroy the Law but to fulfill it (see Matt. 5:17-18). The "new
command" He gave that we love one another (1 John 2:8) was really the "old
one," which they had "since the beginning" (1 John 2:7). Christ did set the
example of a greater love, saying, "Greater love has no one than this, that he lay
down his life for his friends" (John 15:13). So the natural law is only the
Christian's minimal duty; New Testament divine law is his maximal duty.
Natural law prescribes that the Christian is to act justly; divine law commands

him to act sacrificially as well.

Second, the greater responsibility that divine law places on a Christian extends not only to his dealings with other persons in business but also to his business profits. Natural law forbids the robbing of the poor, but divine law adds that he must help the poor. It is not enough to avoid oppressing the poor; he must also be engaged in redeeming them. Jesus said, "Blessed are you who are poor, for yours is the kingdom of God" (Luke 6:20). He added for the rich, "Use worldly wealth to gain friends for yourself, so that when it is gone, you will be welcomed into eternal dwellings" (Luke 16:9). Few Christian businesspersons take this evangelistic use of their wealth seriously.

CONCLUSION

Natural law is the indispensable basis for an adequate business ethic. It is common to both believers and unbelievers, but believers are also bound by a higher law (see 1 Cor. 13). So, while the natural law obligates Christians to gain justly, the divine law urges us to give liberally. Paul reminded Timothy of the special duty placed on Christians who profit in business:

> Command those who are rich in this present world not to be arrogant nor to put their hope in wealth, which is so uncertain, but to put their hope in God, who richly provides us with everything for our enjoyment. Command them to do good, to be rich in good deeds, and to be generous and willing to share. (1 Tim. 6:17-18)

EDITOR'S PERSPECTIVE

Norman Geisler correctly contends that natural law is the only law "common to both believers and unbelievers." He sees the natural law as *the* "indispensable basis for an adequate business ethics." God gave the divine law (special revelation) as a special blessing to His children, not to the world. The natural law, on the other hand, is written on the hearts of all people, even if they do choose to deny and suppress it.

Both Richard Gaffin and Norman Geisler understand the fallen nature of mankind to be so unGodlike in character that the unregenerate could not even sustain a stable social order with an effective economic exchange system apart from God's common grace. Only the constraining work of the Holy Spirit enables people to work together harmoniously. Gaffin and Geisler do not find anything inherent in either the divine (scriptural) law or the natural law that can effectively constrain or produce correct moral behavior in the unregenerate. Their self-control is only made possible by God through His unobserved acts of common grace as He utilizes their natural self-interest, fear, views of prudentiality, natural law, and various other means to affect socially beneficial behavior.

Both Geisler's and Gaffin's views on this matter of reality are supported by the biblical data. Our logic and experience also attest to their validity. Fallen humanity is permeated with sin just as a glass of water is saturated by a handful of salt tossed into it. Our entire lives are radically affected by it. The intellect, will, and emotions are all affected by our sin nature. We are totally depraved. Only God can create a new heart; we cannot obtain a new one by our own efforts.

Furthermore, the sin nature is a radically oriented nature that cannot be free from a self-oriented awareness and concern. It is a nature wholly dependent

175

on self-righteousness apart from its rebirth. "Self" is at the very heart of its orientation, and it precludes the possibility of our having a true, godly righteousness on our own. We are conceived in sin and born in sin (see Ps. 51:5); we are depraved in every regard.

Total depravity does *not* mean, however, that unregenerate persons cannot act in a way to benefit a neighbor or be kind. It does not mean they are consciously manipulating or acting rebelliously at every point. It means they are incapable of desiring, from the core of the heart, that God would be honored and glorified by their every thought and act. They are without any ability to be truly God-centered. They are self-centered.

It is grossly mistaken to confuse self-righteousness with godliness. Socially beneficial human conduct is plentiful. We should thank God for this fact every day. But the standard by which we should evaluate human motives, thoughts, and behavior is not a standard established by society or by ourselves. The standard is God's standard of His own holiness and righteousness. Whose character and conduct can stand in the light of God's perfection and be pronounced good? Those who truly know God know themselves to be terribly sinful.

There is another side to these realities, though. Our first parents were absolutely responsible for their and our fall, and we are responsible for the self-perpetuation of sin. We knowingly suppress the truth God has revealed, whether in nature or in Scripture. We are morally responsible for this. Is there a Christian anywhere, regenerated as an adult, who does not remember willingly violating his or her own natural knowledge of what was right and wrong? Who, apart from Christ, can claim to have never suppressed what was right for the sake of pursuing personal desires?

Dr. Geisler is also absolutely correct when he states, "If there is no natural law, God is unjust." God is the author of the natural law, and He made it evident to us (see Rom. 1:19). With the Fall came the knowledge of good and evil. That knowledge was implanted in the heart of all the unregenerate. We come to life with the ability to discern right and wrong. Dr. Geisler is also accurate when he says the problem faced by unbelievers is not that they do not *perceive* the truth, but that they will not *receive* or act on it. We do know what is right; our problem is one of doing what we know is right.

From the editor's perspective, Dr. Geisler's most powerful argument for the fact that natural law is indeed on the hearts of all humans was his contention that we can see this reality by observing human *reactions* (not actions) to circumstances that offend us. Our desires to be treated kindly, fairly, justly, and so on are manifested quickly when we perceive that we are being mistreated. Our reactions declare that we *do* know what is right.

Having concluded that we are totally depraved, and that we have the natural law of righteousness written on our hearts, we are now ready to address these questions: How are Christians to approach unbelievers in the marketplace? Do we come on the grounds of divine law or natural law? We are called to be salt and light; we must stand before the world so that unbelievers can see our light and glorify God for it (see Matt. 5:13-16). We are to speak up for righteousness and not give way before the wicked in the marketplace (see Prov. 25:26). On what basis, then, are we to do this?

From the editor's perspective, the answer is clear. The natural law, a general knowledge of good and evil, and a conscience are operative in God's image-bearers and have been since the time of the Fall. Our moral responsibility took on a new dimension then. We were made responsible and accountable for our moral judgments, and the ground of our discernment was the natural law inscribed in creation and on every heart where it is written so clearly that we are without excuse when we violate it. Our consciences will bear witness of this truth (see Rom. 2:15).

The written law was given at Sinai to God's children, not to the world in general. One had to be a member of the family to receive its full benefits. There was a special benefit to those who possessed it (see Rom. 3:1-2). The same is true for the Sermon on the Mount and the New Testament precepts. They were given to the Church, not to the unbelieving world. However, the unbelieving world can gain benefits from being with those who subscribe to the precepts of special revelation. God is free to impress unbelievers with whatever He wishes, just as He is free to turn them over to their depraved minds (see Rom. 1:28). Scripture also tells us the king's heart is like water in the hands of the Lord, and it can be turned to do whatever He wishes (see Prov. 21:1).

What has God established to use in the lives of the unregenerate to guide their moral thinking? The answer is, surely, the natural law. That is what has been made universally available, according to God's Word. Romans 1-3 makes it abundantly clear, though, that *none* seeks after God or comes to love God apart from His special grace. Therefore, Richard Gaffin's contention, with which Geisler agrees, that neither the natural law nor the divine law is sufficient, in and of itself, to cause unbelievers to act righteously is also correct. Only by God's constraining common grace does society avoid falling into anarchy and total self-destruction.

On the other hand, God generally uses the natural law written on human hearts to inform unbelievers of what is right and wrong. Therefore, as God's children, we should normally plan to make our moral appeals to unbelievers on the basis of the natural law.

Lot, Abraham's nephew, appealed to the men of Sodom to "not act wickedly" when they came to his home and asked that his guests be turned over to them so they might "have relations with them" (Gen. 19:4-7). Lot's appeal to them was based on the natural law. Paul did not mind appealing to Roman law and justice when he was being tried before Festus; he eventually appealed to Caesar (see Acts 25:1-12). Appealing to the natural law, and manmade law, is most appropriate when dealing with unbelievers in the world.

Appealing to the natural law does not preclude us from referring to God's written moral law, however, when there is still an acknowledgment of the validity of the Ten Commandments and the law of love in the general culture. Our opportunity to do this, though, is simply strong evidence of God's prior common grace. It is our conclusion that the Christian business professional should learn how to apply the natural law to the everyday moral problems encountered in the marketplace.

THE DISTRIBUTION OF WEALTH:
Are There Biblical Directives?

Is God a capitalist? Is God an egalitarian or maybe a socialist? Could God's ideas about the distribution of wealth be totally different from those embodied in any of these systems? Does the Bible favor one economic system over another? Does Scripture's emphasis on personal moral responsibility and accountability impel us toward a free market system where personal choice and its consequences are rewarded both positively and negatively? Or do biblical teachings about the Jubilee and gleaning laws also tell us there needs to be some form of state intervention to guarantee a fairer form of distribution?

Questions about the creation and distribution of wealth are basic to economic life. The world is deeply divided between those who emphasize the individual's responsibility for the creation and distribution of wealth and those who emphasize the collective responsibilities to bring about economic justice. Henry Krabbendam pointed to the tension between "the one and the many" in chapter 6. This tension is central to the problems associated with economic justice, and we are going to examine it in some detail in this section.

The following discussion serves as an introductory excursion into the topic of "distributive justice," the central concern of the series' next book, *Biblical Principles and Economics: The Foundations*. Book 2 will provide an in-depth look at such topics as personal liberty and private property; human equality and public property; biblical incentives that are, and are not, compatible with world economic systems; the compatibility and incompatibility of utility theory with biblical principles; the assignment of poverty concerns to the private and/or public sectors; the "ethics of love" and its ability and inability to function successfully in a free market environment; and other subjects having an impact on the distribution of wealth. The two competing theories on what produces justice in the marketplace—wealth should be distributed according to personal effort and contribution; wealth should be distributed according to personal need or equally—will be examined in that book.

The two chapters in this book devoted to distributive justice look at the tensions that surface when we comprehend the significance of Scripture's emphasis on human choice (our fall and redemption are intricately tied to the doctrine of choice) and simultaneously hear Scripture's call for us to seek economic justice in the midst of the consequences flowing from human inequality and sin in a fallen world. Scripture does reveal God's deep interest in our freedom of choice and His love for those who are disadvantaged—orphans, the poor, prisoners, widows, for example. God obviously expects us to choose to do something to help persons in need. What are we to do, and how are we to do it? These are the important questions.

The great issues associated with the distribution of wealth divide the economic-political-social systems of the world into competing, and sometimes warring, factions. Many biblical themes that speak to justice and righteousness also touch on these issues. God has not left us without help as we try to cope with and comprehend these economic complexities. The prophets of the Old Testament cried out repeatedly against the economic injustices of their day. In the New Testament, Paul and James had some compelling things to say about "riches." Wealth itself is never condemned in the Scriptures, but our attitudes toward it and our use of it are frequent topics.

To help us explore the subject of distributive justice, Udo Middelmann presents the biblical evidence supporting the position that personal effort should be the primary basis upon which wealth is distributed, and Robert Wauzzinski examines numerous assumptions undergirding capitalism in the light of Scripture and finds them lacking. Dr. Wauzzinski does not conclude, however, that a socialistic system is therefore indicated; he finds that it, too, has enormous deficiencies from a biblical perspective. Instead he suggests an alternative system through which the group may seek justice.

Two themes thread their way through the chapter Mr. Middelmann has prepared. He emphasizes the importance Scripture assigns to the fact that God's image-bearers are *choice-makers*. Everybody must make choices about how to behave, and we are all personally accountable for our decisions and actions. This choice-making ability is also foundational to the second theme: all humans are called by God to make an effort to overcome (conquer) the debilitating realities flowing from our fallen nature. We are to work, sacrifice, and improve on what God gave us through creation by the sweat of our brow. We are to subdue and distribute wealth with a view to God's intended purposes.

Mr. Middelmann concludes that if these two realities were fully understood and addressed, distributive justice would stop being thought of in terms of absolute and relative mathematical differences between the wealth of the "rich" and the "poor." This world view assumes such measurements hold the key to the determination of economic justice. He contends this is not the case. He believes if these two realities were grasped, individuals would come into harmony with God's will to the degree that there was a matching of personal competencies with productive opportunities, which would create a production-distribution system of rewards that would allow for the care of self, family, and others.

PERSONAL EFFORT, CONTRIBUTION, AND MERIT AS THE PRIMARY BIBLICAL GROUNDS FOR DISTRIBUTING WEALTH

Udo Middelmann

Mr. Udo Middelmann is Director of the International Institute for Relief and Development, an arm of Food for the Hungry in Geneva, Switzerland. He studied law and theology in Europe and the United States and was a member of L'Abri Fellowship for twenty years with Francis Schaeffer. The author of Pro-Existence, *he writes and lectures widely on Christianity and society, as well as relief and development issues.*

Mr. Middelmann earnestly believes that effective remedies for historical, social, political, and religious hindrances to human development and growth require a fresh examination of the Bible's view of the world. A call for compassion alone distorts that concern. He also believes that any constructive change demands a cognitive analysis of existing conditions before biblical principles can be applied compassionately to fragile human situations. He actively pursues opportunities to reduce human suffering by frequently traveling to all the continents to evaluate, consult, and supervise efforts directed at elevating the quality of life.

In the discussion for the most just and humane society, the title of this chapter introduces two immediately inflammatory words. I do not refer to *biblical grounds*, which can easily be reduced in their impact by seeing them related to a traditionalist's religious value system. That makes them unspecific and scientifically irrelevant, indicative only for one of many moral orientations.

The words *personal* and *wealth* in connection with effort, merit, and contribution are properly understood to reflect a mind-set worthy of the strongest criticism. For some, they represent the core of what is objectionable and evil in our society. They rightly associate these terms with practices and a

182

thought world characteristic of our specifically Western approach to life, to the production and the distribution of wealth. Both words reflect the double focus in our somewhat singular experience when compared with other cultures in the world.[1]

The discussion has been enriched by detailed insights into the practices elsewhere, which have been suggested as new models that would better aid the removal of injustice and poverty. The contrast is well described by the two words *personal* and *wealth*, for against the prevalent submission of the individual to the life, the structures, and the traditions of the group, the "Atlantic mind-set" (Barbara Ward)[2] has stressed the exact opposite. Here, the individual seeks the creation of wealth and surplus outside prescribed, formalized practices.

The discussion is almost always not one of underlying reasons for one view or the other. That would have to deal with different world views and an evaluation of the results of each in the distribution of wealth. Instead, objections are raised on the belief that an emphasis on the person and on wealth is only possible in a philosophic framework that encourages greed, selfishness, unlimited self-interest, and heartless inequality of distribution of the common (or social) wealth. Radical change in ideas and practices is then demanded, for nothing else would affect the world of ideas and the results in a social reality. Until such change, any society could not be called just or humane.

Wealth differentials among people in the same society (or in the human race worldwide) are seen as a fault and require a fundamental and systemic change of distribution. Anything that leads to different results must be abolished, benefits removed, for the sake of creating a world of justice, equality, and equal access to something less than wealth, most often a simple life. This all fits the image of the family of man, of living together in *one* world and facing limited global resources together.[3]

Different systems of distribution must be designed that allow access to life independent of personal effort. The words *personal* and *wealth* continue to be used in a new, more spiritual meaning, when it no longer relates to effort, work, and some of the other elements we shall bring up later, but to the dream of a just society. A modern rendition of the goals of the French Revolution is easily found in this dream, when the *fraternity* of one human race demands an *equality* of relative wealth, produced by people *liberated* from pressures and systems of privileges and burdens.

A philosophy of avarice, competition, privilege, and self-interest is blamed for the tremendous human suffering produced by personal effort, contribution, and giving merit to qualifications. For that reason, a new system of distribution must be advocated, in which the "social limits to growth" (Fred Hirsch) have no influence on the desired equal outcome in distribution of wealth. At the same time it will disqualify the contribution and merit of the selfish and encourage a new human being characterized by altruism, compassion, and spirituality.

The often-heated reaction this phrase provokes can easily be understood, when compared to such a vision. Emphasizing the personal contribution as a means for distributing wealth encourages distinctions of persons and distinctions of wealth. Justice is more related to a person's actions and choices than to the biological existence of human beings and their number. There is no vision of an impersonal justice, but a vision of equals being treated equally and unequals with respect for their differences. Changes in history are the results of significant choices of human beings who reflect their calling as children of a moral, significant, and discerning God rather than impersonal nature, their drives, or the traditions of their societies.

We want to look more closely at the biblical framework and at some of the Bible's specific teachings, for the "Atlantic orbit" also comprises those cultures that have been most affected by biblical thinking.[4] The result of personal effort, contribution, and merit has led here to a most remarkable distribution of wealth for a wide proportion of people. In fact, when there are little personal effort, a lack of motivation, limited desires, few ideas, and even fear, these will often result in the creation and distribution of insufficient wealth.

We shall, therefore, consider the subject from a biblical perspective, which includes specific instruction as well as a control from experienced realities. This way we should be able to find our way in the midst of traditions and accusations and the tension between reality and ideology. Without that, we shall easily find ourselves exposed to guilt without cause and lack the energy and conviction to defend ourselves and the biblical ground for our practices. Without that grounding we will be overcome with poverty of courage, which again will spell disaster for the human family in the long run.[5]

To be a person means to be an actor. *Persona* is the Greek word for "mask," which frees a normal person to play another, to take on a distinct identity. The mask gives freedom for the player from the constraint of his civil life.

In the Bible as well as in daily life, we can observe that small events and the larger sweeping consequences take place as a result of persons making their choices in accordance with the script of their value differentiations. The pursuit of their goals, their work and calling, and their participation and responsibilities are expressions of their choice of the pieces of their basic view of man and society in history.

To be a person results from having an additional factor beyond the givens of the situation in the metaphysical realm, the anchor of values, freedom, and all that is not merely physical. It gives a higher perspective for the struggle than merely reacting to the demands of the moment in its physical components of material needs. It contains an important element of freedom and gives the space for action.[6]

On that insight also rest the recognition of freedom and distinctions between good and evil. Without it, all events follow necessarily and cannot elicit praise or blame. Real differences of a qualitative kind only exist in a designation coming from outside the physical universe. In that metaphysical realm reside the distinctions required for an appreciation that choices have different consequences. Only where a choice can be affected will it also matter to carefully select choices by the different consequences in the real world. And that can only be done by actors choosing their masks, being real persons. They set themselves into a situation of real independence, of distance in order to be "themselves."[7]

It is remarkable that those who would oppose such an emphasis on the person do so from the perspective of being persons. They do not accept the biblical view as a material or historic necessity; rather, they strongly object to it, claiming that we have chosen a wrong mask. Theirs is a vision (as only persons can have) of a world without the significance of personal effort, contribution, and merit. It stands against a reality experienced in which different quantities, shapes, actions, business choices, and opportunities exist and where the result is open, depending on the mask worn and the character portrayed.

It is the vision of society as a unit, expressing a fundamentally impersonal *idea* in which personal choices have been rendered ineffective in the material realm of wealth distribution and reserved to such "personal" areas as attitudes, feelings, and spiritual experiences. But such a vision can only exist in the mind of man. A world where choices do not have effects and where different intellectual and material contributions lead to equal distribution of resulting wealth is a world unknown to man.

In the vision, any affirmation of personal dignity and autonomy is understood to indicate unsocial concerns, which lead to unjust consequences. Only the loner, the asocial, the selfish, greedy, and unloving human being will operate in this way.[8] His will be a *private* concern, *depriving* others of their share, their justice, and their place in the unitary understanding of society. He will create benefits, using privileges and advantages for himself and thereby rob others of their share. The vision is metaphysical, but the reality and the desired result are always only material. Equality is seen basically as a mathematical distribution. Work produces social property created out of common global resources, which are ageless and created for an equal share of all in *one* world. Personal effort, hierarchy of distinctions, and earned or inherited privilege (earned by someone previously) have no place within the vision. There, equal worth and stress-free and no-fault existence are projected to level those efforts, choices, and merits that would produce a disturbing question about the vision of a good society, harmonious social behavior, and so forth.

Similarly, concerns about the distribution of wealth should be replaced by distributive mechanisms. There should not be any more distribution of wealth as a result of personal effort. Where wealth comes into existence as a result of such effort, faulty structures of distribution are assumed that allow for unequal results. The assumption that exploitation is the cause lies at hand. Starting with an impersonal view of society in its material sense, it is not surprising to find an inability to recognize the unique effect of personal intervention and work, and to hear it condemned where it is still recognized. When the goal (equality and justice) is emphasized more than the means (personal effort, etc.), any unequal distribution must have been the result of unfair, immoral actions. Unequal availability of wealth is seen as the result of faulty distribution and constitutes theft and injustice. The thief in turn only appropriates what faulty distribution channels have withheld from him as an equal unit in society. His action is a corrective measure against unjust distribution schemes. He designed his own, much as public theft is instituted through excessive taxes or inflation.[9]

Clearly, the emphasis on the personal effort stresses a distribution of wealth from above, from the level of effort, resulting in wealth for the whole society eventually in different amounts. This is contrasted by a concern for distribution from below, taking as its baseline the biological existence of units in society.[10]

The Bible says remarkably little about business practices and systems for distribution of wealth. Its concern is the reality of human beings in the midst of all of life. The Word of God addresses minds and hearts and calls them to honesty, faith, and realism in a history in which all the effects of the Fall need to be resisted until the return of the Messiah will bring about incorruption and righteousness.

The Bible speaks of human beings in all situations as in need of correct ideas and values, of truth rather than prescriptions for all eventualities.[11] That was a pharisaical problem created by them after the center of their world shifted from a knowledge of God to legalistic systems.

The Bible centers its concern on persons. God and the creature relate as persons first, revealing and believing what is true in the form of concepts, words, ideas. Belief and unbelief start in the heart (and mind). His Word gives us the script for our actions as persons. The result will be a surplus of ideas and a life distributed to each for greater resistance to the scarcity of knowledge and life in a world marked by the Fall and death.[12]

Being addressed as persons with a perception of metaphysical realities, individuals will use opportunities to know and to act, depending on various material and spiritual factors. Different consequences of different actions (or inactions) reveal a basic justice and consistency in a crazy world that is far from being *one*. An individual cannot be indifferent to poisonous mushrooms and expect that the outcome will always strengthen life. Respect for the laws of the land or the laws of creation will lead to a just distribution of consequences. Variation is the result of variant behavior.[13]

The disparity of outcome is acceptable when justice is done to persons' significant choices and when it is, therefore, not a result of arbitrary and contradictory factors. On the other hand, when variations in outcome and distribution are not the result of voluntary and personal actions, other, and again deliberate and personal, ways of caring for the poor are demanded by the theology of the Bible, by its description of life, and by its insights into the complexity of the life story of men and women in society and the link of community. This is demanded precisely because persons' actions have consequences into all eternity, which themselves require resistance out of respect for those affected by others' choices.

The Bible encourages and demands such concerns in a web of friendship, families, work and business relations, markets and civic participation within a community of ideas, values, and goals, within one language and history, one family in Adam to whom one blessing is offered in the faith of Abraham. Precisely because of this view, personal effort must also be made to hinder the logical outworkings of wrong choices in the lives of others. Much of personal existence in work and compassion, in business skills and the creation of opportunities, in law and culture, is such a stand against the persistent results of Adam's rebellion.[14]

The God of the Bible is a Person who thinks, feels, and acts. He is not the ground of *being*, but a Person with a distinct character meriting respect and honor. Definite in His ideas, He created a universe of defined shapes.[15] The Bible speaks not of an expanding infinite unity, but of an increasing number of distinct realities. To God, not all things are the same ultimately. He is unity *and* diversity. He is not a part of His creation; He exists in "before" and "after" relations;[16] and He created a universe of distinct shapes, of man and nonman, of spirit and matter, of ideas and physical forms, of cause and effect as well as the possibility of new causes chosen in freedom of personal existence.[17]

Man, made in the image of this God, is defined by God's intentions and actions. The emphasis on the human being as a choice-maker in the image of the Creator is central to the Bible. Religion and worship do not revolve around an unquestioning approval of the status quo, repeating patterns and harmonized submission. To have dominion challenges the previous order.[18] To worship calls for communication. To speak, to adore, and to obey require differentiation, language, and real choice. Man's relationship with the God of Heaven and earth frees him from finding his orientation in nature with its repetitive cycles and its indifference to personal distinctions. Nature was to be harnessed, discovered, and used. History does not unroll, but is created by each person's story. For that, man was to live by the Word of God, not by the sights in creation. Adam was to notice the distinct relatedness and personality of Eve in contrast to the animals (see Gen. 2:4-24).

With real distinctions, language becomes a helpful and necessary tool.[19] Knowledge is required to direct the effort to understand the place and purpose of human life. Such knowledge elevates and produces distinctions to ignorance, within hierarchies of effort, contribution, and merit. Only on the basis of distinctions is culture a meaningful pursuit.

Adam's call was to dress the garden, cultivate it, and give it his names and designations. This course of action requires and rewards skill, creates a wealth of personal involvement and satisfaction, and rewards the spirit of careful dominion. He was to give shape to what God had left undone. This assignment continues after the Fall, when Adam and Eve were called to resist death in any form and to believe and act in light of the history yet to be created by them and God's additional working toward a new creation.[20]

Mankind was created in the image of the living God. Being alive means more than repeating cycles; there are contributions to be made to progress and refinement, correction and addition, through work and service in the material and the intellectual-spiritual areas of human life.

Just as God thought, spoke, and then it was, so man was to think, define in concepts and words, and then produce the wealth necessary to live in a world of unfinished shapes and later also of scarcity and need. Nature was never to be accepted as found.[21] It called for classification and knowledge of its workings in order to work with it. Just as God had made a *tohu-wabohu* (Hebrew for "chaos" or "disorder") and gave it increasing differentiation in succeeding days, so man was to continue to express his wealth of personhood through choice and action.

A living God sets the framework for growing insight, increased abilities, and honed skill. Wealth in any form did not just exist, but needed to be discovered, gathered, and found useful. Food needed to be grown and picked, relationships started and nurtured, knowledge passed on and multiplied.[22] New problems could be tackled; the future could look different because of the intercession by human choice as an additional component to change the mere extension in time of the past. Personal actions are significant in history and bring about what may exist until then only in the mind of the person.[23]

A living God can speak that word by which man was to live (see Deut. 8:3), giving information necessary to understand life. Therefore, personal interest to find out was rewarded by better knowledge to master a hostile environment. Working by the sweat of the brow against hunger in a fallen world (see Gen. 3:19), creating a new generation of children against the certainty of one's own death (see Gen 3:19-20), and making those practical, moral choices that safeguard life in an antagonistic natural setting after the Fall follow from the biblical perspective on human effort, personal choices, and their rewards to individuals primarily. Secondary factors, such as history, family ties, nature, ideas of community, were all rejected as dominating factors in favor of a partnership with the God who speaks and acts.

Individuals are called to obedience when they sin. Abraham was called out of Ur. People have names and stand before God.[24] Where judgment and reward confront Israel, it is the result of individuals' choices in the past and present: "Not all who are descended from Israel are Israel" (Rom. 9:6); "I am the only one . . . left" (1 Kings 18:22); "As for me and my household" (Josh. 24:15). Personal choices affect the whole family and nation, but their significance to wealth or poverty lies in the creative acts of individual human beings. All events result from an idea expressed in an act by a person, God or the Devil or the man himself, which presents a challenge to the status quo by making something else thinkable. The Word of God deals with reality. It gives options and alternatives worthy of pursuit against the mere semblance of natural states, developments, or growth.

In this sense, the promise of the Messiah broke the finality of death and meaninglessness for Adam and Eve (see Gen. 3:15; 4:1). The dust could be turned to earth, a wilderness into a field. Distinctions could be drawn between what had become and what ought to be. But it would only become that by the effort, contribution, and merit of individuals.

Likewise, disciples were called out of their social context with such radical words as "Follow me." Persons have names; each life is a biography that contributes to the course of what then can be called history.[25]

Living according to the Word (see Deut. 8:3) also means those words that talk about enterprise, which encourage goals and open new possibilities. In Deuteronomy 8:9, that Word would invite individuals to seek iron under the hills and copper under the mountains. God would enable them to get wealth, to organize resources and processes, to seek personal areas of resistance to death by the creation of surplus. Nature provides slim pickings, but where personal choices follow the indications of God's Word, additional resources can be found and turned into rewards (see Gen. 26:12ff.).[26]

With this understanding, the Bible sets a strong opposition to those who would sound a loud gong for material justice of equality because of their view that inequality results from structural problems in the mechanics of distribution. The Bible encourages the creation of surplus in ways other than by using unjust distribution as a means. It is even the goal in a fallen world of brutal realities and the result of personal effort. We are to live seven days on the work of six and twenty-four hours on the work of far fewer. Our effort during a few months of the year should yield a harvest for twelve months. There should be enough to take care of orphans and widows as well, to be hospitable to strangers and generous to brethren in need, storing against spoilage and waste or lean years from time to time. The struggle for life produces surplus and distributes wealth among human beings who are called and driven to reveal the Creator's family rather than to make their home in nature's scarce provisions.

The effort of the vinedresser would bring results. The wall around the field would protect the harvest. Peace in the land would allow a person to reap what he had sown. Spiritual worship and obedience would enable people to create wealth (see Deut. 8:18ff.), and investment would lead to returns.

This is the basis for hope after the Fall to pick up the pieces and to expand the finite set of known dimensions through spiritual encouragement, intellectual insight, and political, social, and economic openness. By comparison, the African mind-set—with its service to traditions, its fear of personal responsibilities, its political, social, and religious bondage—hardly challenges the present for a different future. The notion of a different future is absent even from its languages and grammar. Likewise, a historical dialectic about the inevitability of the historical process will also lead to resignation, little personal courage and enterprise, while the Bible calls all men to know the living God and His mind. Repentance itself is a willingness to make the personal effort to change in order to have life.

The God of the Bible calls us to break out of the again-and-again of paganism, to affect nature's shape and society's condition. There is no room for a despondency that has its origin in a view of historic necessity and inevitability. We are free from the tyranny of circumstances to struggle for life, to teach knowledge and virtue, and to have respectful dominion over various areas of human life.[27]

God frees man from dependence on heavenly bodies and superstition to proceed rationally and with an open mind. He allows man to conquer space through exploration, free from the fear of the unknown, restrained only by responsibility to God, neighbor, and the next generations. There are no guilds, licenses, or professional prescriptions in the Bible. Excellence competed in the market when not hindered by men in power. God, existing in time, encourages the use of time for better commercial and social organization. He frees people to seek better management of nature, calling for thrift and planning (see Gen. 41).

The world was rediscovered as the sphere of a rational Person, God, rather than of a multitude of rival spirits in a fragile balance of powers. God's just rewards, His clear commands, and His faithfulness to His promises set the framework for deliberation, personal effort, and contribution in material things of business or in the formal security of contracts, courts and appeals, righteous measures, and market prices.[28] Justice could be sought in the city gates. Bribes were forbidden, but so was the artificial setting of supposedly fair prices. Agreement, rather than custom and law, was the basis for business in the Old and New Testaments.

The teaching of the Fall and the laws governing much of life must have had a double effect on people of biblical times. First, they would have called a person to responsibility and forced him to evaluate his actions, since the distinctions between life and death, righteousness and sin, culture and barbarism, Jehovah and Baal, were before him. Second, they would have set before the person a standard worth struggling and competing for, in order to gain in the fragile exposure of life to the scarcity of any one moment's experience. The law serves as a corrective *and* as an encouragement and quarry for the additional data required when nature gives us primary data, but when life is more than sense perception and ways of making do.[29] The obscenity of death, the frustration with need, and limited pooled wealth, they all are repelled when the Creator of the universe calls for personal action and effort and masterly competition against them. Craftsmen and builders, hunters and fishermen, judges and kings, were thus under a constant challenge, "impelled from behind by some life-affirming sentiment and drawn forward by some conception of what . . . should be."[30]

Yet such a broadened horizon would also call for self-control and competence to be successful in the task. Even to choose between the good and the poor or evil, self-control and skill, discipline and a recognition of exclusiveness, is required. They affirm quality and lead to competition in judgment, in the selection of a good king, a faithful shepherd, and so on. Hiram from Tyre had to be called as builder, for there was none in Israel of adequate competence.[31]

Personal existence, effort, and contribution require a dynamism that struggles for refinement, for improvement, for a hierarchy of insight. Choices are required that lead to differing results in the lives of people and their children. Without such distinction, civilization disappears and society collapses; productivity is reduced. Only in a world of personal distinctions can culture be different from barbarism, can Abraham live differently from Lot, Jacob from Esau.

Personal effort distributes wealth along the lines of personal stewardship. We are not called to protect and exhibit the world the way we found it for all generations. Rather, we are called to household with creation in continuous exhibition of being children of God instead of nature. Stewardship of God's concerns for human beings results not in maintaining nature, but in struggling in personal choices to win the battle against scarcity in a fallen world.

Scarcity is known to all of us who are familiar with God's Word. As long as death rules, we and creation groan in waiting.[32] In such a situation of scarcity, competition for life against the constant threats to life, relationships, and true worship and obedience is required of us. Life and all other things are brittle, fragile, and easily wounded. We are not surrounded by a friendly or peaceful environment. Health, including economic health, is not there for the asking. It has to be created. The Bible presents it as a battle against sin and death. We are called to compete against death in all its ugly forms. This includes, but is not limited to, the spiritual battle in which the individual must persevere "under trial, because when he has stood the test, he will receive the crown of life" (James 1:12).

Originally, competition calls for the means to strive together, to do what is suitable to achieve a goal or to reach an objective, to win a prize or to make a profit. It requires insight into the characteristic manner in which a challenge is to be met with adequate abilities. Related to competition, competence is that ability to have sufficient means for the necessities of life and the capacity to function in a particular way in response to an aggressor. It is an active demand for some resource in short supply.

Therefore, the Bible describes human beings making choices to stand against natural limitations of any kind when these are the result of the Fall, of sin, or of a broken world. Competition is necessary in order to struggle for that balance required to live, which has been broken as a result of the Fall. Not equality, but an adequate life is the goal. To that end, virtue and knowledge are required. They want to be reached for, ever beyond our grasp, through personal effort. Once found, they produce rich rewards in relationships and material goods and services.

That struggle to live requires competition in order to win against the scarcity of life after the Fall. We compete in order to fulfill our purpose as human beings and live. Nature, also under the curse, provides neither enough nor equally. Nature sheds no tears. She would be a poor and heartless mother— "one large restaurant" in the words of Woody Allen.

With such an emphasis on the personal reality in the universe, the creation and protection of private property is no surprise. The quality of effort defines the quantity of distribution. The significance of personal contributions results in property of people with names. There is no anonymous ownership in the Bible, but real people with real names. People do not own all things equally, in some social property sense, for there is no such thing as "the people." Such undefined egalitarianism would spell tyranny for the individual.[33]

And it is the self in the image of God that God seeks, addresses, and singles out to protect. To work against self does not result in justice discovered; it results in the destruction of personal significance. Biblical property laws protected the use of wealth created and deprived others of access when they had not contributed to it. These laws established responsibilities, but also limited the rights of intervention from the outside. Wealth should be tithed and could be taxed in recognition that God the Creator lay the foundation and that the Levites, the road builders, the teachers, and others in society contributed in varying degrees to the distribution of wealth. But the right to earn, to engage in business activities, and to work the waters of the Sea of Galilee or the Western Ocean in trade and business when the original land could no longer provide adequately for the expanding families and nation was the free choice of all persons.

The absence of a central state, of restricting institutions (the warning was *against* kings who would levy taxes and make men serve them), allowed for free development of individual possibilities. We know of no licensing prerogatives, no divisions of labor except by agreement, and no sacerdotal authorities managing the creation and distribution of private property.[34] The Jubilee defined lease arrangements, but did not limit the sale of harvests and other forms of monetization. Private property was protected because one law ruled all lives equally in the original intent of the law. The distribution of wealth resulted from the choices in the hearts and minds of people, their motivations, and their faithfulness to God's Word.

Distribution of wealth was also protected through the existence of one law and the availability of courts to protect the individual against those in power or the envy of his neighbors. The Torah gave stability to the original definitions of human life and society, limiting the force of ideologies, paganism, and power structures hiding behind authorities or majorities. It gave a common set of values, ideas, and challenges.[35] Contracts could be concluded and were protected. Fines were set and bribes forbidden. Neither the poor nor the rich were to be treated with an advantage. All titles were free and could be transferred, capitalized, and the money reinvested differently. All commodities could be exchanged. Such an open system without market controls, enforced associations, or legal restraints (out of supposed concern for a wider and, on some level, always anonymous public) gave greatest breadth of possibilities for personal economic advantage through effort, skill, and adaptability. Since the Bible centers everything on the moral and the personal in the context of a real creation, we find no equality ideology with the goal of mathematical equality; the concern seems to be genuine respect for individuality[36] (see Deut. 18:8).

Property, profits, and professional options were left to the choices of the individual in the framework of his relationship with a moral God and real judgment in history by God, by the next generation, and by the surrounding culture. With the struggle of life demanding hard work in a world of scarcity, only God could advise and call people to life. Self-sacrifice, sweat and toil, education, knowledge and virtue, organizational skill and the courage to take on the most difficult tasks, the use of time and the daring that brings forth inventions—all broaden the resource base for human life and distribute wealth by individual creation.

With God giving His Word and the encouragement to look beyond the present dimension, calling people to seek so that they would find, to believe so that they would have hope, nothing of human origin should so dilute the result of effort as to deny the intellectual, spiritual, and psychological validity of the framework and weaken individuals in their resolve to resist death and resignation. God promises that "the testing of your faith develops perseverance" (James 1:3). Failure to allow such testing in the areas of faith (and economic and business realities) prevents the truth from being discovered. Ideological definitions will then take the place of real insight and knowledge, just as subsidies and protective isolation will keep a dream alive at public and intellectual expense.

Biblically, different results, as consequences of different choices, would always serve as a form of judgment and lead in certain cases to improvement, adjustments, and renewed realism. "If a man will not work, he shall not eat" (2 Thess. 3:10) describes this well. Truth should be discovered in reality. Consequences should not be kept from originally false or unrealistic choices. Material judgment and practical consequences should do the work of moral justice concerns. The market of reality in God's creation serves well as a testing ground for the truth or falsehood of any proposition.[37] This is similar to the test of prophets and their statements about future events. It is not the *idea* of justice in wealth distribution that brings wealth to people. Only hard work, skill, family relations and, where necessary, neighborly love will work toward a solution of scarcity problems.

The real world, as it is created and as it exerts a form of control on the imagined and projected world of autonomous man, is the real testing ground for the extent and limits of such personal effort for wealth distribution. The Bible describes man's approach to life as if he was a competitor in an athletic contest (see 2 Tim. 2:5), a soldier under orders (see Gal. 6; 2 Tim. 2:3), and a farmer needing skill in order to produce (see 1 Cor. 9:10). Other Scriptures (see 1 Cor. 9:25; Phil. 3:13ff.; Col. 2:18) comment on how to "press on toward the goal" in life.

The illustrations do not suggest a reward for selfishness. They state that the point of effort is to win. Only one person gets the prize for the best effort. The interest lies in winning by doing the job well and thereby also being a challenge to others in their attempts. Similarly, in business we expect a company to put forth and to demand the best effort. The results are the prize of finding the best products and highest return on the invested capital. Complaint about quality cannot be brushed aside with reference to higher spiritual values in not competing with a rival product.

"We expect the highest level of performance of which he is capable. And the reason is very simple. That is what serves the greater social good."[38] In fact, improving the self to win the competition is a noble undertaking. Paul speaks of "straining for what is ahead . . . to win the prize" (Phil. 3:13ff.). His words relate to the spiritual home with God, but include our concern for life after the Fall and being faced with death. Temperance, diligence, enterprise, prudence, frugality, and delayed rewards compete against vice, selfishness, disobedience, and a fundamental irrationality about creation and human life in it.

God's world and our lives are not yet in the final shape. We are in a race to win, challenging our minds and bodies to greater effort for improved performance. Competition serves as teacher, sets new models, and stretches our ideas. Remove the threat of loss or judgment and any reality becomes acceptable, for it removes the distinction between what is and what ought to be. Then death becomes a part of life, and shoddy merchandise, false labeling, and inflated prices are tolerated as socially just and spiritually valuable.

The critique of such an emphasis on the personal and on wealth distribution through effort, contribution, and merit confuses the biblical view of self and competition with fundamental irrationality in selfish people. Together with the self-righteous and often racist views of the health-and-wealth gospel, such irrationality deserves rejection. Yet it must be kept distinct from the biblical affirmation of the personal significance in wealth creation.[39]

The biblical view is not irrational because it places individuals always in a context of family, history, and life after the Fall. Both the Word of God and His creation should be shared by all people, to break the cruel cycle of nature and compounded ignorance about the Creator of a good world. What Adam Smith spoke about in relationship to the free market has much wider and deeper realities in the human context. There are relationships of mutual effect, but not in a finite mathematical world only.

We must resist the moral censure of self by condemning selfishness, for it is characterized more by irrationality than self. It is irrational because it does not respect the givens of creation: families, consequences in history, the rule of law, and accountability in judgment.

Likewise, we must protect open competition without failing to point to the irrational consumerism that leaves no room for strengthening the more human elements in life of relationships. One may compete with one's neighbor and win, but the relationship with the neighbor must not be lost.[40]

The Bible places the life story of individuals into a theology, a history, and a relational context, which needs to be considered rationally. In that context, widows and orphans need to be cared for; enemies should be loved. Nehemiah 8:10 and other biblical references point to such a social and moral reality that does not limit personal effort as the basis for wealth distribution. The problem is moral, not structural, as modern man in his own kind of irrationality wishes to describe it. The evil decried by Amos and Isaiah is not structural and distributional evil. They speak against personal sin of individuals. The people are guilty because they bribe judges and use false weights and measures. Such actions are wrong; they are also stupid, since the victims of these abuses could always find a way to retaliate.

Herbert Schlossberg brings in a timely comment when he says,

> The Bible says almost nothing about poverty as a sociological phenomenon, but says a great deal about evil acts that people do to others. The prophets were concerned neither about social analysis as such, nor about issues of relative incomes, that are the preoccupation of so much governmental and academic analysis: but rather about the ethical lapses that took place in their societies and the impact of those lapses on the innocent.[41]

Failing to see the difference leads to heaping guilt feelings on people whose only fault is that they are not equally poor. The sharing of abundance is a moral, intellectual, and spiritual duty and the consequence of rational insight. That abundance is one of material help *and* moral-spiritual understanding, without which most people in the world are still suffering the results of the Fall and their own irrationalities in spite of all structural adjustments and distributive efforts independent of personal effort, contribution, and merit.

Such leveling interventions fail to produce the imagined result, and they also weaken the evidence of, and motivation for, personal action. They are, in fact, a form of subsidies for those who without fault of their own have fallen on tough times and for inferior, uncompetitive workmanship. They also have the effect of removing the challenge that death presents in any life, to improve, to seek solutions.

Peter gave neither money—which he did not have—nor an invitation to join the early Christian soup kitchens in Jerusalem to the beggar; he provided a solid ground for all of life (see Acts 3). The present solidarity concerns are a distortion in their single concern about material poverty alone. Drawing on wealth created through means such as distribution mechanisms and structural correctives limits the possibilities of effectively removing social problems through investment, training, creation of employment, and the corollary of spiritual and intellectual training leading to motivation and self-esteem.

This position is irrational, for the concern for material wealth without a similar concern for the moral-spiritual wealth has never led to a wealthier society. Yet it explains a certain primitivism in the popular mind-set and the angry reactions against the biblical emphasis on personal effort as the basis for wealth distribution. It accuses economic liberalism and the Christians on the delivery end without noticing the importance of precisely this view at the foundational and productive end. Then the concern for material distribution toward equality takes on a similar selfishness in terms of rights and entitlements, which was critiqued at the outset.

Both destroy the human society; both are equally irrational. Both have a common spiritual view at the beginning in that man is merely a biological fact in a state of nature. For the selfish individualist, only the fit will survive. For the egalitarian, the greater picture of the harmony of impersonal nature serves as guide. Neither has the stuff required for a human society and a world of business in open transactions, market possibilities, and the wider concerns of justice and human life in a world of scarcity. Only a verifiable and rational metaphysical world view can provide that with the encouragements, the sanctions, and an understanding of the nature of man, history, and the world around us. With these qualifications in place, only God's Word and work suffice.

With the biblical understanding, beginning with the personal Creator, a real fall, and the place of the human being in significant history, the many modern centrifugal factors (i.e., of mobility, a futuristic and irrationally selfish outlook, a sensuality that replaces the search for making sense of all of life) can be restrained, ordered, and rejected. The lack of common goals and values, which are so essential for business and human activities and themselves results of a radical pluralism in modern democracies, becomes obvious in the destructive rivalries. The Bible puts a concern for facts and relationships, for history and human realities, back into human grasp and broadens one's understanding of fact and purpose, of business realities and rational-cultural needs. It gives a freedom to human life under God and also in reality of society. It limits the utopian appeal of new societies, which offer a world without problems and all the solutions for the price of present injustice and massive interference with the free flow of ideas and the free exchange of goods and services. The Bible defines the world as fallen, human beings as image-bearers of the personal God of the universe, and life as an effort in battle against death. Against the faith of the egalitarian, the Bible reveals the history of personal significance, of wealth, creation, and distribution through responsible persons.

In a similar way, the Bible sets the rewards for effort in a framework of being content and thankful. De Tocqueville observed that modern man, without the Bible and under the Enlightenment vision of the new and self-made man, tends to be consumed by nervous longing for further things *not yet* owned.[42] Being always driven to possess more or to create a new humanity—the two extremes of unbiblical orientations—destroys the life of which the Bible speaks in appreciation of the personal effort for material and relational wealth.

Both extremes also deviate from the biblical picture in that the first relates more to the struggle for the survival of the fittest in biological and impersonal battles, while the second follows an image of nature as a balanced organism, an equally impersonal reality. The first worships man as god; the second worships the harmony in that idea of nature. Both partake of the fundamental pagan and irrational notion that man should either follow himself or disappear in the oneness of nature, humanity, or simply Being.

CONCLUSION

The Bible attributes the creation and distribution of wealth to personal effort, initiative, and responsibility. Each person should be encouraged through incentives and through teaching of the moral-intellectual and cultural context of human life. Material considerations do not adequately describe human life; by themselves, they further a mentality of the survival of the fittest. Scarcity in wealth includes scarcity in the knowledge of the place and purpose of human life, the individual and society, the limits in a fallen world, and the high calling to assert human creativity in all areas. Making these areas a further part of effort and the creation and distribution of wealth will prevent the form of selfishness and alienation so common today on every level of enterprise.

A deliberate effort is needed to reclaim the hearts and minds of people for the biblical perspective and to place the question of faith back into the context of all of life. To this end, business should be encouraged to strengthen and encourage every possible avenue in which human realities of effort, creativity, and a rational-moral viewpoint can be expressed. Our orientation is not the market alone, though the freedom of the market should be treasured as all other freedoms. Rather, the pursuit of those realities in material business transactions reflect and declare the existence of the God of the Bible. By that I mean an agreed price for a product without moral restraints toward those who cannot afford it, but a selection of products that exhibit one's own moral-cultural purpose. We are disciples and disciplers within a network of rational values.

We are also called to work for wealth and surplus in a fallen world in which scarcity is not only our own future possibility, but also a current reality in the lives of others. If we are to link hands with them now, a hard bargain needs to be made, efficiency encouraged, and initiative rewarded. One can only give what one has earned first in the resistance to the status quo. Adam and Eve could face a larger family because Adam was willing to work the fields by the sweat of the brow. Here again, the knowledge that we do not live in *one* universe with *one* set of known resources, which need to be preserved for *one* humanity, is essential. Moral accusations stemming from that mind-set need to be rejected in light of the better evidence and the scriptural commands.

Wealth is the result of personal effort, sweat, initiative, knowledge, and virtue. The list includes self-sacrifice for future gain, material restraint for spiritual gain, and other organizing and chosen avenues to reach goals. When these things have been encouraged through reward or other forms of recognition, more resources, a livelier exchange of ideas and insights, and a greater benefit for all in material and societal wealth have always been the consequences. In fact, parallel to the Queen of Sheba inquiring of Solomon's wisdom and Solomon's God, most of the world's inquiry and resentment have focused on the singular ability of creating wealth in the wide sense by the culture that has had a direct influence of biblical teaching in the past.[43]

In that culture, the general reward to the free exercise of personal effort, contribution and merit in the form of available created wealth must also be acknowledged. It shows that more can be done to the society at large through such steps in accordance with the biblical teaching in society and in the lives of individuals than through false religious spirituality or imposed systems of distribution. As a spinoff, the degree of private altruism and personal benevolence was in the past in some direct relationship to such grounds for wealth distribution. Mother Teresa is able to assist the poor and dying in Calcutta in her own way only because the wealth created by the personal effort in our society created enough resources (material and spiritual) that can be shared with her. Their own culture does not provide such abilities or concerns. Lasting change in that impersonal outlook of the Indian culture can only come when people are not only accompanied to death, but when their resistance to death is encouraged through personal spiritual and material transformation. No amount of ethical concerns and spiritual exhortation will accomplish a more humane society unless the basic facts of creation, of God's mind and purposes, and of the human creative reality are respected. Without that, only sorrow and common poverty will result. Much of the world is a tragic living example of such poverty.

It can only become worse when businesses are run by false religious concerns without the biblical world view and when the distribution of wealth is not the concern of persons anymore. "A Company run on Biblical norms rather than profits"[44] does not and should not exist with regard to the reward for personal effort and effective creation of surplus. Yet the concern behind such a statement must address that person in the wider obligations established by the existence of God, our high calling as in the *imago dei* and the common battle against sin and the results of sin. Thus, the use and further investment of rewards and profits must be our concern within the wider cultural mandates given to us in Scripture so that we can make the world inhabitable again for man.

EDITOR'S REFLECTIONS

Udo Middelmann makes a very strong case for the biblical significance of understanding the human as a choice-maker. It is, indeed, important. We are accountable to God for our efforts to overcome the effects of the Fall and their constraining influence on the production-distribution functions assigned to us by Him. In fact, the case he presented for human responsibility and effort was so strong that other participating scholars asked Mr. Middelmann where Christ fit into his analysis.

He responded immediately that Christ is at the very heart of his analysis. Christ's love for us, when known and accepted, sets us free from the old bondage to "self" and restores us to a living relationship with God. Knowing God and being loved by Him move us to desire His will, which becomes the very motivating force enabling us to live, once again, as God had originally intended. The Fall brought with it a new dimension to work—toil and sweat (see Gen. 3:17-19)—which many people shun. Redemption restores our motivation, which energizes us to "work heartily, as for the Lord" (Col. 3:23).

The scholars continued to probe, though, as to whether or not Mr. Middelmann's case needed to be balanced by reflecting on other biblical truths that deal with things like the Jubilee and the gleaning laws. What was God's intent when He instituted these provisions? If these concepts were given to Israel when it was a theocracy, are the concerns embodied in them now the responsibility of the state? What, if any, are the responsibilities of the community for those who "fall between the cracks" of society?

The poor are always with us; we can do good for them whenever we wish (see Mark 14:7). Should only individuals consider the needs of the poor? If individuals and private institutions are to seek ways to help the needy, can the state also legitimately act to help the disadvantaged? How do we really help the poor, though, and not enable them to become falsely dependent on artificial props that ultimately enslave them to their helpers? Is capitalism, socialism, or some yet-to-be-defined third economic system the best one in which to address these questions? Dr. Robert Wauzzinski addressed the relationship that ought to exist between individuals, private enterprises, and the state.

Several things should be kept in mind while reading Dr. Wauzzinski's chapter. First, he perceives that many underlying assumptions of both capitalism and socialism are fundamentally out of conformity with biblical revelation. He discusses these differences in some detail and concludes that Christians should discover and operationalize an alternative economic system. He believes a more just system lies between the extremes of capitalism and socialism, and he offers some tentative suggestions on what such a system might look like.

Second, Dr. Wauzzinski correctly understands that the capitalistic economic model was nurtured and sustained in its ascending days on the back of the natural law, which was believed by many to be value neutral. Christians and nonChristians had different reasons for championing the rise of capitalism, but both groups supported it vigorously. The belief that the natural law is value neutral was popular and is still operative today in some quarters. Wauzzinski rejects the naive aspects of this view, for much of what is identified as the natural law is, in fact, a human reaction to natural realities. He is correct in not confusing human reactions with what is natural. Capitalism is not value neutral! Allowing persons with "natural advantages," in a fallen world, to "rule" those with "natural inequalities"—physical, mental, and experiential differences— creates a prima facie basis for wondering if justice will automatically result in such a fallen natural environment.

Finally, Dr. Wauzzinski believes the entire ethos of Adam Smith (and others), who so profoundly shaped the early and prevailing view of capitalism, was saturated with Immanuel Kant's view of man as an "autonomous" being. (Autonomous man has an independent will.) God's influence, presence, and will are greatly diminished in importance in such a view. The will of the community is also subordinated to the will of the individual. Individualism is elevated to a pinnacle of endearment, and self-interest is subtly glorified. This world view was united with capitalism and stands against many biblical truths at various points.

The first part of Robert Wauzzinski's chapter assumes that the reader is familiar, to a degree, with macroeconomic terminology. But even the economic novice should have little trouble comprehending the real thrust of his position. Every thoughtful Christian business professional ought to examine the basic assumptions of capitalism and ask if they are compatible with biblical data.

CHAPTER 11

THE GOSPEL, BUSINESS, AND THE STATE

Robert A. Wauzzinski

Dr. Robert A. Wauzzinski occupies the Edward B. Lindaman Chair of Communication, Technology, and Change at Whitworth College in Spokane, Washington. The Chair is an interdisciplinary one with assigned responsibilities in the disciplines of technology, economics, ethics, and religion, as well as the history and philosophy of science. He has authored a book on the relationship between evangelical Protestantism and the Industrial Revolution, as well as several articles on the general interrelationship of Christianity and economics.

Current forms of opulence theology and economic scandals within the Church should cause Christians to deeply reexamine the role that money plays in our lives. Capitalism and socialist-Marxism[1] are the two dominant ideologies that argue for how wealth should be integrated within society. I will attempt to show why these two ideologies are secular and hence, finally, inadequate for Christians.

Modern economies manifest at least one major cancerous contradiction: "freedom" is often set at odds with "justice." That is, economies that stress self-interest, individual choice, and the power of the market to determine the internal nature of business and tout efficiency seem to generate their own needs for justice or public welfare and social good. Various transfer payments are usually initiated to address the problem of want that arises in part due to the pursuit of freedom and self-interest. Alternately, economies that stress justice, the plight of the oppressed, and the social nature of the production process are weak at motivating workers, putting an end to waste, and limiting the ever-expanding, self-serving bureaucracy. Furthermore, when these ideologies are presented in contrast, a more fundamental tension is manifest. Capitalism abundantly produces while it struggles with distribution; socialism distributes well while it fails to adequately produce.

I will argue that these fundamental tensions grow out of exaggerated assumptions. These secular assumptions affect, nevertheless, the way we produce, consume, distribute our wealth, view ourselves and our world, and interpret the gospel.

PROBLEM DEFINED

The contradiction being referred to is built on the debate between individualism and collectivism. In one system, the needs, freedoms, and choices of the individual become the alleged foundation and glue for society. Collectivism, on the other hand, believes that this individualistic ethic creates vast injustices and inequalities and so attempts to remedy the problem by collectivizing authority and wealth. Let us look at how both systems attempt to tackle the persistent problem of need.

Individualism—the ideology that helped spawn capitalism—values individual desire above all other social aspirations.[2] Indeed, social institutions grow out of individual needs and desires according to this dogma.[3] Central to certain portions of individualism, in turn, is the all-encompassing nature of the social glue of self-interest. Thus, Adam Smith, modern capitalism's initiator, says,

> As every individual endeavors as much as he can to both employ his capital in the support of domestic industry, and so to direct that industry that its produce may be of the greatest value, [the individual] . . . neither intends to promote public interest nor knows how much he is prompting it. . . . He only intends his own security . . . as in so many cases, led by an invisible hand to promote an end which was not part of his intention.[4]

This optimistic quote betrays a secular faith or certainty in the power of a deistic-nonpersonal god[5] to arrange social fate so that, ironically, the self-interest of people becomes glue and tonic for society.

Before self-interest could govern society, however, traditional religion and the rule of revelation had to be "overthrown,"[6] and in their place the radical and complete demands of autonomy had to reign. Autonomy, in turn, replaced traditional morality (at least "morality" was supposed to be present in society) with acquisitiveness[7] as the key economic virtue, with the result that people increasingly turned their heads from Heaven to earth in an attempt to buy happiness.[8] Happiness, or "value," was measured by the expanding yields of mass production as validated by the consumer's vote in the marketplace.[9] The

market, it was thought, could best coordinate and measure individual preference, quality of goods, resource allocation, and price.

Government, according to this ideology, and especially because of the
presiding notion of individual autonomy, governed best when it governed least.
Accordingly, justice was thought to be the maximization of freedom. Individuals granted government the ability to guarantee contracts so that private
property—the supreme gain of individual pursuit—could be established. To the
extent that autonomy—literally self-law—became the law of life, private property became infused with the rebellious spirit. Therefore, this view held high the
banner of economic freedom and regarded economic self-interest as social
gospel,[10] defining contents of justice, freedom, and the relationship of business
to governmental activity.

Capitalism evolved into the twentieth century with a mixed report card of
success and failure until the Depression. The Great Gloom that hung over the
world during the thirties was inspired by chronic unemployment, an unhealthy
distribution of wealth, failure of aggregate or overall supply, a slump in demand
and production, not to mention the increased social malaise brought about by
World War I. Simply hoping the market would correct itself (as traditional
capitalists thought) did not better the situation; the market could not correct
itself. A growing number of economists, led by John M. Keynes, became
sanguine about an unaided economic solution. The market had to be managed
by experts if capitalism was to be saved, thought Keynes.

Keynes aimed his considerable academic acumen at the problem of
depressed aggregate wealth. Because a depressed market could not provide for
an adequate national income, the government (mostly federal) had to intervene
in the market to shore it up. A vigorous economy was thought to result from an
increase in deficit spending, aggregate savings, investment, and consumption,
and from expanding operations. Interest rates, moreover, had to be monitored.
Paper money also had to be properly managed to keep pace with perceived
economic needs.

Keynes functions as a transitional figure between individualism and collectivism because of his seemingly conflicting desires. Although touting capitalism's virtues, he approached collectivism by lumping social institutional spending into aggregate categories. Due to emphasis on an expanding role for
government, the reality of a glutted public sector seemed inevitable.[11] "Public"
was increasingly equated with a lump-sum, government-managed economy.

Keynes, like his capitalistic predecessors, did not disregard economic
autonomy; he simply attempted to autonomously manage it.[12] Indeed, greed
was to be a god in the short run so that in the long run, we would be free to return
to traditional virtues.[13]

Keynes's theories seem to be gripped by a central irony. Since the market is unable to provide sufficient aggregate wealth, the federal government must assume responsibility for market activities; however, if the government does its job thoroughly, the market will thereby shrink in size *as will the responsibility level of many social institutions.*

Freedom, in this view, is again the fruit of acquisitiveness that in the short run frees one from want and in the long run allows one to return to traditional virtues. Justice, or the fair access to these fruits, results from the increasing management of resources by the government on behalf of public welfare. Concomitantly, "social" justice is often equated, perhaps unintentionally, with governmental justice precisely because of Keynes's emphasis on aggregate economics.[14] In Keynes's mind, Smith's naturalistic deity failed and had to be replaced by the economic manager.[15]

We have seen in Keynes's theory an attempt at a creative synthesis[16] between individualism and collectivism. In Marxist-Leninist theory, in particular, and in socialism, in general, a full-fledged collectivism is manifest. The social institution that increasingly predominates in social affairs, especially the part of society that is the brunt of economic oppression, is the state. Just as the individual's wants and needs define social reality for capitalism, so the state corrupts the meaning of many social institutions in a collectivist society.

Marx's view of the world was filtered through the glasses of dialectical economic materialism. History, according to Marx, is built on the sweat of production, which in turn rests on the oppression of the worker by his employer-ruler. Gradually growing enraged by this treatment, the oppressed worker revolts causing, thereby, cataclysmic social change. The revolt and the resulting culture are the very antithesis or opposite of what the ruling class had intended. Eventually, however, a synthesis or compromise is reached between disparate parties that becomes the new social order.

This entire process is anchored in the swelter of production. Friedrich Engels, Marx's long-time supporter and friend, once wrote,

> The materialist conception of history starts from the principle that pro-
> duction, and with production the exchange of its products, is the very
> basis of every social order, that in every society which has appeared in
> history the distribution of the products, and with it the division of society
> into classes . . . is determined by what is produced and how it is
> produced.[17]

Thus, for Marx, history is reduced to a struggle over the fundamental entity of life—wealth.

While society is rooted in the struggle for the control of material productions, production is rooted in labor.[18] Labor transforms the dreams of the capitalist and the raw material into a finished good capable of commanding a profit. Problems arise when the owners of production realize an enormous profit, or the workers surplus value, while paying the workers subsistence wages. This process represents the essence of injustice for Marx.

Marx maintained that capitalists will tighten their wirelike grip over the production process, thereby thoroughly integrating the creation of wealth, out of the fear of losing control. Marx believed that markets and men under capitalism would eventually be controlled. At the same time, private property— the fruit of individualistic egoism, which is allegedly born out of freedom—is built on the sweat of human labor and hence is held irresponsibly. This contradiction of irresponsible freedom and autocratic control will be among the tensions that cause the downfall of capitalism, according to Marx.

Although capitalism would eventually collapse because of its own contradictions, Marx wanted to hasten the demise by revolution. The violent overthrow of the bourgeoisie oppression committed against the worker is conceivable because humans are essentially autonomous and therefore completely capable of determining their own history. That is, the determinism caused by economic enslavement could be negated by the human ability to re-create history by violence. And although the conditions following the revolution may resemble tyranny, the final Communist solution would usher in an era of universal justice or an end to the alienation of the worker from the fruit of his labor. Collectivization is an interim step to this end. Thus, Marx tried to overcome the tension between justice and freedom by siding with justice. It remains to be seen if justice was served through Marx and his followers.

The vehicle for social justice was the state, as we have said. Marx proposed that the state undertake the following measures before its abolition:

—abolition of all private property and application of all rents to public welfare.
—centralization of credit by means of a national bank, thereby giving the state exclusive monopoly of capital.
—centralization of all means of communication and transportation.
—state ownership of factories, instruments of production, and wastelands.

Furthermore, if one were to add to this list the socialist penchant for attempting to dictate the mores of such institutions as schools, families, and churches, we have a clearer picture of how the state has attempted to define social reality.

This brief survey does not begin to adequately cover the history of economics in general or the depth of the individualist-collectivist debate in particular. However, the outline accurately reflects both the individualist-collectivist, freedom-justice of freedom-determinism debate.[20] What follows is a critique of these alternatives with theoretical and practical alternatives.

BY THEIR FRUITS YOU SHALL KNOW THEM

Our Lord maintains that by the fruits of one's life a basic direction and commitment can be discerned (see Matthew 7:15-20). This fact is certainly true in economics; basic secular assumptions result in oppression and poverty. Let us begin with capitalism.

That the study of economics and the practice of business are not value free, as some claim,[21] seems to need no justification. The active presence of commitments, beliefs, social customs, and values is at work in theory and practice. Furthermore, to pretend that these forces are not at work is to attempt to mask autonomy.

The Christian must first question the place given to self-interest. As the Reformer John Calvin has said, "Thus it will come about that we shall not only join zeal for another's benefit with care for our own advantage, but shall subordinate the latter to the former."[22] To believe that social harmony can be realized through an aggregate of self-satisfaction, or self-interest, however necessary, would not profoundly corrupt society and its members, would be sheer folly, according to Calvin. After the fall into sin, self-interest too easily degenerates into disruptive selfishness. Ivan Boesky, who was nabbed for unethical inside-trading on Wall Street, is, therefore, the fruit—not the exception—of capitalism.

Likewise, the secular equation of labor with "factor of production"[23] strips work of its God-ordained blessedness and objectifies it, making labor a calculable "thing" to sell to the highest bidder.[24] Such a "factor" can summarily be paid and stripped of its moral and social responsibilities as well as much of its dignity. To the extent that capitalism has so defined labor, it has ironically undercut the quality of production by reducing the dignity and authority of labor relative to the status and power of management. Therefore, it is currently difficult to rediscover many forms of work as a God-given calling.

Utilitarianism's influence on capitalism and our society must also be questioned. The equation of happiness with consumption and disutility or pain with labor is highly suspect and myopic.[25] Labor is a good gift from our Father; it only becomes tainted in sin. It is subject to redemption and joy in Christ. Moreover, to the extent that utility functions as an "end state" (or goal) in economics, land, labor, and capital function as a means to this end. Accordingly, environmental "tradeoffs," the objectification of labor, and the aggrandizement of capital are tolerated because they bring us "happiness." Could not the operative force of this utilitarian calculus help explain the gospel of health and wealth that is so prevalent in our country today? And would not this definition of happiness help explain how the gospel is reinterpreted by some as the avenue to personal peace and prosperity?

Furthermore, consumption validates production in neoconservative capitalism. The so-called marginalists shifted their entire emphasis in value theory from "absolute" value theory to a theory of exchange.[26] Abandoned are the theories explaining the motivation for consumer spending. Rather, microeconomics is especially concerned with the consumer's demonstrated desire for utility maximization (at the margin). The consumer's preference is simply quantified, not given a value preference. That is, neocapitalism has no demonstrated way, beyond calculating utility states, to account for "morality" *in* and *through* market exchanges.[27] To be sure, morality can be added to the market—and this has been one of the traditional functions of religion within capitalist economies[28]—but this view of the market has no inherent normative principle to differentiate the sale of drugs from Bibles; they both provide different utility options. Or, to say it differently, moral and legal law functions as an *external* restraint, thereby conflicting with the "free" market that is an aggregate of self-interested utility maximizers.

Scarcity is redefined in light of this view of "consumer sovereignty." An "absolute" definition of scarcity is abandoned in favor of a view of scarcity attuned to the "perceived" needs and resources of the consumer. The rational consumer (fictitious ideal type), armed with perfect information, seeks the best quality goods at the lowest possible price. However, the goal is to purchase one's "perceived needs," limited resources notwithstanding. Do real economic means always equal "perceived needs"? Perhaps our current deficit problem can answer that question.[29] Perhaps consumer greed causes the expansion of "needs" beyond means?

If this analysis of consumer sovereignty is attached to the assertion that capitalism is driven by individualism, one can see why capitalism does well on the production and consumption of goods while tending to fail or falter on the distribution and preservation of goods and nature, claims of the free market notwithstanding.[30] Therefore, to correct for the social and economic disturbances caused by the free market, the government has had to (a) increasingly assume a watchdog function over various market activities and (b) use its powers of taxation to command and then transfer monies to those who, for various reasons, are incapable of sufficient utility maximization, even while (c) it supports many markets with subsidies.[31] Such a confused and pragmatic state-business liaison should prompt a radical rethinking of current capitalism's assumptions.

John M. Keynes rethought and redid the traditional *laissez faire* relationship of government and business. To cope with the perceived failures of the market, Keynes became the prophet of the modern welfare state. However, in so doing, he created a kind of aggregate-ism or an exaggeration of aggregate economies to the detriment of socioeconomic reality.

Keynes attempted to rescue capitalism as has been mentioned. Among other things, certain end states like profit and utility maximization are not questioned. Rather, means like labor, capital, currency, and land are treated as technical means to the end of utility maximization, with a resultant loss of personal responsibility. The economy or data circle is viewed, moreover, like a self-contained unit whose internal workings can be fed or made to suffer by the efforts of a group of experts. Economic causes and results are a product of a cause-and-effect network of malleable parts, so it is believed.

Keynes's "tank" or economy leaves very little room for human responsibility even while it attempts to save individual economic freedom through increased state involvement in the market. Keynes considered it problematic if consumers were savings conscious because of the endangerment to consumption. An economy that manifests too little consumption and/or investment often had to be force-fed large amounts of money—like a money-making hen—to achieve the right results. However, the economy cannot be overfed with paper money, lest it "overheat" or manifest inflation. The government's deficit spending is needed to achieve continuous growth. In all these maneuvers, people are the recipients, not responsible agents of public welfare and policy.

One need not look beyond the stock market crash of October 1987 sparked by the fears of foreign creditors over rising federal deficits to critique the greed lying behind federal deficit spending.[32] Indeed, by their fruits you will know them.[33] However, the federal deficits do not appear to be caused by greed. They seem to arise out of the mandates of national defense, social welfare, and the modern corporation's "needs" for massive amounts of capital to meet the demands for investment capital that aggregate savings alone cannot fund. Aggregate savings, in turn, are insufficient because aggregate consumption is too great. Aggregate consumption arises, in turn, out of the very processes set in motion by aggregate analysis. That is, there is little internal interdependence among the factors of the economy because of (a) the autonomous, nearly insatiable desires for wealth that lustfully follow profitable markets (thereby weakening others) creating (b) the need for government involvement in first the weaker markets, then the aggregate market.

Finally, and perhaps most problematically, aggregate analysis in the main blurs economic activities and weakens social reality as it actually exists because of its overpreoccupation with micro-macroeconomic analysis. Neither unrelated individual entities, represented in microeconomics, nor aggregates, represented by macroeconomic theory, are the fundamental economic units. To be sure, persons spend, and governments have a collective influence on markets. However, underneath the Keynesian-inspired macro-micro distinction is an unbiblical philosophical premise: reality is either individualistic or aggregate, and the economic significance of social institutions is not of primary importance. Families, governments, schools, churches, and their *members* are economic. Their activity is profoundly interconnected such that a disturbance in one mode of life drastically affects all others. Thus, the macro-micro dichotomy that resulted from the Keynesian revolution is at best a theoretical device that inadequately reflects diverse reality as we experience it. Furthermore, to the degree that these institutions are not acknowledged and room given for their proper economic functioning, we will be holistically poorer for it.[34] Moreover, as I have noted, to the extent that the government becomes involved in the economy to bolster the market, the market and social reality lose their ability to be responsible.

My critique of Karl Marx's economic analysis will be brief for two reasons. First, orthodox Marxism has never been a serious option for most Americans. Second, its evils seem more transparent, though its critique of capitalism seems prophetic. Christian theoretical analysis of Marxism is necessary.[35] However, a most obvious practical fact of current Marxism best represents the fruit of Marx's theory. There is a demonic irony to the fact that Marx and socialism intended a movement for worker justice while his disciples use portions of his thought and the socialist process to oppress, say, Polish workers through the most repressive of governments! Perhaps Marx's own words found at the end of the *Manifesto* should be quoted to Polish Marxist-socialism: "Workers of Poland unite, you have nothing to lose but your [communistic] chains."

The oppression and the considerable loss of institutional freedom in many socialistic countries are due to the attempted collectivization of social reality; the people, the poor, the worker become the embodiment of capitalistic exploitation. Therefore, it is reasoned, it is just for the group to collectively redistribute wealth and increasingly assume economic responsibility *for* society. Justice is defined, therefore, by the state's collectivization of the means of wealth with the loss of member and institutional freedom. Accordingly, persons primarily find their identity as servants of the presiding group or the state. The state attempts to overcome the conflicts between acquisitive egoism and economic necessity by collectivization and a redistribution of wealth. This is the attempted great reconciliation of man with the fruits of his labor.

The utopian allusion to historical reconciliation is a secularized biblical notion based on idolatrous criteria. Marx's materialistic determinism is myopic and, ironically for Marx, serves to undercut his desire for freedom. Marx's materialistic myopia rests on the assumptions that all social reality depends on economic matters. The theory believes that social institutions will inevitably collapse under the weight of economic demands. The resiliency of private education, the prophetic Church, the family, private markets, and the critical theater in capitalistic countries, in spite of massive capitulations, prove Marx incorrect. Even if, however, Marxist-Leninist doctrine was correct, the means of state domination of social reality is not justified by the end of justice—it only makes the means more bitter.

I have attempted to show how the secularly inspired dilemma posed by individualism and collectivism cannot resolve the freedom-justice question and therefore leaves us with the deadly choice between public welfare and equality versus personal freedom, efficiency, and self-interest. Given this quandary, the best that can be expected is a pragmatic mixture of capitalistic and socialistic economies, or of public and private interests. Governments and business never come to a peaceful relationship.

I will argue in this next section how the gospel, understood in broad contours, can deliver us from this dilemma.

ALTERNATIVES

The gospel, or the revelations of God given for sin, comes to us under the general rubrics of creation, Fall, and redemption. We turn to these categories for our alternatives.

By creation, I do not mean simply nature. Rather, creation signifies the cosmos or the heavens and the earth created by God in order, regulation, and beauty while adorned with splendor.[36] The order manifest in creation represents the lawful might and purpose of the Creator God within all existence.[37] The "Let There Be's" of Genesis 1 are the sovereign vehicle of rule whereby *differentiated* life is called into being by God. In fact, there is a close-knit correlation between the sovereign creating, providing, preserving, and governing activities of the universe.[38] Kingdoms, kings, boundaries, and purposes, through His covenantal or faithful will, are indelibly impregnated into the creation at its inception.[39] Indeed, we can say after God in Genesis 1:31 that the entire creation was created "very good." It is very good because it is differentiated and created with meaning.

I liken this creation to a house with many rooms. The Master Architect has designed each room or area of life with a distinct purpose or meaning that manifests both a delimiting quality and the possibility of sustenance in spite of sin.

These rooms have been called spheres of life.[40] Their possibilities are sovereignly ordained and dependent upon God for their continued existence. They do not arise out of individual desires or needs; still less do they owe their origin to some aggregate or group. The *potential* for government and business, for example, originates in the ordinances of God (see Rom. 13:1).[41] This, of course, does not mean that God ordains a particular *form* of government (democracy, etc.); that would be an idolatrous suggestion. Rather, it does mean that God decrees that a government room universally manifests the need for justice in a particular place and time.

One may object to this interpretation, citing the lack of anything remotely resembling a government in "primitive" cultures. I answer the objection by saying that God is the Sustainer and Creator of the world. "Sustaining is a moving, unfolding, unlocking process, revealing continually a galaxy of diversity."[42] As creation progresses from the garden of Genesis to the city of Revelation, new social institutions are sovereignly ordained for service. Or to say it differently, if we can locate the origin of the family, government, and the Church in the sovereign will of God, why can we not do the same for businesses, schools, sports teams, and so on? And if the family has a God-ordained role and ordinance—to be committed—for its life, why can we not assume the same for other social spheres?[43] And finally, if we say that the state must promote certain activities (defense, taxes, exact laws) and *must not* interfere in other activities (do not tell me whom I am to marry), may we not also say that spheres of influence have their proper tasks and proper limitations as well?

This notion of societal spheres is my answer to the problems posed by individualism and collectivism. Businesses, governments, schools, and churches have their own created meaning and admit to no more fundamental division. The lawful establishment of these institutions and their concomitant ordinances represents the context of freedom. Submission to the will of God—His ordinances and precepts—provides the context for self-interest, freedom, social welfare, and justice; a harmonious blend of justice and prosperity comes only as we surrender our lives to Christ and flee from our autonomy.

Finally, and most importantly, we have Christ, our Logos or Word, who is the Source of all light and life in the creation and the hope of new life after the Fall.[44] Through the Logos, all things were made. Christ's reign effects a cohesion of diverse reality, even the relationship of government and business. Thus, creation and redemption, while distinguished by history and thought, find their proper relation to each other in Christ.[45]

The discussion of the Fall, like that of creation, is related to the discussion at hand and therefore does not claim to be exhaustive. Creation and all of its rooms are cursed because of the sin of humanity. Sin's effects are radical in that they proceed from the heart of sinful humanity,[46] and integral in that all that humanity touches becomes distorted because we and reality are interconnected.

The essence of sin is autonomy.

> In contrast to God's commandment and justice, mankind now substituted his own decisions or his own sovereignty and prerogative to choose. . . . Thus he chooses his OWN way and his OWN judgment and what pleases himself.[47]

The spirit that places self-interest above that of the neighbor's welfare, trusts in mammon over biblical principles (as was the case with Keynes), or uses government to oppress people in the name of justice is the spirit of autonomy and results in fragmentations.

This spirit of autonomy is an austere master. It twistedly[48] demands obedience in all areas of life. An object, a person, a process or, in our case, a room can be trusted in, can be hoped in, and can forcibly lead[49] cultural activities. Thus, Christ had to say, "Ye cannot serve [or worship] God and mammon [or money]" (Matt. 6:24).

We may depict this idolatry or worship of money with the conception of incorporation. Now by incorporation I do not mean the judicial act whereby a business attains legal status. Rather, I mean

> the reorganization of perceptions as well as enterprise and institutions [sic]. Furthermore, it means . . . not only the expansion of an industrial Capitalist system across the [U.S.] continent, the spread of market economy into all regions . . . but also . . . the remaking of cultural perceptions.[50]

The wish to orient society to self-interests and individualism or to direct it to the welfare state and economic determinism represents idolatry and a corruption of our social institutions. Schools become vocational factories; parenting becomes nurturing for success (complete with related anxieties); politicians run on buck-producing, rather than justice-producing, platforms, even while the "gospel of prosperity" prospers.

Mammon, not money as a good gift of creation, is evil. Speaking of the lust for money as portrayed in Luke 12:16-21, Geldenhuys says,

> It becomes greed, unquenchable lust for money or power. It never rests content with the "sufficient" provisions of God. It is acquisitive, material-

istic and linked with autonomy (*my* barns, *my* crops, *my* goods). He had full monopoly and was not a steward of something that was *lent* to him by God for His glory and for his neighbor's need.[51]

Barns, fruits, and goods were not created evil; they are part of God's very good creation. Nor are the amounts the central problem, though the abuses are apparent. Rather, Christ condemns the autonomous greed and acquisitiveness resulting from a self-satisfied, pleasure-oriented callousness to God and to one's neighbor. Perhaps the current American economic "reorientation" that has forgotten or, worse, made welfare objects of farmers, steelworkers, and auto-workers is an example of such callousness. Moreover, perhaps the autonomy of American capital that made promises to labor even while it secretly planned to relocate operations and expand into other markets, thus devastating communities, updates the urgency of Christ's words.

Redemption is our final biblical theme for consideration. I support the orthodox confession of justification by faith alone and its related notions. My intention in this section is to relate our faith to the problems at hand.

The term *salvation* can denote deliverance, liberation, or help. It is the preservation of all things bound up with human existence.[52] In other contexts, it can mean to save, keep, benefit or preserve, or to restore to harmony or health.[53] In the context of speaking of a variety of creational rooms and the myopia caused by sin, salvation is crucial! Salvation means a rediscovery of an ability to harmoniously live out all of God's intentions[54] in such a way that a wholeness and well-being occurs in all rooms. But how is this possible? Isn't salvation primarily a personal affair?

When proclaiming the Kingdom of God—God's reign on earth and through His new people—the Bible announces a new creation.[55] Indeed, in Jesus Christ's death and resurrection, God reconciles us in principle to Himself, our neighbor, ourselves, and the creation. Thus,

> the scope of redemption is as great as that of the fall; it embraces creation as a whole. The root cause of all evil on earth—namely the sin of the human race—is atoned for and overcome in Christ's death and resurrection. . . . Christ is the possibility of restoration.[56]

Accordingly, all of life falls under Christ's reign (see Col. 1:26ff.) and can be sanctified with prayer and thanksgiving (1 Tim. 4:4-5). This dynamic of salvation starts in the heart of a renewed mankind and thereby rents asunder the autonomous dynamic of history in favor of the power of God that is capable of restoring all of life to its created potential.

Nowhere is the intersection of the notion of salvation and creation more relevant than in the idea of stewardship. At least two traditions are used to describe economic activity: pagan-secular and Christian. In the first tradition, economics is equated with self-interest, in greater possession of wealth, even at the expense of others. Economics is equated with stewardship in the Christian tradition. A steward, though having access to all that the owner possessed, did not have final control of the property or its fruits.

Sin disrupts our stewardship. However, we may become renewed stewards in Christ. We may be ransomed from our greed and restored to a liberating service of our God and our neighbor. To have all in Christ means that we can sacrifice all to and for Christ (see Eph. 1:3; 2:5-9, esp. 2:7). The businesses, wages, profits, and dividends, therefore, must be seen in the light of the terrible "price" paid for our salvation; they are *not* "earned." They are most appropriately offered up to Him and our neighbor's need as a pleasing sacrifice. Because we are stewards, our view of wealth has to encompass a concern.for net fertility or growth as well as for the preservation of the world; we are to be as interested in profits as in capital, environmental quality, and human enrichment.

Justice, mercy, freedom, and social well-being come only through the Cross and Resurrection, which is to say that a sacrificial spirit does not count its interests as more valuable than those of another. At their best, capitalism and socialism manifest moments of these virtues when immediate gratification and a bloated bureaucracy, respectively, are overthrown for service of a wise customer and the needs of the disenfranchised. However, when self-interest and the state's oppression cloud sacrifice and renewed life, social agony is bound to follow.

I have suggested that God has established, then redeemed, the potential of social institutions (this being part of the new life in Christ) in general, while government and business in particular are called once again to do justice and stewardship, respectively.[57] In the section that follows, concrete examples of how these precepts are being realized will be demonstrated. Specifically, I will attempt to show how the fundamental notions of land, labor, and capital can be reformed. I will also attempt to show how cognizance of social institutions can greatly enhance economic theory and well-being.

It is clear that one's view of the world and its ultimate authority affects the way nature is regarded.[58] Nature is not a "free gift"; still less is it niggardly. Nor is it a vastly complex machine or a domain to be conquered, as various secular traditions allege. Treating nature in that way greatly undermines its value and contributes to the current ecosphere crises. Rather, the ecosphere of plants, animals, water, rocks, and soil is the physical basis for a notion of land as a concrete sign of the convenantal character of God.[59] It is not for sale to the highest bidder, nor is it fundamentally a wealth-producing entity. It belongs to Another! The market does not give it ultimate or even economic value; it was created with value that the process of exchange only *partially* enhances.

The notion of stewardship simultaneously cripples the treatment of property as private (read autonomous and individual) and collective (read state dominated). Grace prompts the Land Giver to allow room for us on His estate. Accordingly, while one holds the title to some property, and while the state protects certain trusts (like national forests), all gifts come with a price tag to be paid upon receipt of the gift. Use the land to glorify Me and benefit your neighbor, says God. An unbelieving, foolish heart treats property and its fruits as if it belongs to us to dispose of as we see fit. Like our talents, land does not become blessed until it serves another.

Land, like the creation, is created after its kind. The current penchant to see land as wealth-producing tends to treat land in a monolithic way, thus endangering the land's complementary or simultaneous ability to care for all people in a creationally diverse manner. The swampland-to-suburban-mall manifestation we see around us is at best myopic. Such a vision, like the market, often tends to be shortsighted because the time preferences, especially under Keynes, tend to emphasize short-term demands over long-range conservation. Fuel consumption is an example.

Labor, contrary to Karl Marx and David Ricardo, is not the basis of all value, if for no other reason than what I have just said about nature. Labor is also not a "factor of production." Labor is a professional calling before God's face whereby the possibilities and privileges of a specific calling serve to enhance— simultaneously—the production of goods and preserve possibilities for future generations. As we are called in Christ to surrender our entire lives to the Giver of life, we are gifted to competently pursue a career.[60]

Moreover, and this is especially difficult for market economies to calculate, avocations arise that provide meaningful services for little or no remuneration. The market with its cash-nexus myopia cannot account for the mercies of service or value because the monetary side of an avocation is not pronounced while the service side is. Should these services be weakened, we are the poorer for it. For example, if many were to leave volunteer positions at a nursing home, the services would have to be professionalized by the market or by the state with the ironic consequence that resulting tax or payment increases would cause a decrease in disposable income—assuming no other changes. It pays to help your local nursing home!

Because our labor is not fundamentally defined by wage demands, status, and job consciousness,[61] and is given by Christ, we are free to treat *any* labor as a ministry or service. We do not have to be ordained to serve God in our areas of competency. Rather, our labor can have dignity, and we can and should be treated with *respect*,[62] regardless of the position. Perhaps if this respect would become widespread, then the destruction and hostilities caused by the adversarial system would be lessened.[63] Labor and management could then reconcile their differences enough to jointly face the challenge brought on by the internationalization of competition through a process of codeterminating business operations.

Capital is hard to define. Do its functions include that of the owner, manager, investor, director, or the entrepreneur? All of these functions are included, along with attendant machinery, under the rubric of capital.

The problem facing capital is, again, its autonomy. The so-called indifference function suggests that capital can buy and sell labor in the labor market. Capital may or may not prefer one kind of worker over another; still less does it care about the quality of life for the "factor of production." Capital's law is to maximize profit. If this goal can be attained by reducing labor costs—by surreptitiously removing operations—then the goal, *not* a concern for the laborer, determines plant location.

The solutions to this problem are not the nationalization of industry. Because industry depends on a variety of social institutions for existence, it is proper to mandate that a plant closing be made public two years in advance of shutting down. The effect of such a law would be to (a) recognize the reality of the noneconomic responsibility that businesses have to communities because they have received noneconomic benefits from communities, (b) promote mutual understanding and accountability and hence enhance a more complete view of public welfare, and (c) give communities time to attract new businesses.

Capital should view itself as ad-ministration, that is, adding to the service (and not the burden) of the laborer and the community. To the extent that any facet of administration becomes a process unto itself, it becomes an idol that will ultimately corrode the business operation. In this spirit of the need for service by administrators of capital, I paraphrase 1 Peter 5:1-5:

> So I exhort the administrators among you. . . . Steward your employees that labor with you as God's charge to you. Do not do this out of force, but willingly, not for shameful gain, but eagerly, not dominating your employees, but as a servant to your employees. . . . Clothe yourselves in humility and service, for God opposes the proud but gives grace (profit) to the humble.[64]

Institutions fundamentally shape one's identity. Do they shape economic decisions, or are they to be subsumed under the rubric of the individual, aggregate sums, or the group? One example may help introduce this section.

When family commitments fade, transfer payments increase; Aid to Dependent Children is an example of this fact. How should institutional economic analysis tackle this problem?[65]

Let us start with the institution of banks considered from the viewpoint of (a) how they affect national policy and (b) how a Christian might integrate faith with banking. Banks are somewhat unique in that they operate on the supply-and-demand side of the market. Banks can buy and sell money; hence, they both control and are influenced by the laws of supply and demand. Moreover, the announced interest rates of certain leading banks have a ripple effect throughout the industry. Thus as institutions, they affect the national economy.

More to the point is banking's basic dictum. Banks lend at the highest possible rate allowed by law or the market to those who are considered good risks. This norm results in a preference for the wealthier patrons, even while it helps perpetuate poverty because poorer persons are considered too risky. In part, I believe this problem is caused by the risk aversion factor in capitalism.

Fortunately, there is an alternative to this situation. Dwelling House Savings and Loan Association of Pittsburgh, Pennsylvania, founded by Robert R. Lavelle in the 1950s, is located in and ministers to one of the most economically disadvantaged areas of that city. Through offering, on the average, 10 percent loans (even when the prime rate was near 19 percent in the late 1970s) to those considered risky, Lavelle has profoundly altered housing patterns around the nation.[66]

Because Lavelle takes seriously Christ's injunction to live out a life of grace, his lending institution reverses traditional banking orthodoxy. A brochure explains its purpose:

> Dwelling House attempts to reverse the traditional banking rule—by lending to people who may not be "good risks," at the lowest practical interest rate. Our goal is to approach people with respect and through encouragement and patient financial counselling, to help them become good risks. This follows God's command to serve the poor and the needy.[67]

This ministry is made possible by cutting advertising expenses, lowering salaries, minimizing needless facilities, keeping passbook rates at 5.5 percent, and not enacting high-interest certificates. Such sacrifices are hardly to be compared with the holistic richness gained by all who are associated with Dwelling House. Its uniqueness is manifest in its lack of an overriding notion of self-interest and state ownership and its positive influence on the economy and politics.[68]

The importance of the family's economic patterns must also be noted.

Many economists have traditionally treated families as utility maximizers, but this notion creates conflicts. Parenting requires thrift. If, however, there is a contradictory drive to instantaneous gratification, debt follows. This pattern has hurt the American economy. The Japanese do not have this problem because the traditional family virtue of thrift is still operative. The real pool of savings for investment and resultant job creation is a fruit, in part, of this pattern.

Finally, the increased presence of the "working mother" has also affected our economy. Traditional economic theory has created the ideal of a rational consumer. Accordingly, time and choice were in relative abundance, as compared to resources. Because the reverse is true today, convenience generally takes precedence over savings. Whether or not the reality of a two-career family helps is another question.[69]

We have arrived at our last and perhaps most crucial topic. Do we have to choose between the market or the state,[70] or some pragmatic mixture, to provide for our social welfare? I think a biblical view of justice and its relationship to creation and its manifold institutions can address our central dilemma in a fresh manner:

> Public justice as the central task of the state means enacting and adminis-
> tering public policy in such a way so as to safeguard and encourage
> people in the fulfillment of their manifold offices and callings in society,
> the governing task of the state itself being only one of many offices in
> society.[71]

Public justice involves the enhancement of a variety of callings or institutions so that institutional well-being and social well-being are simultaneously bettered.

Public justice from the perspective of sphere sovereignty means that governments may not legislate the capital formation process but may adjudicate how this process affects society. Government should convene representatives from labor-business consumers, environmentalists, the elderly, the disenfranchised, ecclesiastic leadership, family experts, along with the traditional budgetary luminaries. Adjudication should structurally, not pragmatically, enhance institutional well-being in the way it recognizes social diversity as God ordained and not the product of individuals vying for parts of an economic pie.[72]

This approach is not capitalistically *laissez faire* in that through the power of the sword, governments can (to use the biblical phrase) promote the common good necessary within institutions while punishing the evil present.[73] It is not aggregate-bound analysis because while national spending is kept in mind, institutional impact and import are more directly stressed. And finally it is not socialistic because no rationalization is being proposed. Social welfare is not the responsibility of the state; it occurs when adjudication considers the place and authority of society's several institutions.[74]

CONCLUSION

Clearly, then, the tension that has arisen out of individualism and collectivism will not suffice as a Christian foundation for economic theory or practice. Individualism and collectivism rarely, if ever, stand on their own. They must temper their views with elements of the "opposite" belief. Privatization, decentralization, and individual initiative are even now being injected into the Soviet economy. At the same time, in America, economic history "justice" has dictated that the "free" market and its virtues be "balanced" by transfer payments, market subsidies, and "public" interests. And although we are not headed in the near future toward one uniform economic system, the lack of integrity in both positions should cause the Christian pause.

What unique benefits might this perspective provide, say, for worker "needs"? The question can be answered only according to the standards that one deems essential. Thus, I suggest that space to live, freedom of movement, food and related biological processes, a holistic-feeling life, education, a sense of power or efficacy, ability to communicate needs, group solidarity, sufficient resources, access to art, just treatment, family and friends and, finally, faith in Christ (that struggles to realize a vision for all of life) are our needs. Neither government nor business can provide these needs; they are given for life by God. In fact, the social institutions that stand behind these needs must increasingly shoulder their respective burdens. However, businesses should provide sufficient remuneration so that all people feel they have options within these areas of life. Governments should provide sufficient legal space for these institutions to grow and thrive. The more wholeness that is manifest in social institutions, the more will be holistic riches. Day care is a good example. In a more creationally rich society, neighborhood people, businesses, extended families, schools, cooperatives, and churches become potential sources of child care. In turn, parents are freed to serve and develop in other areas, even while they earnestly pursue their parenting.

This approach obviously represents the ideal. But each social institution can call us, as per its own God-ordained room, to wholeness. Churches can preach the Kingdom, families can demonstrate the universal need for commitment, schools can provide wisdom, and so forth. And when these institutions reach their necessary limits, governments can "punish evil and promote the good" by legally limiting, adjudicating, and harmonizing (not coopting) institutional welfare.

Thus, freedom and justice seem to be more integrated in this view. Freedom, ironically, can be known only through submission to the whole counsel of God of which justice is but one aspect. Freedom is found in the limits and possibilities provided by stewardship and not by self-interest. Through institutional sacrifice and responsibility, public welfare is greatly enhanced, the needs of the Kingdom are fulfilled, and self-interest and the needs of institutions are properly harmonized. Consequently, mammon and the more or less tyrannical state bureaucracy have been resisted with the result that the rule of the Great King shines brighter in our midst.

EDITOR'S PERSPECTIVE

Robert Wauzzinski's contention that the ideologies of both capitalism and socialism, in their varied forms, are imperfect models from a Christian perspective is certainly a fair observation. Competition in its self-centered, worldly form, for example, is hard to square with Christian ideals without defining it in such a limited way as to render it meaningless as it really functions in the marketplace. There is no need to redefine competition in an effort to make it a biblically consonant term. Christians sometimes do this, however, in an effort to justify their conduct while overlooking the biblical concern for "attitudes." At its heart, competition is an attitude and not a behavior. After all, Adam Smith did build his arguments for competition on the grounds of self-interest, and Christians need not sanctify this in the affairs of the world. Self-interest, in the lives of those who do not truly love Christ, is hardly a virtue, even if it does "fire" capitalism.

Adam Smith glorified competition, and our culture accepted it as a central tenet of our economic system. Put simply, competition is watching a "rival" while serving a customer with "self" in mind. The Bible recognizes it as *rivalry* between neighbors and calls it "vanity and striving after wind" (Eccles. 4:4).

Collectivist models, on the other hand, have a definition of economic justice they want to impose on the community through regulation or taxation and redistribution. Their efforts rest on the beliefs that human equality should govern the consequences that reflect our natural differences. Egalitarians and socialists often assume that one person's economic advantage has been gained at the expense or loss of someone else. Individual advantages are assumptively suspected of harboring latent, if not active, injustices.

Robert Wauzzinski attempts to redress the various deficiencies in capitalism and socialism by defining an alternative economic system. Is he successful? Does he really identify a third kind of economic system, or does he simply rebalance the quasicapitalistic-egalitarian system we currently live in by adding one more level of consensus-seeking structure? If his concept of sphere sovereignty, where representatives from the different spheres of business (managers, laborers, suppliers, customers, etc.) are responsible for reaching a consensus on the distribution of wealth, does represent a new economic model, then who or what will adjudicate the differences that will inevitably arise in a fallen world among the various interest groups? If the relatively impersonal market that atomizes decisions (capitalism) does not adjudicate, and the government that centralizes decisions (socialism) does not adjudicate, then who or what will? And what will make them or it more just than the existing alternatives? Mankind's fallen nature is the "fly in the ointment" that must be realistically considered whenever we look for a better economic system.

Udo Middelmann's chapter emphasizing the biblical perspective on the freedom God has given each of His image-bearers stands in sharp contrast to Wauzzinski's "new way" where those who represent collective groups seek a consensus. The biblical data Mr. Middelmann points to was integrated historically with Adam Smith's economic concepts, and together they created the capitalistic system of the nineteenth and twentieth centuries. So many Christians have felt comfortable operating within the rubric of capitalism because the Christian concepts of personal freedom (governed and bounded by God's special revelation), hard work, efficiency (good stewardship), personal accountability, thrift, and work as a calling have been compatible with capitalism. But Christians have not always done a good job of attending to the injustices that can occur in any system when it is either abused or allowed to operate without taking note of how our fallen nature can distort our social reactions to the consequences of the "natural order."

The tensions over who or what will govern and adjudicate our systems of justice—economic, political, social, family, etc.—are ancient. The definition and assignment of responsibility, the legitimization of assumed authority (power), and the requirement for accountability are crucial considerations for any social order, for they are central to governance—personal or community. They are concepts associated with *rule*. God is the Sovereign Ruler, but autonomous man wants to rule, so the enmity between them is great.

When we reflect on God's call of Abraham, when God set him apart from the other nations with the intent of establishing a nation of people submissive to His will, we begin to grasp the significance of the contrast between the governance concepts of God and the ideas of men who want to be autonomous controllers of their own destiny.

Abraham and Lot found it necessary to separate because of overcrowding on the land, and Lot's decision to live in Sodom soon placed him in sore conflict with the world view of the surrounding culture. Moses' authority was called into question by those who opposed his leadership—Korah, Dathan, Abiram, and their 250 followers (see Num. 16:1-35). The people of Israel, in the days of Samuel, wanted a king, "such as all the other nations" had; they rejected God's *full* authority (see 1 Sam. 8).

Christians face a very complicated decision-making process as it relates to governance, for we have dual citizenships—a citizenship in Christ's Kingdom and a worldly citizenship. In Christ's Kingdom, as He reigns in His subjects' hearts, there is no biblically prescribed economic system. We must live in a system governed largely by people who do not give their allegiance to Christ.

Christians, upon entering the marketplace, have two levels of responsibility—that of personal conduct in the workplace and that of concern for what system of economics should be sought and maintained so God's mandates can be *best* carried out. (They cannot be perfectly carried out in a fallen world.)

On the level of personal behavior, we are to apply God's revealed principles to everyday problems in the marketplace. For example, if we love our subordinates, we will not allow them to get by with shoddy work; we will treat customers with small accounts with the same respect as we treat those with large ones; we will be careful to pay our workers well; we will not discriminate against persons with handicapping conditions.

Having an impact on the second level—shaping the basic economic system—is a much more complicated process that transcends the capacity of any one person. Christians must act while depending totally on God's common grace for all systems-changes. All economic systems reflect cultural presuppositions, a body of common law, legislative acts, administrative mandates, and judicial precedents, all of which establish the adjudicating process within the larger system. Changes in such basic systems, unless a revolution occurs as advocated and sought by Marx, are generally slow to take place.

Christians should not label specific economic systems as "Christian." God is not a capitalist or a socialist. On the other hand, God does want us to be motivated and excited about our work. He wants us to work hard and discover the wonders of His basic creation. He wants us to enjoy Him and His created order. So our task is to discern, build, and maintain a system that offers the best incentives to see these aspects of God's will carried out.

God has a heart for the poor. People who are precluded by mental and/or physical disadvantages from taking full advantage of the opportunities to enjoy the riches God has so abundantly provided allow the rest of us to demonstrate the true nature of our hearts. Which system will best support a compassionate response to their lot in life? What happens when the percentage of Christians in a culture declines, or is small, and Christian ideals are not the leaven of the marketplace? Should Christians support public welfare under some conditions? Can Christians, who cherish their choice-making responsibilities, refuse (in all cases) to support legislation-enacting regulations, or are there times when Christians should support government regulations?

The editor has no doubt that God has, through common grace, blessed His children in the Western world for several hundred years by enabling us to live in an environment where so much "choice-making" has been so freely allowed in the economic arena by those who adjudicate justice. As the antibiblical forces rise in our culture, however, Christians need to keep an eye on the exercise of *self-control* by business leaders. Self-control in the lives of nonChristians is ultimately a product of God's common grace. Should God withdraw His constraining grace from the affairs of the marketplace as evidence of His judgment, self-control would diminish. If this occurs, should Christian business professionals seek government regulation or allow economic injustices to increase?

For example, is regulation necessary to control environmental pollution in a high-tech society? Should we allow people to trade in the stock market on the basis of inside information? Should the workers and a community be given some reasonable advance warning of a plant closing? Should smoking in public be regulated? Should questions like these be adjudicated in a free capitalistic market, a regulated socialistic market, or a new representative market system where agents from the many stakeholders gather and seek a consensus?

Only the Spirit of God is capable of solving such complex and interdependent problems. In view of a growing world population, the ever-expanding development of "messy" technology, and the increasing interdependency of world economies (a reversal of the safeguards instituted at the tower of Babel [see Gen. 11:1-9]), we should plead with God for a great spiritual revival or the return of our Lord. Who else can govern righteously? In the meantime we are to work with sinful-capable people who seek more autonomy while needing meaningful boundaries of constraint. They live together with the consequences of their natural inequalities while professing equality.

ESCHATOLOGY AND BUSINESS ETHICS

What has the doctrine of the "end things" and "end times" (eschatology) got to do with business ethics? Are not our ethical concepts derived from the character and behavior of God? Is it even possible for historic or future events to shape ethical conduct? Furthermore, is not the Christian community so divided over the interpretation of Scripture when it speaks of the end times that its ethical influence, if any, would be divergent and confusing, not unifying?

Our view of eschatology is one of the three dominant shapers of our Christian world view. This book, and the entire series, is committed to examining biblical truths that *ought* to shape the world view of Christians in the marketplace, and our view of eschatology brings together our beliefs about history and matters of eternity. The future, the focus and subject of eschatology, is absolutely critical to our understanding of the purpose and meaning in life.

God created us with a three-dimensional perspective—past, present, and future. The editor believes that our view of eschatology is as vital to the shaping of our world view and business conduct as are the doctrines of God, man, the Fall, sin, and redemption, for without it the other doctrines are incomplete and devoid of their hope. At least three aspects of our world view are deeply influenced by our understanding of eschatology. First, our view of history and its significance is tied directly to our perception of the end times. Persons who have a circular view of history—Buddhists and Hindus, for example—perceive justice and righteousness from a totally different perspective than do Christians. Justice, in their world view, is an impersonal function of the cosmos, grounded in an impersonal spiritual cosmic law that measures out justice through the phenomenon of reincarnation. Righteousness, in their world view, is measured against the standards established by human experience and reason. Self-righteousness is all that can be known or hoped for. There is no belief in any special revelation or a personal God.

Second, our eschatology profoundly influences our willingness to quietly suffer personal injustices for the sake of righteousness and the name of Christ. Christians have a hope of things to come that is closely tied to our eschatology. It is said of Christ that "for the joy set before Him, [He] endured the cross" (Heb. 12:2). What was that joy? The joy that was sure to come *in the future* when He returned to be with the Father. Our eschatology elicits a trust in God's perfect way of justice. Vengeance can be left to Him; we can trust in His ways so completely that we are set free to even love our enemies.

Finally, our eschatology has psychological and motivational implications for how we assess and prioritize the creation mandates (family, *work*, and worship) and the Great Commission. These implications transcend the scope of this book, but we will look briefly at a few of them at the close of this section.

Dr. William S. Barker and Dr. John Jefferson Davis address the effects of premillennialist and postmillennialist views of the end times on business ethics. Their careful scholarship shows us how our views of eschatology can have an impact on our business behavior. They make no attempt to persuade us to embrace a particular eschatological understanding, but they do point to the importance of recognizing how it influences our world view.

In Dr. Barker's chapter, pay particular attention to the section entitled "Relevant Scripture Passages," where the thoughts of the apostles Peter, Paul, and John are set forth on how they believed eschatology should influence personal conduct. The apostles did not believe the doctrine of the end times was some pie-in-the-sky dream about the by-and-by. They saw it as having practical relevance for daily living.

CHAPTER 12

A PESSIMISTIC VIEW OF THE END OF HISTORY AND ITS IMPACT ON BUSINESS ETHICS

William S. Barker

Dr. William S. Barker is Professor of Church History at Westminster Theological Seminary in Philadelphia. A graduate of Princeton University, Cornell University, Covenant Theological Seminary, and Vanderbilt University, he has previously taught at Covenant College in Lookout Mountain, Tennessee, where he served as Dean of Faculty, and at Covenant Seminary in St. Louis, where he served as Dean of Faculty and as President. He was Editor of the Presbyterian Journal *and Publisher of God's World Publications in Asheville, North Carolina. He has also served as a pastor in suburban St. Louis and in inner-city Chattanooga, Tennessee.*

FOUNDATIONAL QUESTION: How is our view of the world and its significance affected by our theological understanding of the "end times" (eschatology), and how would this perception of reality affect our business ethics?

I. INTRODUCTION

"And this gospel of the kingdom will be preached in the whole world as a testimony to all nations, and then the end will come," said our Lord Jesus Christ to His disciples (Matt. 24:14, NIV). He was responding to their question about when the destruction of the Temple of Jerusalem that He had just foretold would occur and what would be the sign of His coming and of the end of the age.

In one sense, all of us who believe that the end of history is tied to the second coming of Jesus Christ can scarcely be described as pessimistic with regard to the end of history. With hallelujahs we affirm that, as the apostles saw

229

Him ascend, caught up in the clouds into Heaven (see Acts 1), He is going to come again in the clouds, in power and great glory, and every knee shall bow and every tongue shall confess that Jesus Christ is Lord, to the glory of God the Father. How can one be gloomy or pessimistic with a conclusion of the world's history like that?

But the term *pessimistic* as we are using it here refers to our expectations concerning the social structures of this world prior to the return of Christ. Some Christians regard the thousand-year reign of Christ referred to in Revelation 20:1-10 as taking place through the Church before the Second Coming; hence, they are described as believing in a "postmillennial" return of Christ, His coming after the thousand-year reign. Others of us believe that the thousand-year reign on earth will begin with the return of Christ; hence, we are "premillennialists." The pessimistic view of the end of history that we thus hold is that we do not find in Scripture, and hence do not expect, that the Kingdom of Christ will be fully manifested in the social structures of this world until He comes again. There are also "amillennialists," who interpret the thousand years in a strictly spiritual sense, who would share this pessimistic or realistic view of the world with us, although some amillennialists might have expectations closer to the optimism of the postmillennialists. The position represented in this chapter is that Scripture does not indicate a total overcoming of evil in this world until Jesus returns; therefore, while we have confidence in the Lord to accomplish His purposes in His time, our expectations are more pessimistic about the prospects for society.

How does this pessimistic expectation affect our business ethics? Certainly it is true that one's expectations can shape one's attitudes and actions. A person's eschatology, or understanding of the end times, can definitely influence his ethics. The Communist who sincerely believes that the Marxist dialectic of history is inevitably moving toward the dictatorship of the proletariat and the classless society will zealously apply his energies to the revolution that supposedly brings this to pass. In like manner, the postmillennial Christian may be moved by his optimistic expectations to apply himself energetically to the social projects that will contribute to bringing in the Kingdom.

But the ultimate motivator for the Christian is not success; it is obedience out of loving gratitude. It is the love of Christ that constrains us, says Paul (see 2 Cor. 5:14), not our love to Him so much as His love to us, God making Him who had no sin to be sin for us so that in Him we might become the righteousness of God (2 Cor. 5:21). Having Christ Jesus as Savior and Lord means that our activity in this life is directed and motivated by whatever is His intention. If we conclude from His Word that His intention is not to transform society before His return, we are nevertheless vitally concerned to obey His directions, whatever they may be. "If you love me," Jesus said repeatedly in the upper-room discourse, "you will obey what I command" (John 14-16, NIV). We gratefully recognize Christ as our King now. The fullness of His Kingdom may not be realized in this world until He comes again, but until then, we are just as zealous to carry out His intentions in this world.

There is a sense, then, in which Christ's Kingdom is "not yet" for the Christian; its fuller manifestation will be realized only when Jesus returns. But there is also a sense in which the Kingdom is "now," in that Christians live and work in this world as subject to the lordship of Christ, who is their King already. This "now, but not yet" aspect of the Kingdom of Christ will affect the way we conduct our business ethics. The "now" of Jesus' kingship will mean that we always, daily, render obedience to His clear commands in every sphere of life. And the "not yet" of His Kingdom, while not meaning that we expect to bring the social structures of unregenerate man entirely under the lordship of Christ, nevertheless serves as our sure hope and perfect ideal to impel us toward that eternal state, encouraging us onward and keeping us from ever settling for even the best achievements of this world.

What did the Lord want His disciples to pray for in the petition "Thy kingdom come"? The British Puritans of the seventeenth century answered, "That Satan's kingdom may be destroyed; and that the kingdom of grace may be advanced, ourselves and others brought into it, and kept in it; and that the kingdom of glory may be hastened."[1] The "kingdom of glory" is the "not yet" aspect, which we indeed want to hasten. The "kingdom of grace" is the "now" aspect, which entails both evangelism and discipleship, bringing into and keeping in the present Kingdom both ourselves and others; thus we carry out the Lord's Great Commission to His Church in Matthew 28:18-20—making disciples of all nations, baptizing them and teaching them to obey everything He has commanded. Finally, over against the "now" and "not yet" aspects of Christ's Kingdom there stands the kingdom of Satan, which must be destroyed.

The existence of the kingdom of Satan reminds us that we reside in a world of conflict. There is evil at work in this world beyond just the evil of our sinful human nature. One of the reasons why we do not anticipate the establishment of Christ's Kingdom on earth prior to His return is that Satan will ultimately be destroyed only at the end. Until that time, however, we are to oppose him and his kingdom wherever we can. Clearly, we can bring people from the realm of darkness into the realm of light through evangelism. But we have to counteract Satan's dominion in all the areas in which he traps people, whether it be destruction of families, abortion, pornography, poverty, ignorance and deceit, greed, or anything else seeking to thwart the Kingdom of Christ.

This world is not Satan's. He exercises such dominion as he has only by

God's delegation or by temporary usurpation. The earth is the Lord's. When it was created, it was pronounced good (see Gen. 1:31). And even since the fall of man and the curse upon creation, the goodness of God is manifest in nature (see Ps. 65:9-13), even to unbelievers (see Matt. 5:45). The conflict with Satan entails not only a redeeming of people from his clutches to the Kingdom of Christ, but also a reclaiming of this world from the Evil One to its rightful Lord.

Several relevant Scripture passages will help us to see how these themes relate to business ethics for the Christian. From the principles derived from these texts, some biblical propositions will be developed. Then after some particular problems are discussed, we shall consider specific applications of these scriptural principles to business ethics.

II. RELEVANT SCRIPTURE PASSAGES

Peter deals with the problem of the prolonged delay of Jesus' return:

> Since all these things are to be destroyed in this way, what sort of people ought you to be in holy conduct and godliness, looking for and hastening the coming of the day of God, on account of which the heavens will be destroyed by burning, and the elements will melt with intense heat! But according to His promise we are looking for new heavens and a new earth, in which righteousness dwells. Therefore, beloved, since you look for these things, be diligent to be found by Him in peace, spotless and blameless, and regard the patience of our Lord to be salvation. . . . You therefore, beloved, knowing this beforehand, be on your guard lest, being carried away by the error of unprincipled men, you fall from your own steadfastness, but grow in the grace and knowledge of our Lord and Savior Jesus Christ. To Him be the glory, both now and to the day of eternity. Amen. (2 Pet. 3:11-15,17-18, NASB)

Christians are being bothered by scoffers who argue that things just go on as they always have. Peter answers that God's timing is different from ours, but just as He created and brought the judgment of the Flood by His powerful word, so His Final Judgment by fire will come suddenly when men do not expect it.

Out of this context, Peter asks the pointed question, "Since everything will be destroyed in this way, what kind of people ought you to be?" (2 Pet. 3:11). He answers it in three ways. First, in keeping with God's promise, we are to look forward to a new heaven and a new earth, the home of righteousness. Either this earth we know is to be purged rather than utterly destroyed or an existence similar in some ways to present existence is projected—yet characterized by righteousness. In either case our aspirations are not to be bound up in what will be destroyed by God's Judgment. Second, we are to be of a different character from the unbelievers of this world. We are to be spotless, blameless, and at peace with God. We are not to be carried away by the error of lawless men. Instead we are to grow in the grace and knowledge of our Lord and Savior Jesus Christ. It is clear that through our relationship with the Holy God and with His Son, we are to be distinct in character from those who are ignorant of God's law. Third, we are not only to look forward to the day of God, but to speed its coming. How do we do that? Peter says that God is patient, wanting individuals to come to repentance. We are reminded that Jesus said that the gospel of the Kingdom will be preached in all the world and then the end will come (see Matt. 24). We speed the coming of that day, therefore, by carrying out all that is entailed in the Great Commission in both evangelism and discipleship, obeying all Jesus' commands.

Paul pictures us groaning in the process of our sanctification, longing to have the full salvation of our bodies realized, and even the whole creation groaning in this fashion:

> For I consider that the sufferings of this present time are not worthy to be compared with the glory that is to be revealed to us. For the anxious long-ing of the creation waits eagerly for the revealing of the sons of God. For the creation was subjected to futility, not of its own will, but because of Him who subjected it, in hope that the creation itself also will be set free from its slavery to corruption into the freedom of the glory of the children of God. For we know that the whole creation groans and suffers the pains of childbirth together until now. And not only this, but also we ourselves, having the first fruits of the Spirit, even we ourselves groan within our-selves, waiting eagerly for our adoption as sons, the redemption of our body. For in hope we have been saved, but hope that is seen is not hope; for why does one also hope for what he sees? But if we hope for what we do not see, with perseverance we wait eagerly for it. (Rom. 8:18-25, NASB)

The indication is that the created world will be liberated from its bondage to decay that is part of the curse. This destiny of the creation is linked to the glorious destiny of the children of God, with whose freedom the creation will also be liberated. Here the hope of redeemed mankind and the hope for the created world are closely tied together.

John uses the prospect of Jesus' second coming as an admonition to purity. In the wonder of what we will become, we shall see Him as He is and become like Him. He writes,

> Beloved, now we are children of God, and it has not appeared as yet what we shall be. We know that, when He appears, we shall be like Him, because we shall see Him just as He is. And everyone who has this hope fixed on Him purifies himself, just as He is pure. . . . The Son of God appeared for this purpose, that He might destroy the works of the devil. We know love by this, that He laid down His life for us; and we ought to lay down our lives for the brethren. But whoever has the world's goods, and beholds his brother in need and closes his heart against him, how does the love of God abide in him? Little children, let us not love with word or with tongue, but in deed and truth. (1 John 3:2-3,8,16-18, NASB)

The Son of God appeared so that He could destroy the Devil's work, and our purification must include this opposition to the Devil. It also means a Christlike love for our Christian brothers and sisters, including acts of mercy to those in need.

John is saying these things in the context of 1 John 2:15-18, where love of the world is set over against love of the Father and where opposition is also indicated by the appearance of antichrists. The end times are suggested by the reference to the world and its desires—the lust of the flesh, the lust of the eyes, and the pride of life—passing away, while the one who does the will of God the Father lives forever. John has in view the ultimate cosmic conflict, but his point is that the conflict is now, carried out in the Christlike purity that is manifested in concrete deeds of loving mercy.

Paul's comments on work are just as pertinent today as when he wrote them:

> Make it your ambition to lead a quiet life and attend to your own business and work with your hands, just as we commanded you; so that you may behave properly toward outsiders and not be in any need. . . . So then let us not sleep as others do, but let us be alert and sober. . . . But since we are of the day, let us be sober, having put on the breastplate of faith and love, and as a helmet, the hope of salvation. . . . But we request of you, brethren, that you appreciate those who diligently labor among you, and have charge over you in the Lord and give you instruction, and that you esteem them very highly in love because of their work. Live in peace with one another. And we urge you, brethren, admonish the unruly, encourage the fainthearted, help the weak, be patient with all men. See that no one repays another with evil for evil, but always seek after that which is good for one another and for all men. (1 Thess. 4:11-12; 5:6,8,12-15, NASB)

Here, in the context of one of the most stirring descriptions of the Second Coming (4:13-5:4), Paul exhorts Christians to the kind of hard work and self-control that will gain the respect of outsiders. A quiet industriousness will produce independence, which in turn will admonish those who are idle but will also show kindness to all. In another passage Paul also stresses being busy in doing what is right while shunning the brother who is idle (see 2 Thess. 3:6-15).

Ephesians 4:28, which is found in a passage on Christian living beginning with 4:1 and extending through 5:17, is the Bible's economic gospel in a nutshell: "Let him who steals steal no longer; but rather let him labor, performing with his own hands what is good, in order that he may have something to share with him who has need" (NASB). In a section that makes the cosmic contrast between light and darkness and that brands greed as a form of idolatry, this verse declares that (1) we are no longer to steal, but (2) we are to work, (3) doing something that is useful, (4) in order to be able to share with those in need. This is one of the ways in which we are imitators of God in His love, we are understanding the will of the Lord, we are pleasing the Lord, we are living a life worthy of our calling, and we are heirs of the Kingdom. Colossians 3:1-6 echoes many of these themes.

How are we to respond to evil? Paul has this answer:

> Never pay back evil for evil to anyone. Respect what is right in the sight of all men. If possible, so far as it depends on you, be at peace with all men. Never take your own revenge, beloved, but leave room for the wrath of God, for it is written, "Vengeance is Mine, I will repay," says the Lord. "But if your enemy is hungry, feed him, and if he is thirsty, give him a drink; for in so doing you will heap burning coals upon his head." Do not be overcome by evil, but overcome evil with good. (Rom. 12:17-21, NASB)

Being transformed by God's renewing of our minds, rather than being conformed to the pattern of this world, leads to our feeding even our enemies and leaving revenge to God. Once again we are in a context where ethics is associated with eschatology (cf. Rom. 13:8-14). Because we are aware of the ultimate outcome of this world, we are able—even though involved in the cosmic conflict between God and the Devil—to deal with our enemies in the loving spirit of Christ. In a similar passage that describes the conflict in terms of Spirit versus flesh, Paul urges that we not be weary in doing good but, as we have opportunity, do good to all people, especially to those who belong to the family of believers (see Gal. 6:7-10).

Advocating godliness with contentment, Paul warns about desiring wealth:

But godliness actually is a means of great gain, when accompanied by contentment. For we have brought nothing into the world, so we cannot take anything out of it either. And if we have food and covering, with these we shall be content. But those who want to get rich fall into temptation and a snare and many foolish and harmful desires which plunge men into ruin and destruction. For the love of money is a root of all sorts of evil, and some by longing for it have wandered away from the faith, and pierced themselves with many a pang. But flee from these things, you man of God; and pursue after righteousness, godliness, faith, love, perseverance and gentleness. Fight the good fight of faith; take hold of the eternal life to which you were called, and you made the good confession in the presence of many witnesses. I charge you in the presence of God, who gives life to all things, and of Christ Jesus, who testified the good confession before Pontius Pilate, that you keep the commandment without stain or reproach until the appearing of our Lord Jesus Christ, which He will bring about at the proper time—He who is the blessed and only Sovereign, the King of kings and Lord of lords; who alone possesses immortality and dwells in unapproachable light; whom no man has seen or can see. To Him be honor and eternal dominion! Amen. Instruct those who are rich in this present world not to be conceited or to fix their hope on the uncertainty of riches, but on God, who richly supplies us with all things to enjoy. Instruct them to do good, to be rich in good works, to be generous and ready to share, storing up for themselves the treasure of a good foundation for the future, so that they may take hold of that which is life indeed. (1 Tim. 6:6-19, NASB)

He admonishes those who are rich to put their hope in God rather than in their wealth, being rich instead in good deeds by being generous and willing to share. Recalling the words of our Lord in the Sermon on the Mount (Matt. 6:19-24), Paul says that in this way the rich lay up treasures for themselves in Heaven as a firm foundation for the coming age, so that they may take hold of the true life.

The various principles expressed in these Scripture passages enable us to form biblical propositions with regard to how our theological understanding of the end times affects our view of the world and in turn has an impact on our business ethics.

III. BIBLICAL PROPOSITIONS

1. The risen and ascended Jesus Christ is King over this world—This proposition is foundational for the Christian's life no matter what his specific millennial eschatology may be. Jesus introduced the Great Commission by saying, "All authority in heaven and on earth has been given to me" (Matt. 28:18, NIV). Just as this is the basis for our evangelism and missions, so is it the basis for our personal discipleship and every facet of Christian living, including our business ethics. For the Christian, the kingship of Christ has both its "now" and its "not yet" aspects. The full manifestation of His Kingdom of glory will be realized with Jesus' second coming. The Final Judgment is delayed; we can therefore leave vengeance to Him.

In the meantime, we Christians realize the present aspect of Christ's kingship by obedience to His commands, which includes conformity to His example. Just as He came into the world in His first coming so that the world through Him might be saved, so we are in this world to convey the grace of God, who desires that all come to repentance. Our aim is to advance His Kingdom of grace; by obedience to our King, we hasten the day of His Kingdom of glory.

2. There is a conflict between Christ's Kingdom and this world—Although the risen Christ has received all authority in Heaven and on earth, the "not yet" aspect of His Kingdom of glory means that this world, which God so loved that He gave His only begotten Son, is still hostile toward its yet-unrecognized King. The creation is to be included in the eventual revelation of the children of God; therefore, we are to care for God's creation, in which His honor will be ultimately vindicated. Nevertheless, we are not to be bound to what will be judged. "Love not the world," we are admonished in a context of antithesis between love of the world, which will pass away, and love of the Father, who gives eternal life. Thus, until the Second Coming, we exist in an environment of conflict. We live in a world that belongs to the Lord, but still does not recognize or receive Him as its King. This ongoing conflict produces an ambivalence toward the world in the Christian, who must discriminate constantly between what is redeemable creation and what is an integral part of the fallen world that is hostile toward the Lord. Difficult as this discernment may be, it is important to be aware that there is such a conflict.

3. There is a continuing conflict within the Christian—The discrimination that the Christian must exercise concerning the world is compounded by the conflict raging within himself between the flesh, or the old fallen human nature, and the Spirit, who indwells the born-again believer. The covetousness, or greed, which finally put to death Saul of Tarsus (who thought he was keeping God's law) by convicting him of internal sin, is denounced by Paul the apostle as a form of idolatry. Along with immorality and impurity, greed is improper for God's holy people who are heirs of the Kingdom of Christ and of God, and it is to be put to death as belonging to our old nature.

As the Spirit increasingly governs our lives, conforming us to the image of Christ, we manifest the fruit of the Spirit, which is self-control, resulting in honest and useful hard work. And the end result of our work is that we may have something to share with those in need. The underlying motivation for economic activity in the unbelieving world is covetousness or greed, which remains an idolatrous threat for the flesh of the believer, but the profound motive for the Christian's economic activity becomes the ability to perform deeds of mercy for the needy.

4. Behind these conflicts of the Kingdom is our adversary, the Devil—It would seem difficult enough that we must cope with the effects of fallen human nature, both in ourselves and in the world, but the reality of evil is further compounded by the work of Satan, who agitates and takes advantage of the idolatrous tendencies of our flesh and of the world. The Son of God appeared so that He could destroy the Devil's work; therefore—although the Final Judgment is delayed—we are to be joined with Christ in destroying Satan's work in ourselves and in the world. Just as antichrists were already apparent as the Devil's agents in the New Testament world, so we are to function as Christ's agents in this world. But in contrast to the lifestyle of the Devil's agents, that of the agents of Christ's Kingdom is characterized by mercy to fellow Christians in need. Even beyond this, it is characterized by doing good unto all, as we have opportunity, and even feeding our enemies. Because we know that Jesus is coming again, ushering in His Kingdom of glory, we are able to operate now in the spirit of His first coming, leaving vengeance to Him and overcoming evil with good.

The picture the Bible presents to Christians then, of this time before our King's second coming, is one of conflict—between the world and the Kingdom, between the flesh and the Spirit, and between the Devil and the Lord God. During this time between, in which we live out our lives, we are to manifest our allegiance to Christ in ways that will show that our citizenship is in Heaven, not merely in this world. The very fact that we do not expect that Christ will transform the structure of society before His coming again will help us to keep from making our contributions to society ends in themselves. There is the "not yet" aspect of His Kingdom of glory, which will manifest the power of His judgment. Living now in the light of that Second Coming in glory, we are strengthened and encouraged to live in the "now" aspect of His Kingdom of grace, imitating the spirit of His first coming in its mercy toward all who would turn from their sins and trust in Him.

A radical distinction between the Christian and the unbelieving world, therefore, is going to manifest the gospel in every facet of his life, including his business ethics. In contrast to the unbelieving secular world's profit motive, the Christian business professional's motive will be profit, not as an end in itself, but to help others, even his enemies. Thus being an imitator of God and of Christ, as a citizen of the Kingdom of grace, he manifests the gospel and points people toward the righteousness of Christ.

IV. SOME PARTICULAR PROBLEMS

A "pessimistic" view of the end of history, as described above, presents certain problems for Christians who seek to apply their faith to business ethics and to all of life. A few of these will be considered before we conclude with specific applications to a Christian's business ethics.

1. Is there a sacred/secular dichotomy?—It has become popular in evangelical Christian circles in recent decades to deny that there is any distinction between the sacred and the secular. Everything is worship, for example, not just our assembling for prayer and preaching and praise of God on Sundays, but our work on the weekdays, our family life, our recreation. Every part of our lives is lived out before God, and thus everything is sacred. Such affirmation has been made over against a tendency to compartmentalize our lives between Sunday activities, which adhere to Christian beliefs and follow scriptural standards, and secular vocations, which follow standards derived from the world and for which the Bible seems to have no relevance.

Certainly it has been healthy to stress that the Scriptures are relevant to every area of thought and life. Since the fallen world is in opposition to the Kingdom of Christ, we cannot expect the world's standards for any activity to be entirely in accord with God's will. Nevertheless, Scripture does indicate that there are distinctions between callings, even within the Kingdom. As 1 Timothy 3 and Titus 1 show, there are special qualifications for those who are to hold office in the Church, and it is good for a man to aspire to such office. There are priorities, in other words, in carrying out the strategy of the Kingdom. To fulfill the Great Commission, certain roles are absolutely essential, and others are helpful but secondary. The Lord bestows gifts according to His infinite wisdom, and we are not to value people according to their gifts; the important thing is for each of us to develop and use personal gifts to the utmost. Yet some gifts and callings have more immediate application to carrying out God's primary purpose. After Christ's resurrection, it was not enough for Peter and the other apostles to return to fishing and become the best possible fishermen they could be for the glory of God.

It is important to address this problem in the context of the effect of eschatology on business ethics because a more "optimistic" view of the end times, which expects to bring in the Kingdom by transforming the social structures, can lead to a blurring of all distinctions between callings. In our more "pessimistic" view, it becomes apparent that our "secular" calling, while "spiritual" in the sense of being offered to God and carried out according to His principles in the power of His Spirit, nevertheless needs to be consciously related to the overall purpose of the Kingdom of grace to be seen in its proper perspective.

This does not mean that we seek success in business merely to be able to support missions and evangelism, but it does mean that we pursue with vigor and honesty a useful employment so that we can help the needy in every way, including through missions and evangelism. Seeing God's purpose in terms of the Great Commission, with its full breadth of application, helps us to view our own calling in a perspective that makes some distinction in terms of priorities.

2. *Quietism versus activism*—The following analysis I owe to Dr. James Skillen of the Association for Public Justice from his lecture "Christian Action and the Coming of God's Kingdom," which he gave at Covenant Theological Seminary in April 1982. Quietism he equated with a sense of hopelessness about the world. Activism he described as the sense that Christians can so change the world that it will be changed to the ideal. According to Dr. Skillen, the proper view is neither quietistic nor activistic. There is a continuity between this age and the next. We are called upon to be homesteaders and sojourners at the same time. We leave nothing behind, except our sin, and carry everything with us into the Kingdom. A pregnant woman cannot fail to prepare for the baby's arrival.

I am attracted to Dr. Skillen's position and metaphors because I believe they accurately reflect the Bible's picture of how the expectation of Christ's Kingdom of glory should affect us now as members of His Kingdom of grace in this world so influenced by the kingdom of Satan. We know that this world really belongs to Christ and that He will ultimately claim it. In the meantime neither do we despair or withdraw into isolation nor do we expect that the world will dramatically change before the return of Christ. But we do give ourselves fully to the work of the Lord, knowing that our labor is not in vain.

3. *Individual versus corporate application*—In opposing the works of Satan, persons in evangelical circles tend to focus only on individual sins, not on those evils that are primarily evident in the very structures of society. The social gospel movement of the late nineteenth century was sensitive to the corporate evils that worked to the disadvantage of the poor, the laboring classes, or certain

ethnic groups. Partly in reaction to the liberal theology on which the social gospel movement was based, evangelicalism was slow to develop a recognition of corporate evil as well as individual sins and to develop a response to it.

As Christian businesspeople, we need to be aware of the ways in which sin has affected and can affect the structures of society. It is important to emphasize individual honesty and industry, but the industrious businessman who is scrupulous about his own personal honesty may be insensitive to the way in which wage or price structures, or government policies concerning taxation, are affecting people who produce or purchase his product, but with whom he has no direct contact. The internationalizing of business increases the likelihood of this insensitivity. In all such matters we need to remember that the free market is not the final answer to the fall of human nature and does not always accomplish God's will. Over against the old saying *Caveat emptor* (let the buyer beware), Leviticus 25:17 places responsibility on the seller: "Do not take advantage of each other, but fear God. I am the LORD your God" (NIV).

4. *What is the Lord's intent?*—Some could ask us concerning our "pessimistic" view of the end of history, "If you do not believe that God is going to transform society, what is your incentive to do anything to improve society?" Our answer is that our motivation is not success but obedience. Our concern is to discover our Lord's intent and then apply our energies zealously to that end, leaving the results to be determined by Him.

We apply ourselves to missions and evangelism in response to the Lord's intent as indicated in the Great Commission. We preach the gospel knowing that God will use this to reach those whom He chooses, but also knowing that not everyone will be saved. In Muslim lands our expectations may not be very great, but we know that the Lord's intent is for the gospel to be conveyed there, whether great success results or not.

With regard to business ethics, even if we do not anticipate that society's system will be transformed according to Christian ideals, we still have the responsibility to conduct ourselves according to what we understand to be the Lord's intent for economic life. This would have to include honesty and industry in producing what is useful, with a reverence for God's creation, and with the underlying motive of meeting the needs of people.

Bryan W. Ball concludes his book, *A Great Expectation: Eschatological Thought in English Protestantism to 1660*, with the comment that the English Puritans "repeated that particular phrase in the Lord's Prayer ('Thy kingdom come') with more conviction than any other generation in the English church as a whole." Their assurance of the coming of the Lord and His Kingdom shaped and invigorated their efforts in this life even if they would not see the results in their time. He notes, "The unassailable strength of such convictions lay in the assurance that if time was to prove them wrong in detail eternity would prove them right in principle." To this effect, he quotes from Jeremiah Whitaker's *The Christian's Hope Triumphing* (1645):

> The way to cure the bleeding distempers of Christendome is for all men to endeavour to get inward perswasions answerable to their outward professions; for as these main principles are more or lesse beleeved; so is the heart and life of man better, or worse ordered. When the soul is once fully perswaded, that Christ is God, that he is the true Messiah, that there is another life besides this, that the Lord Christ is ready to come to judgement, and his reward is with him; then the soul begins to seek and beg an interest in Christ, to flee from wrath to come, to assure the hopes of Heaven, whilst we are on earth: and this hope, when once truly attained, carries the soul farre above the comforts of life, and beyond the fears of death.[2]

V. CONCLUSION: SPECIFIC APPLICATIONS

The following questions are the kind that might be asked by those who share our "pessimistic" view of the end of history.

1. What positive role can the business professional play in the marketplace if the world's economic-political systems are unredeemable and doomed to be instruments of the Antichrist?

Even though we may believe that the economic-political systems will ultimately be taken over by Satan in the final conflict with the Kingdom of Christ, we are still here to oppose the works of Satan, and we are not willingly or easily to relinquish any territory to him or his agents. We do not know the timing of the revelation of that Man of Lawlessness who will exalt himself over everything that is called God or is worshiped and who will set himself up in God's temple, proclaiming himself to be God. Until such a time, we should do as much as we have opportunity to do in, through, and for the economic-political systems to make them conform to the Lord's will. This world belongs to Christ. Although the world does not recognize Him as King, we do, and fidelity to our King calls for obedience to His intent.

2. If the world's system is unredeemable, why shouldn't today's business professional take maximum advantage of the business system in this life while waiting for the next life?

This question implies that the business system is inherently evil and that we should engage in its evil methods, thereby robbing Satan for the sake of God. But we would quite clearly be letting a good end justify evil means. We cannot thus buy into Satan's methods; instead we must bring Christ's methods to the business system. These will include honesty and industry, kindliness and mercy in relations with people, and even the feeding of our enemies. The radical difference between the ways of Christ's Kingdom and the ways of the unbelieving world should be made evident in our business ethics.

3. Is the professional's primary objective in business to maintain a posture of personal piety while avoiding the contamination of the world?

Certainly one's personal piety should be maintained, and avoidance of the contamination of the world should be apparent to observers. But the primary objective should be to make one's business productive of God's creation, in God's way, for the good of God's creatures. Then if God should bless with a profit, it should be used for the support of one's family, to help those in need, and for the advancement of the Kingdom of grace.

Even though we anticipate that the "not yet" of Christ's Kingdom of glory will continue until His second coming, the "now" of His Kingdom of grace governs our business ethics, our entire economic life, and every aspect of our thought and life. This world belongs to Him. The fact that He will one day claim it as His own—that we look forward to a new earth as well as a new Heaven in which righteousness dwells—enables us now to live in this present age of conflict with the world, the flesh, and the Devil according to the gracious Spirit of our Savior and Lord in His first coming.

A main practical difference between the "pessimistic" view of the end of history and the "optimistic" view is that the latter does not anticipate the return of Christ for a long period of time, whereas our view entails the possibility of His coming soon, within our lifetime. Our view maintains an expectancy that shapes our entire outlook and behavior. Because we expect the return of Christ before the transformation of this world's social structures, we live in the light of the Second Coming, willing to be radically different from the world in our business ethics. We know that our King of grace is already victorious, and He will come as the King of glory.

This is the point of Jesus' parables of the ten virgins and of the talents (see Matt. 25). They call upon us to live in watchfulness for His return, being faithful in our stewardship of whatever He has entrusted to us. Our labor will be neither too little nor too late, but will be fruitful in accomplishing His purposes in this world, both by contributing to the communication of the gospel of grace and by reflecting that we belong to a Kingdom that will one day come in glory.

EDITOR'S REFLECTIONS

Dr. Barker draws our attention to several very important realities that should be encouraging to Christian business professionals. Because Christ was raised from the dead in bodily form and presented Himself to the disciples on numerous occasions prior to His ascension, our eschatology with its hope for the future has substance and is certain. We know God's plans for the future in sufficient detail so that we are motivated to seek and follow Christ's will for us in the "here and now." As we follow Him, our *success* ought to be measured by Christ's standards for success, not the world's standards.

However, Christians should not ignore the world's measures of success. On the contrary, we should accept and correctly use some of the world's measures in the business arena. For example, production efficiency will generally correlate with good stewardship principles in business. Profits can signify that a good product or service has been offered in a constructive manner to the consuming public. Hard work frequently has its rewards. Business success, even from the world's perspective, is not inherently antithetical to the Christian faith, but business success can certainly be sought in unrighteous ways or mistaken for biblical success (i.e., to truly believe in Christ and be conformed to His image, in holiness and righteousness).

Compromise and sin lurk in the recesses of even the regenerated heart, and the world presents us with many temptations (reflecting our old nature) and encourages us to take shortcuts and a short-run view of life. Worldly success can all too easily degenerate into idolatry where "things"—wealth, power, prestige—first become the objects of our attention and then our affections. Our eschatological view of history is a helpful reminder that a larger understanding of our temporal reality is called for than the unbelieving world is able to provide.

Our eschatology is closely linked to our "hope" for the future and serves as both a "constraint" and an "encourager."

More significantly, though, our eschatology calls us to take a long-run (eternal) perspective when we make important decisions. As our culture's world view becomes more and more existential in character, it fosters the "now" aspect of reality. The short run is substituted for the long run. The current "moment" becomes the basic unit of time and carries the greatest weight. Tomorrow is left to take care of itself. Christians, on the other hand, are called to persevere in righteousness in the hope of the tomorrows—eternal life. Short-run sacrifices for long-run gain are an important part of the Christian world view. A positive concept of sacrifice cannot exist apart from an eternal view of life.

God's gift to us of an eschatology deeply influences our world view. Christ's Kingdom is both "now" and "not yet"; the "now" becomes confused and clouded without the hope and focus of the "not yet." The future provides a perspective for the present. Christ's resurrection seals our hope, but our hope is to be consummated in the future. The "today" may be joyous, or full of pain and temptation, but we are called to march on in the hope of what Christ has set before us. We are called to persevere in righteousness, not merely persevere.

We will turn now to the postmillennialist world view of history and consider its implications for business ethics.

Jack Davis believes the postmillennial eschatological view of the end times is the one that squares best with biblical data, and he also believes it creates a positive outlook so that the Christian can best work in response to both the creation and Great Commission mandates, with the hope of some victories in this life. Dr. Davis employed serious humor when he asked the other authors at the Scholars' Colloquium these questions: Is Christ the coach of a team of players with a losing world record whose only hope is to suffer repeated defeats in the world until the big and final game? Is history just running downhill? Was it all uphill until the birth of Christ, or perhaps the time of the Reformation, but now our lives must be lived in the world amidst a slow retreat from the forces of evil? Our answers would reveal much about our world view.

CHAPTER 13

POSTMILLENNIAL ESCHATOLOGY AND ITS IMPLICATIONS FOR BUSINESS ETHICS AND PRACTICE

John Jefferson Davis

Dr. John Jefferson Davis is Professor of Systematic Theology and Christian Ethics at Gordon-Conwell Theological Seminary in Hamilton, Massachusetts, where he has taught since 1975. Dr. Davis earned the Ph.D. from Duke University, where he was a Phi Beta Kappa graduate and Danforth Graduate Fellow. He is the author or editor of nine books, including Foundations of Evangelical Theology; Evangelical Ethics: Issues Facing the Church Today; Your Wealth in God's World; *and most recently,* Christ's Victorious Kingdom: Postmillennialism Reconsidered. *His articles and reviews have appeared in* Christianity Today, Eternity, The Westminster Theological Journal, *and other scholarly and popular publications.*

A s the title indicates, the purpose of this chapter is to explore the implications of postmillennialism for business ethics and practice. The term *postmillennialism* will be defined, something of its history sketched, and clarifications stated with respect to several common misunderstandings of the view. Its biblical basis will be considered, and then its practical implications for the world of business will be explored.

WHAT IS POSTMILLENNIALISM?

Postmillennialism is an optimistic understanding of biblical teachings concerning the future that anticipates a period of unprecedented revival in the Church prior to the return of Christ, as a result of fresh outpourings of the Holy Spirit.[1] Some of the main tenets of this position as it was generally held in the nineteenth century are as follows:

1. Through dramatic outpourings of the Holy Spirit and preaching of the gospel, Christian missions and evangelism will enjoy striking success, such that the churches around the world will experience a lengthy period of numerical expansion and spiritual vitality.

2. This long period of spiritual vitality, known as the millennium (see Rev. 20:4-6), will also be associated with conditions of substantial peace and economic growth in society as a consequence of the growing influence of Christian values.

3. The millennium will also be characterized by the conversion of large numbers of ethnic Jews to Christianity (see Rom. 11:25-26).

4. At the end of the millennial period, there will be a period of apostasy and sharp conflict between the Christian Church and the forces of evil (see Rev. 20:7-10).

5. Earthly history will draw to a close when the following events occur in rapid succession: the visible return of Christ, the simultaneous resurrection of the righteous and the wicked, the Final Judgment, and the revelation of the new heavens and the new earth.[2]

The postmillennial outlook was the dominant view in American Protestantism for much of the nineteenth century, but has important antecedents in the Puritan and Reformed traditions.[3] Though not representative of a fully developed postmillennialism, John Calvin's thought expresses confidence in the spread of Christ's Kingdom. God will show "not only in one corner, what true religion is . . . but will send forth His voice to the extreme limits of the earth."[4] Countless offspring "who shall be spread over the whole earth" shall be born to Christ.[5]

It is commonly stated that the postmillennial outlook came into prominence through the writings of the Anglican scholar Daniel Whitby (1638-1726), but prior to the publication of his influential *Paraphrase and Commentary on the New Testament* in 1703, this approach to prophetic interpretation had been advanced by Puritan writers such as Thomas Brightman, William Gouge, John Cotton, and John Owen in the seventeenth century.[6] Owen, who was dean of Christ Church College, Oxford, and a prolific writer, is frequently considered to be the most able English biblical scholar of his generation.

In America, the postmillennial outlook has been articulated during the period of the Great Awakening by Jonathan Edwards and during the nineteenth and early twentieth centuries by "Old Princetonians," such as Archibald Alexander, J.A. Alexander, Charles Hodge and his son A.A. Hodge, and Benjamin B. Warfield.[7] In an 1859 article in the *American Theological Review* Charles Hodge observed that postmillennialism was the "commonly received doctrine" among American Protestants.[8] Theologians in the South, such as Robert L.

Dabney and James Henley Thornwell, William G.T. Shedd of Union Seminary in New York, the Baptist theologian A.H. Strong, and Patrick Fairbairn from Scotland were all of this persuasion.

During the latter part of the nineteenth and the early part of the twentieth centuries, increasing pessimism in the churches concerning world conditions caused postmillennialism to be largely eclipsed by premillennial and amillennial schools of prophetic interpretation.[9] It has, however, been advocated in this century by conservative scholars such as Loraine Boettner and J. Marcellus Kirk,[10] and even more recently by R.J. Rushdoony, Greg Bahnsen, Gary North, and David Chilton.[11]

SOME COMMON MISUNDERSTANDINGS

Postmillennialism is sometimes confused with nineteenth-century ideas of "evolutionary optimism" or secular ideas of progress. Such a misunderstanding seems to be presupposed, for example, in *Webster's Third New International Dictionary*, which defines *postmillennialism* as "a theological doctrine that the second coming of Christ will be after the millennium which is to come as a result of the *Christianization of the world without miraculous intervention*" (emphasis added). This view (the author's) expects a dramatic expansion of the Christian Church through fresh outpourings of the *Holy Spirit*, not because of merely human agency, organization, or technology. Its hopeful outlook for the future of the Church is predicated on supernatural rather than natural means. The expression *Christianization of the world* can also be misleading. Postmillennialists expect a remarkable increase in the influence of Christian values, but not the conversion of every individual living at any given point in time. It should also be recalled that this view was being espoused in seventeenth-century English Puritanism, long before the rise of Darwinian thought, and at a time when the external conditions of the Church were marked by conflict and turbulence rather than prosperity and peace. Given the historical conditions then prevailing, is it not plausible to argue that the postmillennial outlook of that time was a mere reflection of trends in the surrounding culture?

Neither should postmillennialism be confused with theological liberalism or the "social gospel." Although it is true that the postmillennial vision of the expanding Kingdom of Christ energized much home and foreign missionary activity during the nineteenth century and also spawned many social reforms in the areas of temperance, peace, women's rights, concern for the poor, and abolition of slavery,[12] its roots were to be found within an orthodox theological context that stressed biblical authority and the necessity of individual repentance and regeneration.

During the latter part of the nineteenth century, however, these theological underpinnings were eroded in the more liberal wing of American Protestantism. Leaders of the social gospel, such as Josiah Strong, Lyman Abbott, and Walter Rauschenbusch, placed the emphasis on institutional rather than individual renewal. In the work of Josiah Strong, for example, as historian Jean Quandt has observed, "Christ . . . the giver of grace and the lord of history became Christ the teacher and example. Conversion was replaced by moral effort."[13] The social gospel grew out of a postmillennial framework, but was theologically distinct from it, and should not simply be conflated with it, as is the practice of many twentieth-century authors.

Neither should postmillennialism be confused with some form of "manifest destiny," the idea that America is in some sense the key to God's plan for the evangelism of the world. In the nineteenth century this confusion did at times occur. Hollis Read, a Congregational minister and missionary to India, in his two-volume work *The Hand of God in History*, saw the millennium coming to a focus in a revived American Church, and he believed that the spread of Anglo-Saxon culture and political influence around the world could facilitate the spread of the gospel.[14] As a *global* and *long-term* perspective, however, postmillennialism as here understood makes no near-term predictions concerning the prospects of a particular denomination or the state of the Church in a particular country. The future of the Church *catholic* is no more to be identified with the temporal prospects of a particular political state (e.g., the United States) than was the ultimate success of the early Church identified with the fate of the Roman Empire.

Finally, postmillennialism is not to be identified with the "theonomy" movement in American Protestantism associated with Rushdoony, North, Bahnsen, Chilton, and others. Theonomists argue for the abiding validity and applicability of the criminal sanctions of the Mosaic law. Although these theonomists are postmillennialists, not all postmillennialists are theonomists; the two positions are conceptually distinguishable. John Owen, for example, in a 1652 sermon "Christ's Kingdom and the Magistrate's Power," distinguished the moral and civil components of the Mosaic law in terms of contemporary applicability, holding that only the moral component is "everlastingly binding."[15] The position presented in this chapter is a nontheonomic version of postmillennialism.

BIBLICAL BASIS FOR POSTMILLENNIALISM[16]

In the Old Testament, the expansive nature of God's redemptive purposes is seen especially in the promises of the Abrahamic covenant and in the messianic prophecies. In His covenant with Abraham, God reveals His intention to ultimately bring spiritual blessings to all the families of the earth (see Gen 12:3). God challenges Abraham to believe that his spiritual descendants will eventually be as numerous as the stars of Heaven (see Gen. 15:5-6) and as the grains of sand on the seashore (see Gen 22:17). God's redemptive purpose is seen to encompass all human cultures and is stated in terms that stretch and stagger normal human expectations.

In subsequent Old Testament revelation, it becomes evident that the Messiah will be God's instrument for bringing these blessings not only to Israel, but to the world at large. God the Father promises the Messiah His Son that the nations will be His heritage and the ends of the earth His possession (see Ps. 2:8). The Messiah's enthronement to the place of authority and rulership (see Ps. 2:6-7) is understood in the New Testament to have commenced with Christ's resurrection (see Acts 13:33). A time is coming when all the ends of the earth will turn to the Lord and all the families of the nations (cf. Gen. 12:3) will worship before Him (see Ps. 22:27). All kings are to fall down before God's Messiah (see Ps. 72:11).

While the Messiah is enthroned at the Father's right hand (see Ps. 110:1)— a rulership exercised by Christ since the time of the Resurrection and Ascension—God sends forth the scepter of Christ's Word and Spirit to rule in the midst of His foes (see Ps. 110:2). The exaltation of Mount Zion (see Isa. 2:2) is seen as a foreshadowing of the latter-day glory of a Church revitalized by the Holy Spirit, constituting it a blessing to the world, causing the nations to beat their swords into plowshares and their spears into pruning hooks (see Isa. 2:4). Isaiah 9:6-7 speaks of the spreading reign of the new Davidic king—a prophecy whose progressive fulfillment was initiated with the ascension of Christ to the right hand of the Father (see Acts 2:30-31,33-35). Messiah's reign during the period of millennial renewal will be characterized by peaceful conditions, for "the earth shall be full of the knowledge of the LORD as the waters cover the sea" (Isa. 11:9). The positive temporal side effects of the Church's renewal during this period are further described in Isaiah 65:17-25.

Ezekiel's vision of the miraculously increasing river of water flowing from the temple, bringing new life and vitality to the barren desert (see Ezek. 47:1-12), is understood to point to the great outpouring of the Spirit that was initiated at Pentecost (cf. John 7:37-39), but not terminated by that event. The *increase* in the magnitude of the river is understood to foreshadow yet more expansive outpourings of the Spirit subsequent to Pentecost—in the early Church, in the sixteenth-century Reformation, in the Great Awakening, in the great missionary expansions of the nineteenth and twentieth centuries, and in the Great Revival, which is yet to come. The Spirit, poured out on the Church and then flowing into the world, has life-giving and revitalizing influence throughout the social order.

Daniel's vision of the mysterious stone from Heaven, cut out by no human hand, that breaks in pieces the statue made of gold, silver, bronze, iron, and clay in Nebuchadnezzar's dream, and then expands to become a great mountain filling the whole earth (Dan. 2:31-35), is understood to be a prophetic picture of the victorious Kingdom of the resurrected and ascended Christ, overcoming all worldly opposition and spreading throughout the earth. Daniel's vision of the heavenly Son of Man presented before the Ancient of Days (Dan. 7:13-14) is understood to refer to the reception of the ascended Christ by the Father in Heaven and His commissioning to exercise dominion over all nations.

Both the promises of the Abrahamic covenant and the messianic texts point forward to the Great Commission (see Matt. 28:19-20), where the Church in its missionary activity becomes the instrument in history through which the risen Christ in Heaven progressively extends His dominion over the nations on earth.

An examination of New Testament texts from a postmillennial standpoint can be organized in the following way: first, texts attesting to the greatness and power of the risen Christ; second, texts describing the growth of Christ's Kingdom; and third, texts pointing to the final greatness of Christ's Kingdom.

When Christ commissions the Church to extend His kingship over the nations, He states that "*all authority*, in heaven and on earth has been given to me" (Matt. 28:18, emphasis added); this unlimited authority of the risen Christ is available to the Church in its mission. The invincible spiritual power that raised Christ from the dead and enthroned Him above all temporal and spiritual powers (see Eph. 1:20) is to be at work "in us who believe" (Eph. 1:19), in the believing Church. The "immeasurable greatness of his power" (Eph. 1:19) is to be manifested in the life, preaching, and service of the Church. If God's power is sufficient to raise the dead, and that power is available to the Church through faith in the risen Christ, should not the Church expect substantial success in its missionary task?

The parables of growth show the dramatic growth of Christ's Kingdom from insignificant beginnings and its quiet but pervasive impact on the world. The mustard seed is the smallest of seeds, "but when it has grown it is the greatest of shrubs" (Matt. 13:32). The Kingdom of Christ is like leaven that works until the whole lump of dough is permeated by its influence (see Matt. 13:33).

The Apostle Paul is confident that the spiritual weapons of the Church's warfare have divine power to destroy strongholds (see 2 Cor. 10:3-5). While reigning from the Father's right hand, the risen Christ subdues His foes, a victorious process culminating in the overthrow of death itself at the Second Coming and Final Resurrection (see 1 Cor. 15:22-26).

The final greatness of the Kingdom is envisioned in texts such as Revelation 7:9-10, where John speaks of a great multitude of the redeemed from every tongue and tribe and nation that no man can number. The text indicates that God's promises in the Abrahamic covenant and His purpose in the Great Commission will indeed be fulfilled as the Church pursues its mission in history. Paul looks forward to a time when the fullness of ethnic Israel will be saved (see Rom. 11:25-26).

The phrase "a thousand years" in Revelation 20:4-6 is understood to symbolize a long period of spiritual prosperity for the Church. The "first resurrection" is taken to refer to a period of future restoration and vindication of the Christian cause for which the martyrs died. The book of Revelation makes it clear that the Church in history will face hardship, persecution, and even martyrdom, but in the end all nations will come to worship before God Almighty and the Lamb (see Rev. 15:4). John's vision, which begins with seven struggling congregations in Asia Minor (see Rev. 2-3), concludes with the magnificent vision of a New Jerusalem (see Rev. 21:15-16) whose dimensions—2,250,000 square miles—boggle the imagination and point to the vastness and plenitude of the ultimate result of God's saving purposes.[17]

IMPLICATIONS FOR BUSINESS ETHICS AND PRACTICE

The observations made in this concluding section are bound to be somewhat tentative and even speculative, since theologians and businesspeople are generally not accustomed to having discussions with one another, much less pondering the possible implications of biblical eschatology for business practice! Nevertheless, those conversations must begin somewhere, and such is the present agenda.

Postmillennialism fosters a *global* and *long-range* perspective on history. To that extent, it would support attempts to take *long-range planning* seriously in business life. Admittedly, talk of long-range planning and long-term maximization of profits may seem idealistic to a harassed manager or owner bombarded by daily pressures, who may, in the words of Dennis Cooper-Jones, be concerned only "with generating enough profit to keep the shareholders off his back and provide sufficient capital to service his immediate ongoing needs."[18] Nevertheless, firms employing long-range planning tend to do better than those that do not. Firms also tend to make greater profits after employing such long-range planning strategies than they did prior to their implementation.[19] In other words, there is empirical evidence that long-range planning is not merely a theoretically interesting concept, but it actually pays off in the profit-and-loss column.

A world characterized by rapid change in political relations, science and technology, and financial markets also underscores the wisdom of a long-range perspective. Ralph Cordiner notes,

> In a time of radical worldwide change, when every day introduces new elements of uncertainty, forward planning may seem to be . . . an exercise in futility. Yet there never was a more urgent need for long-range planning on the part of every business, and indeed every other important element of our national life.[20]

Long-range planning can be valuable in "stirring up fresh attitudes and agitating a group's thinking," writes business analyst David Ewing.[21] The discipline of long-range planning can free managers from the urgent demands of daily operations and intraoffice politics, and give the opportunity to review and question policies and procedures that otherwise might never be seriously evaluated.

In a world economy increasingly dominated by high technology and knowledge-intensive activity, the role of *research and development* looms ever more important. Lead time and long-term perspective are critical in such areas. Recent advances in superconductivity—the flow of electricity through metal or ceramic conductors with little or no resistance—are a case in point. The new superconductivity technologies now on the horizon have tremendous economic potential in the areas of transportation, communication, computers, and the transmission and generation of electrical power. If the United States is to be a leader in this new economic and technological frontier, a long-range perspective is critical, according to John Herrington, secretary of the Department of Energy. "Corporations must take a long-range perspective for building an industry for superconductivity, striving for a balance between short-term profits and future development," stated Herrington. "We must be prepared to make a long-term commitment to bringing this and other important new technologies to maturity."[22] In such cases a misplaced focus on short-term profits would run counter to the long-term interests of both U.S. corporations and American society as a whole.

The long-term perspective is also relevant in the area of *cost containment*. In his book *Out of Crisis*, W. Edward Deming, the business consultant whose ideas have been so influential in shaping Japan's postwar industrial success, points out that low quality and high cost are the inevitable results of purchasing solely on the basis of low bid. Instead of concentrating on purchase price to the exclusion of other factors, Deming argues that companies should think in terms of minimizing net cost per hour (or year) of product life. "But this would require long-term thinking," he observes, "not just the cheapest price tag for purchase today."[23]

Deming also notes that in dealing with Japanese firms, American suppliers often fail to understand that the Japanese are less concerned with price than with long-term relationships of loyalty and trust, and the prospects of continuing quality improvements over time.[24] American short-term perspectives can thus be a handicap in penetrating Japanese markets.

The long-term view encouraged by a postmillennial perspective is also relevant to business ethics. In a commencement address given at M.I.T., Kenneth Olsen, founder and chairman of Digital Equipment Corporation, observed from his experience that to an overwhelming degree people wanted to work for an ethical company where standards are clear and honest activity is expected. Olsen stated,

> People are honest with the company when the company is honest with them, and people are honest with the suppliers and the customers when they realize that the company is not interested in . . . [merely] short-term goals. . . . When given the opportunity, people are willing to fend off the short-term pressures, which the financial community puts on so strongly, to look for the long-term good of the company and society.[25]

To the extent, then, that a postmillennial perspective encourages managers to take the longer view, such an outlook can encourage higher ethical standards in American business and in society as a whole.

EDITOR'S PERSPECTIVE

During the discussion of Dr. Davis's chapter at the Scholars' Colloquium, he made the additional observation that the long-term time horizon envisioned by the postmillennialists might well have additional positive impacts on other Christian endeavors, such as scholarship and the development and perpetuation of family businesses. Why would a Christian undertake scholarship or research if Christ's return is necessary to wrest economic or political institutions from the dominion of Satan or is absolutely imminent? Perhaps a mind-set like that was familiar to the Apostle Paul and the people of Thessalonica. In his second letter to them, he reviewed the events that would precede Christ's second coming (see 1:6-2:12), and he followed it with instructions for disciplining those who were "doing no work at all" (3:11). We do not know if there was a direct connection between their eschatology and their failure to work, but it is logical and psychologically plausible.

We could do a lot of speculating about how a premillennialist or postmillennialist world view could have an impact on our business behavior. In fact, it would be good for Christians to ponder how our view of eschatology influences us, but it does no good for anyone to criticize or judge a neighbor's millennial position. The Church is rife, in some quarters, with millennialism being used as a litmus test to determine who really has it all together theologically. This is counterproductive and a harbinger of spiritual pride. Our concern here is with examining the impact of eschatology on our marketplace behavior, not evaluating someone else's theology ("Who are [we] to judge the servant of another? To his own master he stands or falls; and stand he will, for the Lord is able to make him stand" [Rom. 14:4]).

All of us in the Church have received some teaching on the "end times"—

255

Christ's second coming. As noted, though, there is a wide variety of teaching on the subject, and it spans a wide continuum of possible interpretations and responses. We will look first at a couple of these differences, but only for the purpose of self-examination. Then we will look at what all Christians believe in common regarding eschatology, for our commonality is foundational to our motives and conduct that emanate from our world view.

Just how wide is the eschatological continuum? Very! Some people are convinced that Christ's return is so imminent that the only real assignment the Christian has in the world is to evangelize. They devote their full time (and expect others to) to "fishing for men." To them, devoting substantial time to carrying out the creation mandates, especially as they apply to cleaning up the economic-social-political spheres, would be a serious waste of energy.

It is exciting that God has called some people to be full-time evangelists. It is also good that we are challenged occasionally to examine our personal responsibilities in this area. We all need to assess if we are taking advantage of the opportunities God provides us to share the good news of His Son's redeeming love. It is a contradiction of the plain teaching of Scripture, however, to teach that everyone should be almost totally focused on evangelistic endeavors. People who do this have a way of making others feel guilty if they are not evangelistically oriented. Paul's first letter to the Corinthians (see chaps. 12-14) makes the need for a "diverse body" perfectly clear. There has been no new revelation to change this idea.

On the other end of the eschatological continuum are those who are so oriented to the Scripture's call to subdue and rule the created order, and to resist evil wherever it is encountered in the world, that their devotion to this work leaves them little time, energy, or interest in searching for God's lost sheep.

The first group is most often identified with the premillennialists, and the second group with the postmillennialists. The Body of Christ needs some of both interests (evangelists and "world battlers"), but both groups need to be very careful not to carry their positions to such extremes that they become heretical by ignoring other equally important biblical truths.

Other characteristics are associated with these generalized millennial positions. For example, avid premillennialists tend to cultivate a short-run view of world events (all negative events point to Christ's imminent return) and to be rather pessimistic about the Christians' hope of reversing the tide of secularism. History reveals to them that the world is "going to the dogs." On the other hand, fully committed postmillennialists tend to focus on the larger, long-term picture and plan ways to attack and counterattack the Enemy in the political and economic arenas. They see revivals in South America and Asia as evidence that great victories are being won and that Satan is on the defensive.

These broad generalizations probably do not describe the views of most Christians who are somewhat less polarized, but the "logic" and "psychology" of the two extremes do tend to carry their followers in these directions. Church history, however, reveals that something as fundamental as world missions has been the "darling" of both groups at different times in history—the postmillennialists in the eighteenth and nineteenth centuries; the premillennialists in the twentieth century. For the postmillennialists, it was a biblically mandated step in the process of bringing the world (people *and* institutions) under the lordship of Christ; for the premillennialists, it has been an urgent part of the preparation for Christ's imminent return—the gathering of His children, not the affecting of institutions. But we can conclude that postmillennialists tend to have more interest in the creation mandates than do premillennialists.

God's evangelizing *and* subduing-ruling mandates continue to be carried out, though, even in the face of our theological differences. The Lord always accomplishes His ends, even when the Church manifests major divisions within itself on what is most important.

The greatest significance of millennial eschatology, as it affects business ethics, however, rests in our common agreement about eschatology (not the millennial aspect of it). The editor, for one, has never been able to reconcile all the biblical verses that address the "last days." In humor, he acknowledges he is a pro-pan-ig-millennialist. He is for it, it will all pan out, and he is ignorant as to which theory will ultimately prove to be more accurate.

But the editor has never met a Christian who does not believe that (1) history has a *purpose*; (2) our first parents fell, and this event radically affected history; (3) biblical history is devoted to the revelation of God's love and plan of redemption; (4) God's will for our character and behavior in history is set forth in the Scripture; and (5) there will be a conclusion of this age and a new age will be ushered in at Christ's return, which will bring with it an eternal glory for all of His children. Furthermore, there is massive agreement on what fleshes out this agreed-to view of history.

All Christians are long-term optimists. We are strengthened by our eschatology so that we can suffer for Christ by choosing righteousness and thereby reveal Him who dwells in us. There are things that we will even die for, as have martyrs of the past. We are enabled to stand in the marketplace for what is right, despite enormous pressures to compromise God's principles and standards. We are being equipped to follow Christ in the marketplace. Our eschatology provides significant support in this regard by fostering hope that gives us courage.

The most singularly important contribution of biblical eschatology to business ethics is the *encouragement* it brings to God's children to live like Christ in a perverse world where injustices occur on an all-too-frequent basis. We are to stand strong when evil assaults us, for "like a trampled spring and a polluted well is a righteous man who gives way before the wicked" (Prov. 25:26). Reflecting Christ's attitude and conduct during times of real stress provides a powerful testimony to our family, Church, and world of His reality in the world. Even our enemies take notice of righteous courage.

The Romans 12:17-21 passage is central to our interest in eschatology and its fostering of hope for the future:

> Never pay back evil for evil to anyone. Respect what is right in the sight of all men. If possible, so far as it depends on you, be at peace with all men. Never take your own revenge, beloved, but leave room for the wrath of God, for it is written, "Vengeance is Mine, I will repay," says the Lord. "But if your enemy is hungry, feed him, and if he is thirsty, give him a drink; for in so doing you will heap burning coals upon his head." Do not be overcome by evil, but overcome evil with good.

Will we, the disciples of Christ, *trust* God to repay those who treat us unjustly, to direct our paths, to place us in the positions of authority in the marketplace of His choice, to provide us with the standard of living He desires for us, to reward integrity (now or in eternity—spiritually or temporally), and to guard the relationships we have with our customers, competitors, suppliers, and laborers?

The residual of our old nature raises its manipulative, deceptive, cunning, revengeful, controlling, spiteful head so easily when we suffer an injustice or have a great desire for the things of the world. We are tempted to play by the world's rules when we are hurt. We are tempted to compromise "just this once" or choose a "lesser good" under the self-justifying rationalization that our intended actions are really legal or are only common practice in the market-place. We are all too frequently tempted to take things into our own hands and not wait with a trusting attitude for God.

The love of Christ constrains us (see 2 Cor. 5:14). We are children who are prone to wander, but the Spirit uses God's Word (including many aspects of eschatology) to direct, warn, and encourage us. We know that Final Judgment is coming and that everyone will give an accounting to God. We are encouraged by knowing that all will be made right, once again, when we are glorified with Christ. Our eschatology helps provide this world view.

CHAPTER 14

AN ENDING FOR A BEGINNING: BIBLICAL PRINCIPLES IN THE BUSINESS WORLD

Richard C. Chewning

Biblical principles that should undergird a Christian's view of business and the marketplace are not always apparent or easily applied without some effort and practice. Ephesians 4:11-16 speaks of "equipping . . . the saints for the work of service" so that they can become mature and grow up "to the measure of the stature which belongs to the fullness of Christ." Clearly, Christians are not to limit the integration of Scripture in their lives to the activities of the Church and family, as important as they are. They are to manifest Christ's mind in their relationships with their coworkers and their decision making as they follow His precepts in the marketplace. Christians are to be salt and light in every environment.

If people would think about the lives of individuals like Adam, Noah, Abraham, Jacob, Tamar, Joseph, Moses, Ruth, David, Daniel, Matthew, Luke, Lydia, and other prominent figures in Scripture, they would soon realize that the overwhelming majority of them were not "professional churchpeople" or priests. They were the farmers, shepherds, laborers, craftspeople, housewives, merchants, tax gatherers, physicians, lawyers, and others who spent most of their time in the marketplace. The majority of people in Scripture are encountered in their vocations. Our faith is not to be shut up in the functions of the Church, but lived out in the world where those who do not bow their knees to Christ can be confronted by the light of God's truth as it is manifested in everyday life.

We need to be extremely careful when we find ourselves subtly or overtly dividing the world into sacred and secular compartments. God declared all His creation to be "very good" and gave His stewards instructions regarding its management. The fall of our first parents radically altered the conditions under which we were to labor and live in the world, but the Fall did not change the basic mandates regarding worship, family, and work, for they were all reinstated after the Fall.

Yes, we do need to recognize that in these "latter days" the Church has been given the role of gathering and training God's children for service in the world and it is the *only* institution that has been promised that "the gates of hell will not overpower it" (Matt. 16:18). This is not, however, an invitation for Christians to retreat into the Church. No, it is a promise that the *base camp* from which we go out into the world will be guarded by Christ against all odds until His return.

This book has been designed to examine basic biblical truths that can guide Christians when they want to know what God thinks about the marketplace, and wonder what is the best kind of economic system to foster as they strive to be stewards and servant leaders. In Section E (chapters 10 and 11) some biblical principles relating to the distribution of wealth were examined in an effort to determine what kinds of economic *systems* are encouraged by Scripture. The other five sections (A-D, F) addressed issues that relate biblical precepts to *individuals* in the marketplace.

The six basic tensions examined earlier will be revisited now and the biblical principles developed there will be applied to other related questions. This will expand the application of the precepts and principles with the hope of stimulating further thought about their use.

SECTION "A" REVISITED

The tensions that often develop as Christians try to balance the demands of the creation mandates and the Great Commission were the topic of discussion in Section A. Dr. Kenneth Kantzer persuasively argued that God intends His precepts to transform society. He also concluded that working in business is a legitimate Christian calling, for business constitutes a significant "ways and means" of carrying out the stewardship responsibilities given us by God. Scripture also has much to say that has specific application to business, and much of it was given in the context of the marketplace. Dr. Kantzer went a step further, though, and argued that Christians should also carry into the market-place a sense of responsibility for rebuilding their workplace according to God's principles in an effort to create a productive and just environment.

Dr. Philip Wogaman, while generally agreeing with Kantzer's position, issued a strong exhortation for Christians to seek their *identity in Christ*—not in success, power, wealth, and other trappings of the world. Christians are called to become like Christ and exhibit His character in and through their business conduct. In fact, their ability to do that in an environment that commends so many alternative "ends" for consideration offers Christians an extraordinary opportunity to make a real difference for Christ. Those who do not give their allegiance to Christ admire people who hold to impeccable standards of integrity, provided they do not manifest a self-righteous attitude obnoxious to Christians and nonChristians alike. Dr. Wogaman correctly pointed out, however, that these lofty goals of being effective for Christ in the marketplace cannot be realized unless the Christian is growing in personal holiness under the tutelage of the Holy Spirit. Society will not be transformed by a holier-than-thou cadre of self-righteous people.

The editor introduced two additional subjects. First, Christians do not have any biblical authority to present themselves to the world as "Christian" managers. No specific functions of management are distinctly Christian in nature; we are to be managers who manifest Christian character and attitudes. The second matter was the problem of probable outcomes, which is concerned with the distinction between (1) being obedient to Christ because we expect to successfully accomplish a goal and (2) being obedient regardless of the probable outcome because Christ has given us the task. It should not matter if we believe that Satan has been given control over the world's institutions or that Christians are empowered to redeem the world's institutions for Christ before His second coming in order for us to obey God's creation and Great Commission mandates. What we think about our probabilities of success is irrelevant if God has commanded that the work be done. The creation mandates and the Great Commission are both in effect until Christ's return and the Final Judgment.

Building on the concepts set forth by Drs. Kantzer and Wogaman and the editor, how should the following questions be answered? Should a Christian business professional pursue biblical values even if it would have an adverse financial impact on the other stakeholders? Does the Christian in a management position have a responsibility to go beyond the traditional ethical responsibilities associated with avoiding illegal behavior? Questions like these seem to imply that if people are too Christlike, their business interests might be hurt. Is this true? Or put another way, how Christlike can one be in business and still be successful? Are Christ's character and standards of conduct antithetical to business? The following illustration addresses these questions.

Suppose there is an industry practice of pirating advanced research findings from other corporations by hiring key research people from their staff with the full intent of receiving the research information. Are Christians obligated to equate this with stealing? If they could stop their corporation from following such a practice, but could not alter the behavior of their competitors, what should be done? This situation raises the "means" and "ends" issues addressed by Dr. Kantzer and also raises the "source of our personal identity" issue spoken to by Dr. Wogaman. Many people accept the acquiring of proprietary information through the pirating of personnel as a perfectly normal means of competing in the marketplace. It is standard practice.

The editor believes such conduct is absolutely wrong. The practice is an intentional act of stealing. Christians must pursue what is right according to Christ's standards, regardless of its financial impact or whether it is legal or not. "Right" is not financially or legally determined. Using Dr. Geisler's reaction test, how would people *react* if their major competitor hired their research director at the very critical time when important practical product research was being completed? They would hardly react by wanting to bestow their blessings on the departing research director or their competitor. People's reactions would surely declare that an injustice had been done.

Christians have a far better standard by which to judge conduct, though, than that of the reaction test. Besides, the reaction test is an after-the-fact test. We have the plain truth of God's Word. To intentionally take something that is not ours, without the consent of the owner, is simply wrong. A reader may protest and argue that the information belongs to those engaged in research as much as it does to the employer. It is certainly true that many researchers have personally generated much of the information that is being sought, but what is their responsibility to those who have provided them with the resources and environment to make the discoveries while employed? Would they have had the opportunity to support their families while acquiring the knowledge if they had not worked for the employer? What obligations do Christians have toward employers? Can Christians take proprietary information and treat it as their own? What is the difference between walking out of a job with proprietary information and walking out with computers, calculators, and other tangible assets? There is really no *moral* difference!

The most basic problem encountered in moral decision making is the tendency of people to be self-oriented, which opens the door to many rationalizations allowing them to justify their personal desires. When people's primary concern is for themselves, moral issues quickly become "gray" as they turn the issues over in their minds and try to find a way to legitimize their desires. There is far less gray in moral decision making when the strongest desire is to be true to Christ, who would have us consider the rights of others.

Christians can provide a vivid testimony of the gospel's power when we remain faithful to godly standards. Daniel's faithfulness to God while he was in exile opened many doors of testimony for him. Godly conduct in the marketplace will often offer us opportunities to state why we believe and act as we do.

We should see the creation mandates and the Great Commission as compatibly yoked companions, not as opponents to each other.

SECTION "B" REVISITED

The issues and tensions highlighted in this section emanate from the relationship between God's law and God's grace. Dr. Myron Augsburger argued that the New Testament ethic supersedes the Old Testament ethic. He believes Christ's teachings and actions are so demonstrative of God's holiness, justice, equity, righteousness, compassion, and love (qualities the law points to but cannot bring to life) that the New Testament does indeed give us a new ethical standard.

Dr. Walter Kaiser disagreed and argued that the Old Testament and the New Testament are, in fact, one single, unfolding body of truth. The New Testament amplifies, clarifies, and exhibits the Old Testament intentions, but it does not change or supersede them. He believes the same, unchanging, universal principles are embodied in all Scripture, and Christians are to seek these principles.

The editor believes the issue of discerning biblical principles is so important that this entire series of books is dedicated to addressing it concretely, practically, and applicationally, by aggregating Old and New Testament precepts into principles reflecting the whole counsel of God. The two driving forces that are common to all the work are the search for *biblical principles* and their *application* to every area of business and public policy.

The editor strongly believes that the application of biblical principles to business and public policy is honoring to Christ. It facilitates His lordship in the lives of His children as they conduct themselves in the marketplace where His light can drive out darkness. Exactly how, though, does this work in the marketplace?

Biblical principles, as defined in chapter 1, are expressions of biblical truth that are derived from the repetitive and consistent discussion, use, and application of a particular facet of truth, in diverse biblical contexts, by the Holy Spirit. They are similar in nature to the doctrines that make up our "systematic theology"   doctrines of sanctification, justification, grace, forgiveness, Trinity, and so forth. We do not, however, speak of doctrines of truth telling, doctrines of equity, or doctrines of justice. Why? Because these latter concepts are, for the most part, subsets of the doctrine of sanctification. They are concerned with how Christians are to live out their faith in the world, and the Church has simply done a better job of "birthing" Christians than it has of helping them mature and live in the marketplace where so much of their time is spent. Christians are to be "doers" of the Word, not merely learners and speakers of the Word (see Matt.

7:21; James 1:22; 1 John 3:7,18).

Many scholars have been invited to search the Scripture for recurring biblical themes with marketplace applications. The editor began this in 1966 after being convicted that he was not integrating Scripture with his study of business. That stimulated a search for biblical statements that applied to people in the marketplace, business institutions, and economic systems.

After months of study, the observation was made that many ideas and concepts were repeated in several biblical passages. This realization initiated an active hunt to find out how often a precept was presented and this led to scriptural cross-referencing, which became a routine part of the work. As a result, two other significant things became apparent.

The appearance of the same precept in many contexts did not either water down or harden the truth found in any particular passage; rather, it expanded the complexity and richness of the original truth. For example, *love* may be a word of encouragement in one context and a word of sharp discipline, for purposes of restoration, in another context. If we are to come to a rich understanding of love, love must be comprehended in a myriad of contexts.

The Old Testament is particularly helpful in this process, for it is filled with many "case applications" of God's eternal truths. It is presented in a different form, to be sure, than it is in the incarnate Christ, but it is no less the same truth. And while it is true that much more teaching in the New Testament is on the Person and work of the Holy Spirit, whose work in the life of a believer is *absolutely* essential for anyone to correctly discern spiritual truths, it is nevertheless true that the Holy Spirit was present in the believers throughout the time of the Old Testament. He circumcised hearts then, as now.

The two Testaments are absolutely harmonious! Grace and law are not enemies when the law is used lawfully (see 1 Tim. 1:8)—used by the Holy Spirit to build in us the attitudes and behavior that reflect God's character. The law is holy (see Rom. 7:12), but we cannot be holy by trying to keep the law. Our old nature "kills us" when we attempt this. But the law is a great help to Christians when the Holy Spirit shows us the intent, the spirit, and the correct application of the case law in the contemporary context where it is needed. All Scripture is "profitable for teaching, for reproof, for correction, [and] for training in righteousness" (2 Tim. 3:16).

SECTION "C" REVISITED

Dr. Henry Krabbendam and Dr. Vernon Grounds set forth the arguments for holding to biblical absolutes while acknowledging that Christians are moral agents who must apply biblical propositions and principles to situations that require personal, moral judgments. Christians can rarely just slap an absolute on a situation and expect to end up with the truth being properly applied. Properly applied truth has two components: (1) the truth itself, and (2) its use in love.

The editor, it will be remembered, postulated "that the presence of [both] objective and subjective dimensions of reality is necessarily associated with the existence of and administration of biblical absolutes" because of (1) our moral nature that took on a different character after the Fall; (2) our finite limitations that leave us with incomplete information and understanding; (3) the fact that the most moral judgments are choices between multiple "goods," not just good and evil; and (4) the fact that absolutes reflect God's character and behavior, which are hard to see clearly because of our spiritual blindness.

Understanding that there is a proper relationship between the objective biblical absolutes and their moral application, which requires human judgment, should, however, help us work our way through another family of questions. Is the Bible a sufficient guide for business conduct in every historical era and for every type of business situation? What should business professionals do when Scripture seems unclear or is silent on the particular business issue being considered? To what degree are Christians free to carry out business practices in keeping with their biblically informed consciences?

The Bible is absolutely sufficient to guide business conduct in every era of history and in every type of business situation. God's character, the basis of all biblical absolutes, never changes, and man's nature is the same from generation to generation. Our nature is not evolving to some higher moral plane. What changes are the situations—not God, man, or the created order. This does mean there is a greater and greater need to discover God's universal *biblical principles*, though, as we move away from the time and features of the agrarian and theocratic society in which much of the original Scriptures were given. Many Christians who find the Bible hard to apply to their contemporary work environment have simply not been helped to see the underlying principles; they have mistakenly concluded that because Scripture does not specifically discuss certain contemporary topics by name, it has nothing to say about them. This conclusion is fallacious.

What should Christian business professionals do when Scripture seems to be either unclear or silent on a particular business matter? In the short run they should take their questions to other Christians they respect. When the Corinthians were bringing lawsuits against one another, Paul asked, "Is [there] not among you one wise man who will be able to decide between his brethren?" (1 Cor. 6:5). Is there not some Christian who has integrated Scripture with business well enough to be able to give sound counsel?

Two other things can be done over the long haul. The individual should spend some disciplined time looking for specific concepts in the Bible that have application in the work environment. This endeavor should not become a substitute for private devotions, however. When an applicable concept is found, it should be tracked through the Scripture by cross-referencing it to learn its compete sense. Finally, study materials and other Christians can be sought who will come together to seek God's transforming truths to apply in the marketplace.

We can conclude, then, that biblically informed individuals are free to act in keeping with their biblically informed conscience and are, in fact, mandated to carry out their business practices in the light of their discernment guided by God's Word. This is an integral part of God's call of His children to business. We are His agents in the marketplace.

SECTION "D" REVISITED

Is a Christian to raise moral issues in the marketplace on the basis of scriptural law or natural law? The question of how Christians are to posture their moral concerns in the marketplace was the topic of Section D. The extent of our sin nature (depravity) and its effect on our character and ability to make proper moral judgments was the subject Dr. Richard Gaffin tackled. The presence of the moral aspects of the natural law in the hearts of all men was the topic Dr. Norman Geisler addressed. He argued that a Christian should appeal to those with a different faith premise on the grounds of the natural law that is written on their hearts. Dr. Gaffin, while not disputing that people do have the natural law written on their hearts, did argue that this alone, however, is not sufficient to *cause* them to do good. He argued that we are totally dependent on God's "common grace" for any stability in the marketplace.

Building on the material offered by these two scholars, three new and related questions will now be examined. What can general revelation and natural law contribute to business ethics? Would the business professional who follows biblical revelation be ethically superior to people who merely follow natural revelation? And finally, to what degree does the capitalistic system cater to human depravity and, in so doing, thwart God's redemptive activity in the world?

General revelation and natural law contribute greatly in the world to the broad acceptance of what is generally considered to be appropriate social behavior. Numerous cultural mores are commonly found among distant and diverse cultures and are behaviorally compatible with some values set out in the Bible.

For example, the truly distinctive features of the Ten Commandments, when compared with other cultural systems of law, are found in the first four commandments, which focus on God and our normative relationship with Him. These four commandments provide the basis for the ultimate meaning and purpose of the other six. Christians know that the true knowledge of God and His personal relationship with them enable them to live a life reflecting the motives and behavior indicated by these laws. Christians are constrained by the love of Christ, and the Spirit uses the Scripture to guide and help them partake of the very nature of God so they will continue to grow in His likeness (see Heb. 12:10; 2 Pet. 1:4), which will be reflected in their attitudes and behaviors.

General revelation also provides many physical examples of consequences that guide people when they are making decisions that have physical and moral components. Many decisions that are related to our physical self-preservation are clearly aided by observing and learning of the harsh realities associated with the violation of many physical laws. For example, driving a car around a curve too fast has a moral component to it. Moral issues related to product safety, working conditions, and environmental pollution, to name a few, are open to the appeals of general revelation.

Natural law and general revelation must be understood in the context of God's constraining common grace, though, for they are often willfully ignored. Sometimes people are even observed to have gross twists to their "common sense" when they are turned over to their depraved minds (see Rom. 1:24,26,28). So, much of what has been said in the previous three paragraphs can be contradicted with specific case illustrations. Scripture and our personal experience acknowledge, however, that the biblical principles speaking about the evidence of God in our hearts and its frequent rejection are truths pointing clearly to our fallen nature.

Suppose for a moment that common grace was particularly effective during a specific era of history—little white-collar crime, a low divorce rate, and so on. Would Christian business professionals following special revelation be ethically superior to persons following natural revelation during such a period? Yes, mature Christians would have several real advantages.

First, mature Christians have a body of revealed standards in the Scripture that would provide a *broader base* of enlightenment that should translate into an enlarged ethical sensitivity. In other words, Christians should have less trouble with inadvertent sin.

Second, Christians have a very different base of motivation that is pleasing to God and is often perceived in the marketplace as a genuine servant's heart expressing sincere concern for the interests of others. Genuine love is easily discerned, and it does impress its recipients! Thus, opportunities for providing counsel or sharing the gospel are created.

Third, Christians are likely to have very different reactions to personal injustices suffered in the marketplace. The world and its natural law have no substitutes for forgiveness, nor do they provide an eschatology to encourage the unjustly treated person to leave vengeance in the hands of a just God.

Finally, and of greatest importance, Christians are indwelt by the Holy Spirit who uses the Word of God to lead and teach us. We have a Helper who aids us in temptations, helps us guard and conquer our old nature, and gives us wisdom when it is needed and sought. Collectively, mature Christians are more likely to be ethical in the marketplace than are people who reject Christ, even during times when God's common grace is very evident.

To what degree does our capitalistic system cater to human depravity and, in so doing, thwart God's redemptive activity in the world? This question irritates many Christians who are strongly committed to the belief that there is a high degree of compatibility between their faith and the freedoms and benefits provided by a relatively free capitalistic economic system. The question is not asked to challenge that perception. It is designed to cause us to reflect on the threat *wealth* is to those whose identity is not rooted firmly in Christ.

Why did Christ tell His disciples, "Truly I say to you, it is hard for a rich man to enter the kingdom of heaven. And again I say to you, it is easier for a camel to go through the eye of a needle, than for a rich man to enter the kingdom of God" (Matt. 19:23-24)? Max Weber, in *The Protestant Ethic and the Spirit of Capitalism*, quoted Southey's *Life of Wesley* (chap. 29) in which John Wesley (1703-1791) was reported to have written:

> I fear, wherever riches have increased, the essence of religion has decreased in the same proportion. Therefore I do not see how it is possible, in the nature of things, for any revival of true religion to continue long. For religion must necessarily produce both industry and frugality, and these cannot but produce riches. But as riches increase, so will pride, anger, and love of the world in all its branches. How then is it possible that Methodism, that is, a religion of the heart, though it flourishes now as a green bay tree, should continue in this state? For the Methodists in every place grow diligent and frugal; consequently they increase in goods. Hence they proportionately increase in pride, in anger, in the desire of the flesh, the desire of the eyes, and the pride of life. So, although the form of religion remains, the spirit is swiftly vanishing away. Is there no way to prevent this—this continual decay of pure religion? We ought not to prevent people from being diligent and frugal; we must exhort all Christians to gain all they can, and to save all they can; that is, in effect, to grow rich.[1]

The problem is clear. Inherent in the fallen human nature is a drive to be autonomous, independent, and number one. This very essence of pride combines with the natural psychological insecurity found in all fallen humans, which makes the prospects of physical security seem extremely attractive even though it is a counterfeit satisfier of our true need to be both significant and secure. Hence, the plea of the wise person in Proverbs:

> Give me neither poverty nor riches . . .
> Lest I be full and deny Thee and say, "Who is the LORD?"
> Or lest I be in want and steal,
> And profane the name of my God. (30:8-9)

Christians need to be discerning and humbled by the paradox that wealth carries with it both a blessing and a temptation. The root of any problem people may have with wealth is surely attitudinal, but let us not gloss over our spiritual need to frequently take a hard look at our own motives and desires. It is easy to wander into lust and greed. The real question we need to wrestle with is this: What blessings does God want to impart to us and others through the wealth He has entrusted to us as stewards? Earthly treasures are to be converted into heavenly treasures.

Christians need to acknowledge that increasing the standard of living for everyone in a society carries with it a two-edged sword. While economic prosperity resounds to the glory of God and the physical benefit of everyone, it also has the power to simultaneously corrupt and harden the old nature toward the eternal benefits of God. The Bible is clear that wealth is not inherently evil, but it is equally clear that if we perfectly fulfill the creation mandate regarding *work* and do not know and love God, we are spiritually absolutely poverty stricken.

SECTION "E" REVISITED

Distributive justice is a topic almost everyone has an interest in, for it deals with our share of the available wealth. Robert Heilbroner, in his brilliantly written book *The Making of Economic Society*, explained that there have been only three basic ways of dividing wealth throughout recorded history. Some societies have followed a system of "tradition" that satisfies their sense of justice. For example, the oldest son might inherit a double portion of the family estate or, in some cases, even all the estate. Or the hunter who makes the kill gets the choice portion of the animal. Tradition governs the division of available wealth.

Other societies have followed a "command" system where the authority figure or ruler determines the division of wealth. Dictators or totalitarian bodies determine how the wealth is to be used and distributed. Those in power decide if wealth is to be divided according to need, equally, or by rank within the hierarchy.

The third system, the newest in history, provides individuals the freedom to exchange their time, talents, and possessions as each chooses to in the market-place. This "market" system rests at the heart of capitalism. Those of us who have spent our lives in this type of system, however, sometimes fail to remember just how slow, painful, and sometimes even unjust a process it was to establish the market system. Legal rights and claims of ownership of the earth's basic raw materials and tangible assets were slow to develop and be accepted. In fact, the free market system would never have developed, in all probability, if the vast North American continent had not been available for the economic-political-social experiment to take root in. Its real foreshadowing is seen, however, in the more primitive forms of free trade practiced by the Israelites.

The Israelites, who possessed houses they did not build and vineyards they did not plant, were told that the land of Canaan belonged not to them, but to God, and that they were merely aliens and sojourners in it (see Lev. 25:23). They were God's stewards. *Ownership* and *stewardship* are not synonymous for those who do not give their allegiance to Christ, but for those of us who do, the two terms should be synonymous.

It has been evident for thousands of years that people who possess positive physical, mental, and experience-related advantages and who are free to make choices in an environment that rewards their creative efforts tend, on balance, to be more motivated and productive than do those who remain subservient to others in a restricted environment. Udo Middelmann discussed God's creation of His image-bearers as "choice-makers" and highlighted the significance God places on this aspect of our nature. This characteristic was at the heart of his argument that wealth should be distributed according to individual efforts and contributions.

In a fallen world where self-interest is so pervasive, however, we are quickly confronted with the fact that many people who have physical, mental, and experiential disadvantages get "left behind" in the economic affairs of life. The sin nature can drag disadvantaged people down even further than they might otherwise fall, while the same old nature is hardening the hearts of the advantaged peoples toward the true needs of the disadvantaged. Equally tragic, though, is the truth that when God's perspective on human nature is forgotten or rejected, man's self-generated wisdom often becomes foolishness when he sets out to help his neighbor. Impaired wisdom is of little long-run help to the disadvantaged. Even well-intended efforts to help them often fail to stimulate the development of more mature patterns of motivation and behavior that would enable them to eventually help themselves. It takes real wisdom to help people help themselves.

Robert Wauzzinski examined the underlying assumptions of capitalism and socialism in order to determine just how compatible and incompatible they are with scriptural standards. He believes they both fall short of providing adequate means for dealing with mankind's fallen nature, and he suggested an alternative structure for seeking a consensus on issues that so easily divide people when they are allocating wealth. However, he did not address how these differences were to be adjudicated and settled when a consensus was not forthcoming in the system. Who or what is to umpire the world's differences? This big question plagues fallen men, for many injustices are easily observable in all the world's systems of production and distribution.

The next book, *Biblical Principles and Economics: The Foundations*, is devoted to exploring "distributive justice" on a broader and deeper scale, so we don't want to go too far in drawing conclusions here before the scholars have had an opportunity to put the entire issue under the full light of Scripture. We do want to address one other concrete question, though, before we close this section of our review. Do Christians in business have the economic responsibility to try to make employees and other "stakeholders" more equal in society as a whole? Should Christians seek to narrow the gap between those at the top of the economic ladder and those at the bottom?

A study of two Old Testament concepts provides some genuine insight into God's mind on such questions. Both the Year of Jubilee *and* the division of the Promised Land are discussed at some length in Scripture, and they give us some direction, if not definitive answers, for questions like this. The dividing of the land (see Num. 26:52-56; 32:1-42; 33:50-54; 34:1-29; 35:1-15; Josh. 13:1-21:45) reveals two important facts, which create a tension for us as we attempt to practice God's revealed principles. First, the land was divided by lot, but the lot did not favor the larger tribes or leave the smaller tribes with the smallest territory. The lot did not produce a proportional equality between the tribes as measured by the area of their territory. (The editor has not done a topographical or resource study of the territories to see if some other measure of proportional equity may have been manifested through the casting of lots.)

Once the particular tribes got their land, though, the families within the tribes were to be given land according to their size, the larger families getting more and the smaller ones less (see Num. 33:54). So we are presented with a model in which both inequality and equality were present. Inequality was expressed among the tribes when the land was actually divided, but they were to seek a form of equality among the families in a particular tribe. Both equality and inequality seem to be sanctioned, leaving the balance between them to the moral judgment of people and to God's providence.

When we impose the concept of the Jubilee on top of the actual division of the land, we discover another concern that God has for everyone who is called to work and be involved in the distribution of wealth. Simply put, under the plan of the Jubilee, the head of any family was free to make good or foolish decisions regarding the disposition of the property of his immediate family. He was free to "sell" and "buy" the family land, but it was not a perpetual sale. In effect, he could only *rent* it, and then only until the Year of Jubilee. He could not dispossess the future generations of his family. In other words, the sons or grandchildren could not be permanently disinherited of their *right* to the land by the circumstances and decisions of their fathers.

There was to be a new beginning, a reallocation of wealth, every fifty years that was to overcome the concentrations of land that might occur during the stewardship tenure of a previous generation. In essence, the negative consequences of sin and human finitude were to be redressed and not allowed to be cumulative and self-perpetuating. This was to be built into the system and not left exclusively to personal choice. Families were not to be barred from access to the means of providing for themselves by the mechanics of an economic structure—free or otherwise.

The editor concludes that Christians do have a responsibility to seek a just means of preventing an ever-widening gap between those at the top of the economic ladder and those at the bottom when it is caused by the poor stewardship decisions of prior generations or conditions that are perpetrated by the economic structure itself. How is this to be done? The editor has no glib answer for this in a pluralistic society that has little interest in God's concerns. The Jubilee was intended to serve as a form of economic forgiveness, though. It seems as if both spiritual and economic forgiveness are important to God. They should, therefore, be of great interest to Christians.

SECTION "F" REVISITED

The last section focuses on eschatology ("end times") and how it shapes our world view, motives, and behavior. In this context, we looked at the importance of our understanding of Christ's second coming and the role it plays in providing us *hope* for the future, which motivates and sustains us in the present. We contrasted this with those who have a circular view of history and who are less likely to be excited about work and be motivated to seek economic justice for their neighbors when their plight in life is perceived to be a just reward or punishment for their personal conduct in a previous life.

Drs. Will Barker and Jack Davis each explored a particular millennialist view of Christ's Kingdom reign and how this can motivate Christians in the marketplace. Some broad generalizations were made with regard to premillennialists and their tendency to accept a short-run interpretation of world events and their propensity to be more interested in the Great Commission than the creation mandates. It was also concluded that postmillennialists would more likely take a strong interest in the creation mandates and view world events from a long-run perspective.

We determined, though, that the most significant aspect of Christian eschatology is its ability to encourage us to anticipate God's ultimate victory and accomplishment of justice on our behalf, which frees all Christians to follow Christ and leave the ultimate outcome of our works, failures, successes, and hurts to His care. We are enabled to be truly different in responding to the hurts and injustices experienced in the marketplace. We are set free from a self-orientation and enabled to love our enemies, a distinctive mark of Christians. Christ asked pointedly, "If you love [do good to, lend to] those who love you, what credit is that to you? For even sinners do the same" (Luke 6:32-36).

As we move deeper into the end times, however, it is fair to ask if business institutions that have grown up in a culture heavily influenced by Christian values have improved over the centuries in their nurturing of ethical behavior on the part of individual business professionals? Have business institutions been positive encouragers of godly values in society?

The questions cause us to consider some of the consequences of striving to redeem economic structures, but they are not easy to answer for several reasons. First, God has no grandchildren; He has only children. Every generation is born in sin; therefore, every individual must face the call and claims of Christ. One is not a Christian by virtue of being born in a Christian family, although there are many advantages to being born in such a family. But the Christian faith is not cumulative from generation to generation.

Second, the culture can be deeply influenced by the proportion of the general population that is Christian. That is why a reformation or general revival can have such a salutary impact on the culture at large. This, too, depends on both the special and the common grace of God in His redeeming acts. His special grace is absolutely necessary for regeneration to take place, and His common grace is needed if His special grace is to have an impact on the culture at large. For example, "When a man's ways are pleasing to the LORD, He makes even his enemies to be at peace with him" (Prov. 16:7). God can (and has) blessed nations for the sake of His children.

The questions are also hard to answer because the historic records reveal that many individuals with enormous integrity work in business at the same time that many operate with minimal or practically no ethics. No one, to the editor's knowledge, has ever been able to statistically determine the proportions between these groups during a particular time of history.

Furthermore, the changing structure of institutions over the centuries has affected accountability, the size and concentration of economic power, the nature of risk bearing (owner-manager structures versus professional manager structures), and other important variables. These differences make comparisons difficult.

In spite of all these reasons for doubting that a definitive answer can be given to our questions, the editor still wants to make two statements whose implications are to be understood in the light of God's common grace and seen as a byproduct of His special grace, not as a definitive end objective of the gospel message. Have business institutions improved over the centuries in their nurturing of ethical behavior? The editor gives a qualified "yes" answer.

The free market system with its mass distribution can survive only if there is a reasonably positive relationship between the quality of the product and the price of the product, and a high level of general trust in the system of law as a basis for justice. It is next to impossible to be a large, successful economic entity without doing a lot that is right and doing it honestly. It is fair to argue that exposure to *positive* competition serves as an arm of common grace to check the more debased side of human nature.

Have business institutions been a provider of godly values in society? The editor offers the identical type of "yes" answer. It is hard not to believe that the world's population is receiving, century by century, more and more products and services that are genuinely beneficial. Concerns for sanitation, hospital care, orphanages, and education have been evident at times when Christians were sensitive to such social interests and extremely influential in the culture. The editor simply has to say that many positive economic benefits have accrued to society in general as a side effect of Christians' influence on business, science, medicine, engineering, and other disciplines.

COMMENCEMENT, NOT A CONCLUSION

It is too early to draw many final conclusions. There is so much work to be done in the search for biblical truths that can be applied to the foundational issues of business and economics. This book commences that work. The subsequent volumes will build on it and add to it enormously.

The editor is encouraged to see the positive things that have already emerged from the examination of business-related issues and questions under the light of Scripture. Before the series is finished, the whole counsel of God's

Word will have been sought and brought to bear on a host of issues. Individual pieces of God's truth are extremely important to the whole, but our thinking about God's will, as it pertains to the marketplace, needs to focus on the larger principles in order for us to appreciate and foster the balance God is working out in the lives of His children as we (1) simultaneously obey the creation mandates and carry out the Great Commission in the marketplace; (2) seek God's view of the marketplace as it is expressed in both Old and New Testaments; (3) learn the absolute truths of Scripture and discern how to apply them in ever-changing business and economic situations; (4) grow to understand the full impact sin has on us all while simultaneously appreciating God's common grace in providing everyone with the knowledge of good and evil so we can communicate our concerns about moral issues in the marketplace; (5) wrestle with how wealth is to be distributed in a fallen world where personal choice-making is so fundamental but where some people are unable to adequately care for themselves; and (6) differ so completely over millennial beliefs but end up as a "whole body" obeying God's creation and Great Commission mandates.

It is indeed by grace that our individual imbalances are collectively brought into balance when our inadequacies are added together. Oh, how merciful and gracious is our Lord and Savior as He sovereignly governs His creation with the meaningful participation of His image-bearers!

NOTES

CHAPTER 2

1. John Calvin, *Sermons on the Epistle to the Ephesians*, trans. Arthur Golding (London: Banner of Truth, 1973), pages 457-458.
2. John W. Cooper, "Is Capitalism Based on Greed?" *Integer* (Summer/Fall 1987), page 11.

CHAPTER 3

1. J. Philip Wogaman, *A Christian Method of Moral Judgment* (Philadelphia: Westminster, 1976), see esp. pages 1-5.
2. From *Webster's Seventh New Collegiate Dictionary* (Springfield, Mass.: G. & C. Merriam Co., 1967), page 397.
3. Rudolf Otto, *The Idea of the Holy*, trans. John W. Harvey (London: Oxford University Press, 1923).
4. John Wesley's sermon on Christian perfection sets forth his understanding of Christian growth in love.
5. Cited in Walter G. Muelder, *Religion and Economic Responsibility* (New York: Scribner, 1953), page 70. Bishop Lawrence argued that "in the long run, it is only to the man of morality that wealth comes. We believe in the harmony of God's universe. We know that it is only by working along His laws natural and spiritual that we can work with efficiency. . . . Material prosperity," he continued, "is helping to make the national character sweeter, more joyous, more unselfish, more Christlike. That is my answer to the question as to the relation of material prosperity to morality."

The twentieth-century quotation is from Robert Schuller, cited by Dennis Voskuil, *Mountains into Goldmines: Robert Schuller and the Gospel of Success* (Grand Rapids, Mich.: Eerdmans, 1983), page 157. Voskuil notes that this early Schuller quotation is not as characteristic of his more recent statements, although the simple equation of faith with success still marks much of his preaching and writing. Both Lawrence and Schuller appear to have lost sight of the many biblical passages warning against or even condemning wealth, on the one hand, and expressing divine support for the poor, on the other. He would have no part in the casting down of the mighty from their seats or the exalting of those of low degree!

6. The PTL scandal, which erupted in the summer of 1987, inspired both a sense of outrage and a sense of pathos. It was clearly outrageous that vast numbers of innocent viewers of the "ministry" should be led to give generously to support what they took to be a worthy ministry—only later to discover that they were actually supporting a grossly materialistic lifestyle by its leaders. There was a larger pathos, however, in the very grossness of the materialism. For here was obviously an effort by persons of weak faith to shore up their deep sense of insecurity. Gross materialism, in that sense, is generally a "consolation prize" for people who have lost touch with the deeper truths of the gospel. And what a poor consolation it is!

7. Max Weber, *The Protestant Ethic and the Spirit of Capitalism,* trans. Talcott Parsons (New York: Scribner, 1958 [1920]). Weber is sometimes errone-ously regarded as having written that Protestantism *caused* the rise of modern capitalism. Although that interpretation is wrong, he did argue that Protestantism—especially in its Calvinist forms—gave modern capitalism its peculiarly ascetic character.

8. Wesley prided himself on living frugally so he could give away the greater part of his increasing earnings (much of which was derived from the sale of his many books). He appears to have continued to live on exactly the same amount of money through the years; he gave the balance away and thus fulfilled his own principle of "giving all you can."

9. Carnegie wrote that "the growing disposition to tax more and more heavily large estates left at death is a cheering indication of the growth of a salutary change in public opinion" and "of all forms of taxation, this seems the wisest" (in *Democracy and the Gospel of Wealth*, ed. Gail Kennedy [Boston: Heath, 1949], page 5). Lest Andrew Carnegie be dismissed too quickly as a fuzzy-headed liberal, however, he also wrote that "wealth, passing through the hands of the few, can be made a much more potent force for the elevation of our race than if it had been distributed in small sums to the people themselves" (page 6). Carnegie's writing was from the *North American*

Review, vol. 148 (June 1889), pages 653-664.

10. Milton Friedman, *Capitalism and Freedom* (Chicago: University of Chicago Press, 1962), page 133.

11. Martin Luther's essay, "Temporal Authority: To What Extent it Should Be Obeyed," *Luther's Works* (Philadelphia: Mulenburg Press, 1962), vol. 45, pages 81-129, is one of many places where the Reformer emphasizes the importance of a Christian calling to secular work. For example, he writes that "just as one can serve God in the estate of marriage, or in farming or a trade, for the benefit of others—and must so serve if his neighbor needs it—so one can serve God in government, and should there serve if the needs of his neighbor demand it" (page 100). In another characteristic passage exegeting Genesis 22, Luther remarks,

> When we are sure about God's will and believe that He has commanded what we have under consideration, the matter must be undertaken, not with trepidation or hesitation but with the utmost eagerness, even if one had to expose himself to a thousand dangers or to death itself. . . . For it is most certainly true that when anyone in his vocation is convinced in his heart that God desires and has commanded in His Word what he is doing, he will experience such force and effectiveness of that divine command as he will not find in the oration of any orator . . . . And when the heart has been provided with this confidence, it proceeds boldly and is not anxious about the possible or the impossible, the easy or the difficult (*Works* [Saint Louis: Concordia, 1964], vol. 4, pages 103-104).

These may be good words for people in business, although it may not be as easy as Luther thought to be "sure about God's will."

12. Elmer W. Johnson, "How Corporations Balance Economic and Social Concerns," *Business and Society Review,* vol. 54 (Summer 1985), page 13.

CHAPTER 4

1. Emil Brunner, *The Divine Imperative* (Philadelphia: Westminster, 1977), page 388.

2. John C. Cort, "Christ and Neighbor," *New Oxford Review*, March 1987, page 21.

3. Tom Sine, *The Kingdom Connection* (Waco, Tex.: Word, Inc., 1987), page 23.

4. Fulton J. Sheen, *Peace of Soul* (New York: McGraw-Hill, 1949), page 20.

5. R. C. Sproul, *Stronger Than Steel* (New York: Harper & Row, 1980), pages 61-62.

6. Jacques Ellul, *Money and Power* (Downers Grove, Ill.: InterVarsity, 1984), pages 20-21.

CHAPTER 5

1. Douglas Stuart, "The Law(s)—Covenant Stipulations for Israel," in *How to Read the Bible for All Its Worth*, ed. Gordon D. Fee and Douglas Stuart (Grand Rapids, Mich.: Zondervan, 1982), pages 137, 139.

2. Emil G. Kraeling, *The Old Testament Since the Reformation* (New York: Harper, 1955), page 8. The same sentiment was echoed in A.H.J. Gunneweg, *Understanding the Old Testament* (Philadelphia: Westminster, 1978), page 2: "It would be no exaggeration to understand the hermeneutical problem of the Old Testament as *the* problem of Christian theology, and not just one problem among others." See also Bernhard W. Anderson, *The Old Testament and Christian Faith* (New York: Harper & Row, 1963), page 1: "It is no exaggeration to say that on this question hangs the meaning of the Christian faith." See my chapter, "The Old Testament as *the* Christian Problem," in *Toward Rediscovering the Old Testament* (Grand Rapids: Zondervan, 1987), pages 13-32.

3. See Walter C. Kaiser, Jr., *Toward Rediscovering the Old Testament*, pages 26-32, for an extended discussion of 2 Timothy 3:16-17. Also W.A. Bartlett, *The Profitableness of the Old Testament Scriptures* (London: Rivingtons, 1844).

4. Robert Banks, *Jesus and the Law in the Synoptic Tradition* (Cambridge: Cambridge University Press, 1975), pages 203-226.

5. David Wenham, "Jesus and the Law: An Exegesis on Matthew 5:17-20," *Themelios,* vol. 4 (1979), pages 93-96. Also see Walter C. Kaiser, Jr., "The Place of Law and Good Works in Evangelical Christianity," in *A Time to Speak: The Evangelical-Jewish Encounter*, ed. A. James Rudin and Marvin R. Wilson (Grand Rapids, Mich.: Eerdmans, 1987), pages 120-133.

6. C.E.B. Cranfield, "St. Paul and the Law," *Scottish Journal of Theology,* vol. 17 (1964), pages 43-68.

7. See Luke T. Johnson, "The Use of Leviticus 19 in the Letter of James," *Journal of Biblical Literature*, vol. 101 (1982), pages 391-401; also Walter C. Kaiser, Jr., "Applying the Principles of the Ceremonial Law: Leviticus 19; James," in *The Uses of the Old Testament in the New* (Chicago: Moody Press, 1985), pages 221-224.

8. John Goldingay, *Approaches to Old Testament Interpretation* (Downers

Grove, Ill.: InterVarsity, 1981), pages 52-53.

9. Roger Mehl, "The Basis of Christian Social Ethics," in *Christian Ethics in a Changing World*, ed. J. Bennett (New York: Association, 1966), page 47.

10. J.L. Houlden, *Ethics and the New Testament* (Middlesex, England: Penguin, 1973), page 2.

11. M.T. O'Donovan, "The Possibility of a Biblical Ethic," *Theological Students Fellowship Bulletin*, vol. 67 (1973), page 19.

12. Goldingay, *Approaches to Old Testament Interpretation*, page 53.

13. Karl Barth, *Church Dogmatics*, trans. A. T. MacKay (Edinburgh: T. & T. Clark, 1961), vol. 3/4, page 11. For further discussion, see Walter C. Kaiser, Jr., *Toward Old Testament Ethics* (Grand Rapids, Mich.: Zondervan, 1983), pages 24-29.

14. O'Donovan, "Possibility of a Biblical Ethic," page 17.

15. O'Donovan, "Possibility of a Biblical Ethic," page 18.

16. O'Donovan, "Possibility of a Biblical Ethic," page 18.

17. Stephen A. Kaufman, "The Structure of the Deuteronomic Law," *MAARAV* (1978-1979), pages 105-158.

18. N.H.G. Robinson, *The Groundwork of Christian Ethics* (Grand Rapids, Mich.: Eerdmans, 1972), page 321, citing J.H. Oldham, *The Church and Its Function in Society* (London: Allen & Unwin, 1937), pages 209ff.

19. James B. Jordan, *The Law of the Covenant: An Exposition of Exodus 21-23* (Tyler, Tex.: Institute for Christian Economics, 1984), pages 16-19. For a critique of this principle, see Robert P. Lightner, "Nondispensational Responses to Theonomy," *Bibliotheca Sacra*, vol. 143 (1986), pages 138-140. See also Paul B. Fowler, "God's Law Free from Legalism: Critique of Theonomy in Christian Ethics," unpublished paper, pages 24-25.

20. I have been very much indebted and influenced by the various unpublished papers of Michael Schluter, which he so kindly shared with me. Particularly helpful here was his paper "Can Israel's Law and Historical Experience Be Applied to Britain Today?" See also "Guidelines for Applying the Law to Social Polity Today."

21. See Kaiser, *Toward Rediscovering the Old Testament*, for a diagram and discussion of this point, pages 164-166.

CHAPTER 6

1. For this phraseology, see Normal L. Geisler and William E. Nix, *From God To Us* (Walnut Creek, Calif.: ICBI [International Council of Biblical Inerrancy], 1987), pages 1-3.

2. For the customary definition of economics, see John A. Reinecke and

William F. Schoell, *Introduction to Business* (Boston: Allyn & Bacon, 1977), page 4. For the definition I propose, I am greatly indebted to R.E. McMaster, Jr., *Wealth For All* (Whitefish, Mont.: A.N., Inc., 1982), pages 1ff.; and *The Reaper*, August 2, 1984, pages 1ff. A third definition is suggested by E. Calvin Beisner and Daryl S. Borgquist, *The Christian World View of Economics* (Mountain View, Calif.: The Coalition on Revival, 1986), page 3: "Economics is the study of the principles and methods of production, distribution, and consumption of wealth." Note once again the emphasis on wealth rather than scarcity.

3. See Edward Stevens, *Business Ethics* (New York: Paulist Press, 1979), page 202.

4. See Reinecke and Schoell, *Introduction to Business*, page 476.

5. The notion of propositional, objectively valid, biblical truth has run in strong opposition from post-Kantian thought such as neoorthodoxy by virtue of the driving force behind it. This is the freedom (nonobjectifiable)/ nature (objectifying) scheme. Where orthodoxy, in a biblically warranted arithmetic, holds that 100% (God's Word) = 100% (man's word) = 100% (Scripture as *one* divine-human book), neoorthodoxy rejects the latter half of this equation. It maintains that 100% + 100% = 200%. According to neoorthodoxy, the divine and the human sustain a dialectic relationship. Although in true Kantian style they are two poles that presuppose each other (100% + 100%), they nevertheless do not coincide at any one point (200%). Hence the notion of propositional (objectifiable) truth (nonobjectifiable) is simply a contradiction in terms.

6. See Richard C. Chewning, *Business Ethics in a Changing Culture* (Reston: Reston Pub. Co., 1984), pages 20-21. A broad consensus as to what is right or wrong is missing and the conflicting basic ethical assumptions of the various segments of society will not permit such consensus to become a reality (again) any time soon. In fact, ethically society is heading in hopelessly contradictory directions at the same time, hence the charge of schizophrenia.

7. In philosophical terms, this is the issue of the relationship between the particulars and the universals.

8. This is cogently argued by Jacques Ellul, *The Theological Foundation of Law* (New York: Seabury Press, 1969), pages 17ff., 60ff., 75ff.

9. See R.J. Rushdoony, "The Philosophy of the Free Market," *Journal of Christian Reconstruction,* vol. 10, no. 2 (1984), pages 37-38.

10. Rushdoony, "The Philosophy of the Free Market," page 38. See also Gary North, *The Dominion Covenant* (Tyler, Tex.: The Institute of Christian Economics, 1982), pages 1-26, as well as Appendix A, "From Cosmic

Purposelessness to Humanistic Sovereignty," pages 245-321. I am particularly indebted to this appendix for some of the thoughts expressed in this section. Rushdoony and North both argue that the concept of randomness lies at the root of the radical reinterpretation and total restructuring of reality. It was introduced to get rid of (every last vestige of) God who was already in the process of being replaced by nature. Not only did every purpose and standard that originated in God vanish with the concept of randomness, but nature and its inherent design and law structure were wiped out as well. Thus, the stage was set for the reinterpretation and restructuring.

11. It is ironical that a product of meaninglessness turns out to be the sole source of meaning. But it is ill-advised to speak of an "illogical" contradiction. How can man be virtually "nothing" and "everything" at the same time? Apostasy has a "logic" all its own. Man will aspire to take God's place by whatever means. In this context he first dethroned Him by means of the methodological "chaos" of randomness with a view of enthroning himself to create order in that chaos.

12. All the observable trends in modern society can be reduced to these two. The others compromise one way or the other. In fact, they invariably wish to have it both ways. Since the two basic trends are irreconcilable, however, all compromises battle a built-in conflict.

13. The evolutionary biological model lies on the face of it. Just as nature's undesigned and unregulated selection spelled progress and accomplishment, so the uncontrolled and unimpeded competition of the market will prove to have impressive results. See for a further discussion, Stevens, *Business Ethics*, pages 23ff.

14. Writes Lester F. Ward, *Dynamic Sociology* (New York: Appleton, 1907), vol. 1, pages 54-55: "Let us admit, however, as candor dictates, that almost everything that has been said by the advocates of *laissez faire* about the evils of government is true, and there is much more that has not been said which should be said on the same subject" (quoted in North, *The Dominion Covenant*, page 303). What Ward admits in practice, however, he is not willing to yield in principle. Properly trained legislators in the laws of sociology will undo the evils and carry the day.

15. See Gary North, "The Evolutionists' Defense of the Market," Appendix B in *The Dominion Covenant*, pages 323-356, esp. pages 336ff.

16. The threat of discontinuity and (potential) chaos was offset among Canaanites by their fertility religion and in Babylon by the cult. On the other hand, the regimentation of the modern technocratic society led to the hippie movement and the emphasis on existential freedom. This generation saw the

pendulum swing both ways on the university campuses in two decades. The sixties were marked by a revolutionary spirit against the control of the military industrial complex. Since the mid-seventies the main preoccupation became to achieve job security in a changing and disturbing world. The yuppies replaced the rebels. Undoubtedly the pendulum will swing again. Even the Christian is not immune to the influence of the dialectic. Worry is a virtual declaration of the functional nonexistence of God in the face of threatening circumstances. It indicates, "If I am not in control of my own future, nobody is."

17. See H. Krabbendam, "The New Hermeneutic," in *Hermeneutics, Inerrancy, and the Bible*, ed. Earl D. Radmacher and Robert D. Preus (Grand Rapids, Mich.: Zondervan, 1984), pages 549ff., esp. page 553. See also from the same author, "B. B. Warfield versus G.C. Berkouwer on Scripture," in *Inerrancy*, ed. Norman L. Geisler (Grand Rapids, Mich.: Zondervan, 1979), pages 443ff., and "The Functional Theology of G.C. Berkouwer," in *Challenges to Inerrancy*, eds. Gordon Lewis and Bruce Demarest (Chicago: Moody Press, 1984), pages 305ff., esp. pages 310-311.

18. This, of course, is in evidence throughout society. For example, what may seem freedom (of expression in a student newspaper) to the one may have all the earmarks of irresponsibility to the other (the school administration). Vice versa, what may appear to be proper control to the one (the parents) may be like a cast-iron mold to the other (the children).

19. Attempts have been made to anchor natural law in the structure of reality created by God. A broad consensus throughout history regarding basic tenets of morality such as murder, adultery, theft, etc., seems to suggest this. Man appears to be incurably moral. He cannot help but think in terms of good and bad, and in a general way knows the difference between the two.

Further, Scripture seems to support this sense of morality. It presents man in his conscience and thought as excusing and accusing himself and others (Rom. 2:15). Indeed, man practices by nature the things of the law, which are said to be written on the heart (Rom. 2:14-15).

In the face of both the historical realities and the biblical data, therefore, it appears difficult to deny the existence of a "natural law" that is embedded in the created structures and that functions as a universal standard. Now, it must be admitted that man as created in the image of God is incurably moral. He does not simply act morally because it is ultimately in his best interest (out of pragmatic considerations), nor because the environment expects this from him (social pressure). He does so because he has the moral imprint of God's being indelibly stamped on his constitution.

However, this does not justify the construct of a well-defined natural law that is universally accepted and practiced. There is neither a historical nor a biblical warrant for that. History displays an even more bewildering ethical pluralism with patterns of conduct that are increasingly in conflict, while Scripture does not endorse the notion of the law written on the heart of all men. It speaks of "the things of the law" and the "work of the law" in this context (Rom. 2:14-15). Only the regenerate man has the law itself written on the heart (Jer. 31:33). The difference could hardly be more vast.

The state of affairs appears to be this. On the one hand, man experiences the pressure of his constitution. This is a force for good. On the other hand, his rebellious heart seeks to suppress and efface all God's truth, also in the ethical realm. This is a force for evil. The unregenerate man is kept in check by his conscience, his pragmatism, and his society, all instruments of God's restraining influence and continuing benevolence. Unless fully seared, his conscience speaks out for God and morality as part of his constitution. Unless quite reprobate, man will refuse to cut off his nose to spite his face. Unless thoroughly diseased, a society will insist on some semblance of law and order rather than to face dissolution and chaos.

The case of the regenerate man is different. With his rebellious nature removed, he delights in the law of God, which is increasingly written on his new heart and becomes ever more an integral part of him, through the Spirit who effects this by means of the Word. In principle, one can expect anything bad and nothing good from the unbeliever. After all, he does not fear God and is hostile to His law (Gen. 20:11; Rom. 3:10-18, 8:7).

It is clearly unrealistic to have any illusions about the unbeliever. In practice, however, one can assess the sensitivity of his conscience, the pragmatic patterns of his behavior, and the general codes, official and unofficial, of his society. These determine the level of predictable conduct, and with it, the parameters of safe interaction also in the business world.

From the believer, one can in principle expect everything good and nothing bad. It is a matter of biblical realism, however, to reckon with the presence of both indwelling sin and temptation. Acceptable conduct, therefore, apart from his customary behavior and the general societal ethics, can only be expected as long as he centers his life in Jesus (John 15:5), practices the presence of the Spirit (Rom. 15:16), and is empowered through the Word, by prayer, and in the fellowship of the Church. This state of affairs, which seems to conform to Scripture, simply has no place for the construct of a definable "natural law," which is universally valid and accepted.

20. Man seems doomed to spin his wheels throughout his existence. Although life has its pleasantries (enjoy your wife all the days of your meaningless life [Eccles. 9:9]) and its preferable alternatives (two are better than one [Eccles.

4:9]), death is the evidence that it is ultimately going nowhere.

21. For this definition of the fear of God, I am indebted to John Brown, *The First Epistle of the Apostle Peter* (Marshallton, Pa.: The National Foundation for Christian Education, n.d.), vol. 2, pages 115ff., and a tape series "Fear of God" by Albert Martin (Caldwell, N.J.: The Trinity Pulpit).

22. The personal touch seems prominent in the Japanese business model in which the employees are treated as part of the "family" and encouraged to take pride in "their" company. The personal and the human touch, according to R.C. Sproul, *Stronger Than Steel—The Wayne Alderson Story* (New York: Harper & Row, 1980), was characteristic of Wayne Alderson who through the concepts of the value of the person and the dignity of man turned a money-losing steel company into a profitable concern. A businessman in Chicago had the caring touch. He ran his business, which was strictly seasonal, in a way that he did not have to lay off his employees during the winter.

23. This approach that ties down the various case laws to the individual commandments in the Decalogue is predicated upon a specific architecture of t th Exodus 20:22–23:33 (the Book of the Covenant) and Deuteronomy 5–26 (the stipulations in the Hittite treatylike covenant renewal). This came first to my attention in the form suggested by B. Holwerda in the early 1950s. For his Exodus proposal we are dependent upon an unpublished manuscript quoted extensively by C. Vonk, *De Voorzeide Leer* (Barendrecht: Drukkerij Barendrecht, 1966), vol. 1c, pages 392ff. The Deuteronomy proposal is contained in B. Holwerda, *Dictaten: Exegese Oude Testament* (Kampen, Netherlands: 1957). This is a printed class syllabus on Deuteronomy. His thesis is that both the Book of the Covenant and the Deuteronomic stipulations, after the Decalogue is promulgated, constitute a methodical exposition of the Ten Commandments. Apparently he was neither the first nor the last one to propose this. See Walter C. Kaiser, Jr., *Toward Old Testament Ethics* (Grand Rapids, Mich.: Zondervan, 1983), pages 127ff., who points this out specifically in terms of Deuteronomy. He credits Stephen Kaufman for reviving an old idea in a new way and endorses not only his conclusion that Deuteronomy is a "highly structured composition whose major topical units are arranged according to the order of the laws of the Decalogue," but also the actual division that he proposes. While Kaufman's contribution and Kaiser's endorsement ought to be welcomed in terms of the main thesis, it seems to me that Holwerda's suggestion as to the transition points from set of case laws to set of case laws is preferable. Regrettably, he died before he could finish his proposal in the necessary details. So what follows here is partly my own construction. It is presented as the backdrop for the main text

in which certain case laws are tied to specific commandments of the Decalogue: I: 6:1-11:32; II: 12:1-13:18; III: 14:1-29; IV: 15:1-16:17; V: 16:18-18:22; VI: 19:1-22:12; VII: 22:13-23:14; VIII: 23:15-24:22; IX: 25:1-19; X: 26:1-19. Apart from B. Holwerda, *Dictaten*, page 410, I am also indebted to C. Vonk, *De Voorzeide Leer*, pages 492ff., who has a slightly different division. For a further justification of the division I propose here, see my unpublished syllabus, *The Pentateuch*, pages 177ff.

24. See McMaster, *Wealth For All*, page 13.

25. I take it that the way the New Testament interprets and handles the Old Testament is a model for the Church. Just as James introduces a new case law in the area of the Sixth Commandment in the footsteps of the Old Testament, specifically Exodus and Deuteronomy, so the Church should be able to follow in the footsteps of the New Testament.

26. See McMaster, *Wealth For All*, pages 1ff.

27. The issue here is not that the Christian should not endeavor to keep peace with all men. He should (see Rom. 12:18). But "all men" do not intend to keep peace with him *forever*. True Christianity evokes persecution (see John 15:18ff.; Phil. 1:29; 1 Thess. 3:3; 2 Tim. 3:12; Rev. 12:12).

28. *Love* and *truth* deserve to be underscored. There is nothing harsh or blunt about the Christian's "warfare." At least, there should not be (see 2 Tim. 2:24-25). At the same time, he should seek to join the spiritual issue (see 2 Tim. 2:25-26).

29. The One who personified love and truth ended up on a cross. But what a victory that was! This should also tell us something about the *nature* of victory. Sometimes "defeat" really spells VICTORY (see Rev. 12:11; 20:4).

CHAPTER 7

1. Reginald H. Fuller and Brian K. Rice, *Christianity and the Affluent Society* (Grand Rapids, Mich.: Eerdmans, 1966), pages 173-174.

2. Dennis Clark, *Work and the Human Spirit* (New York: Sheed & Ward, 1967), page 168.

3. John H. Leith, ed., *Creeds of the Churches* (Chicago: Aldine Publishing Co., 1963), page 132.

4. Leith, *Creeds of the Churches*, pages 334-335.

5. Leith, *Creeds of the Churches*, page 231.

6. Daniel Callahan, "Post-Biblical Christianity," *Commonweal*, December 6, 1966, pages 291, 293.

7. Allen Hollis, *The Bible and Money* (New York: Hawthorn Books, 1976), pages 5, 9-10.

8. Josiah Stamp, *Christianity and Economics* (New York: Macmillan, 1939), pages 72-73.
9. Gordon D. Fee and Douglas Stuart, *How to Read the Bible for All Its Worth* (Grand Rapids, Mich.: Zondervan, 1982), page 63; cf. pages 84-85, 203.
10. Christopher J. H. Wright, *An Eye for an Eye: The Place of Old Testament Ethics Today* (Downers Grove, Ill.: InterVarsity, 1983), page 162.
11. John Taylor, *Enough Is Enough* (London: SCM Press, 1975), pages 51-54. Cf. Fee and Stuart, *How to Read the Bible for All Its Worth*, pages 141-148.
12. C.A. Anderson Scott, *New Testament Ethics* (Cambridge: Cambridge University Press, 1934), pages 45-46.
13. Clark, *Work and the Human Spirit*, pages 121-122.
14. Quoted in *The Judeo-Christian Vision and the Modern Corporation*, eds. Oliver Williams and John Houck (Notre Dame, Ind.: University of Notre Dame Press, 1982), page 58.
15. John Mitchell, *The Christian in Business* (Westwood, N.J.: Revell, 1962), page 16.
16. Quoted in Walter George Mueller, *Religion and Economic Responsibility* (New York: Scribner, 1953), page 41.
17. Elton Trueblood, *The Common Ventures of Life* (New York: Harper & Row, 1949), pages 85-86.
18. Thomas C. Oden, *Conscience and Dividends: Churches and the Multinationals* (Washington, D.C.: Ethics and Policy Center, 1985), pages 100-101.
19. Wade H. Boggs, *All Ye Who Labor* (Richmond, Va.: John Knox Press, 1961), pages 196-197.
20. Quoted in Mueller, *Religion and Economic Responsibility*, page 44.
21. Mitchell, *The Christian in Business*, pages 101-103.
22. Kenneth Boulding, *Beyond Economics* (Ann Arbor: University of Michigan Press, 1968), page 234.
23. Quoted in Jane D. Douglas, *Women, Freedom, and Calvin* (Philadelphia: Westminster, 1985), page 118.

CHAPTER 8

1. J. Murray, "Common Grace," *Collected Writings* (Edinburgh: Banner of Truth, 1977), vol. 2, page 102.
2. *Westminster Confession of Faith*, vol. 16, page 7.
3. This facet is thoughtfully developed by G.C. Berkouwer in *Man: The Image of God*, trans. D.W. Jellema (Grand Rapids, Mich.: Eerdmans, 1962), pages 179-184.
4. Berkouwer, *Man: The Image of God*, page 184.

5. John Calvin, *Institutes of the Christian Religion*, trans. F.L. Battles (Philadelphia: Westminster, 1960), vol. 1, page 277.

6. Calvin, *Institutes of the Christian Religion*, vol. 1, pages 70, 160.

CHAPTER 9

1. Heraclitus, *Fragments*, trans. G.S. Kirk and J.E. Raven, in *The PreSocratic Philosophers: A Critical History With a Selection of Texts* (Cambridge: Cambridge University Press, 1964), pages 197-201.

2. See Plato, *Republic*, books 4-6 (New York: Pantheon, 1964).

3. Cicero stated that "there is a true law, right reason in accord with nature; it is of universal application, unchanging and everlasting. . . . There is one law . . . binding at all times upon all peoples" (Cicero, *The Republic*, 3.22, cited in *Natural Law in Political Thought*, ed. Paul E. Sigmund [Cambridge, Mass.: Winthrop, 1971]).

4. St. Augustine, *On the Spirit and the Letter*, page 48, vol. 5 of *A Secret Library of the Nicene and Post-Nicene Fathers of the Christian Church*, ed. Philip Schaff (Grand Rapids, Mich.: Eerdmans, 1956).

5. St. Augustine, *On the Good of Marriage*, pages 203, 407, vol. 3 of *A Select Library of the Nicene and Post-Nicene Fathers of the Christian Church*.

6. St. Augustine, *On the Spirit and the Letter*, page 48.

7. St. Augustine, *On the Spirit and the Letter*, page 48.

8. St. Augustine, *Reply to Faustus the Manichean*, 19.1, vol. 4 of *A Select Library of the Nicene and Post-Nicene Fathers of the Christian Church*.

9. Thomas Aquinas, *1-2 Summa Theologica*, 91.2, in *Basic Writings of Saint Thomas Aquinas*, ed. Anton Pegis (New York: Random House, 1944).

10. Aquinas, *1-2 Summa Theologica*, 90.4.

11. Aquinas, *1-2 Summa Theologica*, 90.1.

12. Aquinas, *1-2 Summa Theologica*, 91.1.

13. Aquinas, *1-2 Summa Theologica*, 91.4.

14. John Calvin, *Institutes of the Christian Religion* (Grand Rapids, Mich.: Eerdmans, 1957), 1.3.1.

15. Calvin, *Institutes of the Christian Religion*, 1.4.4.

16. Kenneth Kantzer, *John Calvin's Theory of the Knowledge of God and the Word of God* (Cambridge, Mass.: Harvard Divinity School, 1981).

17. Calvin, *Institutes of the Christian Religion*, 2.2.22.

18. Calvin, *Institutes of the Christian Religion*, 2.2.22.

19. Calvin, *Institutes of the Christian Religion*, 2.2.22.

20. Calvin, *Institutes of the Christian Religion*, 1.5.1.

21. John Calvin, *The Epistles of Paul the Apostle to the Romans and to the*

Thessalonians (2:14), eds. David W. Torrance and Thomas F. Torrance (Grand Rapids, Mich.: Eerdmans, 1979), vol. 8, page 48.

22. Calvin, *The Epistles to the Romans and to the Thessalonians*, vol. 8, page 48.

23. Calvin, *The Epistles to the Romans and to the Thessalonians*, vol. 8, page 48.

24. Calvin, *The Epistles to the Romans and to the Thessalonians*, vol. 8, page 48.

25. Calvin, *The Epistles to the Romans and to the Thessalonians*, vol. 8, page 49.

26. John Locke, *An Essay*, 2.6, in vol. 35 of *The Great Books* (Chicago: Encyclopedia Britannica, 1952), page 26.

27. John W. Montgomery, *Human Rights and Human Dignity* (Grand Rapids, Mich.: Zondervan, 1986), pages 127-129.

28. George H. Sabine, *A History of Political Theory* (New York: Holt, Rinehart & Winston, 1961), page 425.

29. Hugo Grotius, *De Jure Belli ac Pacis Libri Tres*, vol. 2: *The Translation* (The Law of War and Peace) (Oxford: Clarendon Press, 1925), page 8.

30. Grotius, *De Jure Belli ac Pacis Libri Tres*, page 45; cf. page 61.

31. Grotius, *De Jure Belli ac Pacis Libri Tres*, page 13.

32. A.H. Robertson, cited by John W. Montgomery, *Human Rights and Human Dignity*, page 22.

33. Greg Bahnsen, *Theonomy in Christian Ethics* (Phillipsburg, N.J.: Presbyterian and Reformed, 1977), pages 399-400.

34. Bahnsen, *Theonomy in Christian Ethics*, page 445.

35. Frederic R. Howe, *Challenge and Response* (Grand Rapids, Mich.: Zondervan, 1982), page 72.

36. Martin Luther, *The Bondage of the Will*, sect. 94 (Grand Rapids, Mich.: Baker, 1976), page 244.

37. Confucius, *Analects of Confucius*, 25.23; cf. 12.2.

38. C.S. Lewis, *The Abolition of Man* (New York: Macmillan, 1947), appendix, pages 95-121.

39. Paul Kurtz, ed., *Humanist Manifestos I and II*, 1.5 (Buffalo: Prometheus Books, 1973), page 8.

40. Kurtz, *Humanist Manifestos I and II*, 2.3, page 17.

41. Joseph Fletcher, *Situation Ethics: The New Morality* (Philadelphia: Westminster, 1966), page 120.

42. Fletcher, *Situation Ethics: The New Morality*, page 235.

43. Fletcher, *Situation Ethics: The New Morality*, pages 43-44.

44. See Kurtz, *Humanist Manifestos I and II*, 2.7, pages 18-19.

45. Seneca, cited by John T. Noonan, Jr., ed., *The Morality of Abortion: Legal and Historical Perspectives* (Cambridge, Mass.: Harvard University Press, 1970), page 7, footnote.

46. Fletcher, *Situation Ethics: The New Morality*, pages 43-44.

47. Lewis, *The Abolition of Man*, page 56.
48. Alan Bloom, *The Closing of the American Mind* (New York: Simon & Schuster, 1987), page 28.
49. Bloom, *The Closing of the American Mind*, page 39.
50. Bahnsen, *Theonomy in Christian Ethics*, page 445.
51. Contrary to the claim of some, secular humanism is a religion. It claimed to be a religion in its own *Humanist Manifestos I and II* (1933, 1973); it has a journal called *Religious Humanism*; its proponents write books with titles like *Religion Without Revelation* (Julian Huxley) and *Religion Without God* (M.K. Kolenda); the Supreme Court recognized it as a religion by name (Torcaso versus Watkins, 1961).
52. It was not simply the "ministry" of Moses that has faded away, but "the ministry that brought death, which was engraved in letters on stone," namely, the Ten Commandments (2 Cor. 3:7).
53. Jeremiah 12:16-17 is not an exception. For when it speaks of other countries learning the "ways" of Israel and "swearing" by their God, it is speaking about the future kingdom "after" Israel is "brought back" to their own country (v. 15) when there will be a restored theocracy under the Messiah. During this time, there will be a divine law basis for civil government under the reign of Christ. Furthermore, Psalm 147:19-20 says explicitly that God has not revealed His "laws" or "decrees" to any other nation than Israel. Paul referred to Gentiles as those "who do not have the law" (Rom. 2:14).
54. See Roy L. Aldrich, *Holding Fast to Grace* (Findlay, Ohio: Dunham Publishing Co., n.d.), chap. 7.

CHAPTER 10

1. Besides the classical criticism of self, individualism, and dependent realities in Marx and other writers since then, particular mention must be made of the neo-Marxist Frankfurt school under Theodore Adorno, Max Horkheimer, and Jurgen Habermas, who have brought these ideas into the common thought life through their sociological writings and their influence in educational philosophy.

   But such criticism is also found in Ronald Sider and Tom Sine et al., though they would strongly reject any association with Marxist thoughts. Yet the common basis is an assumption that justice is measured in terms of end result, always a material and mathematical consideration. Thus, even with the best intentions, one can be a materialist in outlook.
2. Barbara Ward, *The Rich Nations and the Poor Nations* (New York: Norton & Co., 1962).

3. Such a view of limited global resources in *one* world is not only found in *Global 2000* reports or in the North-South process under Willy Brandt, but also in Tom Sine's *Mustard Seed Conspiracy*, (Word Inc., 1981).

4. For futher discussion, look at P.T. Bauer, *Reality and Rhetoric* (Cambridge, Mass.: Harvard University Press, 1984) and *Equality, The Third World and Economic Delusion* (Cambridge, Mass.: Harvard University Press, 1981).

5. Jean-Francois Revel, *How Democracies Perish* (New York: Doubleday 1983).

6. See Alan Bloom, *The Closing of the American Mind* (New York: Simon & Schuster, 1987); Richard M. Weaver, *Ideas Have Consequences* (Chicago: University of Chicago Press, 1984); Warren Brooks, *The Economy in Mind* (New York: Universe Books, 1982).

7. John D. Watson's view on behaviorism as a form of control of outcome from a materialistic perspective.

8. B.F. Skinner, *Beyond Freedom and Dignity* (New York: Knops, 1971).

9. When the goal is to drive a car, one must make sure that energy has been so organized deliberately by will, personal effort, and new material resources that an engine, a transmission, and wheels on the road are in place. Without the means, the goal can never be reached. It remains wishful thinking and is dangerous in daily life.

10. There must not be a confusion about production and distribution of wealth. The Bible's concern is about economic health through personal effort, etc.

11. Much has been made available about the role of religious values and perspectives in economic and business practices since Weber and R.H. Tawney. P.T. Bauer is helpful here, but also John Mbiti, *African Religions and Philosophy* (London: Heinema & Co., 1983); Max Weber, *The Protestant Ethic and the Spirit of Capitalism*, trans. Talcott Parsons, New Edition (New York: Scribner, 1958); and R.H. Tawney, *Religion and the Rise of Capitalism* (New York: Harcourt, Brace & Co., Inc., 1926).

12. The emphasis on the instruction by God's Word, on obedience, rational and verifiable knowledge, the need for discernment, and the quest for evidence makes the Bible, in the mentality of the twentieth century, a most unreligious document. Yet, ethicists would often rather change the clear statements in Scripture than correct their basis for ethics in light of it. They are the new high priests.

13. See for example, Deuteronomy 28.

14. Against the view that the Old Testament teaches some form of *ursozialismus*. Out of the understanding that mannah was provided only in the wilderness and that milk and honey needed to be created, the blessing of God rested also on "their going out and coming in," a reference understood

to refer to trade, business, and profitable enterprise. See also Meir Tamari, *With All Your Possessions* (Free Press).

15. See Genesis 1; Psalm 8; Isaiah 8:19ff.
16. See Genesis 1:1; Habakkuk 2:3-4; John 7:39; Romans 2:4; 1 Peter 3:20.
17. See Genesis 24; Luke 19:41ff.; Acts 27:27-31; consider Jonah and Nineveh.
18. Genesis 1:28; Deuteronomy 8:9,18; Isaiah 45:18-20; Colossians 2:8-23.
19. Emphasis on the Word in creation, in John 1:1ff., in the concern for truth in John 17:17, but also in having prophets' discourses. Notice George Steiner, *Language and Silence* (New York: Atheneum, 1967).
20. From Genesis 3 throughout the rest of the Bible.
21. The first three chapters of Genesis and therein the whole setting of the rest of God's Word. Here the definitions are given without which the rest has no foundation.
22. Consider the emphasis on family relations, genealogies, and being tellers to the next generation.
23. Michelangelo's *Creation* painting in Rome portrays Genesis 1:27 and 2:17 together. Eve exists only in the mind of God when Adam was made.
24. Lengthy genealogies have their place if people matter as individuals (see 1 Chron.; Matt. 1). Events and choices are related to persons, not streams of cultures: Gideon, e.g., Judges 6-7; 1 Chronicles 1-8; Matthew 1:1-17; David called to be king (see 1 Sam. 16ff.); Amos went into a different kingdom as a shepherd (see Amos 7:10ff.) to speak against and challenge a whole culture.
25. Family relations also include the effect of faith in genealogies: Timothy had Lois and Eunice as teachers (see 2 Tim 1:5).
26. This includes the actions of the Jewish midwives who resisted Pharaoh's orders to follow God's Word (see Exod. 1:17ff.). The nation grew in spite of adverse conditions.
27. Prophecy opens up a different and certain future and reveals the outcome of current choices; it produces hope or repentance. In the Bible, man does not see himself a repetition of the past only, nor as owning the freedom to redefine the future through his actions alone. Rather, the Christian knows that all men stand in the stream of history created through significant choices. The sacrifices looked backward to the Fall and forward to the Messiah. From that perspective, the prosperous could be judged to be not always good (Why do the wicked prosper?) and the poor not always evil (Job).
28. The provisions for correct measures, against bribes for contractual fidelity, and the application of one law for all people are not related to a religious idea, but to the form of the universe. They reflect the final givens of creation

and are therefore not changed by religious or political orders. This frees business to proceed in the same created reality without being subject to the whims of those in power. Quite a different view was held by the medieval Church and is now again being advocated, when discussions are held to define without relationship to the real created world what is a fair price, an honest judge. In Israel, justice was not clouded by an idea of God's preferential bias for the rich or the poor.

29. Richard Weaver's *Ideas Have Consequences* argues this extensively.

30. Weaver, *Ideas Have Consequences*, page 20.

31. 1 Kings 5.

32. See Romans 8:18ff.

33. Paul Johnson, *Modern Times: The World from the Twenties to the Eighties* (New York: Harper & Row, 1983). This book is a valuable study of examples of tyranny against the person, always justified by greater social justice and benefit for "the people." When Jehovah is no longer known, there can also be no definite knowledge of Adam. With the French Revolution, a path was cleared for violence against the person in ever-varied and more brutal searches for the new society. Hitler, Stalin, Pol Pot, and Mao are brothers in brutal social experiments against individual persons and their significance.

34. See the excellent study of Christopher J. Wright, *Living as the People of God: Relevance of Old Testament Ethics* (Leicester, England: InterVarsity, 1983).

35. See Bernard-Henri Levy, *The Testament of God* (Paris: Grassett and Fasquelle, 1979).

36. Equality in the early Church was not mathematically determined. Love, generosity, and sacrifice do not create material equality, nor is it their goal. Acts 2 and 4 and 2 Corinthians 9 speak of enough, not what a materialistic age considers equal.

37. This even extends to the test for prophets and the Messiah (see Matt. 11).

38. André Ryerson, "Capitalism and Selfishness," *Commentary* magazine, December 1986, page 39.

39. Example for a distinction not made in Wayne Bragg, "Beyond Development," *Church in Response to Human Need*, MARC (Missions Advanced Research and Communications Center), (1983).

40. English sports games were, for a long time, based on such an understanding of competition that it required a good loser who was honored equally.

41. Herbert Schlossberg, "A Response to Nicholas Wolterstorff," *Transformation* (June-December 1987), page 20.

42. De Tocqueville is cited in Robert Bellah, *Habits of the Heart* (Harper &

Row, 1985), as one who understood that in older societies, one knew where one stood relative to others because of a network of established statuses and roles, each of which implied an appropriate form of attachment. This changed in the egalitarian and mobile American world. There he found a "restlessness in the midst of prosperity. . . . because they never stop thinking of the good things they have not got." He wonders whether the competition of all against all without the mediating infrastructure of family, community, a wider view of history, and personal responsibilities into the future explains that "their minds are more anxious and on edge. . . . They clutch everything and hold nothing fast" (pages 117ff.).

43. Fascinating studies on this field are found in J.M. Roberts, *The Triumph of the West* (Little Brown & Co., 1985); also Rosenberg and Bridzell, *How the West Grew Rich* (Basic Books, 1986).

44. Reference from an article in *The Wittenberg Door* (October, 1979), page 3.

CHAPTER 11

1. I am using the hyphen between socialism and Marxism because these ideologies share at least one basic dogma, differences notwithstanding. This shared belief will be one of the central themes of this work.

2. Steven Lukes, *Individualism* (Oxford: Basil Blackwell Press, 1973), pages 123-124. Cf. Yehoshua Arielli, *Individualism and Nationalism in American Ideology* (Cambridge: Harvard University Press, 1964).

3. As this belief applies to government, see Roger L. Miller, *Economics Today: The Macro View*, 5th ed. (New York: Harper & Row, 1985), page 111; as it applies to additional social institutions, see Rochne McCarthy et al., *Society, State and Schools* (Grand Rapids, Mich.: Eerdmans. 1981), pages 15-16.

4. Adam Smith, *The Wealth of Nations*, ed. Edwin Cannan (New York: Modern Library, 1965), page 423.

5. For the deistic secularization of the biblical notion of providence as an absence of God's active governance and how deism applies to the economy and Smith's (naive) economic optimism, see Bob Goudzwaard, *Capitalism and Progress* (Grand Rapids, Mich.: Eerdmans, 1979), pages 20ff.

6. The paradigmatic figure of Immanuel Kant often spoke of the Enlightenment as the throwing off of the self-inflicted nonage of yesterday. For an excellent summary of some of the origins of modern economic autonomy, see Bernard Mandeville, *The Table of the Bees: or, Private Vices, Public (sic) Benefits* (Harmondsworth: Penguin, 1970), pages 63-75. For autonomy's effect on the development of Western ideology, see Herman Dooyeweerd, *A New Critique of Theoretical Thoughts*, 4 vols. (Philadelphia: Presbyterian

and Reformed, 1969). For autonomy's effect on economics see Goudz-waard, *Capitalism and Progress*, pages 197ff. and passim.

7. R.H. Tawney, *The Acquisitive Society* (New York: Harcourt, Brace & World, 1920).

8. Philosopher Jeremy Bentham once equated happiness with the "sovereign governance" of pain and pleasure. This utilitarianism in equating utility with pleasure or the act of acquiring and pain with labor decisively influenced subsequent economic theory and social reality. Cf. Robert L. Heilbroner, *The Making of an Economic (sic) Society* (Englewood Cliffs, N.J.: Prentice-Hall, 1962), pages 25ff., 53; and his *The Worldly Philosophers* (New York: Simon & Schuster, 1972), pages 22ff., with Goudzwaard, *Capitalism and Progress*, pages 139ff., 242ff.

9. The reader will recognize neocapitalism's definition of value here. Classic capitalism, like Marx, believed that all economic value originated from labor.

10. The suggestion that economic theory and practice can become a religion is meant to be literal. How much more plain could Andrew Carnegie have been than to speak of *The Gospel of Wealth*? See also Chewning, *God and Mammon: The Interrelationship of Protestant Evangelicalism and the Industrial Revolution in America, 1820-1914* (Pittsburgh: Shiloh Publications, 1985). Although this dissertation became a book, it is no longer in print by this house. Subsequent publishers are being solicited.

11. Mark Blaug, *Economic Theory in Retrospect* (Cambridge: Cambridge University Press, 1978), pages 684-686.

12. Heilbroner, *Worldy Philosophers*, pages 270-272; Robert Goudzwaard, "Towards Reformation in Economics" (Toronto: Association for Advancement of Christian Scholarship), pages 10ff.

13. See, therefore, Goudzwaard, *Capitalism and Progress*, page 138, as quoting Keynes's "Economic Possibilities for our Grandchildren," pages 371-372.

14. Alan Storkey, *Transforming Economics* (London: Third Way Books, 1986), pages 40-45.

15. The term *manager* refers to one overly preoccupied with the control and manipulation of the economy. For a Christian assessment of this phenomenon, see Jacques Ellul, *The Technological Society*, trans. John Wilkinson (New York: Vintage Books, 1964).

16. The reader may question why no mention is made of Paraeto optimality or the more modern attempt to simultaneously realize individual and social desires. The so-called indeference to consumption has no final unique social optimum state because it attempts to "balance" social and individual wants through compensation payments. Moreover, optimality represents a lump of

individual preferred noncomparable optimal states. Comparability of optimal states is extended to the economic act of compensating payments while no normative foundation is given for welfare distribution. See Blaug, *Economic Theory In Retrospect*, pages 618-622.

17. As reported in Heilbroner, *Worldy Philosophers*, page 139.

18. Marx defines *labor* as the "quantity of effort used by the worker in the production of a good."

19. Karl Marx and Friedrich Engels, *Manifesto of the Communist Party* (Moscow: Foreign Languages Publication House, 1957), pages 86, 89. While this quote does not exhaust the gamut of their suggestions, it does note representative ones.

20. The attempts to "Christianize" this debate have been many. One of the more recent thorough projects occurs in John A. Bernbaum, ed., *Economic Justice and the State: A Debate Between Ronald H. Nash and Eric H. Beversluis* (Grand Rapids, Mich.: Baker, 1986). It is striking that Nash draws on classic and neoconservative capitalism for his analysis of justice and, for example, seems to be burdened by individualism and a tension between freedom and justice; see respectively pages 15-16. Likewise, Beversluis, while seeming to "balance" individual and collectivist agendas, actually favors the collectivist's (though not the socialist's) agenda by equating *social* justice with the God-given mandate for the state to do justice; see pages 27, 30, 32.

21. Thus Miller's distinction between "positive" and "normative" economics in a book that is manifestly neoconservative! Miller, *Economics Today: The Macro View*, pages 16-17.

22. John Calvin, *Institutes of the Christian Religion*, ed. John T. McNeill, trans. Ford Battles (Philadelphia: Westminster, 1967), 1.7.5. Cf. Waldo Beech and H. Richard Niebuhr, *Christian Ethics* (New York: Ronald Press, 1955), pages 274-297.

23. G. Bannock et al., *The Penguin Dictionary of Economics*, 2nd ed. (New York: Penguin, 1979), page 268.

24. Selig Perlman, noted labor historian, argues that American labor willingly accepted management's offer, gradually and begrudgingly extended, for higher wages if labor would surrender their social agenda. See his *A Theory of the Labor Movement* (New York: Macmillan, 1928).

25. Goudzwaard, *Capitalism and Progress*, pages 29ff., 140ff., 241ff.

26. Phyllis Deane, *The Evolution of Economic Ideas* (New York: Cambridge University Press, 1978), page 116.

27. Goudzwaard, "Towards Reformation in Economics," page 10. Cf. Benjamin Ward, *The Liberal Economic World View* (New York: Basic Books,

1979), page 34. Ward has also written a related volume, *The Conservative and Radical Economic World View.*

28. See my *God and Mammon* and, from a promarket viewpoint, Warren T. Brooks, "Goodness and the GNP," in *Is Capitalism Christian?*, ed. Franky Schaeffer (Westchester, Ill.: Crossway Books, 1985), pages 19-49. Cf. Paul E. Johnson, *A Shopkeeper's Millennium: Society and Revivals in Rochester, New York, 1815-1837* (New York: Hill & Wang, 1978).

29. The reader may legitimately accuse me of mixing household oranges with governmental apples. The "rational consumer" and related terms are generally related to microeconomic decisions while government spending is often defined in macroeconomic theory. Reality is, however, not this easily compartmentalized.

30. Galbraith notes that in the history of modern markets two seemingly contradictory forces are present *within* the market and *caused* by the market: a synergism of diverse resource allocation and monopolistic hoarding. John K. Galbraith, *The Galbraith Reader*, ed. Lowell Thompson (Ipswich: Macmillan of Canada, 1977), pages 393-400.

31. One needs only to consider the irony of subsidizing tobacco use—a known vehicle of cancer—even while we pay for a portion of the medical expenses of elderly smokers who have used tobacco for years. Moreover, we subsidize this usage in states where the argument for the free market is the strongest!

32. There is a growing consensus among economists that the prolonged period of economic growth enjoyed since the start of the Reagan administration has been fueled by the deficit spending and not by tax cuts. Should this theory prove only marginally true, one of recent history's most remarkable ironies will have occurred: A self-confessed conservative president would have used a manifestly liberal economic approach to bring the U.S. market to the brink of debt!

33. One can legitimately object that Keynes only intended deficit spending to last during the down cycle of a depression, and thus my critique is worthless. However, once the deficit ghost has been let out of the greedy chest, and the fruits from manifold barns have been eaten, it becomes difficult to "get off the wagon" of deficit spending because it is so addictive, especially when government spending "multiplies" or ripples through the economy. And so, neo-Keynesian Paul Samuelson prompted the Kennedy and Johnson administrations to simultaneously cut taxes and increase federal spending with the result that inflation and debt severely tortured our economy. See Miller, *Economics Today*, pages 272-290.

34. I am indebted to Goudzwaard's "Towards Reformation in Economics" and personal conversations with Bob for some of the insights contained in this

section on Keynes. For a free market critique of Keynes, see Gary North, *An Introduction to Christian Economics* (Nutley, N.J.: Craig Press, 1979), pages 53-55.

35. See David Lyon, *Karl Marx: A Christian Assessment of His Life and Thought* (Downers Grove, Ill.: InterVarsity, 1979); and ed. John C. VanderStelt, *The Challenge of Marxist and Neo-Marxist Ideologies for Christian Scholarship* (Sioux City, Iowa: Dordt College Press, 1982). Lyon reminds us that Marxism has greatly evolved in the last 125 years.

36. *Theological Dictionary of the New Testament*, ed. Gerhard Kittel, trans. Geoffrey W. Bromiley (Grand Rapids, Mich.: Eerdmans, 1968), vol. 3, pages 867-895.

37. G.C. Berkouwer, *The Providence of God* (Grand Rapids, Mich.: Eerdmans, 1952), page 54.

38. Albert W. Wolters, *Creation Regained* (Grand Rapids, Mich.: Eerdmans, 1985), page 13.

39. Cf. Psalm 147:15-20; 148:7-14; Proverbs 8:22-23,27-30; 2 Peter 3:5,7.

40. The reader will obviously recognize the thought of Dutch Calvinism and especially the thought of Abraham Kuyper and Herman Dooyeweerd. See Dooyeweerd, *New Critique of Theoretical Thought* (Philadelphia: Presbyterian and Reformed, 1969), vols. 1, 2.

41. James Skillen, "Politics, Pluralism, and the Ordinances of God," in *Life Is Religion*, ed. Henry VanderGoot (Ontario, Canada: Paideia Press, 1981), pages 195-206.

42. Berkouwer, *Providence of God*, page 67.

43. I am obviously talking about general revelation. See G.C. Berkouwer, *General Revelation* (Grand Rapids, Mich.: Eerdmans, 1955). There is no reason why general revelation need conflict with the centrality of the inspired Word or the supremacy of the Word made flesh, even Christ our Lord.

44. Geerhardus Vos, *Redemptive History and Biblical Interpretation: The Shorter Writings of Geerhardus Vos*, ed. Richard B. Gaffin, Jr. (Philadelphia: Presbyterian and Reformed, 1980), page 90.

45. Vos, *Redemptive History and Biblical Interpretation*, page 66.

46. Herman Ridderbos, *Paul: An Outline of His Theology*, trans. John R. Dewitt (Grand Rapids, Mich.: Eerdmans, 1975), pages 119-120,227.

47. G.C. Berkouwer, *Sin* (Grand Rapids, Mich.: Eerdmans, 1977), page 271. Cf. Dietrich Bonhoeffer, *Creation and Fall* (New York: Macmillan, 1959), pages 66, 68.

48. The good creation is twisted or distorted but never destroyed. See Albert Golin and Albert Descamps, *Sin in the Bible*, trans. Charles Schalden-

brand (New York: Descamps, Co., 1964), page 17.

49. The term *lead* may be deceptive. Berkouwer, quoting Herman Bavinck's *Reformed Dogmatic*, says sin parasites off what is good in the creation. It is a life and therefore has not true reality. Berhouwer, *Sin*, page 261. Sin's power to allure is only in its deceptive, addictive power.

50. Alan Trachtenberg, *The Incorporation of America: Culture and Society in the Gilded Age* (New York: Hill & Wang, 1982), pages 3, 5. This critique is similar to Jacques Ellul's notion of the idolatrous technological society, though with one big difference as we will see. For Calvin's and Luther's agreement with the cancerous effect of mammon, see respectively W. Fred Graham, *John Calvin, the Constructive Revolutionary* (Richmond, Va.: John Knox Press, 1971), pages 67-68; and Paul Althaus, *The Ethics of Martin Luther*, trans. Robert C. Shultz (Philadelphia: Fortress, 1972), page 101.

51. Norval Geldenhuys, *Commentary on the Gospel of Luke* (Grand Rapids, Mich.: Eerdmans, 1971), page 355.

52. Kittel, *Dictionary*, vol. 3, pages 966-967, 1004.

53. Kittel, *Dictionary*, vol. 3, page 967.

54. Goudzwaard, *Capitalism and Progress*, pages 205-206.

55. Herman Ridderbos, *The Coming of the Kingdom*, trans. H. deJongste (Philadelphia: Presbyterian and Reformed, 1969), page 167 and passim.

56. Wolters, *Creation Regained*, page 59.

57. I have constantly stressed that social institutions have their own unique character. Because reality coheres in Christ and is therefore holistic, social institutions also have analogous moments of the God-ordained demands within their daily operations. Families, for example, spend money, vote, are responsible for education, and hope, etc. Thus, it is proper to speak of a certain "overlap" of institutional expression that, nevertheless, colors but does not eradicate the original purpose. This notion is corrupted, however, when, as is currently the practice in many Western nations, governments and businesses assume a "partnership" that eventuates in a relationship that makes business dependent on government and government suspicious of the results of the market, results partially caused by federal contracts! Shared responsibility should always enhance respective integrity.

58. Loren Wilkinson, ed., *Earth Keeping: Christian Stewardship of Natural Resources* (Grand Rapids, Mich.: Eerdmans, 1980), pages 101-144.

59. Walter Brueggeman, *The Land: Place as Gift, Promise and Challenge in Biblical Faith* (Philadelphia: Fortress, 1977).

60. Paul Marshall, *Labour of Love: Essays on Work* (Toronto: Wedge Pub. Foundation, 1980), pages 1-19.

61. Perlman, *A Theory of the Labor Movement*.

62. The Value of the Person Ministry in Pittsburgh does just this. See "Labor, Management Honor 'Value of the Person,'" *The Kenosha Labor* (Kenosha, Wis.) September 14, 1978. Cf. Patricia A. Dill, "Christian Perspectives of Labor Management" (tutorial submitted to Chatham College, Pittsburgh, Pa.: 1980).

63. Ed Vanderkloet et al., *Beyond the Adversary System* (Toronto: Christian Labor Association, 1976).

64. Taken from the *Revised Standard Version*. Cf. Luke 12:41-48, esp. vv. 45,48.

65. I am grateful for Alan Storkey's ground-breaking efforts and insights that inform this section. See his *Transforming Economics: A Christian Way to Employment* (New Malden, England: Third Way Books, 1986).

66. Lavelle's bank is located in the Hill District of Pittsburgh. In the 1950s, home ownership was at 12 percent. The City Planning Department of Pittsburgh has now established it at 29 percent, with Lavelle claiming that it is at 40 percent. Dwelling House has become a model of hope for many. More profoundly, Lavelle was the first black realtor to challenge, success- fully, the practice of "redlining," or the racist exclusion of certain pre- arranged neighborhoods from mortgage money and public advertisement.

67. Dwelling House Savings and Loan Brochure: "Meeting People's Need" (5011 Herron Ave., Pittsburgh, PA 15219). For relevant statistical informa- tion, see Rodney Brooks, "Dwelling in the House of Lavelle," *Black Enterprise*, June 1984, page 146.

68. For a further treatment of what constitutes a responsible business, see George Goyder, *The Responsible Company* (Oxford: Basil Blackwell, 1961).

69. Storkey suggests that both parents work 4/5 job time during preschool years (*Transforming Economics*, page 135). This suggestion would obviously have a dramatic effect on the economy as a whole.

70. Hence the "neoliberals." See Sheldon Danziger and Eugene Smolensky, "The Welfare of All the Poor," *New York Times*, October 1, 1987.

71. McCarthy et al., *Society, State and Schools*, page 164.

72. The experienced reader may wonder if my suggestions do not parallel the theories of John K. Galbraith. I am not suggesting that the government preside over a field of competing "countervailing powers." I believe that competition is mitigated when one stops to consider that it is government's office to recognize the room that has been given by God, hence reducing the need for a pillage-the-economic-pie mentality. Moreover, these institutions, insofar as they have economic concerns, arise out of creational distinctives not egoistic self-interest as the latter would fragment political life, even as special interest politics is currently doing. Creational politics, as outlined,

has as its first priority the public trust at stake. Its mandate is to more holistically debate and adjudicate representative economic concerns.

73. In traditional economic theory, the problem of pollution is treated as an "externality." In essence, businesses or persons who pollute are asking others to pay the cleaning bill even while damage occurs. In this environment, governmental action seems appropriate.

74. I have intentionally omitted the debate concerning the different kinds of justice—retributive, proportional, and distributive—because an adequate survey would take us too far afield. I recommend, however, that this topic be considered.

CHAPTER 12

1. *Westminster Shorter Catechism*, #102.

2. Bryan W. Ball, *A Great Expectation: Eschatological Thought in English Protestantism to 1660* (Leiden, Netherlands: E.J. Brill, 1975), pages 237-238.

CHAPTER 13

1. See John Jefferson Davis, *Christ's Victorious Kingdom: Postmillennialism Reconsidered* (Grand Rapids, Mich.: Baker, 1986), for a recent presentation of this view.

2. Clarence Augustine Beckwith, "The Millennium," in *The New Schaff-Herzog Encyclopedia of Religious Knowledge*, ed. Samuel Macauley Jackson, 13 vols. (New York: Funk & Wagnalls, 1910), vol. 7, page 377.

3. Iain H. Murray, *The Puritan Hope: A Study in Revival, and the Interpretation of Prophecy* (Carlisle, Pa.: Banner of Truth, 1971, 1975).

4. John Calvin, *Commentary on Micah*, vol. 4 (Grand Rapids: Eerdmans, 1960), page 3.

5. Calvin, *Commentary on Psalms*, vol. 110, page 3.

6. Peter Toon, ed., *Puritans, The Millennium and The Future of Israel: Puritan Eschatology 1600 to 1660* (Cambridge: James Clarke, 1970), page 6.

7. See Greg Bahnsen, "The Prima Facie Acceptability of Postmillennialism," *Journal of Christian Reconstruction*, vol. 3, no. 2 (1976-1977), pages 48-105, for a review of this position in Church history.

8. Cited by James H. Moorhead, "The Erosion of Postmillennialism in American Religious Thought, 1865-1925," *Church History*, vol. 53, no. 1 (1984), page 61.

9. For discussion and explanation of the various views of the millennium, see

Robert G. Clouse, ed., *The Meaning of the Millennium* (Downers Grove, Ill.: InterVarsity, 1977).

10. Loraine Boettner, *The Millennium* (Philadelphia: Presbyterian and Reformed, 1957); and J. Marcellus Kirk, *An Eschatology of Victory* (Nutley, N.J.: Presbyterian and Reformed, 1971).

11. David Chilton's *Paradise Restored* (Tyler, Tex.: American Bureau for Economic Research, 1984) is a commentary on the book of Revelation from a postmillennial standpoint.

12. Timothy L. Smith, "Righteousness and Hope: Christian Holiness and the Millennial Vision in America, 1800-1900," *American Quarterly*, vol. 31, no. 1 (1979), page 21; see also *Revivalism and Social Reform in Mid-Nineteenth Century America* (Nashville: Abingdon, 1957), by the same author, esp. chaps. 5, 10, and 14.

13. Jean B. Quandt, "Religion and Social Thought: The Secularization of Postmillennialism," *American Quarterly*, vol. 25 (1973), page 396.

14. Cited in Robert G. Clouse, "Millennium, Views of the," in *Evangelical Dictionary of Theology*, ed. Walter A. Elwell (Grand Rapids, Mich.: Baker, 1984), page 717.

15. John Owen, *The Works of John Owen*, ed. William H. Goold (London: Banner of Truth, 1967 [1850]), vol. 8, page 394.

16. See Davis, *Christ's Victorious Kingdom*, esp. chaps. 2, 3, and 5, for detailed analysis of the biblical data. Chapter 5 is devoted to an analysis of Revelation 20:1-6.

17. It is not the purpose of this chapter to respond to the various objections that can be raised to the postmillennial approach here presented, e.g., texts in the New Testament expressing a sense of nearness in the return of Christ or worsening world conditions at the close of history. These issues are dealt with at some length in chapter 6 of *Christ's Victorious Kingdom*, "Contrary Texts in the New Testament," pages 101-116.

18. Dennis Cooper-Jones, *Business Planning and Forecasting* (New York: John Wiley & Sons, 1974), page 123. I wish to thank my research assistant, Stephen Morwing, who helped in the search of the business literature.

19. J. Scott Armstrong, *Long-Range Forecasting: From Crystal Ball to Computer* (New York: John Wiley & Sons, 1978), page 6.

20. Cited in David W. Ewing, *Long-Range Planning for Management* (New York: Harper & Row, 1964), page 63.

21. David E. Ewing, *The Managerial Mind* (New York: Free Press, 1964), page 76.

22. John Herrington, "Energy's Promising Horizon," *Washington Times*, July 29, 1987, page D2.

23. Cited in *Executive Memo* (Washington D.C.: Marrott Health Care Services), vol. 9, no. 3 (1987), page 1.
24. Cited in *Executive Memo*, page 1.
25. Kenneth H. Olsen, "The Education of an Entrepreneur," *New York Times*, July 19, 1987, page F2.

CHAPTER 14

1. Max Weber, *The Protestant Ethic and the Spirit of Capitalism*, trans. Talcott Parsons (New York: Scribner, 1958), page 175.